Politics and Government

Under the editorship of
Richard P. Longaker

Karl W. Deutsch

Professor of Government, Harvard University

Politics

and Government

How People Decide Their Fate

Houghton Mifflin Company · Boston

New York · Atlanta · Geneva, Illinois · Dallas · Palo Alto

To the memory of my mother

Maria Deutsch (1882–1969)

one of the first women
legislators in her time, who
taught me that politics must
serve the peace and freedom
of future generations

Editor's Foreword

Karl Deutsch's *Politics and Government: How People Decide Their Fate* is the work of a master. It should come as no surprise that this major effort by Professor Deutsch is a stimulating mixture of erudition and wit, hard-headed empirical analysis and a broad sense of history. His treatment of the fundamental issues of political science blends the new with the old, systematic analysis with description, and comprehensibility with felicity of style. He simplifies so that students can understand but never underestimates their capacity to learn. The total impact on the student of this analysis of men in politics is a heightened capacity to analyze fundamental processes in political life, extending from the immediate urban political culture in which he lives through the more distant but no less important concerns of the world at large.

Politics and Government is based on a vast knowledge of many disciplines. It is adaptable to a range of courses in political science, the American political process, and comparative government. It is at once practical and theoretical, original yet familiar. The author works from the basic assumption, which few can deny, that contemporary life has become increasingly politicized. Consequently, the informed citizen can cut through the complexity of politics and government only if multiple perspectives are brought to bear on his analysis of the political process affecting him.

The book is keyed principally to the American scene and the American student, and a preponderance of the illustrations and the suggested modes of inquiry are related to the politics of American democracy. There is, nonetheless, a comparative tone which reinforces the author's presentation of basic decision-making theory and systems analysis and which, together with quantitative, historical, and value-oriented perspectives, makes for an informed understanding of the nature of politics and government in contemporary society.

It is a pleasure to be engaged in an intellectual adventure with an author, especially one who, by virtue of his skill in presentation, can help students think for themselves. In this book Karl Deutsch demonstrates not only that realistic political analysis is, in itself, intellectually stimulating but that it is also the first and necessary step toward measured social change.

Richard P. Longaker

University of California
at Los Angeles

Author's Preface

This book was written by one teacher, with the aid of over 400 students, and with the varied advice of over two dozen colleagues, most of them young. The concerned and lively questions, objections, and responses of these students have had the greatest general influence on this book, while the suggestions and criticisms of my academic colleagues have weighed heavily with me on many specific points of fact. Even so, all decisions about the contents of the book were mine, and I alone must be blamed for its weaknesses.

This book aims to make clear the principles of political analysis. It seeks to help the reader to learn to recognize the important questions in public life, and thus in the lives of all of us. It also aims to help him recognize within each question the crucial facts and conditions that make the main difference to what will happen. This ability to recognize the problems and facts that matter most in deciding our fate is only part of politics. For politics involves both knowledge and action. It is, therefore, in part a science, in part an art, in some small part a gift, and in part a matter of personal decision. But most of it can be learned and taught. Those who care enough to learn about politics as much as *can* be learned about it have also an excellent chance to decide actively and responsibly about it, and to master in time the art and gift of acting on this knowledge.

The purpose of this book is to help people begin the study of politics. It is written in simple language, in order to make facts plain and ideas clear. It offers a set of basic concepts, like a box of tools, to be used rather than exhibited. Each concept is defined in terms of some operation that can be repeated and tested by different people regardless of their preferences. By demonstrating the meaning and use of concepts, the book also introduces the reader to the development of concepts and encourages him to form his own concepts where they may help his thinking. Relevant concepts and clear meanings will not make all of us agree in politics, but they may help us know what our disagreements are about. They may help us to avoid arguments over mere words, and to concentrate on arguments about issues that matter.

To keep track of key concepts, those introduced in each chapter are listed at its end, together with suggestions for additional readings. Some concepts also are highlighted in the chapter section heads and subheads which have been designed to outline the argument and aid in review. Finally, the index will help readers to trace the different aspects of a concept as it appears in the context of various chapters.

Though this is a book for beginners, it seeks to be a modern one. Too often, the time between an advance in research and its appearance in textbooks has been far longer than it should be. Political science includes a good deal of the traditional political wisdom of mankind, some of it going back 2,000 years or more. But its main concern is with the world in which we live, and with the political knowledge that may help people make political decisions here and now—decisions about their own fate and the fate of future generations.

Political science in our time is rapidly changing. It is now undergoing the kind of revolution which economics underwent a generation ago, through the work of Lord Keynes, the rise of national income accounting, and the development of the quantitative science of econometrics. The questions "how much? how fast? how soon? and how likely?" which are asked in economics are now also being raised in politics. And increasingly often, they can be answered. To introduce beginners to these new developments in political science and thought, many problems are presented in simple language but from an advanced point of view. Where an argument hinges on figures and series of quantitative data, these appear in the text or in tables and charts.

Politics is a matter of both facts and values, of self-interest and loyalties to others, of concern and competence. If it is true that men see most easily that which they wish to see, it is also true that in order to survive they often cannot do without the truth. It is the central concern for truth, for knowledge that can be verified and policies that work, which turns the study of politics into a science and its practitioners into political scientists. Without this concern for evidence, politics remains a clash of opinions, pressures, power, propaganda, or mere force. With a concern for truth, politics can become a search for solutions and new discoveries, for new ways of working together and deciding our own fate.

Insofar as political science is a science, it is an applied one. Its tasks are practical, and its theories are both challenged and nourished by practice. In these respects, political science resembles such other applied sciences as medicine and engineering. Each of these applied sciences draws on a wide range of fundamental sciences for facts and methods to deal with its own tasks. Engineers call on physics, mathematics, chemistry, and other disciplines to help them build bridges which will stand and machines which will work safely. Physicians and surgeons turn to biology, chemistry, physics, anatomy, physiology, psychology, and many other fields for knowledge to help them to keep people alive and healthy. Political scientists similarly call on all sciences of human behavior, such as psychology, sociology, economics, anthropology, history, and the theory of communication. They do so in order to help people keep themselves at peace, free, and able to cooperate, manage their conflicts, and make common decisions without self-destruction.

Even an introductory book requires a good deal of information from the other social sciences. Interlocking information of this kind is presented throughout the book. Particular attention is paid to history. For history is not only the past tense of politics. Rather, it is to politics and government what nature is to biology or physics. It is the source of a major part of all political experience. The comparison of different peoples and political systems, of their structure and behavior, requires a knowledge of at least the essentials of their past. It is often quite possible to describe and predict the routine politics of a country without referring to its past. If nothing more is at stake than a minor shift in votes, it often can be read off adequately from a few recent polls. But when a nation faces a major crisis, when great changes seem imminent and fateful decisions are being made, then a nation's past, the memories and character of its people, can be decisive. Thus the United States and Germany responded differently to the Great Depression; France and Britain responded differently to the Nazi attack in World War II; and Russia and the United States are responding differently in some ways to the challenges of modern technology. History does make a difference, and this is why historical information commands extensive attention in this modern comparative and analytical treatment of politics and government.

The book is divided in three parts. The first and longest presents in nine chapters a set of basic concepts for analysis, together with some comparative data and some classic theories of politics. The emphasis is on political stakes and participation; the control and self-control of political systems; political machinery, communication, and development; and the evaluation of political performance. The main focus of attention is on the advanced countries of the world. There are references, in addition, to problems of developing countries, but it is a central thesis of this book that the political development of the world's major industrial nations is by no means finished.

Part Two takes a closer look at five major political systems: the United States, the Soviet Union, Britain, France, and the German Federal Republic. In each case, historical and current analysis are combined in seeking to answer such questions as these: What main conditions helped shape the present national political system? How does this system work and how well does it serve the people of its nation? What major unsolved problems does the country face? And what can people in other countries learn from its experiences?

The final part is brief—a concluding chapter looking to the unfinished business of politics which confronts us now and will confront us tomorrow.

In addition to the students and young faculty members referred to earlier, I am indebted for sustained help to David V. J. Bell and Richard P. Longaker, who read the entire manuscript and made many valuable suggestions. I am also indebted for substantial aid on some major points to Carl J. Friedrich. James Chapman and Sheldon Kravitz checked many details of research. Specific chapters were read by Merle Fainsod and Abram Bergson on the Soviet Union; Jean Blondel on Britain; Roy C. Macridis on France; and Dieter Senghaas on the German Federal Republic. Other men, as the text shows, have influenced my thinking. I cannot mention all, but must acknowledge my gratitude to Robert A. Dahl, Harold Lasswell, Seymour Martin Lipset, Talcott Parsons, and the late Norbert Wiener.

Editorial and art work was contributed by Susan Granoff and Rose Mary Corbett; secretarial work by Nancy J. McDowell and Alice Bahrenburg; and valuable coordination by Frank Shelton.

None of this would have produced any kind of book without the help and counsel of Arthur W. Hepner who became an invaluable source of energy and judgment—and a treasured friend.

Throughout the time of writing, the patience, encouragement, and lively insight of my wife Ruth have meant more to me than I can say.

With all these helpers contributing to whatever assets this book may have, I alone am left to answer for its liabilities. I can only hope that, with its weaknesses, this book will encourage others to carry forward the study of politics and government as is here conceived: as processes of collective human self-direction.

K. W. D.

Cambridge, Massachusetts

Contents

Part One
Basic Concepts for Analysis

Part Two
Five Modern Countries

Part Three
Today and Tomorrow

List of Figures

List of Tables

Politics and Government

How People Decide Their Fate

Basic Concepts
for Analysis

Part One

The Nature of Politics

All of us know that politics affects our lives, but do we know the full extent of its importance? Clearly, we live in an age of growing *politicization*. Many matters that did not involve politics in the past, or that did not involve it directly, now are seen as political issues. Many decisions which in earlier times did not need to be made, or were made automatically by custom, or were made by private individuals, now must be made by public agencies and by the political process.

Politics, in one sense, is the making of decisions by public means, in contrast to the making of personal decisions privately

by individuals and the making of economic decisions in response to such impersonal forces as money, market conditions, and resource scarcities. The collection of all decisions made by public means constitutes the *public sector* of a country or society. In our own time, public sectors have been growing in all countries.

A World Politicized

Our cities are webs of politics. The water we drink, the air we breathe, the safety of our streets, the dignity of our poor, the health of our old, the education of our young, and the hope for our minority groups—all these are bound up with the political decisions made at City Hall, in the state capital, or in Washington, D. C.

What is true of the politics of cities is even truer of the politics of nations. One year before the outbreak of the French Revolution, the France of the Bourbon kings collected through municipal, provincial, and national taxes approximately 8 per cent of the gross national product (the sum of all goods and services produced, measured in current prices). A hundred years later, the Third French Republic still collected through government taxes, approximately 8 per cent of the gross national product, although the gross national product by then was larger and the spending policies presumably more prudent than those of the Bourbon kings. To-day, in contrast, the French government collects and redirects the spending of 40 per cent of the gross national product and has been doing so since the late 1930s. Therefore, during the past several decades, France has been five times as political, in terms of the share of politics in allocating the resources of the people, as it was eighty years ago.

In the United States in 1970, approximately 31 per cent of the gross national product will be collected in municipal, state, and federal taxes. Very possibly not all of the monies that flow through the public sector are included in this figure, for, in countries that depend on private enterprise, governments have tried to minimize the size of their share of the national economy in the mind of the public, even though they cannot reduce it in reality. In West Germany, a country well known in the 1960s for favoring private enterprise, between 39 and 47 per cent of the gross national product passed through the public sector, depending upon the particular type of bookkeeping used. In Sweden the share of the public sector in the gross national product in the 1960s was 54 per cent, and in 1968 the Swedish voters by an impressive margin elected a government pledged to extend this sector and its services further. All these figures apply to non-Communist countries. In Communist countries, the political sectors of the national economies are, of course, still larger, though they do not equal 100 per cent anywhere in the world (see Figure 1.1).

Almost everywhere, people feel daily the effects of national political decisions. Such decisions go far to determine the lunches eaten by school children, the level of wages, the prices of many commodities, the cost of credit, the value of money, and the career chances of young people. Political decisions also influence the quality of life—its security or insecurity, its ugliness or beauty—and other political decisions determine the relations of countries with each other, and thus the likelihood of peace or war.

The world itself has become more politicized. In the late nineteenth century, there were perhaps 50 sovereign states; today there are about 140, and the number may increase further in the decades ahead. A good deal of the world's trade and its communications are being influenced—indeed channeled—by political decisions. But far more is at stake than economic gain. Strategically, the world has become one: guided missiles with nuclear warheads can be delivered halfway around the globe in forty minutes. What little military security is left now depends upon deterrence among those countries that already have nuclear weapons and the means for their delivery. And in the long run it will depend upon the proliferation or nonproliferation of such weapons and means among those countries that do not as yet possess them. If civilization should be destroyed and most of mankind killed within the next twenty to thirty years, we shall not be killed by plague or pestilence; we shall be killed by politics. Politics has become, literally, a matter of life and death.

Politics and Government

Because politics is the making of decisions by *public means,* it is primarily concerned with *government,* that is, with the direction and self-direction of large communities of people. The word "politics" stresses the process of decision-making about public actions or goods—about what is done and who gets what. The word "government" stresses the results of this process in terms of the control and self-control of the community—be it city, state, or nation. Any community larger than the family contains an element of politics. In fact, "politics" derives from the Greek word *polis,* meaning city-state, and to the Greeks, the *polis* was the most meaningful community above the family level.

Government: The Helmsman Concept. Government is related to both the old art of steering and self-steering and the new sciences of information and control. The Greek word for the steersman or helmsman of a ship was *kybernetes.* "Governor" and "government" derive from this term,[1] and so does the word for the science of communication and control, *cybernetics.*

The similarity between the tasks of steering and government has been recognized almost since the beginning of political thought. In *The Republic,* Plato explicitly developed this analogy in his "parable of the ship." The man most expert in navigating around reefs, wrote Plato, might fail to win a popularity contest among the crew in the election of a captain. Aristotle also frequently used this analogy; for example, in his *Politics* he wrote that the limits to the size of an efficient state should be the same as those for the size of a ship—neither should be made too large to obey its rudder.

It is not surprising that the image of "the ship of state" should have become firmly entrenched in political thought. The direction of both ships and organizations requires mastery of much of the same kinds of knowledge and techniques. The helmsman of a ship must have information about many things. He must know, first of all, where the helm is or where he can put his hand on the tiller. He must know where he himself is in relation to everything in his ship; and he must know what he has to do to stay in control of it, for if he loses control all other information is irrelevant to him. Second, the helmsman must know where his ship is, where it is moving, and what kind of a ship it is. Third, he must know where the

---

[1] Webster's *Third New International Dictionary* notes that the word "govern" comes from the old French *governer* which is from the Latin *gubernare* (to steer, pilot, govern) which, in turn, is from the Greek *kybernan.*

Figure 1.1

Growth of the Public Sector

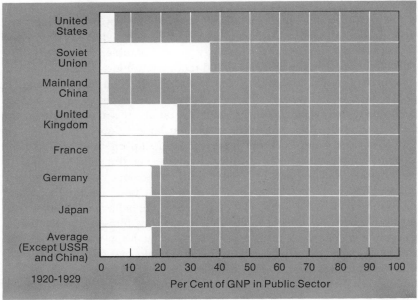

n.a. = not available
[1]*Expenditures by central government, excluding Social Security and public enterprises, as percentage of national income (average for decade).*

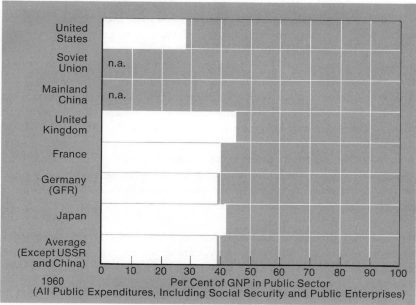

Sources: W. Zapf and W. Schneider from standard sources, Harvard University, 1969; B. M. Russett et al., World Handbook *(New Haven: Yale University Press, 1964), p. 63.*

relevant environment of the ship is—the reefs, sandbars, shoals, currents, and channels of navigation—and where his ship is in relation to all of these. Finally, he must know where he wants to go. He must have some image of his goal, purpose, or preferred course; and he must know at each moment whether the actual movement of the ship is carrying him closer to his objective or farther away from it. Putting together these four kinds of knowledge and acting upon them constitutes the process of navigation.

Something very similar constitutes the process of government. Anyone who directs the affairs of a country—or of any large organization or community—must know how to stay in control; what is the basic nature and the current state of the country or organization which he is controlling; what are the limits and opportunities in its environment which he must cope with; and what results he wishes to attain. Combining these four kinds of knowledge, and acting upon them, is the essence of the art of government.

Like other complex tasks, steering and government often involve a division of labor. Flying a modern airplane and getting it safely from takeoff to destination requires two jobs, not one: the manipulation of the controls and the charting of the course. Both the pilot's and the navigator's contributions are essential. This remains true even where modern automatic equipment can replace the navigator, or indeed the pilot. The two tasks of orientation and control still must be performed.

In politics, too, the task of maintaining control is supplemented by the no less indispensable tasks of orientation and navigation. A chief executive and his foreign minister must be aware of what their own people will stand for, as well as what the legislature and various important parties and political groups will accept. However, they must also be aware of what foreigners will stand for. They must know, or try to know, what the effect of a national action will be in some distant theater of the world. They must know not only what policies will be successful at home but also what policies will succeed in some strange country ten thousand miles away. In World War II three great countries—Germany, Italy, and Japan—were brought to ruin by their governments because each of these governments, though highly expert in securing and holding power within its national boundaries, proved tragically incompetent in assessing realistically what the rest of the world would stand for and what policies could or could not succeed in the international arena.

Aids to Navigation: Maps and Ideologies.   In order to orient ourselves in a difficult and often bewildering world, we frequently have recourse to maps. Maps present a simplified image of the real world. Any map of the New England coastline must be a great deal simpler than the coastline itself. Any diagram of the anatomy of a cat must be much simpler than the cat; the only completely realistic picture of a cat, the mathematician Norbert Wiener once remarked, would have to be a cat—preferably the same cat.

What maps are to the navigator, ideologies are to all of us. An *ideology* is a simplified picture of the world. We may hold such a picture fairly explicitly in our minds, or we may take it more or less for granted and embody it in our feelings rather than in our precise thoughts. However explicit or implicit, an ideology serves as a map by which we guide our behavior. Ideologies therefore have a direct significance for politics, which seeks to govern behavior. Sometimes we are suspicious of ideologies because we feel they are misleading. Yet all of us have ideologies, although some of us tend to divide them into two categories: orthodoxy (our beliefs) and heterodoxy (the other fellow's beliefs)—or our side and the wrong one.

Certainly, we cannot wholly do without ideologies. An ideology is an instrument for making the world look simpler and more consistent than it is. Human beings find it hard to accept and hold in their minds several pieces of information that seem to contradict one another. When we are expected to believe several things that do not fit together, we feel uncomfortable. Psychologists then say that we are suffering from *cognitive dissonance*. Their experiments show that people tend to reduce or abolish cognitive dissonance, either by attempting to reconcile intellectually the seeming contradiction or, more often, by suppressing or forgetting the piece of information that does not fit. Ideologies thus become guides to the selective perception and recall of information. Not only individuals but also groups of people, small or large organizations, entire peoples, societies, and nations try to reduce or abolish their particular cognitive dissonances by repressing or denying inconvenient bits of information—even if these happen to be true and vital to their prosperity or their survival.

Not all ideologies, however, are equally resistant to new information, or equally impervious to truth. Indeed, we may call an ideology *extreme* when it rejects or resists any piece of information, however true and important, that does not fit it. And we may call an ideology *moderate* or *reasonable*—even if we do not happen to agree with it—when it keeps the way open for additional pieces of information that might serve to temper it in the direction of greater realism. Political scientists, like all other scientists, test any item of knowledge by its consistency with many different facts, each of which, in turn, has been verified independently.

The difference between extremism and reasonableness thus hinges on the capacity to recognize reality and to test the truth of opinions. *Extremism* always involves a tendency toward self-deception, regardless of the virtues of the cause it is supposed to serve. Senator Barry M. Goldwater, in running for the presidency in 1964, overlooked this point when he proclaimed: "Moderation in the pursuit of justice is no virtue; extremism in the pursuit of justice is no vice." This problem is as real for those on the far left as for those on the far right of the political spectrum.

A reasonable ideology, on the other hand, permits broad and objective tests for truths. The question is: does it permit the truth of a piece of information to be tested against a wide range of different kinds of evidence from the outside world—that multiple and interdependent *reality* which exists whether we like it or not—or does it test it only in terms of its consistency with a preferred doctrine? To the extent that an ideology permits this kind of multiple verification, it is likely to be more *realistic*. Its adherents have a better chance to learn to act effectively, and its values have a better chance to be attained through realistic action.

Politics, Interests, and Values

Politics and the Pursuit of Interests.   Most of the time, people are interested more in rewards than in sacrifices. One of the fundamental truths about politics is that much of it occurs in the pursuit of the interests of particular individuals or groups. In the analysis of politics, the concept of interest has played a central role since the early sixteenth century. The word "interest" entered the language at that time. It comes from the Latin word *interesse*, meaning "to be between," as wheat grains among chaff, or meat between bones and gristle. This meaning implies that among (or between) a welter of nonrewarding things and events, there are certain rewarding elements which must be sifted out. To ask "What is my interest?" is a Latin way of asking, "What's in it for me?" A special application of this notion developed in the later usage of the word "interest" for the payment which debtors make to their creditors for the use of money. The creditor's "interest" was the reward which he extracted from the financial situation of the debtor. In general, then, anyone's "interest" in a situation consists in the rewards which he can extract from it.

The concept of interest, however, is ambiguous. It implies a claim or *expectation of reward.* But such a claim or expectation has both subjective and objective sides. On the *subjective* side, it describes a *distribution of attention.* People are interested in whatever they pay attention to. If we say that a picture, an advertisement, a book, or a play is holding the interest of its audience, we mean that it holds their attention, and usually people pay attention to things by which they expect to be rewarded. Looking at the picture of an attractive girl in an advertisement may be its own reward, but more often we pay attention to some message or some piece of information, or to some concrete situation in real life, because we think that from it we may derive some reward in the future or because it may help us to prevent damage or penalty to ourselves.

The *objective* side of interest is the actual *probability of reward.* In the behavior of animals, attention and the likelihood of reward are closely connected. We all know that when a cat watches a mousehole intently, there is usually a mouse in it, for cats are fairly realistic animals. Governments often are less realistic. Both national and international politics are rich in instances of political groups, parties, and even governments having paid a great deal of sustained attention to policies and situations which proved to be completely unrewarding. History is full of such examples. The Japanese warlords thought it was in their interest to attack Pearl Harbor; Napoleon and Hitler each thought it was to their interest to invade Russia. Each of these decisions brought about the defeat of a nation and the downfall of its leaders. This pattern goes back thousands of years. King Croesus of Lydia in Asia Minor asked the Greek oracle at Delphi whether he should attack the kingdom of Persia. The oracle replied, "If you cross the river Halys [which formed the border between Lydia and Persia] you will destroy a great kingdom." Croesus attacked, and a kingdom was destroyed—his own.

What is true of governments also has been true of smaller groups such as labor unions, business investors, and real-estate speculators. Their records show that though people have often guessed shrewdly about their interests, they also have often guessed wrong. Mine workers unions in many countries have opposed the introduction of automated coal mining equipment. Yet where such equipment has been introduced in cooperation with the unions, mine workers' wages have risen and mine workers' sons have been absorbed in more attractive occupations. In the 1930s many businessmen thought that President Roosevelt's administration would greatly damage their interests. Yet, when Roosevelt died, business income had greatly increased and there were many more millionaires in the United States; the depression had not shattered the fabric of national unity; and the United States, with relatively fewer casualties in the war, had gained more power in the world arena than ever before in its history. By 1945 American businessmen thus ended up with a bigger and more secure share of the world's wealth and power than they had enjoyed in 1933. Their interests had been well served.

Despite these instances of statesmen, governments, and groups who were spectacularly mistaken about their interests, the classic concept of interest is most nearly applicable in cases where the distribution of attention and the probability of obtaining a reward come together. We speak in these cases of a "true" or *well-understood interest,* in contrast to some imagined or presumed interest which turned out to be unrealistic.

Politics and the Allocation of Values.   Politics deals with the interplay of interests—the claiming and distribution of rewards, that is, of values. Different individuals and groups, or even countries, acting in politics and pursuing their interests may cooperate or compete in regard to the *allocation of values.* Indeed, politics has often been defined as the process by which *values*—things or relationships which people would like to have or to enjoy—are allocated in a society in an authoritative manner—in a manner that will stick and can be relied on—that is *legitimate* in the sense of fitting people's beliefs of right and wrong. A famous book on politics by Harold D. Lasswell bore the title *Politics: Who Gets What, When, How?*

In the past, political theories sometimes have been formulated in terms of a single value which the theorist believed various political actors were trying to get. For nearly two thousand years, from the fifth century B.C. until about the fifteenth century A.D., most political theory dealt with politics in terms of *rectitude* or *justice,* that is, with the question of how powers, responsibilities, and rewards in society ought best to be allocated for the common good. From the sixteenth century onward, notably in the works of such writers as Machiavelli and Thomas Hobbes, politics was usually conceived in terms of *power,* that is, with the question of how powers, responsibilities, and rewards in society were actually allocated; and it was held that power was the key value through which all other values could be obtained. In the nineteenth century in the days of Prince Metternich after the Napoleonic Wars, and again in the twentieth century after World War II, some political writers have tried to see politics mainly as the pursuit of *stability*—the attempt to keep each society and the relations between societies much as they then were. Still other theorists might think of politics as the study of change, growth, and *development.* In general, however, all attempts to view politics in terms of a single value, or a single overriding human concern, have been unsuccessful. They have failed to give an adequate picture of the richness of the political process and of its unending surprises.

Politics and the Plurality of Needs: Eight Basic Values.   Perhaps the most realistic approach has been that of Lasswell, who suggests that there exist at least eight basic values, all of which people will pursue— although with varying degrees of interest—and none of which they can do entirely without in either politics or life. Lasswell's eight values are *power, enlightenment, wealth, well-being* (or health), *skill, affection, rectitude* (which involves both righteousness and justice), and *deference* (or respect). People want to be powerful; they have a natural curiosity and want to increase their knowledge; they desire wealth; they value health and the sensual joy of well-being; they enjoy a feeling of skill, of a difficult job well-done, and they possess what Thorstein Veblen called "the instinct of workmanship"; they all need affection (in fact, psychological research has shown that small children may even die if one tries to raise them without a minimum of affection). People also want to feel righteous in terms of their own conscience, and usually also in terms of their religion or philosophy or the system of right and wrong that prevails in their society and which they have made an internal part of their own personality. Finally, most people want to be respected outwardly by their neighbors and to receive due deference from them. People enjoy being permitted to go first through a door, being invited to sit at the head of a table, and having due and respectful attention paid to their communications and messages.

In addition to these eight substantive values which most people and groups pursue, people also desire certain ways of enjoying them, such as security and liberty. If somebody enjoys a value he usually likes to have it in *security,* that is, he wants to be able to rely on having it in the future. We not only value health, we want to stay healthy; we not only enjoy power, or wealth, we want to continue to keep it. And to those who have few or no substantive values to enjoy, such as the unemployed, the very poor, or the desperate, security has little meaning.

The other manner of enjoying values is *liberty* or spontaneity, that is, the ability to act in accordance with one's own personality, without having to make a great effort at self-denial or self-control and without being subjected to external constraints. Thus people like "doing what comes naturally" to them. They enjoy being healthy but dislike a confining diet or health regime; they may enjoy power or wealth but may balk at excessive self-denial or forced savings, or some Spartan or Prussian discipline, demanded of them in order to increase their power or wealth. But different actions may seem "natural" to different peoples. Each people may tend to act out spontaneously whatever habits or cultural patterns it happened to learn earlier. Quarrels over the meanings of liberty, therefore, have been frequent.

Politics and Legitimacy: The Compatibility of Values

People do not and cannot live by any single value alone, but values are not always wholly compatible with each other. It is possible for someone to increase his wealth only by working so hard that he injures his health. Or he might make money in ways that reduce his feeling of righteousness or diminish the respect he enjoys in the community. This raises the problem of legitimacy. Earlier, we spoke of legitimacy as compatibility with one's beliefs of right and wrong. Now we can explore this concept in somewhat greater depth. *Legitimacy* is the promise that the pursuit of one value will prove compatible with the pursuit or enjoyment of other values.

We say that the pursuit of a value is *legitimate* if, and only if, we have reason to expect that it will not inflict intolerable damage upon any other value which is also vitally important to us. It is legitimate, therefore, to make money provided that this pursuit does not involve a grave moral wrong or a serious loss of respect in our community or a severe impairment of our health. To the extent, of course, that different people prize different values, their ideas of legitimacy will differ. Some may believe that it is legitimate to be concerned about righteousness, respect, and health only so long as these concerns do not interfere with the making of money. Legitimacy, then, is a relative, rather than absolute, concept. It is the promise to any political actor of a viable configuration (that is, an organized set) of *his own* values.

Legitimacy is thus not an absolute thing or quality but a relationship among values within a situation that makes them compatible or puts them into conflict. As the situation changes, legitimacy may change, too. Since legitimacy may vary with time and place, it may vary among groups, and different views of legitimacy may lead to conflict among groups or may intensify existing conflicts.

Conversely, agreement about what actions or what values are compatible go far in facilitating the creation or preservation of communities. So long as there is agreement about what is legitimate, politics and government will function more smoothly. Where legitimacy is lost, agreements break down or are reduced to matters of expediency that can be broken when convenient. The consequences may be tyranny, revolution, secession, or some other form of break-up.

The concept of legitimacy is commonly applied to the manner in which a government, ruler, or office-holder has attained his office. The tenure of office is called legitimate if the incumbent has been put into his position or job by a "legitimate" procedure—by a procedure which those whom he governs will consider compatible with the configuration of their own values. According to this view, his tenure of office is legitimate because of the way he obtained it, not because of what he does with it.[2] In some political cultures, rules of hereditary succession determine who is the legitimate ruler; in medieval monarchies there were great disputes about who was the rightful heir to the throne. In the United States or the Soviet Union, by contrast, being a son or close relative of the chief executive does not in itself establish any legitimate claim to political office and may, in fact, arouse suspicions of the illegitimate practice of nepotism. Such suspicions of nepotism were voiced when President John F. Kennedy appointed his brother Robert as Attorney General and when Chairman Nikita Khrushchev's son-in-law, Alexei Adzhubei, was made editor of the Soviet Union's chief government newspaper, *Izvestia*.

The concept of legitimacy proposed in this book is broader. It deals with the substance of what exists or what is done in politics, and not only with the procedure by which political power is obtained. This broader usage of legitimacy is close to what many writers have called *justice*—by which they mean the compatibility of a political action or practice with the configuration of values prevailing in a particular community.[3] In our book, the terms "legitimate" and "just" will be used interchangeably. People feel that a government is just or unjust, legitimate or illegitimate, not only by how it came to power but also—and mainly—by what it does. If its actions or omissions violate their basic values, they may conclude, as St. Augustine did in *The City of God*, that "a government without justice is a great robbery."

[2] For an elaboration of this view of legitimacy as the right to act or to rule, see Carl J. Friedrich, *Man and His Government* (New York: McGraw-Hill, 1963), pp. 258–59.

[3] See Friedrich, *op. cit.*, p. 254.

Since legitimacy promises a compatibility of values and actions in pursuit of them, it also promises the compatibility of public goals and practices with the private values and personalities of individuals. Where this is so, and government and its laws are held legitimate, individuals cannot break the law without psychological damage to themselves. They will feel the pangs of conscience. Where a law, or the government, or the entire political system appears illegitimate, people will defy it without qualms.

To the extent that most people share many basic values within the same culture they can also share a view of legitimacy. To the extent that some basic values are shared across cultures, international and even world-wide ideas of legitimacy are possible. But this does not mean that there exists only one legitimate set of beliefs. Within most cultures, as well as across them, there are several viable value configurations and several acceptable ways of life. Sometimes, these differing views of what is legitimate can co-exist. The great world religions, such as Hinduism, Buddhism, Judaism, Christianity, Islam, as well as various types of philosophy, have existed side by side for many centuries and have all proved viable in practice.

Politics and the Habits of Compliance

By what means does politics accomplish the direction and self-direction of societies and the allocation of values within them? Primarily it functions through the habits of the great mass of the population of complying with the laws and commands of government; and these *habits of compliance* are reinforced and strengthened by the probability of enforcement of the law against those who may transgress it. Compliance habits are the invisible partner of government, but they do more than 90 per cent of the job. If most automobile drivers were not in the habit of stopping at red lights without a traffic policeman being present, the law about stoplights would be impossible to enforce at any reasonable cost. Similarly, the habits of most people *not* to murder their neighbors, *not* to burglarize houses, and *not* to steal cars are what make it at all practical to enforce the laws against the very small minority of people who still occasionally do these things.

In order to maintain the compliance habits of the many it is not necessary to achieve perfect enforcement against the few who are violators. Of every ten known murders in major U. S. cities no more than five are followed by conviction. Although there are apparently six chances in ten of getting away with murder, these odds are still not high enough to make murder an attractive undertaking.[4] Something similar holds for most other types of crime. The enforcement rates are imperfect but they suffice to keep the amount of crime down to some tolerable level.

[4] In the United States in 1967, one murder was committed for roughly every 24,000 people; in many advanced countries the frequency is much less.

When the compliance habits of the population decline or disappear, laws may become unenforceable. Generally, laws become difficult to enforce when less than 90 per cent of the population will obey them voluntarily. That was the story of prohibition. A little more than 50 per cent of the American electorate tried to outlaw the thirst for alcoholic beverages of a little less than 50 per cent, but the widespread lack of compliance with the resulting laws made them impossible to enforce; this, in turn, encouraged further disobeying of the laws. Certainly, the probabilities of enforcement can help in the development of compliance habits, though it should not be forgotten that compliance habits are the biggest and strongest part of the combination with enforcement, and that the effects of laws and enforcement threats are, on the whole, relatively marginal.

We use laws to control human behavior because they are cheap to pass and, so long as most people obey them voluntarily, not too expensive to enforce. Laws, the habits of compliance with them, and the probabilities of law enforcement enable a society to continue to function. Within limits, we can change society by changing laws, so long as these will be obeyed. But the greatest changes in society come about through changes in habits of compliance. Slavery was abolished in the nineteenth century not because of legislation but because the entire cultural and social climate of the Western world had begun to change. No one legislature could have legislated such a change, but once the change came, laws took their proper place in accelerating the abolition of slavery and in making abolition stick. The great reforms of the world cannot be started by legislation, although they can be helped by it. Legislation is only one of the elements contributing to the deeper change in the thoughts and feelings of individuals, of groups, and of whole societies which transforms one cultural or political epoch into another.

Politics and Priorities

The Art of the Possible.   Politics is indeed what nineteenth-century statesmen called it: *the art of the possible.* Any politician or statesman to be effective must know what can be done politically at any particular time and place. He must know what laws and behavior people will accept, what they will regard as legitimate, and what their habits of compliance will permit to be enforced. And he must know what laws and behavior people will continue to support for a long enough time to achieve the desired results.

What is practical—that is, possible—at any particular time and place depends on people's fundamental habits and values and, to a very important extent, on their *scale of priorities*—on their beliefs of which things should come first. So long as Americans in the early nineteenth century thought that the protection of property, including property in human slaves, was more important than the setting free of slaves and the freedom of all individuals, the abolition of slavery was not practical politics in the United States. It took a generation of unruly young men—many of them bearded—to change the limits of the possible. For years, abolitionists were called unrealistic and extremist, and, from the point of view of their contemporaries, no doubt they were. Indeed, like all extreme political causes, abolitionism attracted the types of people who found it easier to take extreme positions and make extreme demands than to work patiently at the possible. But the extremists—including some angry and violent men like John Brown—did fulfill a mission in history. Their deeds and misdeeds, their crimes and their sacrifices, all contributed to one result: they changed the sense of urgency among their countrymen. They helped to rearrange priorities. And they opened the way for responsible statesmen and practitioners of the art of the possible, like Abraham Lincoln, to find a practical solution to the problem of abolishing slavery while at the same time keeping the Union together and making the new political arrangements work.

At the beginning of the Civil War, the hero of the Italian National Revolution, Giuseppe Garibaldi, offered to fight for the North if Lincoln would immediately announce the abolition of slavery. Lincoln might well have appreciated the contribution which Garibaldi's military talent and heroism could have made, but he felt, probably quite realistically, that he needed even more urgently the support of Delaware, Maryland, and Kentucky, indeed of all the border states, and that he could get their support at that time not on the issue of slavery but on the issue of union. Accordingly, Lincoln waged the Civil War as a war for the preservation of the Union and retained the support of the border states throughout. He had to do without the support of Garibaldi, but he did abolish slavery in 1863—and he won the Civil War.

Reordering Priorities.   In our own time, we may occasionally face similar problems and similar decisions. A Brazilian student chafing under dictatorship in his country said that he thought he and his contemporaries had to become a "sacrificed generation." He felt that they would have to sacrifice their immediate political effectiveness by making extreme demands in order to free the way again for a more continuous and evolutionary type of politics in years to come. Whether this will prove true for Brazil remains to be seen; so does the extent to which similar problems may have to be faced at certain times in the United States.

The United States is now engaged in a great reassessment of national priorities. Its people have not yet fully decided whether poverty in South Chicago is more urgent or less urgent than political stability in South Vietnam. If it becomes clear that the wealth and resources of the United States do not permit it to deal with both these problems on the scale which each demands, some people may find a role in trying to call upon the consciences of their countrymen and persuading them to change their sense of priorities and values. But, in the end, if the United States and the world are to be changed constructively, it will be done by people who have mastered the art of the possible, by people who can make coalitions and keep them and who can not only *demand* that the world be changed for the better but can actually bring such change about.

Politics and Learning

The Capacity to Learn. All self-direction is crippled without self-correction. The ability to correct actions and errors is crucial for all self-steering and self-government. To the extent that we are able to correct or improve our behavior by making more complex responses to the world around us, we say that we have the capacity to learn. *Learning capacity* is the ability of a person or group to give a reliable new response when an old stimulus is repeated. (We can even build machines today which have some learning capacity in this sense.) This is the opposite of the kind of nonlearning that occurs when a person or group reacts with the same response to anything that happens. To some members of the John Birch Society, everything is a Communist threat; and, to some Communist Party Secretaries in the Soviet Union, everything is a Western plot.

All learning ultimately requires reallocating some of the resources of the learning person, group, or system. This is often a costly and painful process, because it is often neither cheap nor easy to change old habits and arrangements. The more we learn about the relationship of the races in the United States, the more we recognize that our habits need change and that our resources need redistribution, although whether we are prepared to make the necessary changes and sacrifices is another matter.

The *politics of dogma* tries to avoid the costs involved in modifying old ideas or in accepting new ones. Here the political process serves mainly to defend cherished beliefs and illusions, and here politics is based on the assumption that no new information is either possible or desirable. The politics of dogma usually seeks to preserve existing practices and institutions, but this is not always the case. Those persons or groups who advocate particular forms of change but who have closed their minds to all other forms also practice the politics of dogma. The critical factor is not the attitude toward the status quo, but the attitude toward learning.

In contrast, the *politics of discovery* begins with the proposition that though we know something about ourselves, our needs, and our capacities and about the world in which we live, we do not know all there is to know. We still have need for additional knowledge and, indeed, actively seek it. We regard the political process as a means of obtaining new knowledge, and we are willing to act upon this knowledge once obtained, despite the price we may have to pay for such action. A similar stress on discovery has characterized the growth of modern science. As the style of thinking and acting that seeks discoveries spreads into political behavior, our politics may become less dogmatic and more oriented toward the making of political discoveries and personal sacrifices.

Viewed over the longer term, politics has the function of coordinating the learning process of a whole society. That is to say, when a new problem arises and confronts a people or a country, or some other sizable social human group, and old answers are useless in coping with it, or when a new response to an old problem becomes necessary because some critical threshold has been passed—as when the forests have been cut down to the point where soil erosion threatens and new trees have to be planted—then the society has to learn a set of new habits.

Whenever a society has to acquire new habits it will discover that not all people can learn at the same speed. Some individuals and groups learn very quickly, many learn at more nearly the average or modal speed of the society, and some are particularly slow or resistant. But if the society as a whole has to make a response, its behavior may have to be coordinated. Here the power of government can play a vital role. By offering rewards for the behavior needed, or by using penalties to accelerate the stragglers, it can help the society to respond more quickly and uniformly than in the absence of such assistance. This function of politics may well be perennial, so long as human societies meet new conditions and have to learn new habits of response to them and so long as human beings differ in their speed of learning. The hopeful theory of both anarchists and Marxists that the state someday will "wither away" and that all government and all politics will become superfluous is not likely to be realized. Even though many present-day tasks of government may one day disappear, in some respects politics and government have a perpetual function to fulfill in the ordering of human affairs.

Accelerating Social Learning.   Politics has the task of coordinating human expectations and social learning in such a way as to help society attain its goals. Attainment of goals, according to the sociologist Talcott Parsons, is one of the fundamental functions of every social system. But society not only tries to attain the goals it espouses at a particular time; it can set new goals and try to attain them.

This setting and changing of goals is different from merely trying to attain the goals one has. Indeed, it may be crucial for a society not to turn political commitment into idolatry—not to make its current goals into little tin gods to be worshipped. It was a simple psychological process that made American pioneers in the nineteenth century write on the sides of their covered wagons the slogan "California or bust." But when a modern government writes on its flag some policy goal with the invisible subscript "or bust," the situation becomes dangerous. In the nuclear age it may be important for governments to realize that goals cannot be treated as absolutes in either domestic or international politics. Rather, our social and political goals must be thought about, discussed, reevaluated in the political process, and in time changed—one hopes for the better. Such changes in the goals of a society, however, may also involve some changes in its structure.

Self-Transformation.   Eventually it is possible for a society not only to change some of its patterns and a few of its goals, but also to become changed in so many aspects and with respect to so many goals, that one may speak of its *self-transformation*. Western societies, in particular, have repeatedly exhibited this power of self-transformation. Medieval Western Europe in the tenth century was transformed substantially as a result of the Roman Papacy's rise to independent political power and the Church's acquisition of freedom to run its affairs without undue interference from secular governments. Since that time, Western civilization has been different from anything it was before and from any other civilization in the world. For hundreds of years, Western man usually had not one but two authorities above him, and he experienced not only the problems but also the responsibilities and opportunities of making his own decisions.

Centuries later, the American Revolution was described by John Adams as fundamentally a change in the habits and customs of the American people, and Adams felt that this transformation was more important than what had happened on the battlefields of the War of Independence. Great and bloody revolutions have occurred in other countries as well: in England in the seventeenth century, in France in the eighteenth, and in Mexico, Russia, and China in the twentieth. Yet major changes also have occurred without significant violence. British Parliamentary and voting reforms transformed the country between 1832 and 1884. The American age of reform between 1890 and 1910, and again the reforms of the New Deal in the 1930s, were epochs in which the American political system and, to some extent, American political culture became transformed. Whether change comes violently or peacefully, it is likely that any large society that wishes to retain its vitality must retain its power of partial or far-reaching self-transformation. This is true even though the governments of many societies, and notably of dictatorships, would much prefer to pretend that they and the institutions on which they are based are going to last forever.

The Unity of Politics

The concept of politics has been explored from a variety of perspectives. We have observed that politics involves the self-direction of communities, the allocation of values, the search for legitimate patterns of compatible values and policies, the art of the possible, and sometimes a fundamental resetting of priorities; it also involves the coordination of social learning, the attainment of the goals of a society, the changing of these goals, the setting of new ones, and even the self-transformation of an entire country, its people, and its culture. But all these are different aspects of a single process: the common decisions of men and women about their fate.

The many different aspects of politics are appropriate topics of the study we call political science. This study enquires into the stakes of politics, the participants in politics, the nature of states and nations, the varieties of political thought, the functions and structure of the political system, the development, administration, and execution of policies, the making of political decisions, and the evaluation of political performance. These are topics to which we turn our attention in the next chapters—without losing sight, we hope, of the unity that gives all these studies purpose and meaning.

Key Terms and Concepts

politicization
politics
public sector
gross national product
government as steering
cognitive dissonance
extreme ideology
moderate ideology
extremism
reality
realism
interest
values
authoritative

justice
power
stability
Lasswell's eight basic values
security
liberty
legitimacy
habits of compliance
scale of priorities
learning capacity
politics of dogma
politics of discovery
self-transformation

Additional Readings

Aristotle. *Politics.*

Easton, D. *Framework for Political Analysis.* Englewood Cliffs, N. J.: Prentice-Hall, 1965.

Eayres, J. *The Art of the Possible: Government and Foreign Policy in Canada.* Toronto: University of Toronto Press, 1961.

Festinger, L. *A Theory of Cognitive Dissonance.* Stanford, Calif.: Stanford University Press, 1962.

Lasswell, H. *Politics: Who Gets What, When, How?* Cleveland: The World Publishing Co., 1958.

Mannheim, K. *Ideology and Utopia.* London: Routledge & Kegan Paul, 1936.

Plato. *The Republic.*

Weber, M. *Politics as a Vocation.* Philadelphia: Fortress Press, 1965.

The Stakes of Politics

The philosopher William James persistently asked one question about an idea or institution—"What difference does it make?" We would like to know what difference politics makes, and within the sphere of politics what difference a particular political institution or action may make. But before we can answer these questions, we must ask *to what* does politics make a difference? What is at stake in politics? What can be changed, rearranged, or redistributed by politics? The present chapter deals with these matters. The next chapter then asks, *to whom* does politics make a difference? This, in turn, leads us to the study of political participants and interests.

Chapter 2

The Political Allocation of Resources and Opportunities

What is directly at stake in politics emerges from an examination of the political, or public, sectors of most countries. Generally speaking, in most of the advanced non-Communist countries, the public sector directly involves approximately 40 per cent of the national income or 35 per cent of the gross national product.[1] Since about one-third of the capital stock of a modern society (roads, school buildings, research laboratories, and the like) is now in the public sector, roughly a third of the wealth of society is directly at stake in the politics of highly developed non-Communist countries.

[1] Roughly speaking, the *gross national product* (GNP) is the sum total of all goods and services produced in a country, measured in current prices. The *national income* (NI, or net national product, NNP) is calculated by subtracting from the GNP the sums required for replacement and amortization of the worn-out capital equipment of the society—amounting to between 10 and 20 per cent of GNP in highly developed countries—and by adding or subtracting the net gains or losses from dealings with the rest of the world. In the case of some advanced countries, such as Britain, the gains from foreign trade and services may amount to as much as 5 to 10 per cent of GNP. For further discussion, see Paul Samuelson, *Economics,* 8th ed. (New York: McGraw-Hill, 1970).

As for employment, the public sector directly controls between one-twelfth and one-eighth of the jobs or the work force. In Communist countries, the public sector involves roughly two-thirds of the national income or the gross national product, and very often more than half of the work force. But since most Communist countries still have a large agricultural work force (working either on collective farms or on agricultural cooperatives, as in Russia, or even on small owner-operated farms, as in Yugoslavia or Poland) the Communist countries have a mixture of public employment, cooperative employment, and self-employment.

The indirect stakes of politics are larger. Politics can make the difference between inflation and deflation by determining price levels, the values of people's savings, employment levels and employment opportunities, and the chances of vertical mobility, of moving up or down in society. Politics also can make the difference between more racial or religious discrimination or greater equality. Politics affects all aspects of life and even life itself. It affects the look and the smell of our cities. It affects the safety and the dignity of people in the streets. It affects our experience of justice or injustice. It affects our life styles and our life expectancies. In 1968 politics in the form of foreign policy was one of the ten principal causes of death in the United States. One of its operations, the Vietnam War, in that year killed about as many Americans as were killed by criminal homicide. For every American killed in 1968 by lawless violence at home, another American was sent to his death by the lawful operation of the political system. This politically-caused death rate was highly concentrated, however, among young men between the ages of nineteen and twenty-six.

All these results of politics are produced by the interplay of the political process with the entire society. What happens to all of us happens because of the continuous and pervasive interaction of political behavior and political decisions with the economic, sociological, and cultural patterns of society—those habits, practices, and institutions which we so often and so superficially consider "nonpolitical."

Power: A Net and a Fish

There are, as we noted in Chapter 1, at least eight values which most people desire: power, respect, rectitude, wealth, health, enlightenment, skill, and affection. Let us look more closely at these values, each of which forms one of the basic stakes of politics. To begin with, there is power.

Power can be thought of as the instrument by which all other values are obtained, much as a net is used for catching fish. For many people, power is also a value in itself; in fact, to some of them it is often the prize fish. Since power functions both as means and end, as net and fish, it is a key value in politics. But it is a key value only in the context of other values, because men do not live by one value alone.

Power has been defined as the capacity to change the probability of outcomes; this is the definition proposed by Robert Dahl. Another definition is that power is the participation in decisions about severe sanctions, that is, about major rewards or deprivations; this definition is preferred by Harold Lasswell. In either case, *power* is the ability to make things happen that would not have happened otherwise. In this sense it is akin to causality, that is, to the production of a change in the probability distribution of events in the world. And since the world is changing already, power deals with the change of change—or second-order change. Thus power involves our ability to change the changes that are already under way and would continue without our intervention.

Hand in hand with the subject of power goes the question of influence. If we ask who has power in politics, we also ask who has the most influence. Lasswell defines politics as "the study of influence and the influential," and he defines influence as participation in decisions about relatively milder sanctions. Based on this definition then, influence is a broader and milder form of power. Other writers use the words "influence" and "power" nearly interchangeably. Often, however, we think of influence as also involving some appeal to the thoughts and feelings of the person to be influenced. *Influence* then tries to get inside the personality of a person, whereas power operates upon him mainly from without. If Arthur M. Schlesinger, Jr. or John Kenneth Galbraith were disfranchised in a Congressional election because he had moved before it was to be held, he still might be able to *influence* the results of the election through his writings, but without a vote he would have no *power* to affect the outcome. Although not everyone who has influence has power as well, everyone who has power also has influence.

To say that the essence of politics is power and influence is to state a partial truth, but not the whole truth. Short-run politics and short-run history is the story of changes among the *elite*—the few who currently hold most power. In the long run, however, the greatest developments in history have been brought about by changes among those who were believed to be powerless—by changes in the needs, habits, and actions of the many.

Power Over Nature; Power Over Men.   Power consists mainly in power over nature and in power over men. These two kinds of power often interact. In the course of history it has turned out that when men increase their power over nature, they can use this greater power as a means of increasing their power over men. When men learned to tame horses, they became riders on horseback and used their new fighting skill as horsemen to subjugate other men. When the Assyrians and Egyptians learned to irrigate and thus to control rivers, this power permitted the centralized monarchies in Assyria and Egypt to pile up the agricultural surpluses that maintained the bureaucracies and armies of these huge irrigation states. In more modern societies, the development of ships to cross the oceans (and later planes to cross the skies) often was transformed into power over colonies and colonial peoples, and sometimes into power over the poor and oppressed in the home countries of the nations whose rulers set out to conquer the world.

These two kinds of power differ in important ways. Power over nature is something men can share. Power over men is something for which men must compete. Machiavelli said that a prince who advances another prince's power diminishes his own. Put in mathematical terms, Machiavelli and thinkers in his tradition have seen power as a zero-sum game. A *zero-sum game* is a game in which the payoffs to all players add up to zero; it is a special case of a fixed-sum game where all payoffs add up to a constant sum. Whatever one competitor wins in a zero-sum game he can win only from the losses of a rival, so that any winnings of anyone must come out of the losses of others. A zero-sum game is a merciless form of competition. What is good for one player must be bad for some other player. And insofar as power in politics is of this competitive, Machiavellian, zero-sum character, the contest for power is without end or mercy. Fortunately, power is not only of this kind.

Power over nature is something which mankind can collectively increase and has increased for the last half-million years. It is a *variable-sum game,* one in which players compete with one another but all can win jointly at the expense of the bank, or of nature. We all have been winners from increased power over nature, from the development of vaccines, irrigation, dams, and other great contributions to human life. By the same token, of course, people also can lose jointly to nature as they have lost in countries depleted by famine, pestilence, or soil erosion.

Even within human society, people can share in the positive by-products of increases in power over men. It is possible to increase such power to the degree that men expand their capacity to act, to do things, to coordinate their behavior, or to comply with other people's wishes. Moreover, a tyrant ruling a million powerless illiterates has less power to affect the outcome of many events than a democratic ruler governing a million high school graduates, because the high school graduates can do more things than the illiterates. It is not merely the greater education that enables the high school graduates to do more. Equally important is the greater experience a democratic country gives its people in making their own decisions and in thinking and acting for themselves.

One of the most important questions of political analysis, therefore, is whether a particular power situation is primarily a zero-sum game or whether it is possible to discover variable-sum aspects within it, so that different players can all win or improve their positions jointly.

Power and Voting.   Whether a power situation is primarily a zero-sum game or a variable-sum game, it is useful to know how the chips of power are divided up among the various participants. As a simple example of the distribution of power we can ask, who has the vote? At the beginning of the century only about 25 per cent of the American people could vote. Even today, when there are over 120 million adults in the United States, registered voters number less than 90 million. That is to say, there are nearly 30 million adults in the United States—or nearly one-fourth of all adults—who are, for all practical purposes, disfranchised. On election day they cannot vote, even if they want to. They are effectively disfranchised through a host of different institutional arrangements, registration laws, residence requirements, and time-consuming procedures for registration. Such requirements and procedures in effect disfranchise not only many poor, but also many well-educated professional people, employees, and students, who change their address[2]—as do about one-fifth of the American people every year.[3] The situation is made worse by the curious habits of southern registrars in the presence of black voters, or the habits of northern registrars in such riot-torn cities as Newark, New Jersey where the majority of the population is black, but the majority of registered voters is white. In addition to the nearly 30 million disfranchised adults living in our country, there are another 8 million adults who are registered voters but who disfranchise themselves by not taking the trouble to vote.

Those who are enfranchised and do vote are typically members of the upper-income and middle-income groups, particularly those who stay put in their localities and those in small towns and on farms. The actual voters are also the older people. Voting is heaviest among those over thirty-five, and the median age of the American voters is forty-two. The young may or may not want to trust people over thirty, but to win an election, one must swing people of the median age of forty-two.

It is these voters then who may decide whether the United States shall fight a war in Southeast Asia, or whether the United States is to outrace the Soviet Union in increasing its supply of intercontinental nuclear weapons. The male students who in 1968 rang doorbells for Senator Eugene McCarthy in the New Hampshire primary had to shave and get a haircut, and the female students had to wear dresses, in order to win 42 per cent of the vote for their candidate, and to bring about the retirement of Lyndon B. Johnson from the presidency. They had, in effect, to persuade the economically comfortable, home-owning, white voter of forty-two.

In a representative democracy the young are a permanent minority. Young men of the age most sensitive to the draft, men between twenty-one

[2] The residence requirements for voting in a presidential election have been removed in many states, so these people are not formally disfranchised, but the discouraging effect of cumbersome procedures remains. In many other democracies, voter registration is universal and automatic, and the share of disfranchised adults is much smaller.

[3] Between March 1963 and March 1964, 19.6 per cent of the population one year old and above moved to a different house within the United States.

and twenty-six, constitute less than 4 per cent of the total population. When we combine this percentage with the percentage of young women in that age group, we get nearly 8 per cent of the population. But because so many of the young change their residence, or take jobs or go to college away from home and do not bother to cast an absentee ballot, or sometimes even to register, only less than 5 per cent of the electorate is in the age group whose lives and future are most immediately affected by the draft. This compares with about 30 per cent of the electorate over fifty years of age. Foreign policy is often shaped, therefore, by those ideas which were internalized twenty or thirty years ago by voters who are now over fifty, and certainly by those internalized ideas of voters now over forty-two. Thus, through the workings of the electoral system, the views and preferences of the older generation enjoy a disproportionate weight over the lives and bodies of the young (see Figure 2.1).

This state of affairs is not something radically new, but in a mass democracy it is something that becomes more seriously new in a period when international relations as well as domestic politics are rapidly changing. The more rapid the change, the harder becomes the communication

Figure 2.1

Voting Participation by Age Groups: United States, 1964, 1966

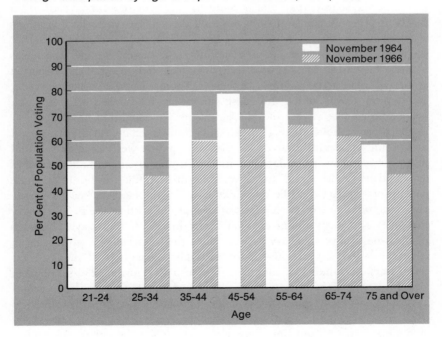

Source: U.S. Bureau of the Census, Current Population Reports, *Series P-20, Nos. 143 and 174, 1965 and 1968.*

among age groups, and the more serious the effects of unequal representation of different age groups by the electoral system.

If, as time goes on, democracy is to be made more vital and viable, people will have to find ways of improving such representation. Perhaps the most radical among the young will revive one of the ideas of John Calhoun, a conservative statesman of a hundred years ago, who developed the notion of *concurrent majorities*. According to this view, a national law should be valid only if also backed by a concurrent majority of the representatives of the section most directly affected, such as the South in Calhoun's day; today such groups as the young, the poor, or the big-city dwellers might qualify as concurrent majorities. Perhaps somebody will think of a better idea. But it is clear that the present method of representation, though it has worked well for many things and in many respects, has some serious imperfections. Much remains to be improved. Indeed, we may have to look for some improvements quite quickly.

Motives and Opportunities for Power.   Other inequalities in the distribution of power stem from differences in motivation and in opportunities. More often than not, a group that is disadvantaged and partly powerless will be disappointed when it first tries to exercise power. When its attempts to exercise power prove unsuccessful, a considerable part of its members will conclude that such efforts are not worth the trouble. They will either lapse into apathy or become advocates of an extreme radicalism that will prevent them from coordinating their efforts with those of others of more moderate views—who are apt to be more numerous. Whether they stay at home and say there is nothing to be done or isolate themselves at some far end of the political spectrum, in either case the disappointed group will cease to be politically effective. Thus, it is those very groups that are denied power which are most vulnerable to the loss of motivation needed to get the power they lack and perhaps ought to have.

Of course, among those motivated to claim a share in power, not all have equal opportunities to do so. Even if everyone were sufficiently equal in power to get his candidate automatically placed on the ballot, some of us would be "more equal" in power than others. The candidates of some persons or groups would be more likely to win the election because of the power or influence of the persons or groups supporting them. The party machines and party financiers would certainly have their say. The mass media would have their say as well, since they determine a great deal of what the voters see and hear and read. The owners of the media, their advertisers, and their staff members (who usually have a different point of view from that of the owners or advertisers) would all have a disproportionate influence on the election's outcome. Thus, even within a representative democracy, the political preferences of a truck driver from Jersey City or a stenographer from San Francisco carry less weight than the preferences of a network newscaster or a top executive of Ford or General Motors. Power and influence make that difference.

The Test of Reality. The more powerless a group is, the more important it is for its members to study the significance of power, and to seek ways of getting more. But the more powerful its members become and the more power they acquire, the more important it becomes for them to study the limits of power.

What determines the outcome of the actions of all those who can vote, nominate, elect, pass laws, and administer them—in short, of all those who have power? There is an ultimate test: external reality. A government can have the power to pass a tariff, but the world economic situation may determine what actually happens after the tariff is passed. An administration can initiate a financial policy, but the world may produce a run on the nation's currency which may throw national finances into disarray. A nation may start a military action in some distant country, but what then happens there may make a great difference to the policy that originally looked so well-conceived.

There may also be a difference between the power to force outcomes on other groups and the power to produce change in oneself or one's group. Some psychologists have spoken of the difference between power *over* people and power *with* people. The latter is the power to coordinate, to pull a group of people into phase, so that their efforts reinforce each other. So long as the sailors on the *Bounty* could not coordinate their actions, Captain Bligh was irresistible. Once they managed to coordinate their efforts, Bligh was out of a job. If they could have coordinated their activities even better, they might have got to a more comfortable island than Pitcairn.

The power to promote mutual coordination and cooperation among people may help them to discover their own strength. It may help them to discover many other things as well. In such a widening context of discovery and sensitivity, power can be used to serve creativity, to aid the production of new combinations of thoughts and actions which are relevant to the needs of the people concerned. When this happens, power becomes, not self-narrowing or self-defeating, but an instrument of human liberation.

Some Other Stakes: Respect, Rectitude, Wealth, Health, Enlightenment, Skill, and Affection

Respect, and with it, status, prestige, and authority, is a value which is perhaps even more sought after than power. Relations between races, among cultural, ethnic, or religious groups, between management and labor, between generations, and among nations in the world all involve the allocation of respect. This value seems intangible but is not. Its results are readily observable. *Respect* involves the precedence given to people, the priority given to their messages, and the preference given to their wishes. Indirectly respect affects employability, trust, career chances, and the likelihood of society responding to people's needs. The more respected a group is, the better off it is likely to be. The more that respect is denied a group, the worse off the group is apt to be.

In the short run, disadvantaged groups are often denied respect. In the process of their seeking to obtain their rights, they, in turn, often deny respect to those who are privileged in relation to them. Thus we find young white policemen calling mature black men "boys" and young black men calling policemen "pigs." Here a denial of respect which was originally one-sided has become mutual. Sometimes the pursuit of respect can be a zero-sum game in which there is very little respect available in the community and every one of the struggling groups despises the other: in 1968 embattled parents in the Ocean Hill and Brownsville sections of Brooklyn, New York and embattled teachers in a teachers' union mutually screamed insults at each other. But sometimes the pursuit of respect can be converted into a variable-sum game in which a society is able to give a reasonable amount of respect to everybody and to find ways in which everyone can get a reasonable priority for his *urgent* needs and be listened to at least a reasonable part of the time.

Respect (or deference) often is closely related to a third value at stake in politics: the value of *rectitude* or morality. Rectitude can be a competitive zero-sum value. In a conflict between two quite different and equally intolerant ideologies, each group of adherents may believe that all members or adherents of the other are heretics, madmen, traitors, deviationists, class enemies, or spawn of the devil (depending on each group's favorite invectives), to be repressed, expelled, or even murdered. The ability of a more tolerant society to find room for and to maintain several varieties of views of rectitude can convert the pursuit of rectitude into a variable-sum game.

Of course, there are limits to such mutual accommodation. As Abraham Lincoln pointed out: a wolf may have one definition of freedom or righteousness, and a sheep another. In a modern industrial society, it is almost certain that people will develop more than one religion, more than one philosophy, more than one ideology. The problem of permitting people to act righteously in terms of their own conscience in a society in which not everybody shares the same views of righteousness is crucial to the survival of modern societies.

Many conflicts about respect and rectitude are intensified by poverty, and eased by wealth. Quite often it is possible to create more opportunities for respect and rectitude, and even for power, if there is more wealth in a society. Because it is difficult (and possibly dangerous) for an automobile driver to decide at a traffic crossing whether at any given moment the east-west or north-south traffic should have priority, a society may use a traffic policeman or a traffic light to determine which of the two lines of traffic is to be permitted to move. A richer society can build an overpass, thereby permitting both traffic streams to proceed at full speed, without the presence of a policeman. This is one case which fits Karl Marx's prophecy that in a more abundant economy the government of men would be replaced by the administration of things. Here indeed the enforcement of law is replaced by the maintenance of concrete—and it works.

Wealth, then—the total supply of goods, services, and facilities and re- sources for production—is a decisive variable for the range of options before a society. At the beginning of the 1970s, the world had an average per capita gross national product of about $800 and a median gross national product of less than $400. These data cover 120 countries, over 90 per cent of mankind. But it is perfectly clear that world income is unequal- ly distributed. The 1968 United States per capita income was about $4,000. At present, one-seventeenth of mankind, the American people, has one-third of the world's income, and another one-seventeenth, the people of the Soviet Union, has one-sixth (see Figures 2.2 and 6.8).

World income is steadily increasing. The average growth rate in the world is 2 per cent per capita. These data are again drawn from only 120 countries, but they cover most of the world's population. Although starting points have been fantastically unequal in different nations, present growth rates vary far less. This fact affords some comfort, for it means that in terms of proportionate income levels, world inequality is not increasing rapidly. If one country is only one-tenth as rich as another, and the incomes of both are growing at the same rate, the ratio between the two incomes will remain unchanged. But though there is little or no change in relative terms, the absolute gap between rich and poor countries is widen- ing. If a country with a $200 per capita income doubles its income in twenty-five years, it will have $400, whereas the United States will go from $4,000 to $8,000. Proportionately, the difference will be the same. In absolute figures, the gap will have widened enormously.

It is important to see whether it is possible to achieve a gradual reduc- tion of inequality in the world at large, as has been done inside most of the modern countries. The figures have not yet been computed, but as a guess, perhaps one-third of 1 per cent of national income in modern countries, or 3 per cent per decade, moves out of the top 10 per cent of income receivers each year and becomes available for distribution among the poorer 90 per cent. In a highly unequal country, the top 10 per cent receives half the income or more. In the United States, the top 10 per cent receives 30 per cent of the income; in India, between 34 and 36 per cent; in Puerto Rico, 40 per cent; and in Guatemala, 47 per cent. In a more egalitarian, non- Communist country like Israel, the share of the top one-tenth is 24 per cent. If 2 or 3 per cent per decade moves out of the top sector, by the end of the century only about 24 or 25 per cent of the income may be going to

Figure 2.2

Power and Income of 120 Nations, 1966

Top area of each brick corresponds to national population; height corresponds to per capita GNP; and volume corresponds to total GNP.

Sources: *Adapted from K. W. Deutsch,* Nationalism and Social Communication *(Cambridge: MIT Press, 1966) by permission of MIT Press; Economic Bureau, U.S. Arms Control and Disarmament Agency,* World Military Expenditures and Related Data, *1966, Research Report 68-52, 1968.*

rman Democratic
public
1   1,658

Albania   1.9   366
Yugoslavia   19.7   457
Hungary   10.2   1,179
Romania   19.1   867
Bulgaria   8.3   918

ria
3
74

Soviet Union   233.1   1,531

Mongolia   1.1   439

China (mainland)
772.0   104

North Korea   12.4   234

Japan
98.9
986

Turkey   31.9   295
Israel   2.6   1,454
Lebanon   2.6   476
Iraq   8.3   268
Iran   25.5   252
Afghanistan   15.4   88

South Korea   29.1   131

Pakistan
117.0
115

Nepal
10.3   75

Burma   25.2   67
Laos   2.7   70

China (Taiwan)
13.3   235

Jordan
2.0   266
us
730

North
Vietnam
19.5   77

Saudi Arabia
4.4   380

Yemen
5.0   103

Thailand
32.9   141

South
Vietnam
16.5   126

Philippines
33.5   171

Ethiopia
23.0   65

India   501.6   74

Cambodia
6.3   139

Ceylon
11.5   147

Malaysia   9.7   311

Kenya   9.6   116
Uganda   7.7   92

anzania   11.5   75

Malagasy Republic   6.1   110

Indonesia   107.4   100

odesia
4   227

Data c. 1966

Australia   11.5   2,178

New Zealand
2.7   2,046

the top one-tenth of income receivers. (Their relative share of income will thus have declined; however, thanks to general economic growth, their absolute income will have increased greatly.)

Governments and the political process play an ever larger role in the growth and redistribution of income within each country. At the beginning of the century the federal government of the United States received as revenue about 4 per cent of the national income, and state and local governments collected another 7 per cent, adding up to a total of 11 per cent. Today the federal government and its agencies gather nearly 20 per cent of the national income (including spending on the Vietnam War), and state and local governments get roughly another 12 per cent, making a total of about 32 per cent. That is, every year for the past seven decades, about one-third of 1 per cent of the national income has moved into the government sector. The data for France, Britain, India, China, and the Soviet Union are similar.

Wealth to a certain extent can buy *health* and *well-being*. It is closely related to life expectancy, and to the economics of living and dying. In a comparison of sixty-seven countries in the early 1960s, about 75 per cent of the variance in life expectancy could be predicted from their respective per capita gross national products. In poorer countries life expectancy for females at birth was low. It was twenty-six years in Mali and thirty-two in India, in contrast to seventy-five in Sweden and seventy-three in the United States. In the United States a female baby at birth had about a seventy-five–year life expectancy if born white, but only a sixty-five–year life expectancy if born black. Yet the matter of life expectancy is not entirely dependent on wealth alone. People in Sweden, whose national income is but half that of the United States, and in Britain, whose national income is also far behind that of the United States, both have higher life expectancies than Americans. The difference can be attributed to politics. Sweden and Britain both have national health programs; the United States does not.

Wealth also buys *enlightenment*. A comparison of eighty countries in the early 1960s shows that about two-thirds of the variance in their levels of literacy is predictable from per capita incomes. Mass literacy levels, among people fifteen years and older, range from 1 per cent in Mozambique and 5 per cent in Ethiopia to 98 per cent in the United States, and slightly more in northwestern Europe. There are similar contrasts in regard to college and university students—the educational elite. In 1960 the number of these students per 1,000 population amounted to about 20 in the United States, 7.5 in Japan, 6.7 in France, 5.4 in the Soviet Union, but only 2.6 in Spain, 2.2 in India, 1.3 in Brazil, 0.3 in Ghana, 0.05 in Ethiopia, and 0.03 in Rhodesia and Nyasaland. Thus the availability of higher education, too, varies with national income, but less so than the existence of health or of literacy at the mass level.

In short, though wealth is important, it does not decide everything. In the areas of health and enlightenment, there are genuine political choices to be made at every level of national income; and the quality of life in each country is determined to a significant extent by the political choices which its people make.

The availability of *skill* also varies greatly among countries, regions, and ethnic groups. One of the reasons for this variance is politics. Black Americans for a long time have been excluded from apprenticeship in many skilled trades, particularly in the construction industries. Some unions, such as those of the automobile workers, steel workers, and garment workers, have welcomed black Americans and encouraged their training. By the start of the 1970s, the full and free access of minority Americans to all skilled trades had become an explosive political issue. To a milder degree, immigrant or foreign labor have been used mainly in unskilled trades in Britain and West Germany, and there, too, political disputes have arisen over the practice.

In a more general sense, skill is involved in the composition of a national work force and is affected by public policy, both directly and through the educational system. Some nations let their schools teach enlightenment but neglect skill. Other countries try to make a large portion of their people skilled. In the most advanced countries, unskilled and uneducated labor is becoming unemployable. The training of young high school dropouts is becoming increasingly a task of government.

There is an even greater range of choice and uncertainty in regard to the last of the basic values that are at stake in politics. This is the value of *affection*—the value which, in the form of friendship, Socrates believed to be at the basis of all politics. (Centuries later, St. Augustine wrote that a population becomes united into a people by having a common object of their love.) But affection cannot be bought by money, nor can it be compelled by power. It must be given freely; and it can only be won by a process of wooing, communication, help, and understanding. Affection among people from different regions, groups, and backgrounds still is an essential element in making a political community. It can be learned in common experiences that are meaningful and rewarding to all partners, but the speed and nature of its coming cannot be predicted. Politics can do much to destroy it, and something—though much less—to encourage it. But where politics does succeed in its efforts at healing, conciliation, and accommodation, the resulting growth of affection among individuals and between them, their government, and their political institutions, is one of the most important prizes of the political process.

Value Enjoyment: Who Gets What and How

In addition to these substantive values, people also desire certain ways of enjoying them. One of the primary stakes of politics is the manner in which any value can be enjoyed. There are perhaps two such ways. As we noted in Chapter 1, if somebody enjoys a value he usually likes to have it in *security,* so that he can count on continuing to enjoy it. Ever since the rise of the state, people have used political organizations to protect social arrangements, persons, and property. The more unequal or unjust the society was, the heavier was the machinery necessary for protection. Slave-owning societies used the state to protect and perpetuate the institution of slavery. Societies badly divided into rich and poor have used the state in part to preserve this unequal division.

But at the same time, security has required the protection of values other than wealth and power. As cities have grown and population density has increased, public health has needed additional protection, for protection against epidemic is a common interest of all social groups. As industrialization has progressed, the efficiency of the technology and the economy also has needed increased protection. The more elaborate and improbable the methods of production have become, the more important it has been to safeguard the conditions necessary for the continued functioning of this delicate technological and economic structure. Today the earth has approximately 3.5 billion people on it, or about twice as many as could be fed by earlier, traditional methods of agriculture. We could not now keep alive a large part of mankind if we did not have modern technologies and modern economies. Thus, mankind's security, health, and essential supplies of food and energy are now partially a task of the political sector.

We also like to enjoy a value in *liberty.* Liberty may mean many different things to different people. In different times and places, even the same people have felt one aspect of liberty to be more relevant to them than others. (For this reason, the great conservative thinker Edmund Burke claimed that it was more useful to speak of specific "liberties" than of liberty in general.)

In the days of Adam Smith toward the end of the eighteenth century, the most salient aspect of liberty seemed to be a negative one: the *absence of restraint.* A century later the simple absence of a prohibition sounded to many as a mockery. Thus, the French writer Anatole France noted, "The law in its majestic equality prohibits the rich as well as the poor to sleep under bridges, to beg in the streets, and to steal bread." France, and others, realized that the removal of unjust laws did not necessarily lead to justice, particularly when the conditions underlying the laws remained unequal.

Since the end of the nineteenth century, liberty has been defined not merely as the absence of restraint, but as something positive: the *presence of opportunity.* It is not enough to be told that you are not forbidden to drive an automobile: if you are to take advantage of this liberty, there must be an automobile available for you to drive.

Another positive aspect of liberty, stressed by the German philosopher Hegel in the early nineteenth century, is the *capacity to act.* To give a driver's license and an automobile to a blind man would not be helpful. He also would have to be given sight.

Closely related to the presence of opportunity and the capacity to act is the availability of an effective *range of choices*. The richer, more meaningful, and more rewarding the choices before an individual the freer he is. These choices must be meaningful to the people who have to choose, that is, they must correspond to their needs and memories. But to be both meaningful and rewarding to most people, such choices must include possibilities of employment, the availability of capital equipment, and opportunities to obtain information and enlightenment.

Another aspect of liberty is *spontaneity*, that is, the ability to act in accordance with one's own personality, without having to make a great effort at self-denial or self-control and without being subjected to external constraints. This refers to the compatibility of the choices offered with the personality structure of the chooser. It relates to how well the available choices fit his particular, personal needs, and often the particular culture with which he has become familiar, in which he has grown up, and which has become part of his personality. Since spontaneity to so many people is the essential part of liberty, and since it is so closely tied up with culture and familiarity, the existence of a sense of spontaneity has sometimes masked the absence of real liberty. Rousseau noted this when he observed that the Poles felt free so long as their nobles were Polish; when their nobles began to emulate French fashions and culture, the Poles called them tyrants. Thus, a regime that was familiar seemed congenial, and therefore acceptable. But spontaneity means more than acting in harmony with the familiar. It also means the opportunity to change one's mind—and to change it freely, even playfully, without narrowing external constraints of political pressure or economic scarcity, and without excessive internal constraints of one's own personal anxieties, ideology, or culture.

In sum, liberty involves the opportunity for *many-sided cumulative growth*. Liberty means a sequence of choices and steps such that one ends up having more choices than before, fewer restraints, more present opportunities, an increased capacity to act, think, and choose, and a wider play of spontaneity. What we call government and politics—the flow of compliance and defiance, of support and opposition, of rewards and penalties, of permissions and prohibitions play a decisive role—but not the only role—in making possible such a creative or liberating sequence of developments.

Clearly, politics can make a difference. It determines much of the allocation of resources and opportunities, up to one-third or one-half of the wealth of many nations, and corresponding shares in other values. Every major value can be at stake in politics: power, respect, rectitude, wealth, health, enlightenment, skill, and affection. And politics can decide much about the manner in which we may enjoy our values—whether in security and liberty or not.

But politics can do still more. Ideally, politics is engaged in a triple game to maintain mankind's chances of life, to enhance and improve them in this age of ideological rivalry, and to change the unjust distributions of values toward more viable, more just, more ethically acceptable distributions, suited to man's growing up in the industrial age. Finally, politics has the task of developing forms of coordination and public self-control—forms that will enable people to make sure that what ought to be done, and can be done, will in fact get done while there is still time.

Key Terms and Concepts

gross national product (GNP)	rectitude
national income (NI)	wealth
power	health
influence	enlightenment
zero-sum game	skill
variable-sum game	affection
concurrent majorities	security
respect	liberty

Additional Readings

Banfield, E. *The Moral Basis of a Backward Society*. Glencoe, Ill.: Free Press, 1958.

Brown, H. *et al. The Next Hundred Years*. New York: Viking Press, 1966. Chapters 5, 6, 18.

Lane, R. *Political Life*. New York: The Free Press, 1959.

Lasswell, H. and A. Kaplan. *Power and Society: A Framework for Political Inquiry*. New Haven: Yale University Press, 1950.

Lasswell, H. *Politics: Who Gets What, When, How?* Cleveland: The World Publishing Co., 1958.

————. *World Politics and Personal Insecurity*. New York: The Free Press, 1965.

Oppenheim, F. *Dimensions of Freedom*. New York: St. Martin's, 1961.

Rappaport, A. *Fights, Games, Debates*. Ann Arbor: University of Michigan Press, 1960.

Wittfogel, K. *Oriental Despotism*. New Haven: Yale University Press, 1963.

The Participants in Politics

Who participates in politics? Let us go back to Lasswell's notion of politics as the study of influence and the influential. The quickest and cheapest way to find out what a country is likely to do when facing a major decision is to ask its top man. In the United States the man to ask would be the President; in England it would be the Prime Minister. But to know what policy a country is likely to adopt, it is not enough simply to ask its President or Prime Minister what he thinks he can do politically. One also has to know what support his preferred policy is likely to get from the heads of his executive departments, and from the top officials under them.

Chapter 3

When the President of the United States wants to get something done, he needs the cooperation of one of his administrative agencies to draw up a plan of action, and he needs people and facilities to put the plan into effect. If the head of the agency and its top-level officials are unenthusiastic about the plan, they can consume a remarkable amount of time going through the motions of carrying it out without actually doing so. Several Presidents have ordered the Department of Defense to insist that all major defense contractors follow fair employment practices by allocating a proper share of jobs to qualified blacks and members of other minority groups. Specifically, the Department was told to withhold contracts from firms which failed to comply within a reasonable time with the government's standards. To date, these orders are still awaiting full implementation— and many blacks, including men trained in skilled trades by the armed services themselves, are still waiting to be hired.

In many ages and countries, chief executives have similarly depended on the people around them to carry out their wishes. In the 1770s and 1780s, King Louis XVI of France wished to bolster the finances of his government which was tottering into bankruptcy. Twice he appointed bankers—first Turgot, and then Necker—to reduce expenditures and increase government income by collecting taxes from the nobles and clergy. Both men were thwarted by the opposition of these two groups and of the courtiers surrounding the King. Both men were dismissed; the government eventually went bankrupt; France fell into revolution; and the King was beheaded, as were many of the courtiers who had influenced and controlled his decisions.

Monarchs, Presidents, and Prime Ministers thus depend on a number of individuals for advice and for the implementation of their policies. They depend on their cabinets, on the permanent undersecretaries in the various departments or ministries, on the top people in the civil service, on the top people in the military, on the top people in the various interest groups, and, under constitutional systems of government, on the heads of important legislative committees. Taken together, all these add up to what we call the *top elite.*

Dictators, too, usually depend upon a top elite of key people who surround them. On the surface, one man may seem to rule, as Hitler and Mussolini claimed to, and as Stalin appeared to. Or the highly visible rulers may be a small committee, such as the Politburo of the ruling party in a Communist country, or a military junta of Greek or Latin American officers. Behind the scenes, however, such conspicuous rulers depend on their chiefs of police, the commanders of strategically located military units, the chief propagandists and heads of the mass media, the top-level bureaucrats, the leaders of political and cultural mass organizations, and the heads of the main economic, financial, and technical organizations, firms, and interest groups.

Most of the major industrial and financial enterprises in non-Communist countries are owned, of course, by private corporations. In Communist countries they are owned by the state. In either type of country, however, their top managers are likely to be influential, and therefore to belong to the top elite.

Top Elites and Mid-Elites

Who Are the Top Elites?   Members of the top elite are frequently identifiable by the so-called *position method.* That is, they fill positions so strategically located in the decision-making system of a country that, unless they are unusually incompetent, they almost cannot avoid having considerable influence. These people control the decisive traffic intersections of the message flows and communication streams of government. Those who decide whom the President sees, for instance, his top White House assistants and others, belong to the top elite. Between 150 and 200 incumbents of such top positions—in government, in the major political parties, in the major interest groups, and in the major occupational divisions—daily make decisions for millions of people.

In Western-style democracies, these groups are free to oppose each other openly. In Communist countries, such as the Soviet Union, a single party has all the publicly acknowledged power. In such countries, the people who want more money spent on rockets must bargain behind the scenes with those who want more money spent on artificial fertilizer so that all can unanimously vote an agreed policy at the public session of the Supreme Soviet. Thus, before such public ceremonies, there is a good deal of bargaining, negotiation, and even wire-pulling and pressure politics.

Some non-Communist countries, too, are governed by a single party, or else by a party which is so much stronger than the others that it virtually rules the country. The people of Mexico and India (and of Turkey between 1920 and 1960) have concentrated most of the visible power in the hands of a single party, whose leaders accordingly hold an important place among the top elite. In all such countries, however, the top elite also includes other members, military or civilian, who owe their position mainly to groups other than the ruling party.

The top elite can also be identified by *reputation*. The question here is not who has the top job but who has the reputation of making the decisions. It may be that the man in the top position, who signs a particular decision or decree or act or bill, is simply a rubber stamp, signing whatever his first assistant puts before him. In time the word will spread among the knowledgeable that the real power in this particular department rests not in the hands of the chief, but in those of his first assistant or of someone even further down the line.

In American history the personal friends and informal advisers of a President have been called, usually by those who did not like them, the President's "Kitchen Cabinet," in contrast to his officially appointed Cabinet. Historians and contemporaries frequently have argued among themselves about the membership and influence of "Kitchen Cabinets," raising such questions as whether Harry Hopkins had as much or more or less to do with the formulation of President Roosevelt's foreign policy than Secretary of State Cordell Hull. Students of the reputed top elite of the United States in the mid-1960s might have done well to include in their list the names of two Washington lawyers, Mr. Clark Clifford and Mr. Abe Fortas, both of whom were said to have had much influence within the administration of President Lyndon B. Johnson. Mr. Clifford later became President Johnson's last Secretary of Defense, and Mr. Fortas was appointed by the President to the Supreme Court. (In Mr. Fortas's case, his reputation for political influence cut two ways. When President Johnson nominated him in 1968 as Chief Justice, senatorial critics of the close personal relationship between the two men prevented his confirmation for this higher office.)[1] In every American administration during this century, men of reputed influence have frequently wielded great power, and the

---

[1] In response to criticism of some of his financial dealings with potential litigants (which were not illegal but raised questions about his ethics), Mr. Fortas subsequently resigned from the Supreme Court.

same is true of other countries insofar as we can tell from our knowledge of their political processes.

The set of people identified as the top elite by position usually overlaps with the set of people so identified by reputation. In only a few marginal cases do people in top jobs possess less influence, and others more, than their formal titles would lead one to believe. Taken together, there are roughly fifty top elite members per million people in Western-style democracies such as the United States, Britain, France, and West Germany. In a country of 200 million like the United States, about 10,000 people constitute a fairly broad *top elite*. Cutting this down by another factor of ten, to five per million, we could try to list the *central elite*—the one thousand most influential people in the United States. Knowing the views of these one thousand would enable us to predict reasonably well what might or might not be acceptable in American politics during the next few months, or even during the next year or two. Selecting the top one hundred elite members might not be quite enough for a country the size of the United States. Even the most influential hundred men would yield an imperfect prediction; and any number much smaller than one hundred probably would yield little or nothing reliable.

The top elite in the Soviet Union possibly could be similarly determined, but it might be a little bit broader. About 15,000 people would correspond in importance to the 10,000 in the United States. For a nation of about 50 million people—or one-fourth the population of the United States or the Soviet Union—the comparable top elite might be between one-third and one-half of the United States figure. For a still smaller country, such as Switzerland or Denmark, with about six and five million people respectively (or between one-thirtieth and one-fortieth of the United States), one still might have to include among the top elite about one-fifth to one-fourth of the American number. In any country, no matter how small, the top elite probably would amount to not much less than 100 or 150 people. We do not know, however, whether a smaller number of elite members would suffice in a small but poor country, such as Ecuador, Cambodia, or Tunisia. There is some reason to think that this might be so, particularly if only a small portion of the population took part in politics, but the matter requires more research.

These, then, are the people in every country who already have their hands on the levers of power. They acquire their position and influence because they are acceptable to, and have the confidence of, a good many of the members of a broader elite. In the United States there is a handy yardstick for measuring this latter kind of elite. The gentlemen who publish the fat volumes of *Who's Who in America* every two years say they pick three people for every 10,000 people in the total population. This corresponds to 300 per million population, or three out of about 6,000 adults. *Who's Who* lists well-known writers, artists, and other public figures. Its editors make a special point of saying that it lists only creditable achievement. This excellent work of reference is therefore probably deficient in listing the top personnel of the Mafia, although some Mafia members may have considerable power in politics.

We may think of the different layers of the elite as if they were the officers of an army of political influence. In such an army, the voters— about one-half of the population—serve as private soldiers. Political activists correspond to sergeants, about one for every fifteen to twenty voters. At the other end, the central elite corresponds to three-star generals who lead corps or armies, and the top elite is equivalent to two-star generals, each of whom leads a division of at least 15,000 voters. The larger elite at the *Who's Who* level then parallels the colonels and lieutenant colonels, with about one for each regiment of about 2,000 voters. A lower layer of the elite corresponds to the lieutenants, one for every platoon of about twenty voters. It is these "lieutenants" of the voters and the social system whom we call the mid-elite. The pyramid of political influence is shown in Figure 3.1.

Is There Really a Mid-Elite?   The mid-elite is a statistical artifact. It is obtained by taking a sample of the total electorate such as the Gallup or Harris polls would construct, and then as a result of this sample selecting

Figure 3.1

The Pyramid of Influence

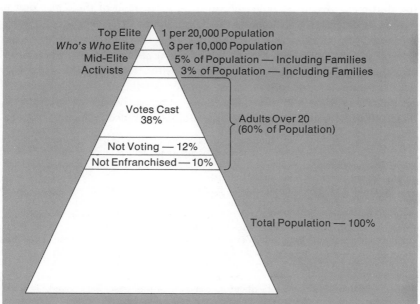

the top 5 per cent of the adult population in income, education, and occupational status.[2] As shown in Figure 3.2, these three categories will not completely overlap. Those persons who are in the top 5 per cent on all three tests form the *core of the mid-elite;* and they have fairly good reason to be content with their condition.

Those for whom one or two of the three tests are negative may be thought of as belonging to a *marginal elite.* In one sense they belong to the elite, but in another they do not; and often they feel somewhat discontented. On the whole, people whose educational rank is much higher than their income tend to be somewhat more critical of existing relationships; they tend to be liberal or radical in their political beliefs. People whose income is significantly higher than their education also tend to be dissatisfied with their status and prestige, but usually they are more to the right of center in their politics.

Allowing for these differences and incomplete overlaps, we can say that the views of the top 5 per cent of a country's adult population, as identified by some combination of income, occupational status, and educational level, would tell us a good deal about what was and what was not politically acceptable in that country.

But would these statistical artifacts or constructs help us to discover living, acting groups or strata in politics? To how much reality do such statistics correspond? The answer is a question of fact, to be discovered by research; and it will vary among different periods and countries. In most countries it is fairly difficult to carry through a policy against the desires of the mid-elite. It can be done, however. A great deal of the legislation of the 1930s, together with some of the legislation of the 1960s, was probably rejected by a majority of the core of the mid-elite, and by the top 5 per cent of income receivers, although significant minorities in these groups may have backed it.[3] The marginal mid-elites, however, were probably divided: the top 5 per cent of voters representing the most highly educated people in the United States quite likely were on the side of the reforms. Thus, on these political issues the educational and income elites disagreed.

[2] Occupational status distinguishes professional and managerial occupations, self-employed persons, white collar and clerical occupations, skilled labor, farmers, unskilled laborers, and other occupational categories. Professionals, managers, and high-level self-employed are potential elite members.

[3] Before the 1936 presidential election in the United States, the *Literary Digest* polled a sample of telephone subscribers (who included most of the mid-elite) about their political preference. The *Literary Digest* announced that the Republican candidate, Governor Alf M. Landon, would defeat President Franklin D. Roosevelt by a landslide. Landon carried only Maine and Vermont; and soon thereafter the United States had one magazine less. None the less, in November 1969, the Gallup poll telephoned 501 people on their responses to President Nixon's speech on the Vietnam War and reported that of the three-quarters of the telephone subscribers who had listened to him, 77 per cent agreed with him or about 57 per cent of the subscribers polled. This was then reported in some newspaper headlines as indicating the approval of 77 per cent of the American people—a prize example of inaccurate polling and reporting.

Figure 3.2

Core and Marginal Groups in the Mid-Elite

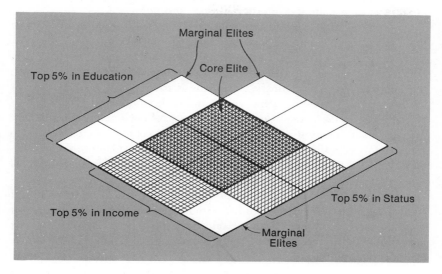

Most of the time, however, when there is no acute crisis or major reorientation, the top 5 per cent on all three criteria show a higher degree of consensus, and their views are thus quite important.

Nevertheless, there is some reason to think that often there is a real difference between the political thinking and behavior of the mid-elite and that of the mass of the voters. When school desegregation was ordered by the United States Supreme Court in 1954, members of the mid-elite in such states as Arkansas were more willing to comply with the law of the land than were many of the rank-and-file white voters. This limited the power of the mid-elite. Even where there is little or no such difference, and voters and mid-elite agree, this may be because the mid-elite simply shares the feelings of the voters, or else the voters have chosen to follow the lead of their betters. Either way, it may be important to know what the mid-elite in a country or city will accept, because such knowledge may tell us what the top elite can afford to do today, and the voters may approve tomorrow.

Who Else Counts in Politics?

The Relevant Strata. In former times and places one did not have to reach farther down into the social body than the top 5 per cent—or at most the top 10 per cent—to find out what could or could not be done in politics. In the last third of the twentieth century this has changed. One must dig more deeply into the social body. For centuries, the concept of *politically relevant strata* was important; today it is indispensable. What are the strata of the population which count in politics? Who must be taken into account in order to prevent a policy from turning out to be utterly unrealistic or a complete disaster in domestic politics?

In most countries today, the politically relevant strata include more than just members of the various elites. A longshoreman in Lagos or London or New York is not an elite member, but by going on strike at a crucial moment he can make a major difference to the economic or even the political life of his country. The same is true of railroad personnel or the workers in large enterprises or key industries. During the brief period of liberalism in Czechoslovakia in 1968, it was of decisive importance that the workers in the most important large factories voted in their meetings to support the liberalizing policies of the Czechoslovak Communist government and its dismantling of much of the old Stalin-type machinery of repression. They threw their weight to the side of the students and intellectuals who were pressing for preserving and continuing the more liberal course, and they continued to do so throughout the rest of the year, after these policies were halted from the outside through the entry of the Soviet army into their country. Even though policies may change, these strata continue to be relevant.

In representative democracies, registered voters who actually vote are part of the politically relevant strata. In the United States in 1968 the

Table 3.1

United States: Presidential Election, 1968

		Number in Millions (rounded) [1]	*% of Total Population*	*% of Voting Age Population*
	Total Population	201	100.0	—
	Voting Age Population [2]	117	58	100
Who Votes	*Registered Voters*	87	43	74
Who Votes	*Actual Voters in Election*	73	36	62
Who Votes	*Registered Voters Who Did Not Vote*	14	7	12
	Disfranchised Population (Population of Voting Age Not Registered to Vote) [3]	30	15	26
	Population Below Voting Age [4]	84	42	72

[1] All figures except those for total population and population below voting age refer to civilian noninstitutional population.

[2] To the noninstitutional population of voting age, another 3 million must be added, comprising the inmates of jails and hospitals, and members of the armed forces stationed overseas.

[3] Includes those who do not know if they voted and are not reported as having voted. Also includes less than 1 per cent of noncitizens of voting age.

[4] Includes institutional population of voting age.

Sources: U. S. Department of Commerce, Current Population Reports, Population Characteristics, Series P-20, No. 174, August 8, 1968 and No. 177, December 27, 1968.

actual votes cast comprised about 36 per cent of the total population; 7 per cent did not vote though they were registered voters; another 15 per cent were not registered; and about 42 per cent were below the age of voting. (In developing countries as much as 50 per cent of the population may be below twenty years of age because these countries have higher birth and mortality rates.) The 73 million who cast their votes in the 1968 presidential election clearly were politically relevant. And perhaps another million people, although not voting, took part in politics in some other way. They also can be considered politically relevant people. These two groups combined, these 74 million voters and participants, constituted 37 per cent of the total U. S. population of 201 million (see Table 3.1).

In the Soviet Union the voting age is lower. The voting population is about 150 million or 65 per cent of the total, and almost all qualified voters dutifully cast their votes on election day. Thus the number of voters exceeds the number of people making up Russia's politically relevant strata (see Table 3.2). We can determine these strata through the following calculations: roughly speaking, 55 per cent of the Soviet population— or 128 million—live either in cities over 20,000 (50 per cent) or in small towns (5 per cent). To stay in power, a Soviet regime needs the support of much of this urban population. Within these cities and towns approximately one-sixth, or 9 per cent of the population, may not be capable of forming an effective part of public opinion, because of age or health or lack of social connections, and perhaps an additional one-sixth may not be interested. But two-thirds of the urban population, or 36 per cent of Russia's total voting age population, are politically relevant adults. By adding to these 54 million people about 20 per cent of the rural population, we obtain approximately 74 million people who make up the Soviet Union's politically relevant electorate. If a Russian government is well

Table 3.2

U.S.S.R.: Elections to the Supreme Soviet, 1966

		Number in Millions (rounded)	*% of Total Population*	*% of Voting Age Population*
	Total Population	232	100.0	—
	Voting Age Population	150	65	100
Who Votes	*Registered Voters*	144	62	96
	Actual Voters in Election	144	62	96
	Disfranchised Population (Population of Voting Age Not Registered to Vote)	6	3	4
	Population Below Voting Age	82	36	55

Sources: U.S. Bureau of the Census, International Population Reports, *Series P-91, No. 13, 1964;* The Current Digest of the Soviet Press, *Vol. 18, No. 24, 1966, p. 3.*

advised, it keeps an eye on the mood and behavior of those 74 million out of the country's population of 232 million. Its politically relevant electorate is thus about 32 per cent of the total population. Curiously, the share of the total population which politicians need to watch carefully is between 30 and 40 per cent both in the United States and in the Soviet Union.

In Western Europe, where there is automatic registration of voters, where there are few or no conspicuous racial minorities, where populations are relatively homogeneous, and where high levels of literacy have existed much longer than in either the United States or the Soviet Union, the politically relevant strata are likely to fall between 50 and 60 per cent of a country's total population (see Tables 3.3, 3.4, and 3.5).

Activities and Activists.   Of course, being relevant in politics doesn't mean being active in politics. Ithiel Pool and his collaborators have proposed six tests for identifying the political activist. An *activist* is a person (1) who is a member of a political organization; (2) who gives money to a political organization or candidate; (3) who frequently attends political meetings, whether of committees or of larger groups; (4) who takes part in electoral campaigns; (5) who writes letters on political topics to legislators, political officeholders, and/or the press; or (6) who talks about politics to people outside his immediate circle of family or friends. Pool and his collaborators consider a political activist to be anyone who fulfills at least three of these six conditions. Based on these not very stringent tests, we can count 3 per cent of the population in most countries as political activists. This seems to be the case in a number of Western countries. Not all

Table 3.3

United Kingdom: Parliamentary Elections, 1966

		Number in Millions (rounded)	% of Total Population	% of Voting Age Population
	Total Population	55	100.0	—
	Voting Age Population	41	75	100
Who Votes	Registered Voters	36	65	88
Who Votes	Actual Voters in Election	27	49	66
Who Votes	Registered Voters Who Did Not Vote	9	16	22
	Disfranchised Population (Population of Voting Age Not Registered to Vote)	5	10	12
	Population Below Voting Age	14	25	34

Source: *Central Statistical Office,* Annual Abstract of Statistics, *No. 105 (London: Her Majesty's Stationery Office, 1968).*

Table 3.4

France: Presidential Election, 1965

		Number in Millions (rounded)	% of Total Population	% of Voting Age Population
	Total Population	49	100.0	—
	Voting Age Population	32	65	100
	Registered Voters	28	57	88
Who Votes	Actual Voters in Election	25	51	78
	Valid Votes Cast	24	49	75
	Registered Voters Who Did Not Vote	4	8	13
	Disfranchised Population (Population of Voting Age Not Registered to Vote)	4	8	13
	Population Below Voting Age	17	35	53

Source: Annuaire Statistique de la France, 1967.

Table 3.5

German Federal Republic: Elections to the Bundestag, 1965[1]

		Number in Millions (rounded)	% of Total Population	% of Voting Age Population
	Total Population	57	100.0	—
	Voting Age Population	40	70	100
	Registered Voters	39	68	97
Who Votes	Actual Voters in Election	33+	59	83
	Registered Voters Who Did Not Vote	5+	9	13
	Disfranchised Population (Population of Voting Age Not Registered to Vote)	1	2	3
	Population Below Voting Age	17	30	43

[1]All figures exclude West Berlin.

Source: Statistisches Jahrbuch für die Bundesrepublik Deutschland, *1967 and 1968 editions.*

activists are members of the elite, however. On the other hand, all political activists belong to the politically relevant strata—unless their views are so far removed from current opinion that they cannot find any significant group of supporters or allies.

In the Soviet Union the situation is a little different. At the beginning of the 1960s, the Russian Communist Party contained about 13 million members, almost 6 per cent of the Soviet population. Communist Party members are expected to be extremely active. They talk politics to their co-workers, they donate money in the form of party dues, and they attend meetings—frequently. In short, they fit all those tests that would gladden the heart of Pool and his collaborators. In addition to the 6 per cent that belong to the Communist Party, more than 7 per cent of the Soviet population belong to the Communist youth organization, the Komsomol. Of course, not all Komsomol members are as active in politics as the Party leadership wants them to be. But if about one-half of the Communist youth is at least sufficiently active in politics to fulfill Pool's activist tests, and if practically all Communist Party members can also be called activists, then the Soviet Union, and similar Communist political systems, have a 9 per cent share of activists.

This high proportion of activists shows, in part, what makes Communist systems different in so many ways from other political systems. Communist governments encourage more intense politicization and a drawing of many more people into political life. But even though this political life is high in activity, it is modest in variety: there is only one legal party and policy. The high level of activity, and the unceasing demand for it by the ruling party and government, cause some discontent among some people who would like to have more time for their personal affairs, or who would prefer to write their poetry, paint their paintings, or pursue their scientific research in a less political manner. But this same high level of activity may produce some valued results for the Communists, and some personal rewards for many of the activists. Such rewards may range from promotion up the employment ladder in government or industry to gains in social standing and prestige, and to the personal feeling of doing important work and of being needed and wanted. For these reasons, much of this political activism is voluntary. If we ask why the governments of Russia, China, North Korea, or North Vietnam in critical times have shown political and organizational capabilities higher than many foreign observers had expected, one part of the answer may be that they have approximately three times as many political activists as do Western countries.

All of this applies to a far lesser degree to countries where a Communist party or regime has failed to become popular with any major section of the population. Where a minority is small and politically isolated, even the most intense activity cannot make up for the lack of popular support. Communist or pro-Communist regimes collapsed easily in northern Iran in 1946 and in Guatemala in 1954, just as Communist guerrillas were defeated in Greece, Malaya, and the Philippines in the 1940s. A comparison of these failures with Communist successes elsewhere, such as in Yugoslavia, Cuba, North Korea, North Vietnam, Russia, and China, suggests that the presence or absence of popular sympathies can be decisive for the success or failure of activist zeal.

Another condition, in addition to the rewards or encouragement a society gives those who participate in political life, may very well influence the levels of political activity, particularly in highly developed Western countries. A political activist habitually spends time and attention (as well as other resources) on politics. The lower the opportunity cost of this time to him, the more he is willing to spend it on a political activity. *Opportunity cost* is the value of the alternative uses to which resources could be put. On the whole, a substantial businessman, a highly skilled surgeon, a medical doctor, a successful lawyer, or a research scientist usually has very attractive opportunities for allocating his energy and working time. Very often a reasonable income affords him attractive opportunities for allocating his leisure time. Thus many members of the middle- and upper-income groups in most countries have a high opportunity cost of time. Moreover, in Western-style democracies, where personal affairs, consumer choices, and spontaneous and free behavior command a vital sector of activities, the pressure on people to do what the government wants them to do is less than in Communist dictatorships.

For these reasons, not many of the highly educated and well-to-do in affluent Western countries ordinarily put much time into politics. Neither do many of the poor, because they either lack motivation (having suffered too much, knowing too little, and being too busy keeping body and soul together) or lack rewards (having received too little satisfaction out of politics, as their earlier efforts were too often ineffective or the results disappointing). And even the poor take opportunity cost into account: a poor person might prefer watching television or visiting a bar to talking politics—particularly if politics in the past had not produced any early and visible improvements. The result is that only a minority of people become ward heelers, machine politicians, local committee members, or persons who run the affairs of small towns. Thus, the professional people on the one hand and the poor on the other are underrepresented in the political process in many Western democracies, whereas many members of the lower middle–class, particularly long-time residents of local communities, choose politics as one of their favorite indoor games.

Spurs to Political Action. Of course, many people who usually do not put much of their time and attention into politics can be stirred up to do so. So long as they are reasonably contented or only mildly discontented with the outcome of the political process, they will pursue nonpolitical interests. If, however, they find themselves seriously disturbed, these people may shift very large blocks of their time and resources into political activity. In this way the political process may become transformed. Mass unemployment in the 1930s pushed many industrial workers who had not been politically active in the mid-1920s into political activity. In response to the Great Depression, and to the new political opportunities provided by the New Deal in the United States, there was not only increased union activity, but also a growth of labor political education committees, voter registration drives, and union voting in factories. As a result, a new element now had to be reckoned with in the American political process—the influence of labor.

Similarly, an acute wave of fear about urban riots or, in the words of the Republican campaign slogan of 1968, about "crime in the streets," moved a great many ordinarily nonpolitical middle-class and upper-class voters into politics and politicized an even broader strata of suburbanites and lower middle–class voters. One of the most powerful instruments ever invented for the politicization of students has been the draft; some might consider General Lewis B. Hershey as one of the founding fathers of student politics in the United States. Many students who ordinarily would have given a good deal of time and attention to other matters entered into politics because so many things of importance in their lives clearly depended on the outcome of the political process.

If many different groups move into politics, they may use their new activities to paralyze and checkmate one another so that the outcome does not significantly change, or else they may succeed in coordinating their activities so that what one group does reinforces the activities of another group. Coordinated activities can transform, sometimes very radically, the outcome of the operations of a political system. To a considerable degree, they can even transform the structure of the system itself.

"Politics as Usual": A Plurality of Interest Groups

Most of the time, most people are not highly active in politics. They leave this to small interest organizations to which they delegate their representation. Many years ago student governments existed to represent the interests of students who were not active in politics, to complain from time to time about the food in the campus cafeteria, and to exert some pressure for a bigger student activity building or for a marginal relaxation of dormitory rules. Recently, student governments have been doing a bit more. Farmers, union members, and business organizations, as well as students, all have their own interest groups.

Indeed, most of the more elaborate political systems from ancient times onward have contained some interest groups. The ancient kingdoms in the river valleys of India, Mesopotamia, and Egypt took into account two interest groups: warriors and priests; the warriors sought to become nobles, and the priests, or more exactly, their monasteries or temples, sought to become landowners. Similarly, ancient Chinese civilization distinguished scholar-bureaucrats from warriors. In many European countries further developments in the Middle Ages led to the rise of merchant interest groups and guilds of artisans. Occasionally, as in England, Norway, Sweden, and Switzerland, yeomen, free farmers, or peasants organized as interest groups with some representation in the political process.

From the nineteenth century on, industrialists have been a powerful interest group, first in England and eventually in most private enterprise countries in the world, with corporate managers often replacing the old-style owners. In modern private enterprise societies under constitutional governments, industrialist groups are paralleled by farmer and worker groups. As people become more politicized, the number of interest groups tends to rise. Recently, at one end of the social scale the poor, and, at the other end, university students and faculties,[4] have formed new interest groups.

Within large interest groups there are smaller, special interest groups. The cotton farmers of the South who favor the lower-priced spreads which usually contain cottonseed oil have different views from the dairy farmers of Wisconsin who seek to promote Wisconsin's own natural product, butter. In four states, at least, farmers' interests are closely tied to tobacco, whereas in other states farmers might rather not court lung cancer.

The Politics of Bargaining. The political process then, in one sense, is the result of the bargaining among different groups. This definition furnishes the basis of Robert Dahl's model of a modern Western political system.[5] In such a pluralistic society, any number can play. Each special interest can set up its own group, its own office, its own organization; each can hire secretaries, each can buy mimeograph machines and begin to churn out releases, each can retain lobbyists in Washington to provide legislators with ample though one-sided information and to take legislators to lunch or find more substantial inducements for legislators to vote the way the interest group desires.

But in a society like that of the United States where almost every substantial interest group is organized, two serious problems arise. First, if most interest groups are organized, heaven help the residual groups that are not—the tenants in the slums, the poor, and some of the ethnic minorities. Until recently, none of these was organized in an effective manner. Lacking organization, they got the worst in most of the political bargaining, and many of the older interest groups were quite content to keep it that way.

Secondly, when almost everybody is organized, society reaches a point where almost nothing can be done. Groups with limited power usually find it easier to veto someone else's proposal than to push through any positive policy of their own. When this happens, politics becomes negative,

---

[4] In the United States today, there are more staff and students occupied full time in the universities than there are people occupied in farming.

[5] See Robert A. Dahl, *Modern Political Analysis*, rev. ed. (Englewood Cliffs, New Jersey: Prentice-Hall, 1970); and his more detailed books, *Who Governs* (New Haven: Yale University Press, 1961) and *Pluralistic Democracy in the United States* (Chicago: Rand McNally, 1967).

and interest groups turn into veto groups. Even where positive policies are possible, any substantial proposal has to be cleared with every relevant interest group. And the larger the number of organized groups, the more of them that must be consulted, the longer are the resulting delays, and the harder it becomes to turn any idea into action.

From Immobility to Emergency.   Pluralistic interest organization can lead, therefore, to creeping immobility. The society becomes harder and harder to move, and attempting reform or innovation becomes as frustrating as swimming in a sea of molasses. Eventually it becomes so difficult to get things done that some device must be found for breaking the deadlock. This device is the *emergency*. In an emergency, we cannot spend our time consulting all the interest groups: we must do something quickly. If there is a real emergency, we greet it with relief. If there is none, we are tempted to invent one. Thus, the politics of a highly pluralistic, highly organized society, a *polyarchy* as Dahl would call it, becomes a cycle of alternating states of immobility and emergency (see Figure 3.3).

In recent years in the United States the emergency usually has been a foreign policy emergency. Since World War II, Presidents of the United States have presented Congress with images of cold war emergencies and dire threats to national security, in order to induce the legislators to appropriate funds for foreign economic aid and other aspects of foreign

Figure 3.3

The Immobility-Emergency Cycle: A Danger in Polyarchy

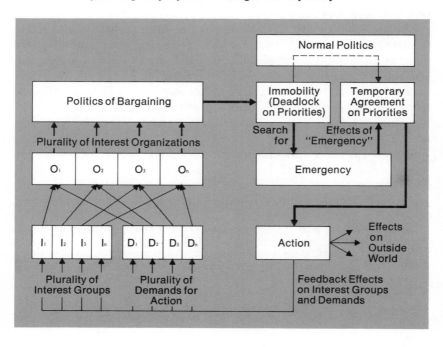

policy. However, if a minority group inside the country finds that foreign policy emergencies, by focusing attention away from domestic matters, do not work in its interest, such a group may be desperate enough to create its own emergency at home. Then suddenly things get done. The black poor and urban slums got much more attention, and a little more money, after the riots in Watts (Los Angeles), Detroit, Newark and other cities. In this case, the original outburst was a real emergency, not a fabricated one. Thereafter, the fear of a "long hot summer" resulting in mass rioting was used by civil rights groups as a means of obtaining desired programs and funds.

Not only governments, but universities also, have exhibited the immobility-emergency pattern. By the spring of 1968 a report on the role of students in the university had lain on the desk of the president of Columbia University for eight months. Then the emergency created by a student revolt on campus greatly accelerated the speed with which pieces of paper moved through the system. Alumni, trustees, corporations, faculty members, students, and a new president—albeit at a grievous cost in time, effort, and in estrangement, conflict, and bad feelings within the faculty and elsewhere in the university community—enacted in months changes which had been talked about for years.

But there are limits to the degree to which such a tactic can be used. Nothing is as destructive in politics as a mood of permanent emergency. To be sure, the group that creates an emergency finally will get some action, but it may not be the action it wanted. It may arouse numerous people who were previously nonpolitical and who now may be hostile to the aims of the group. In 1968 more votes were cast for Governor George Wallace, a spokesman for racial discrimination, than there were black people of any age throughout the country. It is a test of skill in politics to know what can be done, how far to carry an activity, and at what point one may become trapped in a situation where overwhelming strength is brought to bear against the objectives and authors of the original emergency tactics.

From Interest Elites to an Establishment. Most of the time, a small amount of inter-group activities, bargaining, and piecemeal decision-making goes on between emergencies. To carry out these activities almost every interest group, sooner or later, develops leaders, secretaries, professionals, or people whose names have become prominent among its members. In this sense, each interest group tends to develop an elite of its own. If *interest elites* become used to working with each other, to knowing each other, to exchanging views and small courtesies among each other, they may coalesce into an establishment. One might argue that an *establishment* is the ensemble of those interest group elites who have learned to work together. Union leaders and management may learn how to conduct negotiations with each other. Leaders in the mass media may come to know leaders in most other fields, from literature to finance, and to work with them.

This cooperation can sometimes be a good thing; it makes things smoother and gets things done. But it may sometimes be a very bad thing. These groups, used to each other's needs, may become increasingly preoccupied with each other, insensitive to the needs of outsiders, and impervious to new recruitment and to new ideas. Or the members of various interest group elites may identify more and more with each other and less and less with the interests of the groups they represent. Thus some labor leaders, whose incomes and styles of life have set them apart from their own union members, may feel that they have more in common with the representatives of management than with the workers whose interests they are supposed to protect.

Political Parties and Party Systems

Political Parties: Stable Coalitions Among Interests.   Interest groups *articulate* the interests of their members. They put into words the vaguely felt needs, fears, and expectations of their constituents and translate these feelings into specific demands for legislation or other government action. Once individuals are aware that they share a common concern with an interest group, many of them pass from a passive audience of potential adherents into the group's active members and supporters. In the 1930s Dr. Francis Townsend aroused the concern of many elderly Americans about their lack of security for their old age. Large numbers of them joined his Townsend clubs and engaged in political agitation for a Federal old-age pension of "thirty dollars every Thursday," until Social Security legislation was enacted in 1935. Then as now, the average levels of benefits were much lower than the elderly had demanded, but the most urgent needs of most wage earners were covered. It was not the Townsend groups, however, which enacted Social Security. It was the Democratic Party through its majority in Congress under the leadership of the Roosevelt Administration which did so, and it was the Republican Party in the Eisenhower Administration which twenty years later extended Social Security coverage to additional millions of Americans. Interest groups may raise a demand, but political parties transform the demand into action.

Political parties are key organizations for getting social and political results. They do so by aggregating several different interest groups into a stable coalition which is stronger and more powerful than any single interest group by itself. Every major political party represents a combination of such interest groups. In some parties the main component groups are held together only loosely by *"logrolling"*—that is, by the trading of political favors. Other parties from time to time proclaim dramatic slogans in order to rally support in a manner acceptable to all their interest groups. The Republicans of McKinley's day promised their voters a "full dinner pail." Britain's Conservatives under Stanley Baldwin in 1935 campaigned for "safety first." West Germany's Christian Democratic Union under Konrad Adenauer in 1957 insisted on "no experiments." Each of these was a conservative slogan on which a wide range of different interest groups could agree so long as each of them wished to preserve some particular set of existing arrangements. On the other hand, such slogans as Franklin D. Roosevelt's offer of a "New Deal" in 1932 or John F. Kennedy's vision of a "New Frontier" in 1960 were general appeals for change, designed to unite a wide variety of different groups each desiring some particular change.

Still other parties seeking to hold their coalitions together go beyond slogans to more permanent principles, such as "liberalism" or "conservatism." "A party," said Edmund Burke, "is a group of men united to promote the common good in accordance with a principle upon which they are agreed." In Burke's view one such principle was *conservatism,* which implied, first, that any changes attempted should be extremely small, slow, and cautious and, second, that property should be overrepresented in politics, as against talent "out of all proportion." Burke's principle seemed well-designed to unite noblemen, landowners, established churches, favored business interests, and other interests profiting from existing conditions in late eighteenth-century Britain. This kind of conservatism, however, was not an excuse for simply doing nothing. It demanded slow but constant change after the necessity and practicality of change had been demonstrated by experience. "A conservative," said a later writer, "is someone who will never do anything for the first time."

More or less elaborate ideologies, as well as simple principles, may unify a party. These ideologies, however, must also unite the main interest groups on whom the party depends. Thus Britain's Labour Party's Socialist platform serves to link trade union members who mainly want higher wages; intellectuals and white-collar workers who want more government planning, nationalized industries, and public enterprises; women and older people who want more public medical and welfare services; and young voters who are opposed to armaments and compulsory military service. A far more complex and rigid ideology was professed by the Russian Communist Party in the days of Lenin and by the latter-day Communist parties ruling Russia and China. Communist ideology, too, is aimed explicitly at maintaining a coalition of workers, peasants, and intellectuals. In practice it must also accommodate some of the interests of the large bureaucracies and military establishments that have developed in Communist countries.

Party Systems and Participation. In some countries a single party has a monopoly of legal political activity. Under such *one-party* systems, almost anyone who wishes to participate effectively in politics must join this party and try to rise in its ranks. Often a one-party system is combined with a dictatorship; competing parties are suppressed by force and the founding of new parties is punishable as a crime. If a one-party government is also willing and able to control all other organizations affecting public life, from labor unions to sports clubs and youth groups, and if it controls all mass media, all education, and even much of the leisure time of its people, and if it accepts no exception from its claim to power, then it is often called *totalitarian*. The Fascist Party of Mussolini's Italy, the National Socialist (Nazi) Party of Hitler's Germany, and the Communist Party of Stalin's Russia exercised power in this manner. Totalitarian parties and regimes differ according to the main policies and purposes which their "total" efforts at political mobilization and control are meant to serve. The chief aim of the Fascists and the Nazis was military conquest; the major aim of Russia's Communists was rapid industrialization. But some of their political methods—and the resulting human costs—were similar.

In milder cases a one-party system may give the ruling party its formal political monopoly but tolerate a number of other long-established interest groups with political potentialities, such as landowners, industrialists, the military, and some major church organization. They may then also respect a sphere of privacy for their citizens. These less extreme one-party systems are sometimes called *authoritarian*. Franco's Spain with its Falangist Party and Peron's Argentina (1943-1955) with its Peronistas are examples.

A third group of one-party systems is involved in rapid change. Such systems are most often found in developing countries. Some of them have a legal monopoly, as did Mustapha Kemal's People's Party in Turkey from the 1920s through the 1940s. Others tolerate small opposition groups, but in fact predominate, controlling most government jobs and wielding most of the influence in public matters. India's Congress Party and Mexico's Party of Revolutionary Institutions are ruling parties of this kind; and France's Gaullist Party might have liked to win this status.

One-party systems tend to be most successful—and most likely to be accepted by the population—when the supply of political activists and leaders is small relative to the size and urgency of the tasks a country faces. When there is much to be done quickly, and few people to do it, the doers are likely to be organized as a single team of leaders, that is, as a single governing party. If much of what has to be done is backed by popular consent, and the ruling party does it tolerably well, the one-party system is likely to enjoy public support.

When the number of political activists and potential leaders and the number and variety of active interest groups are much larger, not all participants can be accommodated within a single party. Under these conditions, a *two-party* system may offer twice as many opportunities for political participation. Each major party may represent a full team of potential leaders. In a sense this resembles the two-platoon system in football. One set of players is on the field while the other platoon is in reserve, sitting on the bench. When the first platoon is temporarily retired, the other platoon takes over. Thus the game may be pursued with unceasing vigor before either platoon gets exhausted. The platoons have special skills—one for offense and the other for defense—and their joint performance can be formidable. A two-platoon team is stronger, not weaker, than a one-platoon team.

In a two-party system, one party may specialize in initiating change and the other in slowing or consolidating it. Or one party may press for a more active foreign policy and the other may emphasize affairs at home. Again, one party may stress the need to develop public services or public enterprise while the other may speak for the private sector. One party may speak for producers, both management and labor, who want higher prices; the other for consumers, such as creditors and housewives, who want lower ones. For a two-party system to work well, there must be a great deal of overlap among the different specialties and interests. Both teams must still play for the same side, and both players and spectators must know it. Where this does not obtain, the two-party system may deteriorate into mutual hostility and even into civil war, as it did in Austria between Socialists and Catholic conservatives in 1934. The United States and Britain have long provided examples of functioning two-party systems.

Under a two-party system, a large number of interest groups is aggregated into only two major parties. Most interest groups may find, therefore, that neither party fits their needs perfectly. Almost every group will have to compromise in order to squeeze under the umbrella of one of these big *parties of action*. The costs of compromise are the frustrations the interest group accepts; its rewards are what the party can get done for it. If the party can accomplish much, many different groups will be likely to stay within it. If either major party or both of them achieve only little, a large number of interest groups will become intensely dissatisfied. Each of them may then back a smaller party custom-tailored to its needs and prejudices. Smaller specialized parties may accomplish little for their clients, but may serve them at least as *parties of expression*. They may voice their members' interests and act them out symbolically, and thus make their members feel better even if they gain little else (see Table 3.6). Where parties of action fail, parties of expression are likely to become more frequent.

A *multi-party* system, such as is found in many countries of Western Europe, is a mixture of parties of action and parties of expression. Its largest parties can get enough done to keep operating but not enough to unite as many as half the voters and interest groups of the country. Its small parties voice sufficient protests and demands, interspersed with occasional bits of accomplishment, to hold the support of their specialized

Table 3.6

A Typology of Party Orientations

		Methods	
		Action	*Expression*
Goals	*Power*	Republican and Democratic Parties (US) Conservative Party (UK) CDU (GFR) and Gaullists (France)	Liberal Party (NYC) Liberal Party (UK) Free Democrats (GFR)
	Policy	CPSU (USSR) CPCPR (China) Labour Party (UK) SPD (GFR)	Socialists (Norman Thomas, US) American Independent Party (George Wallace, US)

constituencies—regional, occupational, religious, or ideological. To govern the country, several parties, usually both large and small, must form a coalition. Such a coalition then agrees on a program of legislation, and on a distribution of government offices to be filled. Coalition agreements on these matters often are made in writing, even though they are not always publicized. When the program of the coalition has been carried out, or agreement among members ceases for some other reason, the coalition is dissolved and another is formed in its place. France, Germany, Switzerland, and Italy have been governed by changing coalitions for almost a century.

In substance, formal coalition governments among several parties resemble the informal coalitions of interest groups within a one- or two-party system. They differ from the latter two in the relative ease with which they can be dissolved and re-formed. Multi-party systems may be more flexible and less stable than one- or two-party systems, and they may offer a wider range of opportunities for political participation. This openness to participation, however, much like stability, flexibility, and accomplishment, may depend more on the organization and quality of each party than on the particular party system in effect. The differences in openness and effectiveness among political parties often are as great or greater than those among party systems as a whole.

Party Membership, Finance, and Administration.   The character of any political party is primarily determined by seven things: (1) the interests it serves; (2) the aims it professes; (3) its real aims; (4) the size and nature of its membership; (5) the main sources of its voters and other political support; (6) its chief sources of money; and (7) the internal bureaucracy and administrative machinery that runs it.

We have already discussed the first two points, the coalition of interest groups within a party and the party's professed aims and principles. Sometimes the professed aims of a party and its actual aims are the same. Such parties are mainly *policy oriented*. Their leaders and members want to make sure that certain laws are passed or certain policies implemented, regardless of who wins the legislative or administrative power to do these things. They want to determine *what* gets done, no matter who gets the job to do it. Minority parties in the United States often have been of this type. In the course of a long life Norman Thomas ran six times for the presidency of the United States on the Socialist ticket. He was always unsuccessful in the sense of never winning an election, but when he died in 1968 the newspapers pointed out that nearly all the reforms for which he had campaigned had become law; over the years they had been enacted by the major parties who had defeated him. If Norman Thomas ever had ambitions of power, they had failed, but his policy aspirations were in large part successful.

Other parties, as well as many individual politicians, are mainly *power oriented*. Their professed aims, in the form of policy statements and platforms, frequently are different from their real ones. These parties care little what laws and policies are enacted, so long as *they* are sure to be in charge of them. If a policy-oriented person would rather be right than be President, a power-oriented party will change many of its policies and even, discreetly, its principles in order to get elected or to stay in office (see Table 3.6). In such cases it may do less for some of the interest groups it has served in the past, while doing more to win the favor of others. Thus it may change in part the nature of the interest coalition it represents. (Conversely, a party may hold fast to its policies and principles but the actual interests of some of its constituent groups may change. In the past, southern Democrats in the United States favored free trade since their region had little manufacturing industry and imported most industrial goods from the North or from abroad. After 1950, as industry grew in the South, an increasing part of southern interests turned protectionist and asked for tariffs and quotas to keep out competing foreign goods. Southern legislators then had to choose between changing their policies or losing their support.)

Parties also can be characterized by the size and nature of their membership (see Table 3.7). Some parties are primarily *membership* parties. If these are also mass parties, they will organize a substantial part of their voters as members on a more or less permanent basis. Thus the German Social Democratic Party (SPD) in the 1960s had a core of about 600,000 members, while drawing about 15 million votes in national elections. These 600,000 paid regular dues; many attended monthly meetings and

Table 3.7

A Rough Typology of Party Structures

	Stable Mass Membership	Intermittent Supporters and Skeleton Membership
Bureaucratic "Machine-Ruled"	SPD (GFR) Labour Party (UK)	CDU (GFR) Conservative Party (UK) Republican and Democratic Parties on national level (US)
Open	Membership parties in early stages, e.g., New Democratic Party (Canada)	FDP (GFR) Gaullists (France) American Independent Party (US)

volunteered to carry on the many routine tasks of the party such as addressing envelopes, ringing doorbells, distributing handbills, turning out for larger meetings and parades, and bringing voters to the polls. With such a large and dependable body of volunteer labor, a membership party needs less money to hire campaign staffs at election time and to buy publicity and advertising space in the mass media. The popularity of membership parties holds fairly steady in public opinion polls between elections.

In contrast, a *skeleton* party maintains only a small membership and a small staff between elections. On the eve of an electoral campaign, however, skeleton parties recruit a much larger staff, some volunteer and others paid, in order to run a big campaign and to rally its potential voters who have heard little from the party during the period between elections. Such parties rely much more heavily on posters, newspapers, radio, television and other forms of mass publicity. As a result, skeleton parties need a great deal of money.

A membership party can afford to run relatively colorless candidates who have proven their dependability and "party regularity" over many years. The voters will elect these men, not because of any personal qualities, but because they trust the party that has nominated them: "A lamppost could be elected to Parliament from Bombay on the Congress Party ticket," runs a popular Indian saying. The colorful Winston Churchill, turned out of office in 1945 by the colorless Clement Attlee, was left to complain bitterly that he had been defeated by "a sheep in sheep's clothing." In fact, he had been beaten by Attlee's British Labour Party which had won the confidence of Britain's voters.

Skeleton parties usually nominate candidates who can rapidly gain the attention, respect, and confidence of the voters. Thus they frequently seek candidates who are attractive as well as colorful, or who are already well known. Since the voters' impressions of its candidates are so important to the success of a skeleton party, the party may often emphasize its candidate's image, sometimes to the exclusion of his ideas. At the end of the 1940s, both the Democratic and Republican Parties sought General Eisenhower as their presidential candidate. Neither party knew for certain the General's ideas on government or his political leanings, but they were sure that the American voters would find him irresistible. And they were right.

In the United States, both the Republican and Democratic parties are largely skeleton organizations on the national level but maintain more permanent machines in state and local politics. Some regions also have party organizations and clubs in which a somewhat larger number of members meet regularly. Most Republicans and Democrats, however, are registered by party preference without paying membership dues or attending meetings. Individual voters become "members" of parties by simply indicating their party preference at the time they register to vote, and they may change this preference at any time they please. In many states all such registered "members" of a party have the right to vote in party *primaries* which nominate the party's candidates for public office, and they often elect the delegates to the party's national convention which then selects its candidates for President and Vice-President of the United States. (In other states the election of convention delegates is left to the "regulars" in the local party clubs.)

Parties differ not only in the varying amounts of money they need, but also in the sources from which they get it. Since membership parties get much of their money in small but regular amounts from their members, they are less dependent on individual "fat cats" or party donors. Moreover, such membership parties as the British Labour Party or the German SPD, and liberal parties in general, get financial support from other mass organizations such as labor unions and cooperative societies. Conservative parties frequently obtain financial support from big business and industrial organizations, as well as from particular business firms and individuals. Most of these funds, whether given to liberal or conservative parties, are given in expectation of some favors in return. In politics, as in business, there is no such thing as a free lunch.

With the growth of mass electorates and the mass media the cost of large political campaigns is steadily rising. In effect, the entrance fee for major candidates is getting steeper. In the United States this has favored the persistence of millionaires in politics, such as Franklin Roosevelt, Herbert Lehman, Averell Harriman, Stuart Symington, and the Kennedy brothers among the Democrats; and Robert Taft, Barry Goldwater, George Romney, and the Rockefeller family among the Republicans. Politicians who start out with smaller personal fortunes such as Harry Truman, Lyndon Johnson, and Hubert Humphrey among the Democrats, and Thomas E. Dewey, Dwight D. Eisenhower, and Richard M. Nixon among the Republicans, must attract millions of dollars from private individuals, business interests, and, to a lesser extent, organized labor.

If this trend continues, fewer people will be able to participate effectively in politics, and special interests will prevail more often over the common good. A possible remedy would be the public financing of campaign expenditures, in some proportion to the number of votes polled by each party at the previous election, or the number of bonafide signatures on the nominating petitions of a new party. Legislation of this kind was enacted in the German Federal Republic in the mid-1960s and resulted in a markedly greater independence of political parties from the main sources of private financial support; and it may well lead to broader and more varied opportunities for political participation. Similar reforms have been proposed for the United States.

Parties can be more or less "open" or machine-ruled (see Table 3.7). Within every party there is a difference between the members who devote only their free time to politics and the full-time professionals on the party's staff. The latter, together with some holders of political office who in fact devote much time to party matters, form in each party the bureaucracy— the *machine* as it is called in American cities, the "apparat" as it used to be termed in Communist usage. In general, the bigger and more self-contained the party bureaucracy, the less is the influence of rank-and-file members. "In other clubs," wrote the playwright Bertolt Brecht about the Communist Party, "the members elect the secretaries. In our club the secretaries elect the members." In the United States, too, the desires of party members often take second place to those of the bureaucracy. The rank-and-file Democrats in the primaries of 1968 gave strong support to Eugene McCarthy and Robert Kennedy as presidential candidates, but the party professionals at the machine-dominated Chicago convention nominated Hubert Humphrey, who led the party to defeat. In so doing, they may have remembered the old politician's rule: If you must choose between losing control of the party and losing the election, "lose the election."

It would seem, then, that party bureaucracies always prevail over the rank-and-file membership. An *iron law of oligarchy,* asserting just this, was proposed in 1911 by the Italian sociologist Roberto Michels. But such a law would hold true only if old political parties were immortal and no new ones could be founded. In fact, however, the more rigid a monopoly becomes in politics or in business, the more likely it is to lose control. Although party bureaucrats may prefer losing one or several elections rather than making concessions to new developments and new voters, they cannot go on losing too long or their party will decline and other parties arise to take its place. Individuals who wish to reform an existing political party must judge carefully whether they will do better to continue participating within the party or to leave it and try to form a new one. Party leaders, in turn, must decide whether to discourage and drive out opposition or to accept enough reforms to keep participation attractive to the young.

Scope and Domain: Key Dimensions of a Political System

The chapter to this point has been a quick sketch of some of the things one might want to ask when looking at any political system. One might ask: Who are the elites? Which are the politically relevant strata? What is the party system and which are the important interest groups and parties within it? If we consider these matters together with the changing stakes of politics, the changing volume of activities controlled, and the benefits or values redistributed by the political process, we begin to get a rough notion of different kinds of political systems. This set of dimensions points up the radical difference between the political systems discussed by the great political theorists of the past and the political systems of today.

The Greek city-state was a state large in *scope*—that is, in the variety of human activities which it tried to control. Greek government may have redistributed 15 per cent of the income of Athens or perhaps more. The Athenian state was concerned with theaters and art, with education, with religion, as well as with politics and law. Its *domain*—the territory and people it controlled—was small. Athens may have had only 270,000 inhabitants, and the people who were theoretically citizens may not have exceeded 50,000 in number. In actual fact, not more than one-tenth of its citizens were politically active. At the Athenian plenary meeting that condemned Socrates about 1,500 votes were cast for the prosecution and a smaller number for the defense, so that the total number of votes cast in Socrates' trial must have been below 2,500. The political activists in Athens may actually have been only 0.5 per cent of the total Athenian population; the politically relevant strata, the citizens who could have been stirred up, may have been about 20 per cent.

Rome of the Caesars had a much smaller scope. It did much less for the education of the mass of the people, much less for their arts, much less for their religion. It mainly kept the peace, built a few roads, collected taxes, and maintained Roman law in one-half of the empire. (In the other half of the empire the government left the local laws alone.) The Roman government may have reallocated not more than 5 per cent of the national income of the Roman Empire. If so, its scope was only one-third that of the Greeks' (see Figures 3.4 and 3.5).

The domain of the Roman Empire, on the other hand, was fifty times larger, or more, in terms of both land and people. Adding to the quarter of a million Athenian inhabitants all the dependencies of Athens at the peak of its power, the population of the Athenian empire still did not reach a total of more than one million people. The Roman Empire at its peak

Figure 3.4

How Big is "Big Government": The Government's Share

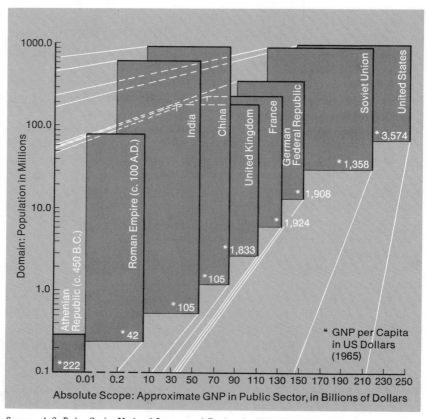

Sources: A. S. Becker, Soviet National Income and Product in 1965: The Goals of the Seven Year Plan *(Santa Monica: The Rand Corporation, 1963); Joint Economic Committee of the U.S. Congress,* An Economic Profile of Mainland China *(New York: Praeger, 1968); United Nations,* Demographic Yearbook, 1967; *United Nations,* Economic Survey of Asia and the Far East, 1965; *United Nations,* Yearbook of National Account Statistics, 1967; *United Nations,* Economic Survey of Europe in 1966; *K. W. Deutsch,* The Analysis of International Relations *(Englewood Cliffs, N.J.: Prentice-Hall, 1968).*

contained 50 to 60 million people, and it maintained much of its size for centuries. This was an unprecedented extension of domain, purchased only partly by a much lesser reduction in scope. The domain had grown fifty times, while the scope had shrunk by two-thirds. Probably less than one-half of 1 per cent of the adult population in the Empire was in politics. The politically relevant strata were probably less than 5 per cent of the total. Roman government was based on the political indifference of the mass of the population.

Fifteen hundred years later, in 1785, we find that the scope of the government of the Bourbon kings of France was larger than that of Rome, though smaller than that of Athens. About 8 per cent of the national

Figure 3.5

How Big is "Big Government": The Government's Job

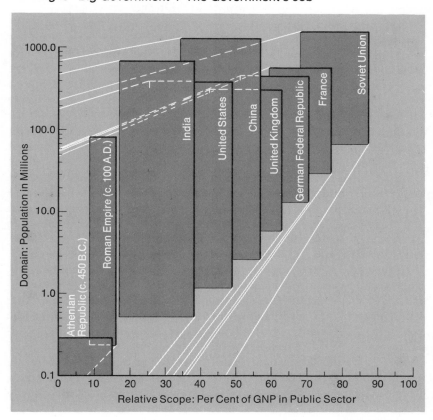

Sources: A.S. Becker, Soviet National Income and Product in 1965: The Goals of the Seven Year Plan *(Santa Monica: The Rand Corporation, 1963); Joint Economic Committee of the U.S. Congress,* An Economic Profile of Mainland China *(New York: Praeger, 1968); United Nations,* Demographic Yearbook, 1967; *United Nations,* Economic Survey of Asia and the Far East, 1965; *United Nations,* Yearbook of National Account Statistics, 1967; *United Nations,* Economic Survey of Europe in 1966; *K. W. Deutsch,* The Analysis of International Relations *(Englewood Cliffs, N.J.: Prentice-Hall, 1968).*

income was redistributed through government taxation and spending. The domain, 25 million people, was fairly large, though less than that of Rome. The dependencies were negligible in 1785, since the French had just lost most of their empire. The politically active population before the French Revolution was approximately 0.1 per cent, about one-fifteenth of what it had been in Athens. The politically relevant strata in 1785 were about 1 per cent of the population—only the nobles and the clergy. This situation did not last. Four years later, a great many more people became politically relevant.

If we compare the France of the Bourbon kings with the France of 1968, we find striking changes. The scope of government, measured by the share of national income distributed by the political process, has risen five times, from 8 per cent to about 40 per cent. The domain has nearly doubled. France has 50 million inhabitants. The politically active population of France, as in other Western countries, is at least 3 per cent. Since about one-fifth of French voters favor the Communist Party, and since there is a fairly high level of union and other activities, the proportion of activists may be slightly higher. French student unrest may have contributed another 100,000 activists or so. Since about 50 per cent of the French population or about 77 per cent of all adults, actually vote, the politically relevant strata today are one hundred times as large as they were in the Bourbon era.

In the United States about 30 per cent of the gross national product goes to the political sector, and 200 million people reside in one federal union. Another 200 million people in Latin America and Southeast Asia depend fairly directly upon the political will of the American people. The United States has thus become a quasi-empire, deciding the fate of about 400 million people in the world. Its political activists are 3 per cent of the metropolitan population and its relevant strata are a shade below 40 per cent.

In the U.S.S.R. the scope of the government sector is much larger still. The central government alone spends more than 51 per cent of the income. Added to this, the budgets of the constituent republics, the other subdivisions of the government, municipalities, and the rest bring the portion of the Russian gross national product that goes through the political sector to 70 to 75 per cent. The direct human domain, 232 million people, is a little larger than that of the United States, and there are another 80 to 100 million people in the satellite countries—East Germany, Poland, Czechoslovakia, Hungary, and Bulgaria—who are fairly directly dependent on the will of the Soviet government. The activists are 9 per cent, the politically relevant strata about 32 per cent.

Clearly, the one thing that is changing the politics of the world is a huge shift from mass apathy to mass participation. Ancient, medieval, and even absolutist eighteenth-century politics were based on the participation of between 1 and 10 per cent of the population. In Western Europe during the first half of the nineteenth century, only 10 per cent of the adults of a country could vote. Today approximately three-quarters of 1 per cent of the population in every developing country every year is shifting into mass communication, activity, and modernity and thus is likely to become relevant in politics. By the end of the twentieth century, more than three-fourths of all adults in the world's highly developed countries, or more than one-half of their total population, will be relevant in politics. This shift to broader participation is under way today. It already has transformed the entire nature of politics and has engendered vast new hopes and dangers. Now begun, it will be almost impossible to stop.

Key Terms and Concepts

top elite
position method
reputation method
central elite
mid-elite
marginal elite
the pyramid of influence
politically relevant strata
activist
opportunity cost
emergency-immobility syndrome
polyarchy
interest elite
establishment
logrolling

Burke's definition of conservatism
one-party system
totalitarian system
authoritarian system
two-party system
parties of action
parties of expression
multi-party system
policy oriented party
power oriented party
membership party
skeleton party
primaries
scope
domain

Additional Readings

Acheson, D. *Present at the Creation.* New York: Norton, 1969.

Dahl, R. A. *Congress and Foreign Policy.* New York: Norton, 1964.

————. *Who Governs? Democracy and Power in an American City.* New Haven: Yale University Press, 1961.

De Sola Pool, I. *et al. Candidates, Issues and Strategies: A Computer Simulation of the 1960 and 1964 Presidential Elections.* Cambridge: MIT Press, 1965.

Deutsch, K. W., L. J. Edinger, R. C. Macridis, and R. L. Merritt. *France, Germany and the Western Alliance: A Study of Elite Attitudes on European Integration and World Politics.* New York: Scribner's, 1967.

Heard, A. *Costs of Democracy.* Chapel Hill: University of North Carolina Press, 1960.

Hoopes, T. *The Limits of Intervention.* New York: McKay, 1969.

Horowitz, I. (ed.) *Power, Politics and People: The Collected Essays of C. Wright Mills.* Oxford: Oxford University Press, 1967.

Lipset, S. M. *Political Man: The Social Bases of Politics.* New York: Doubleday, 1959.

Mills, C. W. *The Power Elite.* Oxford: Oxford University Press, 1956.

Polsby, N. *Community Power and Political Theory.* New Haven: Yale University Press, 1963.

States and Nations

Anyone can participate in politics as an individual, but most people participate through groups and organizations. When the labor union leader Joe Hill was executed in 1925 in Salt Lake City on what he insisted was a framed-up charge of murder, he had these last words for his friends: "Don't mourn me; organize!" Before and since that day, millions of men have known that strength grows from organization. The most powerful kind of organization in the world today is the modern nation-state. To understand the nation-state—its origins, its nature, the ways in which it is partially controlled by interest groups, and the ways in which it tries to control itself as a political system—is to understand much of the heart of politics.

Chapter 4

States and Nation-States

A *state* is an organized machinery for the making and carrying out of political decisions and for the enforcement of the laws and rules of a government. Its material appendages include not only officials and office buildings but also soldiers, policemen, and jails.

In the classical theory of nineteenth-century laissez-faire liberals, as well as of Marxists, the enforcement function was the essence of the state. Everything else was thought to be peripheral. Whether or not this view was true one hundred years ago, it does not fit the facts today. Most modern states spend less than one-third of their budgets on law enforcement, including the maintenance of criminal courts, police, and the national defense. About two-thirds of the activities of the *general government sector*—national, provincial or state, and local—are now devoted to social services, welfare, education, economic aid, and to the maintenance of the economic infrastructure, such as schools, roads, airports, and other parts of the transportation system. (The *economic infrastructure* is the collection of all facilities necessary to make the economy function.) Even in Communist states the tasks of production planning, economic regulation, the allocation of investments, and the providing of social services, education, and public health take a larger amount of money and manpower than the mere enforcement function.

Nonetheless, the enforcement function remains important. If an ethnic group—whom we usually call a *people*—tries to acquire enforcement capabilities in order to police the compliance habits of its members, it becomes politicized. Such a politicized people is often called a *nationality*. If some members of this people control a *sovereign state*—that is, a state which recognizes no higher decision-making power outside itself—we speak of a *nation* or *nation-state*. All of these concepts will be examined in greater detail later in this chapter.

The Changing Relevance of Race.   At some times and places, the visible and inheritable physical marks which distinguish a race became associated with the formation of a people. Where this has happened, we often can tell at a glance to what people a person belongs, and thus often his political majority or minority status in the state. At other times and places, the lines of nationality, loyalty, language, and culture all cut across the lines of race: in such cases, race may have little or no relevance in politics.

In all cases, *race* to the anthropologist means a collection of persons who have some similar inheritable physical characteristics. Most of our physical characteristics, of course, are common to all mankind. We are one single biological species, not several. Unlike lions and tigers—or horses and donkeys—human beings of all races can produce fertile offspring when they interbreed. We are divided into blood groups, but these cut across all races and all political views. Moreover, our heredity is combinatorial. Two or more of our inheritable traits may go together in some individuals but need not do so in others. Some tall people have poor coordination and awkward reflexes, but others do not and excel at basketball. After centuries of argument, no conclusive evidence has been found that intelligence or creativity goes with having a long nose or a short one, being fat or thin, blond or dark-haired, straight-haired or curly, or having skin that is white, black, brown, red, or yellow. There is even less connection between inherited physical traits and such human qualities as kindness, honesty, or competence in politics.

Observable physical traits often do make a difference, however, in how people are treated. In Egypt and Morocco they make little difference; in Brazil and India only a little more; in the United States, they matter a good deal; and in Rhodesia and South Africa, they matter most of all. The most important thing about many such physical traits is that they furnish us with an automatic signaling device for identifying a collection of persons quickly and without cost and effort. We then can file in one place in our mind—we can *associate*—all our experiences with persons of similar physical appearance. By these means we can quickly produce stereotypes and prejudices which eliminate the need for thinking. If in some country many black people are poor and unschooled, we may quickly associate blackness with poverty and lack of education.

If a racial group has a distinct culture in common, then it is an ethnic group as well. Its members would be an ethnic group even without any similarities in physical appearance. If American Negroes all became white tomorrow and resembled a group such as the Irish with no predominant physical traits, most Negroes would still form an ethnic group—and they might still be subject to the same sort of discrimination faced by poor Irishmen in English and American cities in the nineteenth century. Furthermore, many members of this now-white group might well retain a sense of ethnic cultural cohesion and identity, much as many Irishmen have done.

The importance of race in American politics today derives in part from this coincidence, in the case of black Americans, of racial traits with genuine cultural and historical distinctiveness—indeed uniqueness—as a people. In addition, this particular people, vulnerable to easy discrimination through its physical appearance (and its association with the stigma of poverty) has been the victim of severe economic and social inequality, and often of outright political oppression.

"Race" is the label under which this combination of conditions is perceived. But race need not be associated only with the difficulties of being a Negro in America. Assets and sources of pride are also perceived in this manner. What other peoples would call their history, their culture, their songs, and their sense of belonging together—all this many black Americans may experience as pride of race.

Old Peoples and Young States.   These distinctions among peoples, races, nationalities, states, and nations are relevant in our own time because of the rapid changes world politics has undergone. Most peoples in the world are reasonably old, in the sense that their average age as a people can be measured in generations. Most of them go back several centuries and some, such as the Chinese, have had a recognizable identity for more than 2,000 years. The major Western European peoples, too, go back a millennium or more. By the year 1000 A.D., a recognizable Italian language and Italian people had been put together. The French similarly trace their continuity back at least to the ninth century A.D., and so do the Germans. The American people go back at best about 350 years if we consider the first Pilgrim stepping ashore at Plymouth Rock as a 100 per cent American. If we assume more realistically that the American people came fully into existence in the middle of the eighteenth century, approximately fifteen years before the American Revolution, then we must consider the American people as about 200 years old.[1] The Ghanaian people within Ghana's present borders is only twenty or thirty years old (although some peoples within Ghana have a much older tradition). Many other peoples are as young or even younger. But on the whole, the age of most peoples in the world, and certainly of the major peoples, can be measured in terms of centuries.

States are much younger. So are political regimes. (By political *regime* we mean the basic political order under which persons live, such as a monarchy or a republic, a despotism or a democracy, or capitalism or communism in their political aspects.) New states have arisen, and some states that have existed for a long time have become thoroughly transformed in their political arrangements. The China of the emperors and the China of Chiang Kai-shek were both very different from the China of Mao Tse-tung. If we consider such differences as radical changes in regime, then we discover that the majority of all persons throughout the world over thirty years of age are older than the political regimes under which they live.

In this world of rapid political change, the United States is a striking exception. No other major country has changed its constitutional form so little since 1791. To most outsiders, its politics may seem remarkably conservative. Other countries whose present constitutional forms are old, though younger than that of the United States, include Britain (since the Reform Bill of 1832), Sweden, and Switzerland. These countries, too, are exceptions in the modern world.

For there has never been a period like ours. In past recorded history, the political system under which most persons in most places lived was older than the individual. It is only in our time that most of the world's adults over thirty are older than their political regimes. At a time when states and political systems are changing so quickly, it is important to distinguish the slower-changing *habits* of peoples and language groups from the faster-changing *institutions* of politics, economics, national sovereignties, national identities, basic political regimes, and even of social systems.

The Changing Number of States.   A state is to a people, a German nationalist once wrote, as a suit of clothes is to a man. Just as a healthy man will wear out many suits in his lifetime, a people, he thought, should survive many states and political regimes. (Of course, he was writing before the age of nuclear weapons.) What he said is not quite true, but there is some truth in it. Not only have political regimes come and gone faster than the peoples living under them, but the number of states, too, has changed strikingly.

[1] See Richard Merritt, *Symbols of American Community, 1735–1775* (New Haven: Yale University Press, 1966). Another interesting work on this topic is Max Savelle, "Nationalism and Other Loyalties in the American Revolution," *American Historical Review,* Vol. 67, No. 4 (1962), pp. 901–923.

In the years 1815 to 1871, the number of sovereign states tended to decline. In Asia, during these years, many principalities in India, Indochina, and elsewhere were replaced by the colonial rule of a few European powers. Between 1871 and 1900, much the same happened in Africa: a few colonial empires took the place of a multitude of petty principalities, small tribal communities, and states. Earlier, in the Western hemisphere, the empires of the Aztecs in Mexico and of the Incas in Peru, together with many independent tribes in South and North America, had been swallowed up in the vast expansion of the Spanish and English colonial empires from about 1500 to 1775. In the latter year, most of the Western hemisphere was under the flags of only these two powers. In Europe the minimum number of sovereign states was not reached until about 1871, and in Asia and Africa not until about 1900. For the four centuries from 1500 to 1900, the replacement of many small and backward political units by ever fewer, larger, and more modern states seemed to be the general historic trend (see Figures 4.1 and 4.2). The successful independence movements of a few small nations, such as the Swiss, the Dutch, the Belgians, the Norwegians, and the American colonists, appeared to be but minor exceptions to the general rule; and the United States in the end seemed to confirm the apparent pattern by expanding clear across its continent and absorbing whatever peoples lay in its way.

But this general picture is deceptive. From 1810 onward, republics, finally reaching eighteen in number, replaced the Spanish empire in Latin America. From the Ottoman Empire, five Balkan states emerged between 1804 and 1912—Serbia (now the core of Yugoslavia), Greece, Rumania, Bulgaria and Albania; since World War I at least ten Arab nations have done likewise, leaving behind a much smaller and more nationalistic Turkish republic. Scandinavia, which contained two sovereign states, Sweden and Denmark, in 1800, now has five, Norway, Finland, and Iceland having emerged into sovereignty in the interim. Europe consisted altogether of about fifteen sovereign states in 1871, approximately twenty-five shortly before World War I, and over thirty by the 1930s. The world at large reveals a similar pattern. In Africa and Asia a plethora of new states arose from the French and British empires. Indeed, since 1945 the number of sovereign states around the world has more than doubled to well above 140 at the last count (see Figures 4.3 and 4.4).

The historic trend has now reversed itself. Where before many states were giving way to few, more recently few states have been giving way to many. But this has not been a mere swing of the pendulum. The many states and state-like units that were submerged and swallowed up in the past were economically backward and their populations were politically apathetic. The many new states have all experienced at least some touches of economic modernization, industrialism, and mass communications. Their populations are far more numerous and active in politics than their forebears were, and they feel a greater need for that high degree of mutual

Figure 4.1

The Growth in the Number of Sovereign States: Modern States Independent Before 1770

Figure 4.2

The Growth in the Number of Sovereign States: Modern States Which Became Independent Between 1771 and 1890

Figure 4.3

The Growth in the Number of Sovereign States: Modern States Which Became Independent Between 1891 and 1945

Figure 4.4

The Growth in the Number of Sovereign States: Modern States Which
Became Independent Between 1946 and 1969

communication, understanding, and solidarity that turns populations into peoples, and eventually peoples into nations.

An Age of Nationalism.   It is these developments that have made most of the twentieth century an age of nationalism. *Nationalism* is an attitude of mind, a pattern of attention and desires. It arises in response to a condition of society and to a particular stage in its development. It is a predisposition to pay far more attention to messages about one's own people, or to messages from its members, than to messages from or about any other people. At the same time, it is a desire to have one's own people get any and all values that are available. The extreme nationalist wants his people to have all the power, all the wealth, and all the well-being for which there is any competition. He wants his people to command all the respect and deference from others; he tends to claim all rectitude and virtue for it, as well as all enlightenment and skill; and he gives it a monopoly of his affection. In short, he totally identifies himself with his nation. Though he may be willing to sacrifice himself for it, his nationalism is a form of egotism written large.

Although nationalism today is a widespread state of mind, it is in partial conflict with human nature. Children are not born with it; they have to be carefully taught. In most periods of history, nationalism has been weak or nonexistent. It teaches us to prefer distant strangers who share our language and culture to any of our next-door neighbors who do not. It stresses a community of outlook and interest across class lines, but denies any such community across ethnic or national divisions—and stigmatizes a sense of international community as treason to the nation.

Actually, most persons do not think in a nationalist way. In a mass survey undertaken by UNESCO—the United Nations Educational, Scientific, and Cultural Organization—respondents in nine countries were asked, first, whether they felt they had much in common with people in their own class in other nations, and, second, whether they thought they had much in common with people in their own nation but in other classes (see Figure 4.5). According to the doctrine of nationalism, most people should have answered "yes" to the second question and "no" to the first; according to theories of class conflict, they ought to have answered the other way around. In fact, they did neither. They answered in accordance with their own personalities. Those who liked and trusted people did so across both class lines and national boundaries. Those who disliked and distrusted foreigners thought little better of their own countrymen.

Even if most people are not extreme nationalists, nationalism has altered the world in many ways. Nationalism has not only increased the number of countries on the face of the earth, it has helped to diminish the number of its inhabitants. All major wars in the twentieth century have been fought in its name. This is even true of the limited wars since 1945, though the ideologies of both communism and anti-communism have

Figure 4.5

National and Class Solidarities: Nine Nations in 1949

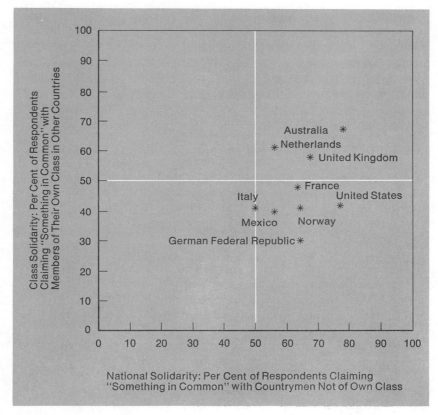

Note that people identify both with class and nation but national solidarity is higher; and that top left-hand quadrant—high loyalty to class, low loyalty to nation—is empty.

Source: W. Buchanan and H. Cantril, How Nations See Each Other *(Urbana: University of Illinois Press, 1953).*

played a role in many of these. In a speech at Montreal in 1966 Secretary of Defense Robert McNamara stated that more than three-fifths of the 149 conflicts which the Defense Department had counted had occurred *within* the non-Communist world. These were primarily conflicts engendered by nationalism.

Nationalism is in potential conflict with all philosophies or religions—such as Christianity—which teach universal standards of truth and of right and wrong, regardless of nation, race, or tribe. Early in the nineteenth century a gallant American naval officer, Stephen Decatur, proposed the toast, "Our country! In her intercourse with foreign nations, may she be always in the right, but our country, right or wrong." Nearly 150 years later the United States Third Army, marching into Germany following the collapse of the Nazi regime, liberated the huge concentration camp at Buchenwald. Over the main entrance to that place of torture and death, the Nazi elite guard had thoughtfully written, "My Country, Right or Wrong."

From Countries to Peoples

The Concept of a Country.   For those who live in it, a country is an area of multiple interdependences. In economic terms, a country is a multiple market for goods and services. An increase in the price of bread or of textiles, an increase in wages, a change in employment, or even a natural catastrophe, has a tangible effect on the lives of all its inhabitants. This is true in emotional as well as material terms. To an American, a hundred Americans killed in a mine explosion or landslide represent a disaster. But to most American newspaper readers, 10,000 Iranians killed in an earthquake are a statistic.

A *country* is a geographic area of material, economic, physical, and psychological interdependences. This is why statesmen at a conference table cannot arbitrarily make a country that will endure. The Congress of Vienna in 1815 and the Paris Peace Conference in 1919 tried to redraw the boundaries of many countries and to create some new countries, but not all of these lasted.

Some political geographers have tried to find "natural frontiers" to define a country, but frontiers that seem natural to one country may seem quite unnatural to another, particularly if both covet the same frontier. The French, for instance, asserted for centuries that the Rhine was a natural frontier of France, because they wanted the German-speaking territories on its left bank to be incorporated into their nation. German patriots, however, countered that the Rhine was a German river, not a German boundary.

By and large, there are few natural frontiers. A natural boundary at most imposes major obstacles to transport and frequently is characterized by thin settlement. And yet a thinly settled boundary region can become a heartland when people have learned to drain its swamps, clear its forests, or irrigate its dry pastures. Similarly, a mountain chain separates two countries only so long as people do not know how to build bridges over its gorges and roads over its passes. Thus, in the early Middle Ages Switzerland was not a country but a frontier region. As roads or passes were built and pass traffic made St. Gotthard the medieval equivalent of the Panama Canal, Switzerland became a country.

Depending on changes in settlement and in technology, a geographic feature can be either an obstacle or a bridge. Centuries ago, the skin-and-wicker boats of the ancient Irish were unable to cope with North Sea navigational conditions, and Ireland was sharply separated from England and Scotland. But after the English and Scotch learned to build better boats and the Vikings and Normans started sailing the seas, Ireland eventually became part of Britain. Nowadays, reinforced by differences in religion and general culture, the most critical Irish boundary is on land, not at the seashore: Ireland is divided in two, six counties forming British or Northern Ireland and twenty-six in the south forming the Irish Free State. These two nations, the British and the Irish, are, as Bernard Shaw put it, separated by the same language to which they tend to attach different political meanings.

A country need not be inhabited by only one set of people. It can be populated by several races speaking different languages and having different cultural traditions. Nevertheless, all these groups live in the same country. To the extent that they do, their fates are linked. Bohemia, until World War II, was a single country of two peoples, Czechs and Germans. India was also a single country before its partition into India and Pakistan in 1947. Today the United States includes persons who call themselves the Negro or black people, others who feel a certain affiliation with the Jewish people, and still others who point with pride to their Irish, Scottish, Spanish, or other roots. It is thus evident that one country can contain or include several peoples.

It is also possible for the same person to belong to more than one people. A Scotsman is a Scot and a Britisher; a black militant American belongs to both the black people and the American people. Many an American Jew will feel both a special kinship to Israel and a patriotic loyalty to the United States. Multiple loyalties are thus not rare occurrences and may remain compatible indefinitely.

Patriotism: Solidarity by Territory. Usually in the past, a country was largely inhabited by people who had been born there. Most people did not distinguish between their country of residence and their country of birth. The country of birth in a patriarchal society was called the fatherland, the *patria;* and ever since the days of the Romans, people have been told that it was sweet and honorable to die for their *patria.* Loyalty to a fatherland, however, was not strong in the early Middle Ages when people had loyalties mainly to their tribes. It emerged in Western Europe only in the thirteenth century and at that time was assiduously fostered by the Church. The key change came when Pope Honorius III decreed that a kingdom, like a diocese, could not be divided nor any part of it alienated or sold off to someone else.[2] Applied first to Hungary and then to France, the decree established the notion that kingdoms were indivisible, that a kingdom was a unit, and that the Crown united a country regardless of the whims or policies of the king who happened to wear it. These views

[2] See Ernst Kantorowicz, "Pro Patria Mori in Medieval Political Thought," *American Historical Review,* Vol. 56, No. 3 (1951), pp. 472–492.

became accepted in much of Western Europe between 1240 and 1500. Eventually, they formed a major principle of European politics: that a country belongs together and though rulers may come and go, countries remain intact.

If we think of a country as the place where we were born, we attach to it many of the warm sentiments that we attach to childhood and to the memories of our parents; and we begin to have strong feelings of loyalty to the country and to anything to which the symbols of the country are attached. Those who believe that the interests of their countrymen ought to take precedence over the interests of others, are called patriots. *Patriotism* means giving preference to the interests of one's countrymen regardless of their race, language, nationality, or religion.

Patriotism sometimes leads to rather striking interpretations. After World War II, a chapel in Philadelphia was to be dedicated to the memory of four chaplains of various creeds. On a sinking troopship these men had given their lifebelts to some G.I.'s and had gone down with the ship. The architect for the chapel proposed an auditorium in which the congregation would sit before a fixed podium decorated by an American flag and the flag of the State of Pennsylvania, and a rotating stage would bring up the appropriate altar or sanctuary for a Roman Catholic, Greek Orthodox, Protestant, or Jewish service. At the push of a button, a machine would interchange the religious symbols before the fixed flags.

The promoters considered this architectural scheme perfectly normal and sensible. Not a voice was raised against it. But think of what would happen if somebody built a church with a fixed altar and a rotation device which would exchange national flags! No doubt, a number of patriotic societies, beginning with the American Legion, would accuse the promoters of political blasphemy. It is quite clear that in the middle of the twentieth century we are more inclined to worship the gods of the tribe and the nation-state than the universal symbols of religion.

If successful, patriotism can unite people of different languages, different races, different religions, and different backgrounds to serve the interests of one country. Let us remember that by "interest" we mean both a distribution of attention and an expectation of reward. A patriot will pay attention to the things that concern his countrymen, and he will try to work for the rewards he expects them to receive.

Peoples and Nationalists

Nationalism: Solidarity by Language, Culture, or Descent. People sometimes do not attach their main allegiance to a geographic unit. Instead they think mainly of their social group and their ancestors. Such people do not ask *where* they were born or where they are living. They ask *who* their parents were. Very likely these people are nationalists.

In its classic form, *nationalism* stresses one's origin by descent and birth; it involves the belief that one's people share a common descent. In actual fact, the bloodlines of mankind have been mixed up a good deal. This holds true not only in such "immigrant" countries as the United States, Canada, and Australia. If we go far enough back in history, it is equally true of all European countries. Ultimately, it is true of the entire world. As we have learned from experience with blood transfusions, there are indeed different blood groups; but these do not coincide with any particular race or nation.

It has been said in Central Europe that a nation is a group of persons jointly misinformed about their ancestry and jointly hostile to their neighbors. Nevertheless, if people believe that they belong together through ancestry, their belief is likely to be reinforced by something observable. They often "prove" their ancestry by producing pieces of paper. When the Nazis introduced elaborate race legislation, they gave rise to a brisk trade in documents, some genuine and some less so. Language, too, is observable—we know what language people speak. We also can observe the culture that has become part of people's personality. We can observe people's associations in terms of friendship and relatives, whether these are relations by blood, adoption, or marriage. We can even observe the probabilities of intermarriage. If the memories of ancestors, subject to error as they may be, coincide with the language group, the culture, the group of friendship and associative ties, and the probabilities of past and future intermarriages, that is, if all these pieces fall into place, then we can say with confidence that we have identified a people.

The Concept of a People.   Probably the simplest way to define a *people* is to call it a group of persons who share complementary habits of communication. The individual members of the group have a wide range of common ideas and notions and can communicate on many topics. A Communist Frenchman and a Nationalist Frenchman may, for instance, differ on many points about politics, one of them perhaps admiring General de Gaulle and the other deploring him, but they might nevertheless find common ground on many things: the definition of a good dinner, the proper way to court a girl, and whether to wear a hat or a beret. Frenchmen of different ideologies still can communicate clearly on thousands of topics with a high degree of mutual understanding and responsiveness. They recognize each other as Frenchmen regardless of their politics.

A people, then, is a group with complementary communication habits whose members usually share the same language, and always share a similar culture so that all members of the group attach the same meanings to words. In that sense a people is a community of shared meanings. The word *liberté* to a French Swiss means much the same thing, local self-government, as *freiheit* means to a German Swiss. But to a North German, *freiheit* might easily mean subjection to a familiar tyranny, as in the days of the German emperor or of Hitler; and to a Frenchman, *liberté* might mean membership in a highly centralized republic governed by a charismatic general as president. What distinguishes the Genevois from the Parisian, and makes the Swiss a people, is the group with whom each shares the meaning of words rather than those with whom they share the mechanics of grammar and vocabulary.

The individual who believes that the interests of his own people should take precedence over the interests of other people is an *ethnic nationalist.* German nationalists in World War I hoped that Americans of German descent would side with the emperor against the United States on the grounds that blood was thicker than water. This calculation proved to be mistaken. There were millions of Americans of German descent, but they functioned as American citizens just as much as any other American group. The assimilation of people of German ancestry to the language and culture of the United States had succeeded. They had become members of the American people. Thus the Nazis obtained little pleasure from the ancestry of Dwight David Eisenhower when he led the United States armies into Germany in World War II. Again and again, the process of assimilation has triumphed thoroughly over mere ties of ancestry.

Politicization and Ethnic Self-Rule. Governments today are engaged in such widespread activities as providing vaccines, old-age pensions, Medicare, roads, and many other things and services. As a result, the governmental sector has become bigger, and a larger part of human life *politicized* (see Chapters 1 and 2).

As government becomes more important to them, as more and more of society's goods and services become subject to allocation through the political process, a people may wish to associate with a state that its members can call "their own." They may find that it is essential to live in a state that is staffed by their own kind, administered in their own language, and run in terms compatible with their basic culture. They want it to be *their* state, in a sense, regardless of whether the state is democratic or not.

An Arab living under the dictatorship of President Nasser in Egypt will find that his government at least is predictable. He can look into his own heart and say, "Well, the man who's governing me is an Arab and I can find out what he will do next by thinking what I would do if I were in his place." Back in the 1920s, Egypt was governed by English officials who were efficient and law-abiding. Most of them were incorruptible, and since the government was constitutional there were fair chances for a hearing of one's complaints. Yet the English were not predictable to the Egyptians because they did not react as Egyptians would in a given situation, nor could an Egyptian identify with his rulers. Moreover, they were not accessible to them through other than legal channels. By contrast, even under dictatorship, Egyptian officials are likely to have cousins who know the cousins of ordinary citizens. They are thus accessible to many Egyptians through family ties, through friendship, and if need be through bribery.

People want to be governed by an accessible, predictable government that is compatible with their values and functions in congenial ways. Then they can say, "our government," even if this government does not permit free debate or free discussion. And they are likely to defend it against any attack by foreigners.

Nationalities: Peoples Moving Toward Nationhood. If a people tries to acquire a state or gain political power at the local, district, or regional level, its members form a *nationality.* Poland was a nation in a very limited sense in the eighteenth century. The petty nobles, who thought of themselves as Poles, were running the country, but most of the peasants under them had no share in administrative affairs and few had an active interest in gaining power. Although the country of Poland was geographically large and the Polish people were numerous, the Polish nationality was small and shallow. It involved only a thin social layer of people who sought and obtained political power. Then the country was divided in the late eighteenth century among her neighbors Prussia, Austria, and Russia. And for the next 150 years Polish patriots tried to make Poland a single entity both as a country and as a nation. Since Polish groups were always trying to attain political power and since they did exercise some pressure or control over their members, it is fair to say that certain of the Poles constituted a nationality in those days. Indeed many Poles insisted on saying they were a nation even though they did not have a state. They regained their state in 1918; and since that time Poland has been a full-fledged nation-state.

A *nation-state* is the strongest organization for getting things done. Usually it commands a good deal of popular support and can count on a fair amount of popular compliance. The government's orders are couched in words the people can understand, communication is fast, and common cultural patterns facilitate teamwork. Where there exists a single people, nation-states—whether capitalist or Communist—have become the normal instruments of running modern industrial societies.

Multi-Ethnic States

Many sovereign states are not composed of only one ethnic group, however. More than half of the world's states for which we have information include linguistic or ethnic minorities amounting to more than one-fifth of their population. Such *multi-ethnic states,* as they are called, are liable to become politically divided in their domestic affairs. If their population is also sharply divided into social strata, the risk of such conflict increases.

Double Trouble: Ethnic Plus Social Cleavages.   Most societies are in fact divided into social strata. Even the United States is stratified, despite its historic reputation of having greater social mobility and a wider distribution of wealth than most other countries. Of the six social classes listed by such sociologists as Lloyd Warner and Morris Janowitz, the three top strata combined—upper upper, lower upper, and upper middle—contain about 10 per cent of the U. S. population. (By way of contrast, however, these three strata accounted for only 3 per cent of the populations of many European countries [such as Germany] in the 1930s.) Below these three top strata, sociologists frequently find a large "lower middle" class, but hardly anybody wants to admit membership in it. Nevertheless, it is quite numerous, composed of small entrepreneurs, small businessmen, small craftsmen, and white collar workers. The "upper lower" class consists of skilled workers and such, comprising about 30 per cent of the population, and the "lower lower" are the unskilled workers and the poor. Middling farmers would be among the upper lower class or the lower middle class, depending on farm size and income, and the farmer who owned a two thousand–acre wheat farm and a private airplane would "make it" into the narrow upper strata.

Where nationalities are divided, they are not likely to be evenly split by social strata. Switzerland is the one country whose different language groups are about equally divided on all social levels. But in most countries one language or ethnic group is much "more equal" than the others. In the days of the Austro-Hungarian Empire, for example, about 80 per cent of the upper level in Bohemia were German and 20 per cent were Czech. In pre-1960 Algeria, 90 per cent of the top jobs were held by Frenchmen and 10 per cent, at most, by Arabs. The farther down one goes in the social scale, the smaller becomes the share of the favored group until at the bottom there are only very few of the favored. In its sociological profile the disfavored group looks like a pyramid; the favored group looks like a pyramid standing on its head. Similar profiles have long been observed between whites and blacks in the South of the United States, and to a growing extent in the big cities in the North.

Modernization, Mobility, and Ethnic Conflict.   Now consider what happens when a country with this kind of profile becomes modernized. All the children begin to go to school. Mass media, shop windows, advertising, and all the rest begin to exercise a powerful demonstration effect.[3] Everybody begins to discover what life could be like. Industry lures people from the countryside and offers them more attractive jobs in the cities; and how

[3] *Demonstration effect* is the sum of the effects which the demonstration of modern products, practices, and living conditions have on the aspirations and habits of people previously unfamiliar with them. Prominent among these effects are a rise in economic demand for new goods and a rise in political demands for new rights, services, and opportunities.

Figure 4.6

The Curve of Inequality: Family Incomes in the United States, 1964

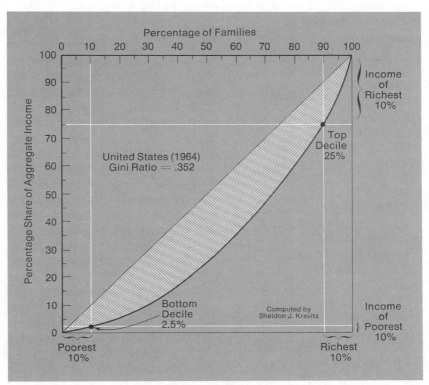

Source: Bureau of the Census, Trends in the Income of Families and Persons in the United States, 1947–1964, *1967.*

can you keep them down on the farm once they have seen Scranton, Pennsylvania!

Now that people want to move, they also want to move upward in society. The modern industrial society teaches people not to take their class position as God-given, but as somehow the result of their own efforts. Class status becomes achieved rather than ascribed or inherited. This means that energetic young individuals now want to move up, and feel resentful if they fail to do so. However, when they try to move up in a multi-ethnic country, they often bump their heads into another nationality group occupying the next higher level in society. And nationality groups, by definition, tend to be exclusive. For, a people (or nationality group) acts not only as a community of communication and a community of mutual predictability of behavior, but also as a community of mutual trust. When we know exactly what someone will do, we trust him, or as Rudyard Kipling once said of his countrymen, we "know the lies they tell."

Figure 4.7

Gini Indices for Unequal Distribution of Power and Wealth: (a) The Unequal Economic Power of Nation-States; (b) The Unequal Distribution of the World's Wealth

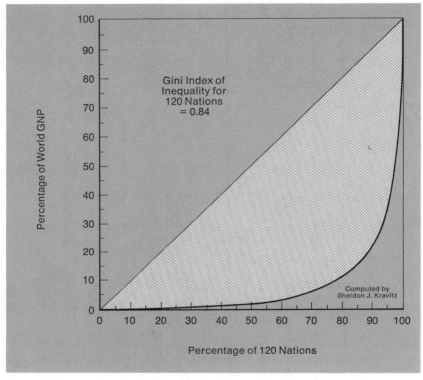

When a young Arab in Algiers wanted a job from a Frenchman, the Frenchman usually found that he could trust another Frenchman more (unless the work was menial). This is an example of overt ethnic discrimination, but discrimination can take more innocent forms. In the United States today, someone decides that having a rich vocabulary in French is excellent proof of good college material, and that a university that requires a knowledge of French for admission has "high standards." On the other hand, an excellent knowledge of the vocabulary of Negro slang is considered irrelevant for college studies (even though it might suggest a good deal of "verbal aptitude"). Enrolling Negroes who don't know French but who possess a rich ghetto vocabulary is considered, therefore, a "lowering of the standards" of a university. College board exams examine people in French, but not in Negro culture—even though the latter may be more useful for future teachers or principals in urban schools. In the name of higher standards such examinations may keep many otherwise qualified Negroes out of the "better" colleges.

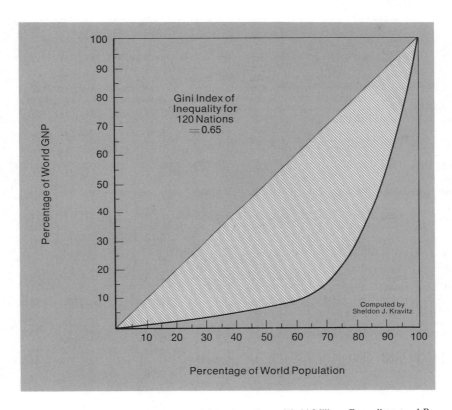

The graph shows a Lorenz curve with axis labels "Percentage of World GNP" (vertical) and "Percentage of World Population" (horizontal), with text "Gini Index of Inequality for 120 Nations = 0.65" and "Computed by Sheldon J. Kravitz".

Source: Economic Bureau, U.S. Arms Control and Disarmament Agency, World Military Expenditures and Related Data, 1966, *Research Report 68–52, 1968.*

What people regard as objective standards are usually culture-bound. For disfavored peoples and races, these culture-bound standards may become tremendous obstacles in the way of social elevation. They may even hurt the psychic self-image—the sense of personal worth—of the members of the disfavored nationalities. The result is social conflict, often long and bitter, driven by disappointed hopes and deep personal emotions.

A favored nationality may sometimes also be motivated by the vision of upward mobility. It may think that if it could conquer another country or colony it could spread itself out like a tree over even more populations. And by adding a new colonial area, it could broaden the opportunities for middle-class jobs for its own people. To the extent that it succeeds in doing this, the favored nationality acquires a sociological profile resembling a mushroom cloud with a thin stem and a wide crown, overshadowing the chances of others. It may then further impoverish the people in the con-

Table 4.1

Distribution of Personal Income Before Taxes in Twelve Countries (Ranked by Inequality Index)

Country	Year	Percentage of Income Going to		Ratio of Top to Bottom Decile	Gini Index of Inequality	Average Net Change in Gini Index Per Decade (rounded)	Net Change in Income Share of Top Decile
		Top Decile	Bottom Decile				
France	1962	36.8	0.5	73.6	0.52 }		
						0.07	2.7%
	1956	34.1	0.7	48.7	0.48 }		
German Federal Republic	1964	41.4	2.1	19.6	0.47 }		
						−0.05	−2.1%
	1960	43.5	2.0	21.8	0.49 }		
	1955	44.0	1.7	25.9	0.51 }	−0.04	−0.5%
						(−0.01)	(2.4%)
	1950	34.0	1.0	34.0	0.45 }	0.12	10%
Pre-war Germany	1936	39.0	1.0	39.0	0.49 }	−0.01	−5%
Finland	1962	32.5	0.5	65.0	0.47		
						0.06	3.6%
	1952	28.9	1.0	28.9	0.41		
Netherlands	1962	33.8	1.3	26.0	0.44 }	−0.01	−1.2%
	1952	35.0	1.3	26.9	0.45 }		
						−0.08 (−0.02)	−3.3%
	1946	38.3	1.0	38.3	0.50 }		
	1938	38.7	n.a.	n.a.	0.48 }	−0.03	−0.4%
United Kingdom	1964	29.3	2.0	14.7	0.40 }	0.00	−1.1%
	1954	30.4	2.0E	15.2	0.40 }		
						−0.04 (−0.01)	−2.6% (8.7%)
	1949	33.0	2.6E	12.7	0.42 }		
	1938	38.0	n.a.	n.a.	0.43 }	−0.01	−5.0%
Sweden	1963	27.9	1.6	17.4	0.40 }		
						0.02	0.6%
	1954	27.3	2.0	13.7	0.38 }		
	1945	34.1	0.9E	37.9	0.48 }	−0.10 (−0.05)	−6.8% (11.6%)
	1935	39.5	n.a.	n.a.	0.54 }	−0.06	−5.4%

Distribution of Personal Income Before Taxes in Twelve Countries (Ranked by Inequality Index)

Country	Year	Percentage of Income Going to		Ratio of Top to Bottom Decile	Gini Index of Inequality	Average Net Change in Gini Index Per Decade (rounded)	Net Change in Income Share of Top Decile
		Top Decile	Bottom Decile				
Denmark	1963	27.1	1.7	15.9	0.39		
						−0.01	
	1953	28.0	1.4	20.0	0.40	−0.05	−0.9%
							10.5%
	1939	37.6	n.a.	n.a.	0.50	−0.07	−9.6%
Israel	1963						
		27.0	1.4	19.3	0.37		
	1964						
						0.03	1.4%
	1957						
		25.6	1.8	14.2	0.35		
	1958						
Norway	1963	24.9	1.0	24.9	0.36		
						−0.07	−2.7%
	1957	27.6	1.1	25.1	0.40		
United States (family incomes)	1964	25.0E	2.5E	10.0E	0.35		
						−0.02	−1.3%
	1955	26.3E	1.3E	20.2E	0.37	−0.02	3.0%
	1947	28.0E	2.0E	14.0E	0.38	−0.01	−1.7%
Yugoslavia (households)	1963	25.4	3.3	7.7	0.32	—	—
Hungary	1962	21.5	4.5E	4.8	0.27	—	—

E = Estimated   n.a. = not available

Sources: United Nations, Economic Survey of Europe in 1965; *United Nations,* Economic Survey of Europe in 1956; *Bank of Israel Research Department,* Saving Survey, 1963/64; *U.S. Department of Commerce,* Trends in Income of Families and Persons in the United States, 1947–1964.

quered country, pressing them or their children down into lower-level jobs. The nationalist movement of the natives seeks to prevent this stratification, or to reverse it.

In such ethnic or racial conflicts there is no built-in stopping point. We begin with nationality A, the favored one, prevailing over the other. But suppose, through some combination of events, that B, the former under-dog, now gets on top of A. Then B will try to corner most of the top jobs for its own people and turn the people of A into the drawers of water and the hewers of wood. This can be done by outright discrimination, by examining and selecting candidates according to the standards of the now dominant culture. Where North African Arabs once were examined in French for civil service jobs, both they and the children of French settlers now may be tested in Arabic.

In many countries, nobody is as solicitous for equality and social justice as the spokesman for an oppressed nationality. And nobody is as callous as the same spokesman, once his nationality succeeds in getting on top. Such nationalists have an interchangeable attitude toward justice. Touchingly concerned for it so long as their own group has been trampled upon, they often show utter unconcern for others when positions are reversed.

A Curve of Inequality.   Such ethnic or racial struggles are expressions of underlying social conflicts. Their intensity grows with the extent of economic inequality and social tension in a society. We can measure the inequality of income among individuals, families, or classes by drawing a so-called *Lorenz Curve* (see Figure 4.6). In this diagram the percentages of population in a country are measured along the horizontal axis and the percentages of income along the vertical axis. If every per cent of people had exactly the same per cent of income, the curve of distribution would be a straight line, coinciding with the diagonal. The more bent the Lorenz Curve, the greater is the area between it and the diagonal, and the greater the economic and social inequality. In a country that manages to move toward more equality the Lorenz Curve will flatten, and the area of inequality will shrink. The area between the Lorenz Curve and the diagonal thus permits us to calculate a single number called the *Gini Index,* after the Italian economist Corrado Gini. This single number is a measure of the extent of social or economic inequality prevailing in a country.[4]

The greater the inequality among classes, or strata, the greater the motivation of ethnic groups to compete for improvement. The less inequal-ity, the less the driving force for conflict. Lack of employment and gross inequality of opportunity are two engines that accelerate conflict among nationalities.

Within most of the advanced countries, stratification has been declining. The richer and more advanced a country is, the closer it moves toward reasonable equality. Very well-to-do countries have a Gini Index of about 0.4; very poor countries have a Gini Index of about 0.7 or higher, but they may keep these data hidden (see Table 4.1). As the table also shows, Communist countries enforce a higher degree of equality, but they do so at

[4] For details of calculation, see H. R. Alker, Jr., and B. M. Russett, "Indices for Comparing Inequality," in R. L. Merritt and S. Rokkan, *Comparing Nations* (New Haven: Yale University Press, 1966), pp. 349–372.

the cost of other values. On the whole, economic growth works better with higher equality, up to a Gini number of perhaps 0.3. What happens beyond that, no one as yet knows.

A Lorenz Curve and a Gini Index can also be made for the world as a whole (see Figure 4.7). International equality has so increased since 1910 that the world is now about as unequal as the worst governed nation-state within it. In the United States, the richest state, Connecticut, has three times the per capita income of the poorest state, Mississippi. In the world as a whole, the difference among countries is not three to one, but sixty to one. The world is extremely unequal, and thus, if economic equality is at least one criterion of good government, extremely badly governed.

A multi-ethnic nation-state with high inequality and high stratification is unstable; it invites major conflicts among language groups, nationalities, and races. A world that is highly unequal does the same. Western Europe and the United States have 80 per cent of world income; all the other countries of the world must scramble for the remaining 20 per cent. If large nation-states such as the United States are explosive, then how explosive is the rest of the world?

Key Terms and Concepts

state
economic infrastructure
race
regime
nationalism
country
patria
patriotism
people

ethnic nationalist
nationality
nation
nation-state
multi-ethnic state
cleavage (social, ethnic)
demonstration effect
Lorenz Curve
Gini Index

Additional Readings

Black, C. *The Dynamics of Modernization.* New York: Harper & Row, 1966.

Buchanan, W. and H. Cantril. *How Nations See Each Other.* Urbana: Illinois University Press, 1953.

Deutsch, K. *Nationalism and Social Communication.* Cambridge: MIT Press, 1962.

Geertz, C. (ed.) *Old Societies and New States.* New York: The Free Press, 1963.

Lipsitz, L. "If, as Verba Says, the State Functions as a Religion, What are We to Do Then to Save Our Souls?" *American Political Science Review,* Vol. 62, No. 2 (1968), pp. 527–535.

Rustow, D. *A World of Nations.* Washington: Brookings Institution, 1967.

Ward, B. *Rich Nations and the Poor Nations.* New York: Norton, 1962.

Aspects of Political Community: Three Classic Theories

Many men look upon their nations as more than instruments. They are seeking a sense of community and of belonging to something bigger than themselves. To feel that one truly belongs to a group of people, and in particular to the society in which one is living, means far more than merely being mechanically included in it. An outside observer may lump people together in the same census category because they share some superficial characteristic, such as "un-married" or "born before 1930," but they will not necessarily feel that they belong to each other in any deeper sense. Indeed, they may look upon one another as strangers and upon their society as a strange land in which they see themselves as homeless aliens. This is the feeling of *alienation,* so well-known to modern poets, philosophers, and young people in many lands.

Chapter 5

The Concept of Community

The sense of *belonging* is the very opposite of such feelings of alienation. It means to look in a special way upon one's society, that is, the group of people among whom one lives and makes one's living by taking part in the division of labor. We look upon our society as a community which we accept and within which we feel accepted. We are at home in it; and home, as Robert Frost once wrote, is where they have to take you in.

A *community* is a group of people whom one understands and by whom one is understood. It promises—and often delivers—a breakthrough in communication from person to person. It is *particularistic* rather than universal, for not everyone belongs to it but only its own particular members. It is *ascriptive* rather than achievement-oriented, for a person is accepted in it for what he is rather than for what he does; and once he is in it, he does not have to earn his membership again and again. Finally, it is *diffuse* rather than specific, for it accepts a wide range of responsibilities, rather than being limited to a single task. Its members can turn to it in whatever respect they may need its aid. A ski club is a specific organization which takes no interest in its members in summer, but a community, like a family, cares for its members at any time, and tries to help them meet their needs.

Could there be a community large enough to have the powers of a nation, and yet small enough to be a kind of larger family? And could enough of these true communities be set up to include all mankind? Men have sought answers to these questions for many years, both in thought and in practice. Some of the great political thinkers of the last two centuries have proposed some answers, based on their own points of view. Their efforts may suggest to us insights relevant to our own problems.

Rousseau: A Prophet of Individualism and Community

Perhaps the most relevant eighteenth-century thinker for the problems of nationality and community was Jean Jacques Rousseau, the watchmaker's son from Geneva. Rousseau was an itinerant, not quite a beatnik though sometimes a hippie, and sometimes a man bent on making a career. So sensitive was he that a contemporary called him "the skinless man." He could be incredibly diligent, but he quarreled prodigiously and at times was illogical. The author of major books, he was the herald of the most elaborate doctrine of civic duties we have had in the world.

Discovering the Individual and His Emotions. Rousseau was perhaps the first writer who rebelled against the rationalist and enlightenment-oriented climate of the eighteenth century. By emphasizing the profound importance of human emotions, he tried to bring back into politics and social thought a consideration of the whole personality of human beings, not only their rational parts. He was, among other things, a theorist of education. Before Rousseau, most of the breed from Plato to Locke and Hartley, and the theorists and psychologists of association, had thought that the task of education was to find some perfect, desirable pattern which one could impose upon more or less defenseless children until they were formed and shaped to fit their culture. In other words, education had been considered the knowledge of the shaping, forming, and molding of children. A Quaker theorist wrote in the seventeenth century, "children are accursed creatures." The only good thing many people could say about children then was that they were getting older every day.

Rousseau took a different view. One would have to go all the way back to the New Testament and its words, "Unless you become like little children . . ." to find a parallel outlook. He believed there was something very important in being young and that education should consist of bringing out what was already inside the young person rather than impressing upon him what was in society. Inside every individual, according to Rousseau, was something original and unique that made him different from everyone else, and from the standardized beliefs and habits which society taught people to copy from each other. Education, for Rousseau, was a process that occurred not from the outside in, but from the inside out. For that reason, he thought that education should be based upon sincerity and spontaneity and that it should encourage self-activity, autonomy, independence, and genuine personal experiences among the young.

From the Individual to the Community.   In education Rousseau was a radical libertarian, but in political theory he was a theorist of community. In his opinion, the more you let people live as individuals, developing their whole personalities and following their emotions, the more you discovered their need for community, and the more salient and urgent the problem of community became. Clearly, Rousseau could not try to be a thorough-going theorist of individualism without realizing the crucial importance of the problem of community. Human beings are so built that they can be individuals only with the help of and within communities. Communities, on the other hand, can make human individuality richer and freer or they can stifle it. Not surprisingly, many of the great theorists of individualism were also the great theorists of the search for more promising or more hopeful forms of community.

Rousseau tried to make his theory of community wholly rational and logical. His famous book, *The Social Contract,* is an heroic effort at such rational, logical thinking. He based it on the assumption that communities are created by an act of will of human beings. Rousseau had every reason to think this way. He was a citizen of Geneva, which had been a city in the Holy Roman Empire and had become a republic by means of a political revolution—an act of the political will—in the year 1526. The independence of Geneva had been confirmed by alliances with Bern and Zurich, by the voluntary conversion of the city to Calvinism, and then by its fighting off the efforts of its former overlords, the princes of neighboring Savoy, to reconquer Geneva and make it part of their state. By voluntary political ties to Switzerland, Geneva had also avoided being incorporated into France. Thus by an act of the political will Geneva had become a republic, and by sustained acts of political will the republic had been preserved.

Rousseau was aware of other states similarly created. Eastward from Geneva, the city states of Bern and Zurich, and the entire Swiss Confederation, were also political entities created by acts of will. In Rousseau's

own time, of course, there were the American colonies, not yet independent, but clearly rooted in voluntary efforts and agreements. Most of the
first colonists had willed to go to the New World. And by acts of will, by
treaties, that is, by "social contracts," Massachusetts Bay Colony and the
colony of Connecticut had been formed.

The Sovereignty of the People.   Rousseau assumed, therefore, that
a state came into existence by explicit or tacit agreement. Explicitly,
people said, "We want to be a state, a community"; by tacit agreement
they chose to stay inside such a community and not emigrate. For Rousseau the state and the people were therefore one. The people, in turn,
were one through common customs and habits. He assumed that whenever
an individual decided that he belonged to a people he already had decided that this people should be sovereign and that, being sovereign, it
should run its own affairs. According to Rousseau, the people therefore
constituted the state. Having created the state, the people ought to control
it and change it as they pleased. This is the doctrine of *popular sovereignty.*

Under this doctrine, the people owe nothing to the magistrates, the
rulers. Legislators are merely enactors or messengers of the popular will;
civil servants are servants of the people. The people can decide whether to
continue the present political institutions or to change them. An echo of
Rousseau's thought appears in Lincoln's First Inaugural Address: "This
country, with its institutions, belongs to the people who inhabit it. Whenever they shall grow weary of the existing government, they can exercise
their constitutional right of amending it, or their revolutionary right to
dismember or overthrow it." This is Rousseau's popular sovereignty theory
in radical form.

To be so powerful against its officials, a people also must be powerful in
relation to its own members. Accordingly, Rousseau argued that in order
to have such a sovereign people which completely controlled the state and
guaranteed the same freedoms to all its members, the people had to make
very great claims upon the individual. Rousseau asserted that in the social
contract every individual surrendered himself totally to the community.
This formally unlimited surrender was limited in its effects, however, by
the fact that every other individual did likewise. And no individual,
reasoned Rousseau, would make more oppressive demands upon his neighbor in the name of popular sovereignty than he would willingly accept for
himself. Moreover, he thought, since any sane man's will could only
accord with his own interests, the state would never make unwarranted
demands. It would use its claim upon the person, time, loyalty, and
property of its citizens only as necessary. Uniformity in the outlook and
interests of its citizens, mutuality of their claims, rationality in their
thought, and realism in their perception of what was necessary thus would
assure that the unlimited claims of the state would be moderate and
limited in practice.

The General Will vs. the Will of All.   The state, as Rousseau saw it, would be steered and controlled by the general will of the people. The *general will* is the sum of all those interests which people have in common. Yet, as Rousseau was careful to point out, most individuals also had some interests which were private or personal or special for themselves or for their families, and which were different from those of their neighbors. These different special interests, the *particular will* of individuals, according to Rousseau, could not be the basis of government: they could only be the basis of some political faction. So long as their common interests clearly were more important to individuals, these persons could form a community and make it work. Within such a true community, each individual had both a higher and a lower self. The former was the source of the general will and the latter was the source of the particular will. The majority of these particular wills, not based on the common interest of the whole community, Rousseau called the *will of all.* To Rousseau obedience to the general will was both a higher moral duty and more in line with a man's true interests than indulgence of the particular will, so long as he lived in a genuine community.

Rousseau assumed that in any group of persons there would be an overlap of interests. But, the overlap could be small or large. If it were large enough, the general will would be strong. If the overlap were small and the special interests greater, the general will would be feeble. According to this view, any group of persons which had enough interests in common to permit the establishment of a general will could form a people, but if the overlapping interests were too few or unimportant, then one people could not be formed. At this point, reality would decide. The size and significance of a group's common interests, as against the permanence and the power of its divergent ones, is an empirical question of fact. Hence, Rousseau's notion is tied to a potentially verifiable question: do these persons indeed have common interests?

Rousseau believed that it was possible to have many such groups of persons, those with enough common interests to form a general will. However, the formation of a general will seemed to require relatively small communities of about the size of the city state of Geneva or a small republic. Rousseau was not sure that large unions, communities of millions of people, could have an overwhelming body of common interests.

The general will could not be forcibly obtained. It had to be arrived at by the independent judgment of each citizen, as he saw his own interests. In order to form the general will, said Rousseau, each individual had to vote in complete independence from all others. Because individuals differed from each other, their views were also likely to differ to some extent. But since these views were all based on the same common interests, they would all be scattered around some mean or middle value which also would be the most popular.

Modern statistics have long had technical terms for these three magnitudes. They call the *mean* the arithmetic average of a collection of measurements. The *median* is that measurement which falls exactly in the middle of the collection, so that there are as many larger findings above it as there are smaller ones below. Finally, the *mode* of a collection is that group of measurements within it containing the largest number of cases. Many observations in nature and society produce findings which show a bell-shaped *normal distribution,* or *standard error curve,* in which mean, median, and mode all coincide (see Figures 5.1 and 5.2). Approximate examples are the height of men, the height of women, the distribution of "intelligence" (or rather, expected success in college, as measured by college aptitude tests), the scattering of rifle shots around the bullseye of a target, the numbers that come up in a crap game with two dice (unless they are loaded), and the distribution of attitudes in a community whose voters are in fundamental agreement. It is the last of these situations that politicians refer to when they say that they wish to keep to the "mainstream" or to the "middle of the road."

Rousseau, it seems, was beginning to think in terms of this new science of statistics, which had been developed by Blaise Pascal, Jacques Bernoulli, and others. He was particularly attracted to the theory that large numbers of people or large samples will cancel many inaccuracies or accidental errors and will therefore provide a more accurate total result, and that measuring something not once but ten times, and measuring each time independently, makes the resulting average figure more accurate than the result of a single measurement. Rousseau hoped for a precise, accurate, sensitive perception of common interests or the general will through the creation of a people sufficiently uniform and small enough in

Figures 5.1 & 5.2

Bell-Shaped Curve   *Skewed Curve*

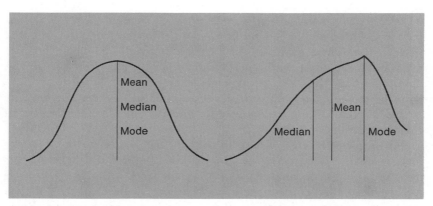

The bell-shaped curve depicts a normal distribution. There can also exist a skewed curve which reflects an asymmetric distribution.

number to have common interests, and yet sufficiently independent from one another and large enough so as not to be swayed by accidental passions or mistakes.

If people formed factions or cliques, this hope could no longer be fulfilled. Common interests and a general will would prevail only *within* each faction, but not *among* the factions. No longer would there be as many votes as individuals, but only as many votes as there were parties or factions. These votes would then be moved not by the common interest of all, but by the special interests of each faction, group, or party. In such a faction-ridden society, even a majority vote would no longer represent the general will, but merely the *will of all,* and and the will of all might be both unjust and unrealistic for the community as a whole.

By contrast, the general will, said Rousseau, was always right by definition, because it consisted in discerning what should be done in the true interests of the community. Given realistic, well-educated, well-informed, thoughtful, and independent citizens, the vote would very likely reach a verdict leading to this result. On the other hand, if citizens were not as well informed as they should be, there might be a wide gap between what the majority of the people might want and what was good for them.

The Logic of Reality, and the Logic of Coercion.

Of course, the real peoples of the eighteenth century—and for that matter of the twentieth century—were not all that well educated or that wise. Very often even the outcome of a popular vote might not be in the popular interest. In seventeenth-century Brandenburg, poor farmers had tried to eat potatoes raw and had suffered stomach-aches as a result. It would have been easy to get a majority of these peasants to agree that potatoes were no good and to vote against them. It was only after a tyrannical Prussian king had marched soldiers with fixed bayonets into the villages to force the peasants to boil the potatoes before eating them that the German farmers took to potato eating on a grand scale. Ignorance has often been more popular than knowledge. For several centuries the equivalents of Gallup polls would have registered landslide majorities for the proposition that the world is flat. These examples show that it is possible to obtain popular majorities based on a grievous misperception of fact. However, if we accept the proposition that there can be emergency situations in which the majority of people cannot discern their true interests or form an adequate picture of reality, we open the way for an emergency dictatorship by an enlightened minority.

This is precisely what Rousseau's theory did. Rousseau spoke of the logic of facts—"*la logique des choses.*" He said things had a logic of their own, and it might be necessary to act in accordance with the *logic of reality* rather than with the logic of popular illusion. In this sense the French revolutionary leader Maximilien Robespierre was a true disciple of Rousseau. He thought he knew what had to be done to save the French

Revolution. Those who did not share his "enlightened" insight had to be constrained to obey; if need be, they had to be beheaded. Rousseau had furnished the arguments for Robespierre's line of reasoning.

It was quite possible, Rousseau said, for an individual to have a common public interest while also having a private interest which went in the opposite direction. The government and the people then had the right and duty to constrain him, and by doing so, they would force him to be free. This sounds like casuistry, but it is not. Consider a young man in a sports car in a great hurry; he would like to collect his girl and get her to a theatrical performance in time. He speeds over a dangerous intersection, a policeman stops him, and hauls him off to jail. Rousseau, looking down from heaven, would say, "The young man has been forced to be free." Rousseau would explain to the listening archangels that the young man, most of all, wants to be alive; indeed, his girl wants him to be alive too. To be sure, the young man has a personal, transitory interest in hurrying up, but he has a fundamental and enduring interest in staying alive. He also has an enduring interest in not killing other people.

The general will, then, once it is joined with an assumption of superior knowledge, opens the way to an emergency dictatorship. It can then be used to justify compulsion, constraint, the draft, and the forcing of people to die for the good of the community. Rousseau said that since the state defended the lives of its citizens every day by maintaining security, it was only taking back the lives it had preserved in the preceding months and years in drafting men for military service. Nothing but the collectivity's own self-restraint could limit its claims against the individual; and such claims could be made not only by a majority that thought it represented the general will, but also by any minority that regarded itself as so enlightened that it knew a people's true interests better than the people itself. Thus Rousseau the libertarian, Rousseau the emotionalist, Rousseau the individualist, became, perhaps unwittingly, an apostle of almost unlimited collectivism.

Burke: Conservatism, Experience, and Continuity

Rousseau's thought found its counterpart in a thinker who shared his view of the political importance of emotions and customs, but who temperamentally was his opposite—Edmund Burke. A brilliant Irishman, a great orator and writer, Burke rose to prominence through his association with some of the leading noblemen and political leaders of eighteenth-century England. He saw the world from their point of view and put their case with power and conviction. Indeed, he went them one better: few members of the corrupt English nobility of the age of George III were as profound, enlightened, and responsible conservatives as he would have liked them to be, although some later English statesmen and military leaders came close to his ideal.

Rousseau was an ideological forerunner of the French Revolution and its aftermath. Burke became the ideologist of the counter-revolution. But Burke did not differ much from Rousseau in some respects. He shared Rousseau's doubt about the perfection of rationalism and rationality. He also shared Rousseau's view of the importance of popular feelings and traditions. But Burke differed from Rousseau decisively in his view of human knowledge.

Burke's Theory of Knowledge.

Burke's Theory of Knowledge.   Burke, following the philosopher David Hume, assumed that the truth could be only tentatively proposed by convention and only imperfectly confirmed by experience. Truth was never established by being self-evident; it was never fixed and immutable. Human abilities to discern reality and to recognize their own real interests, Burke insisted, were quite weak.

Mankind, said Burke, is wise: the individual is not. Therefore, people should never demand liberty in general but only specific liberties that have stood the test of time. When a madman had burst his bonds, asked Burke, should I congratulate him upon the recovery of his liberty? His image is indicative of Burke's view of human nature. To Burke, the average person was feeble, weak, giddy, and comparable to a madman. Thus the common people—and, of course, the young—must be constrained for their own good.

Popular sovereignty was abhorrent to Burke. In a democracy people assumed that anything was moral which their neighbors considered moral. "Nothing," Burke wrote, "is as shameless as a democracy." (History does not wholly contradict him. If the Athenian democracy thought that unwanted babies should be left to starve in the marketplace and the Athenian people walking by found this perfectly acceptable, this was what the Athenian democracy considered as moral. A majority of voters in some parts of the Deep South might condone murders by the Ku Klux Klan. In some years, there were majorities in parts of Germany for some of Hitler's crimes—against peace, against the Jews, against other peoples, and against his domestic opponents.)

The aristocrat, said Burke, has more of a sense of shame because he must ask himself what posterity will think of his actions; the anonymous citizen in a popular majority has no such thoughts. (In fact, Burke's division between nobles who think of the future and commoners who do not has not proven valid. When Churchill spoke to the British electorate in 1940 he said, "Let us bear ourselves so that later generations will say, 'this was their finest hour.' " Churchill treated every British voter as a person with a stake in posterity.) But Burke assumed that all peoples and all governments—monarchies and aristocracies as well as democracies—were fallible. Because they all would make errors and be inconsistent, they needed to follow experience, beaten paths, and ancient precedents.

Institutions as Makers of a People.   If Rousseau assumed that a people could be created all at once by an act of the will, Burke thought that a people could be produced only slowly. Rousseau thought that a people made its *institutions*—that is, its more permanent organizations and practices, such as property, government, or class distinctions—and could change them freely. Burke asserted that the institutions made the people. Changing the institutions quickly and greatly would destroy the people.

Burke said, "The idea of a people is the idea of a corporation. It is wholly artificial and made, like all other fiction, by common agreement. The particular nature of that agreement is collected from the form into which the particular society has been cast. When men break up the agreement which gives its corporate form and capacity to a state, they are no longer a people." Therefore, by deduction, if the French made a revolution against a Bourbon king, they would no longer be French.

In Burke's view, property institutions and social arrangements were the essence of a people. Rousseau's view was, on the contrary, that once a people decided to be together, all political institutions were mere instruments which could be changed at pleasure. If Rousseau's ideas lived on in the thought of Lincoln, Burke's ideas were closer to the beliefs of those southerners who fought for states' rights and for their "peculiar institution" of slavery. Burke said that when people gave up their corporate agreement, or changed their social system, they became a number of "vague, loose individuals." Many a weary step was to be taken before they could once again form themselves into a mass which would have a true political personality. For men to act with the weight and character of a people, they had to be in that state of habitual social discipline in which the wiser, the more expert, and the more opulent led the weaker in judgment, the less knowing, and the less wealthy. That is to say, class rule and class privilege were, for Burke, the very essence of a people.

Man's Slow Learning vs. Fast-Changing Reality.   Burke's reasoning contains some strong points and some weak ones. He argued that a state and a people were a partnership not just for a few limited purposes, like the trade in pepper or salt; rather, they were a corporation for all memories, for all art, for all science, and for all perfection in the community of the living and the dead. Burke thus assumed the people to be a general purpose community in the broadest possible sense; and there are some good reasons to think that he was largely right.

Another strong point of Burke's was his awareness of the weakness of people, of their difficulty in recognizing reality. Only very slow learning processes through practical experience, he assumed, would help people to recognize reality; and experts, specialists, and the various privileged classes would play a decisive role in guiding them. Men's needs were not abstract but concrete; and so were the remedies for them, if any existed. For food one should turn to the farmer; for health, to the physician; but neither health nor food, he said, would be provided by abstract theories. Government, too, had its experienced practitioners: the nobles, bureaucrats, rich men, and other rulers who had long been in power.

Burke also assumed that the elite in a society would be more realistic than the common people. This assumption does not seem to have been warranted; in many cases it is the poor in a country who know at what points the social system does not work. If one wants to know what is wrong with the slums, one does not run an opinion poll in the suburbs. Moreover, even where the members of an elite have seen at first hand the need for some urgent change, they often have refused to make it, for fear of losing some income, property, or privilege.

Burke's own view of statesmanship was different. Unlike many conservatives since his time, he was no standpatter. He accepted the need for change, but he insisted that change come slowly and in small doses. He saw change as a process similar to the task of rebuilding one's own house while continuing to live in it and depending on its uninterrupted protection against snow and rain. To the impatient radical, Burke would have pointed out that even if the roof leaked one could not afford to tear it down. To the complacent conservative, he would have suggested that one could not forget that the roof was leaking and that repairs had to be started soon. Burke was a true *conservative;* he wanted to conserve things even while changing them. In the main thrust of his thought he was not a *reactionary;* he did not try to reverse the changes that had gone before and to turn back to some real or imagined past. And he would have been utterly amazed at some people in our own time who call themselves "conservatives" and advocate the use of nuclear weapons that might blow up the world.

But Burke believed that the rate of learning for a society had to be very slow, and without proof or examination, he assumed that the needed rate of learning, and also the actual rates of change in technology, and in the economic, technical, and political environment of a community, would all have to be slow.

A Burkean type of state is therefore at best slow-changing and slow adapting. In a fast-changing world, it cannot survive. It will quickly fall behind, and if it cannot speed up, it will perish. In this sense, Burke's counsel for being infinitely slow and cautious in making changes is a counsel of perfection. It may be too good for the wicked, fast-changing world in which we live.

A Permanent World of Nations.　　Burke himself, of course, had no such fears. He thought that since changes would be slow, most states and nations could be strong enough and wise enough to survive them indefinitely, unless they ruined themselves by their own folly. Since each state differed from all others by its unique history and interests, Burke believed that clashes among such states would be inevitable and war among states a normal part of politics forever.

Like Burke, Rousseau thought that nations might survive indefinitely. Unlike Burke, he believed that war among them could be abolished. The main movers toward war, as Rousseau saw it, were the princes of Europe. Once their power was taken away, peace among the nations of Europe might be preserved. But that would require that all states become true democratic communities. Moreover, each sovereign community would have to be small and homogeneous in language, culture, class, and status, so that no groups of ambitious and undemocratic rulers could arise and push their countries into new wars.

Both Burke and Rousseau contributed to the ideas of nationalism. But Burke's adherents thought that aristocracies and wars would have to be preserved, while Rousseau's followers hoped to abolish them. The quarrel between these two basic views of politics played a part in the wars and revolutions of the first half of the nineteenth century. And it contributed to the development of the mind of a third theorist who was to advance a new proposition: that the previous history of mankind was no more than pre-history; that it would soon come to an end; and that it would be replaced by a new era of true history which would be radically different.

Marx: A Theorist of World Community

For most of his lifetime, Karl Marx was a German intellectual in exile, writing page after page in the library of the British Museum in London. In his own day he was often ridiculed, but almost ninety years after his death an American journalist called him "the least funny of the Marx brothers." At the beginning of the 1970s, over a billion people—close to one-third of mankind with nearly one-third of the world's income—were living in fourteen countries under governments that revered his name.

Marx was born in Trier in western Germany, the son of a lawyer. His parents had been Jewish but the family adopted the Lutheran faith when he was a child. Marx studied philosophy and became an adherent of the great German philosopher of change and conflict, Georg F. W. Hegel, but he soon developed ideas of his own which in time became an elaborate philosophy and political doctrine.

Motives and Sources of Marx's Thought.   One of his early concerns, like Rousseau's, was with the alienation of the individual from his neighbors and from the society in which he lived. From the plight of the individual, Marx soon turned to the evils of society and politics, and to the possibility of revolution as a remedy for them. For the rest of his life he was an ardent revolutionist. Even many lost revolutions won his sympathy, but unlike some recent revolutionists he never willingly urged men to risk their lives in uprisings he knew to be hopeless. He wanted to be the theorist of a successful revolution, one that would produce more fundamental changes than any that had gone before.

For this purpose he turned to science. Just as Newton had discovered the laws of motion of physical bodies, so Marx proposed to discover the laws of motion of society. Like most scientists, he made ample use of the work of his predecessors. He cheerfully expropriated ideas which he found useful. He took his economics from the English and the Scots, most of his politics from the French, and most of his philosophy from the Germans. Like Burke, he insisted that truth was concrete and that past historic developments determined much of present reality. Also like Burke, and like Alexander Hamilton in America and Victor du Pont in France, he believed that man's attitudes and actions were determined by economic interests and class position. Marx added to this doctrine two further propositions: first, that the strength and interests of classes would change rapidly with technological and economic change; and, second, that the interests of the chief classes of every society were necessarily opposed to each other, so that the struggles between classes formed the foundation of all history and politics. There is a touch of irony in the fact that Marx's revolutionary doctrine of class struggle was partly derived in this manner from conservative ideas.

If all past history was the history of class struggles, as Marx believed, then it was not meaningless chaos. Like British economists Adam Smith and David Ricardo, Marx assumed that there were objective economic tendencies and laws, similar to the laws of supply and demand, and that these laws would work themselves out despite (or even because of) the struggles and confusions of individuals.

A New View of Man's Development. These considerations led Marx to a new view of human history. Originally, he thought, man had made himself human by inventing tools and using them in a process of labor which suggested still additional inventions to him. Thus the invention of tools was what had contributed to man's transformation from tree dweller and caveman to the machine users of his time and ours. Through millennia of pre-history, men had lived under a system of primitive communism, in hordes or tribes which knew neither social classes nor private property in land or in persons. They knew no slavery because no slave could produce enough to make it worthwhile to keep him in bondage. Only later, as labor became more productive, had slavery begun to pay. At that stage it had become worthwhile for some men to claim land as their own and to exact tribute from others for the opportunity to work it. Property, slavery, and social classes were thus not rooted in human nature;

products of progress in the past, they would be done away with by further progress at some time in the future.

In Marx's sweeping view, man's development would thus lead from the small, classless, and propertyless communities of "primitive communism" through a sequence of property-based and class-divided social systems to a future world-wide community of economic abundance. In this new and enlarged community, property distinctions and class divisions would once again disappear or become insignificant. But even this world-wide community of abundance, which Marx called "communism," was not to be the end of man's development. Once men had moved from the age of economic scarcity to a world-wide age of plenty, they could aim at the full and free development of all the potentialities and powers of every individual. This human development, said Marx, was "an end in itself." But he frankly conceded that neither he nor anyone else could foresee what this future development actually would be like. He only felt sure that it would mark man's leap from "the realm of necessity into the realm of freedom." At that point, he believed, man's pre-history would end and his true history begin. What this true history would be, Marx did not know, but he was certain that it would be more interesting and worthwhile than all the centuries of "pre-history" in the past.

As to this "pre-history"—which most historians call "history"—Marx saw it divided roughly into four major stages: primitive communism, feudalism, capitalism, and socialism. After the last of these four, a fifth stage, communism, would mark the transition to economic abundance, classlessness, and the beginning of true history.

Following upon primitive communism and the first appearance of relatively large-scale private property and social classes, a privileged group of landowners, chieftains, and warriors had arisen to lord it over their poorer neighbors, in time reducing many of the latter to bondage as debtors, serfs, or slaves. The masters had desired to transmit their wealth and power to their children. Class privilege then had become inherited like the property upon which it was based; and it had been glorified by the dubious claim of superior descent or blood, such as the proverbial "blue blood" of European aristocracy.

In many times and places, Marx thought, societies had shared certain broad characteristics. They had had a class of large landowners which served as the basis of a warlike aristocracy while exploiting the tillers of the soil. Although the detailed arrangements of such social systems might have varied a great deal across different countries, periods, and cultures, Marx called them all "feudal." He thus used the concept of *"feudalism,"* derived from medieval European history, in a broader sense than many historians use it.[1] The stage of feudalism in the political and social history

[1] See Rushton C. Coulborn, ed., *Feudalism in History* (Princeton: Princeton University Press, 1956).

of most countries, as Marx saw it, corresponded to a particular stage in the development of their technology. A hand mill, he said, corresponded to a society of nobles and serfs; a steam mill, to a society of capitalists and workers.

In Marx's view, as technology progressed from muscle power to machine power, and from handicrafts to factories, capital became more important than land, cash and credit more important than blue blood and nobility, and a bankbook more important than a coat of arms. Once these changes had occurred, a new middle class of merchants, businessmen, and of capitalists would rise in power and prestige, and eventually take the leadership of society away from the nobility. Society would then pass from the stage of feudalism to the stage of *capitalism*. This was what Marx believed had happened in many countries of his time.

The new ruling class would now consist of "burghers" or, in the French term which Marx preferred, of *bourgeois,* who collectively made up the *bourgeoisie.* (If they still preferred to call themselves "middle class," Marx would have thought them excessively modest.) Within the bourgeoisie, the rich and the super-rich would make up the top layer, or the *big bourgeoisie,* of bankers, large factory owners, and the like. Beneath them would be their far more numerous but far less affluent colleagues, the *petty bourgeois,* who shared much of the outlook of the richer businessmen but, alas, neither their security nor their prestige. These small businessmen, shop-keepers, artisans, and other small employers of labor might envy and resent their big competitors, but they would quarrel even more with the wage earners they employed and whose demands for wage increases or shorter working hours threatened their own slender profits.

In Marx's image of the world, however, these wage earners were the chosen people, or rather, the chosen class of destiny. They owned no significant property in land, machines, or major tools, and thus no substantial "means of production." The clothes, household goods, and other person-al articles they owned did not make other workers dependent upon them, and thus did not count in the distribution of economic and political power. The ancient Romans had called such poor, propertyless freemen mere "offspring begetters" or *proletarii;* hence their kind became known in the nineteenth century as *proletarians* and their class as the *proletariat.* Marx accepted this usage with enthusiasm, but reversed its values. A *bourgeois* existence tied a man to the present and the past; a *proletarian* condition gave him a stake in the future.

Being propertyless, as Marx saw it, the proletariat had to be internation-al in its point of view. "The workers have no fatherland," he wrote, "one cannot take from them that which they do not possess." The interests of workers in all countries were the same: better wages and working conditions in the short run, but beyond that a rise to political power, the overthrow of the old order of property and privilege, and the establish-ment of a new society. "Proletarians of all lands, unite!" Marx and Engels wrote in the *Communist Manifesto* in 1847, "You have nothing to lose but your chains. You have a world to win."

If the workers were predestined to become internationalists in outlook and action, the middle classes were apt to become nationalists, at least for a time. As capitalism replaced feudalism as the chief social and economic system, local markets gave way to national markets, local dialects retreated before the standardized national languages, feudal or absolute monarchies[2] were replaced by constitutional governments which safe-guarded private property and competition, and the nobility was replaced by a national bourgeoisie as the leading class in society, politics, and culture. In ousting feudalism, according to Marx, capitalism thus built modern nations. All this, however, said Marx, was merely transitional. National markets would give way to a world market, and national litera-tures to a world literature. Nation-states were thus destined to become obsolete.

Within each country, the effects of merciless competition were sure, in Marx's view, to turn most members of the middle class and the peasantry into proletarians. "One capitalist," Marx noted gleefully, "ruins many." In time, almost the whole population would be proletarian, united and disciplined by the experience of factory labor, and motivated by increasing misery to end the capitalist system that kept them poor and oppressed. Opposing them would be an ever-smaller handful of ever-richer capitalists, who would become ever-easier to overthrow. In the end, as Marx envi-sioned it, "the knell of private property sounds. The expropriators are expropriated."

In each country, the workers would seize power. For a transitional period, they would exercise a *dictatorship of the proletariat*, "by the vast majority and in the interests of the vast majority," and advised, no doubt, by helpful intellectuals like Karl Marx, and in general by "the best elements of the bourgeoisie" who by then would have come over to their side. Since the proletarians were internationalist by nature, the countries they now ruled would all cooperate in a fraternal community of socialist nations. This state of *socialism* would still know scarcity, social classes, and the state. But these, too, would soon pass. Technology would have pro-gressed under capitalism, and this progress would be accelerated in the socialist stage. Soon, therefore, an economy of abundance would usher in the next stage—*communism*—and with it the stateless and classless future of mankind.

[2] A monarch was called *absolute* if he was held to be "absolved" from all human laws. His pleasure was the supreme law in his realm. As to divine law, only the monarch ruling "by the grace of God" was entitled to interpret its meaning. An absolute monarchy existed when a monarch already had forced his nobles to obey him, but had not yet been compelled to share power with the middle class or the masses of the people. Absolute monarchy survived until the seventeenth century in England, until the nineteenth century in the rest of Western Europe, and until 1917 in Russia. At the start of the 1970s, it still existed in Saudi Arabia and Ethiopia.

Some Second Thoughts.   This entire vision seems to have been present in Marx's mind by 1847, before he reached the age of thirty. But in 1875, about a generation later, Marx put down some careful second thoughts.[3]

Economic and political development, it had turned out, were taking much longer than had been expected. The development of capitalism and the path toward socialism and communism seemed far longer and more complex—steeper, more winding, and more fogbound—than had been anticipated. The distinction between *socialism*—the expected first stage after capitalism—and *communism* (the later stage) now loomed much larger and more important.

Capitalism, Marx now saw, could last a very long time. It could reach high levels of development in some countries while still in its beginnings in others. The growth of imperialism appeared to be increasing the longevity of capitalism. It now seemed possible that for a time there should be entire "nations of capitalists," such as England, profiting from the exploitation of entire nations of peasants, such as India—and doling out some of these profits to the English workers as a payment for their cooperation in this scheme of things, and for their failure to play the revolutionary role Marx earlier had predicted for them. Only after many years, Marx now thought, would capitalism collapse and an eventual chain of world wars, depressions, and mass suffering bring the workers of the privileged countries back to the revolutionary path.

In addition, Marx now saw that socialism would still be a social order of scarcity and partial injustice. It would demand work from everyone "according to his abilities," but it would pay only according to the work performed, and thus not in accordance with needs. The skilled worker would earn more than the unskilled (Marx considered skilled labor a multiple of unskilled labor, so that one hour of a skilled worker's time might be worth four hours of an unskilled worker's). Highly skilled work, such as that of professionals, engineers, or scientists, by this principle might have to be paid still more highly—regardless of how each had acquired his skill in the first place. Parents who could give their children a better education could thus equip them with a chance for a better income than the children of their less fortunate neighbors. And these differences in income might find expression in differences of personal property, such as clothes, furniture, and housing—though not in the major means of production.

The reason for Marx's second thoughts is clear. To escape forever from economic scarcity, mankind had to produce much more than it did. Labor had to become vastly more productive. New capital equipment and skills had to be created and accumulated by vast efforts. For all this, people had

[3]He did so mainly in a critique of the program of the German Social Democrats, called *Critique of the Gotha Program* (1875).

to be motivated, not only by words but also by tangible rewards, distributed unequally but in proportion to the work they actually did.

During this stage of socialism, with its inevitable residual injustices, the state would still be needed. It would be needed not only against external threats from surviving capitalist countries, or against domestic efforts of the old capitalist classes to restore their rule; the socialist state would also be needed to enforce its own laws and its own partly unjust distribution of incomes and opportunities even against members of the revolutionary proletariat and the working population.

Only later, after this socialist stage would have accomplished its task— and Marx did not say how many decades or generations this might take— only when the productive equipment of mankind would have been vastly increased, and when "the springs of wealth would flow more freely," would it be possible to enter the final stage—that of communism. In that stage, most goods and services would be so abundant that they would not have to be distributed by being priced and sold unit by unit. In the distant communist economy of abundance each man would work according to his ability; but now at last he would receive—or rather take—according to his needs. Thus Marx's notion was that eventually most consumer goods would become so abundant that the question of allocation would become irrelevant. Nations would disappear, allocation problems would vanish, and we would have a single unified mankind.

What the Theorists Did Not Foretell: The Tendency of Communities to Split

Rousseau, Burke, and Marx all centered their attention on what united men into communities, and on how these communities were developed and maintained. None of the three thinkers concerned himself much with the splitting up of larger communities into smaller ones. But by focusing only on the integration, and not on the division, of communities, the three theorists overlooked an important part of the political and social process.

We know now that there is probably a law of cultural and national differentiation which holds true very generally. If communication within a small group is much larger than external communication, then the internal group will in time develop a communication code of its own. This is the mathematics of the Tower of Babel. If in a mountain village people for hundreds of years speak frequently to each other, but rarely to strangers, the dialect of the peasants will become unintelligible to people from other valleys. If in a computer center at Harvard or Michigan the programmers talk mostly to each other and rarely to outsiders, their programming conventions will become unintelligible to the people working the same IBM computers at other centers.

These thoughts have major implications which most of Marx's followers have overlooked. His principle of socialism—payment according to amount of work—also applies to the international division of labor among Socialist countries. A rich Socialist nation like the Soviet Union, well-equipped with skills, capital, and improved land, will expect to be paid for its exports in accordance with their value, even if they go to a poorer Socialist country. A poor country of this kind, such as the Chinese People's Republic, lacking skills and equipment, can only produce exports of much lesser value, even if they should require greater human effort to produce. There is, therefore, a likelihood that a significant degree of inequality and potential injustice will persist among Socialist countries. If their states and armed forces have the task of defending these inequal Socialist patterns of distribution at home and abroad, they may also have to defend them against each other. What seemed to be only a theoretical implication in Marx's writings in 1875 became an ominous reality in the clashes between Soviet and Chinese Communist troops on the Ussuri River in 1969. Marx's seemingly complete theory is still highly vulnerable and leaking at the seams.

But the followers of Burke and Rousseau have done no better. States have arisen, split up, and been replaced by others much faster than Burke's theories would have predicted. The trend toward popular participation in politics has become more powerful than even Rousseau had expected, but the size and power of many states is much vaster than anything Rousseau foresaw for his small republics. Conflicts among states ruled by governments with mass support have been more bitter and frequent than Rousseau envisaged, and the risks habitually taken by great powers in the nuclear age are vastly greater than anything Burke would have considered prudent, or indeed sane. The problems of nationalism and international conflict—of national community and world community—are still a challenge to men's understanding and statesmanship.

Key Terms and Concepts

alienation	conservative
belonging	reactionary
community	primitive communism
particularistic	feudalism
ascriptive	capitalism
diffuse	bourgeois (noun-individual; adj.)
popular sovereignty	bourgeoisie (noun-class)
general will	big bourgeois
particular will	petty bourgeois
mean	proletarian (noun-individual; adj.)
median	proletariat (noun-class)
mode	absolute monarch

normal distribution curve

will of all

logic of reality

institutions

dictatorship of the proletariat

socialism

communism

Additional Readings

Aristotle. *Politics.* Book V.

Burke, E. *Reflections on the Revolution in France.*

Friederich, C. J. *Nomos II: Community.* New York: Liberal Arts Press, 1959.

Marx, K. *Communist Manifesto.*

McIlwain, C. H. *Growth of Political Thought in the West.* New York: Macmillan, 1932.

Rousseau, J. J. *Considerations on the Government of Poland.*

The Political System: What Holds It Together

Theorists have interpreted the world of politics in many ways. In this age of nuclear energy and space navigation, however, our task is first to survive in this promising and dangerous world of politics and second, to change it for the better. For both tasks, we must understand how this world works, what makes it go, and what persons, groups, or relationships produce its outcomes, good or bad. Which of these are crucial for the prediction of political events or their possible control? In the course of time many answers have been proposed to this question, but most of them have been unsatisfactory. The most recent, and perhaps the best available, answers have been organized around the concept of the political system.

Chapter 6

In studying a political system we must ask first what it is and then what it does. A *political system* is a collection of recognizable units, which are characterized by cohesion and covariance. *Cohesion* means sticking together, or forming a whole. Two units cohere if many of the operations on one of the units have definite results on the other. Thus a tug at one end of a chain will be transmitted to other links, and the turn of a key will turn a lock. Symbols may cohere in a system, such as the alphabet, and men may cohere in a people or a state. *Covariance* means changing together. If one unit changes, the other does, too. Thus a man and his shadow move together, but we must find out separately whether a change in the man causes a change in the shadow or whether by moving the shadow we can move the man—which of course we cannot. In social science, as in all science, discovering covariance is one step toward discovering not only what goes together but also what causes what. Benjamin Franklin forcefully advised his fellow signers of the Declaration of Independence that even if they lost cohesion, they most certainly would not lose covariance: "We must, indeed, all hang together," he told them, "or most assuredly, we shall all hang separately."

To the extent that units are cohesive and covariant, we say that they are *interdependent* and that their fates are tied together. We may then call them the *components* or parts of the system—bearing in mind that some or all of them may be quite capable of existing outside the system. Thus keys and locks can exist separately but work together—as do the parts of more elaborate systems, such as an automobile or a stereo music system.

The Frequency of Transactions and the Interdependence of People

The Concept of a Transaction.   A system is thus held together from within, in contrast to a mere collection which can be held together from outside by some external means. A system is made by interdependence; and, among people, interdependence is made by transactions. A *transaction* is a chain of events which begins in one place or unit and ends in another. The units thus connected are partners in this transaction, but their influence on its result need not be equal. Such transactions may include a transfer of material objects, as in the trade of wheat, iron, or textiles; or the transfer of energy, as in the transmission of electric power; or they may involve the transfer of services, as in the repair of automobiles or watches. An important class of transactions involves the movement of people, such as commuters who go to work every day, or other forms of travel for business, pleasure, education, or migration. Another important class of transactions comprises primarily the transfer of information, as in the flow of letters and telegrams, telephone calls, newspaper circulation, and in radio or television broadcasts.

The transactions among the parts of a system can be observed and measured. In principle, therefore, they are accessible to the methods of scientific investigation, which can be repeated and verified by different observers regardless of their prejudices. A system usually can be recognized by the fact that at least some kinds of transactions occur much more often among the parts within it than between some parts of the system and the world outside it. The *relative frequency of transactions* is a test for the existence of a system and for deciding whether a particular unit belongs to it.

Boundary Lines and Boundary Zones.   The fact that certain transactions are more frequent within a system than outside it gives rise to the concept of boundaries. *Boundaries* consist of those components, groups, persons, or areas in space where the frequency of transactions falls off to an observable degree. If this frequency falls off suddenly, the boundary will look like a *line*; if the transactions fall off gradually we may speak of a *boundary zone*. We can observe such boundary zones in the density of settlements, in the frequency of traffic, around local shopping centers, or even between countries. When students go hitchhiking northward from New England to Quebec, or westward from Cologne in Germany to Paris in France, they will in each case notice the automobile traffic thinning as they near the frontier of each country. These frontiers are areas which have been thinly settled for centuries, and which therefore have formed historic boundary regions. A country, in general, is a good example of this type of frequency system; it is held together by many kinds of transaction flows which are most frequent at its center but fall off toward its boundaries.

Something similar can apply to a group of individuals. It, too, may have a core and a periphery with a boundary zone. The members of a nuclear family—husband, wife, and their young children—usually have much more to do with one another than with people outside this close-knit group. In contrast to past centuries, today the importance of the "extended family" has declined. The nuclear family may have few or almost no transactions with greataunts or second cousins. Aunts and first cousins are somewhere in between. As a rule, the members of the nuclear family see them less often than they see each other, but in many cases more often than strangers or more distant relatives. These closer relatives thus form a kind of boundary zone around the nuclear family; they are its *marginal* members.

Many large groups, such as a people, often show a similar pattern. Most Americans carry on more transactions with other Americans than with other persons. This is even true of many of the two million "overseas Americans" who may be living abroad in military garrisons or business enclaves and orienting their lives to their compatriots around the PX facilities or the American Club.

Most boundaries are relatively stable over time. They stay in the same place, and we can easily remember where they are. Some frontiers among European nations have not changed for centuries. The main part of the frontier between the United States and Canada has remained unchanged for 150 years, and the frontier between the United States and Mexico has stayed the same for more than 100 years. But this is not true of all boundaries. If a system is growing, its frontiers may be moving and expanding rapidly, through settlement, conquest, or conversion, while its frequent transactions will continue to combine to maintain internal cohesion. Thus the United States, Canada, Russia, China, and many Latin American countries have continued to expand their boundaries without most of their people feeling that they had to give up either their national cohesion or identity.

The relationship between the frequency of transactions and the boundary of systems is illustrated in Figures 6.1, 6.2, and 6.3. In all such cases—whether they involve geographic areas, small groups, or whole peoples—the frequency of transactions is a source of cohesion which holds together a system of human relations. (A country is thus not held together

Figure 6.1

Boundary Line I

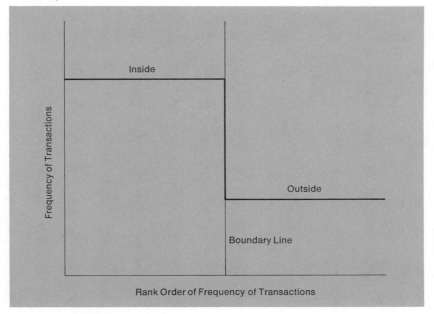

Discontinuous change in frequency.

by its "rocks and rills" but by the relations among the people who inhabit it.) Insofar as people are held together by frequency transactions they are likely to matter more to one another in politics. They are likely to make a greater difference to each other's political behavior, either in conflict or in cooperation.

The Importance of Transactions: Who Gets Rewards

Not all transactions are equally important. Indeed some very frequent ones may be politically trivial. (For instance, in most countries, sports have little direct political significance, although they may acquire it under particular conditions, such as the Czech-Russian hockey game following Russia's occupation of Czechoslovakia in 1968.) The importance of any transaction to any person depends on the difference it makes to the *values* he gains or loses from it, or those which he expects so to gain or lose. The greater the rewards or penalties that people get from certain transactions, the more important are these transactions to them.

More generally, the importance of transactions depends on their *side effects.* The latter are effects that accompany some events or transactions, and that vary with their amount. Traffic has the side effect of noise. Above

Figure 6.2

Boundary Zone I

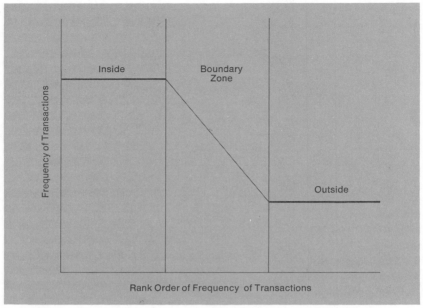

Discontinuous change in frequency at edge of zone; continuous change within zone.

a certain level, district size may influence the availability of candidates for elective office. In a large district, canvassing requires much time, staff, and money, making candidates more dependent on private means, donors, or machine support. Some side effects may occur only above certain levels of frequency. Thus a road or railroad may be worth building in a district if there is a sufficiently high level of traffic or business for it, but below this amount of traffic, no road will be built. Similarly, a secondary school may be worth building in a community if there are a sufficient number of school children, but below this number of school children, no secondary school will be built. Such numbers, frequencies, or levels of demands are called *critical levels,* or *thresholds.* Below any such threshold, some important side effect is negligible, but above this threshold, it becomes significant. Thresholds mark those stages in a process where small changes in one kind of thing or event make a big difference in another. Where such thresholds exist, they may influence the boundaries of a system, even if the frequency of transactions itself is changing only very gradually. Some relations of this kind are shown in Figures 6.4, 6.5, and 6.6.

The Covariance of Rewards: Solidarity Systems. In addition to the frequency of transactions, the components of systems are linked by a second relationship: the *covariance of rewards.* Such covariance exists if, when something rewarding to one component changes, the rewards to other components are also likely to change. This is another example of how the fate of one component is tied to the fate of other components if all belong to the same social or political system. A reward is *positive* if it increases the values enjoyed by a component, or if it reduces that component's inner disequilibrium or tension. It is *negative* if it reduces the values received by a component or increases its inner disequilibrium or tension.

Some systems are connected by a positive covariance of rewards. What is good for the United States is also likely to be good for General Motors. The reverse of this proposition—that "what is good for General Motors is good for the country"—does not follow with compelling necessity, though in the 1950s this statement was attributed to a General Motors executive, Charles E. Wilson, when he was Secretary of Defense. Systems whose components are connected by a positive covariance of rewards may be called *solidarity systems.* The interests of wage earners are solidary if they all stand to gain from a better union contract. Conversely, if all employers in a wage negotiation join forces to gain or lose together, their interests, too, are solidary. If people act in accordance with the saying, "all for one and one for all," we say that their behavior shows solidarity. In international relations, allies act in solidarity if each allied government feels that the gains of the others will bring gains to itself, that its interests are closely

Figure 6.3

Core and Periphery I

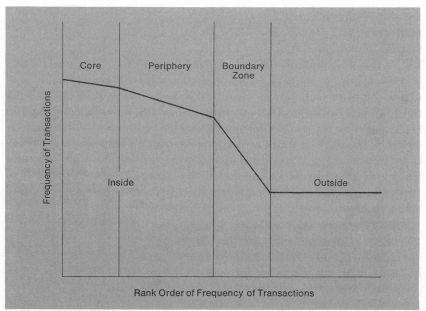

Plural zones: discontinuous change among frequency zones; continuous change within zones.

Figure 6.4

Boundary Line II

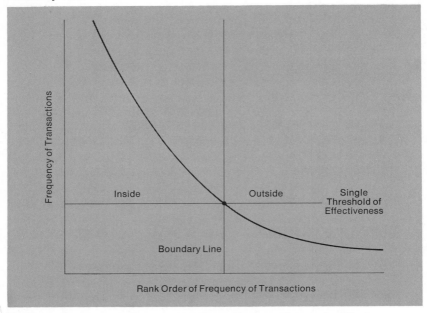

Continuous change in frequency; discontinuous change in effect.

linked with theirs, and that it has to act accordingly. Since national states often think that they have distinct national interests, the degree of solidarity found in their alliances is often slight and relatively unsatisfactory. The Duke of Wellington is supposed to have said that Napoleon was not really a very great general because he had won only against alliances.

If several individuals or groups experience high levels of transactions with a positive covariance of rewards, they may wish to increase their ties to each other, at least to a moderate degree. We may speak of them as being favorable candidates for *integration* into a common system that includes them all. The states of Western Europe, for instance, are already connected in many respects by high mutual transactions and a positive covariance of rewards. To the extent that this is the case, it should be easier to promote further integration of these countries into a single political system, such as a confederation of Western Europe.

Negative Covariance: Conflict Systems. The covariance of rewards, however, may be negative. In a very frequent flow of transactions—or in a single transaction of great consequence—something may be rewarding to one partner in the system, but penalizing to others. If students are made to compete for rank in class, the ability of one student may be rewarding to him but may penalize those students who cannot do equally well. When several men apply for the same job, hiring of one of them will certainly be rewarding to him but will penalize the other applicants (unless they can get better jobs elsewhere).

When several units are closely connected by a negative covariance of rewards that suggests the relationship of a cat to a canary or a wolf to a sheep, we speak of a *conflict system*. Groups locked in conflict are part of one system. The fate of one cannot be understood or predicted without knowing something about the actions of the other.[1] They belong together, but in a rather unhappy sense. During World War I, the French war veteran Henri Barbusse wrote, "Two armies fighting each other are one great army in the act of suicide."[2]

A system is likely to be more stable and durable if the transactions which maintain it are not only high in number, but also of many kinds. For the system to last, these transactions, on the whole, must be rewarding rather than penalizing to the subsystems and individuals composing the

Figure 6.5

Boundary Zone II

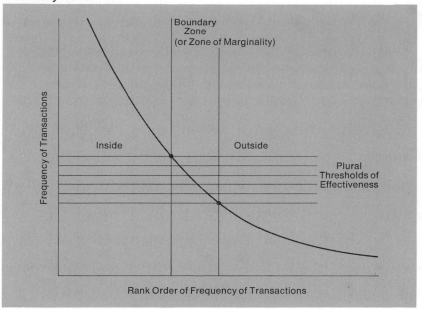

Continuous change in frequency; discontinuous change in effect at edge of zone.

[1]A conflict system is thus a type of zero-sum game. See Chapter 2 for a discussion of zero-sum games.

[2]Henri Barbusse, *Under Fire: The Story of a Squad* (New York: E. P. Dutton, 1917). When the book was first published in French in 1916, Barbusse was a pacifist. Later he became a Communist, hoping that communism would abolish war. He did not live to see Russian and Chinese Communists fighting each other at the Ussuri River.

Figure 6.6

Core and Periphery II

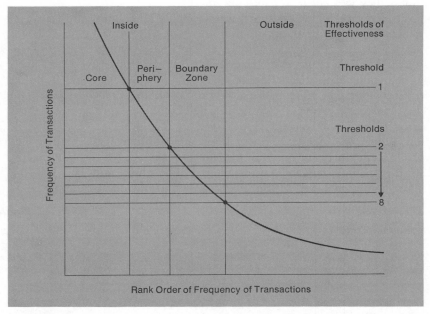

Continuous change in frequency; plural thresholds for discontinuous changes.

system. Systems riven by conflict, therefore, are less likely to endure. Where conflicting groups remain together in one system for a long time, it is very likely that they have some common interests, which make them want to continue their association despite the conflict. Karl Marx and his followers have made much of the antagonism of interest between employer and employee, as well as between property owner and the propertyless. However, Marx himself admitted the possibility of a degree of common interest between the two, at least by implication, in the famous sentence in the *Communist Manifesto* in which he spoke of the "class struggle" as ending either in the victory of one of the two classes, or in the common destruction of the contending classes. Since neither class wishes to be destroyed, both have a common interest in survival, even if it means continuing the struggle. Out of this consideration, Russian Communists, and even Chinese ones, have found it necessary in the nuclear age to think about "coexisting" peacefully in a single international system with capitalist countries.

Mixed Covariance: The Dilemmas of Political Reality.   Barbusse's comment about two armies illustrates the mixed nature of rewards in most situations of interdependence in the real world. Though their soldiers fight for opposed countries or causes, where victory for one implies defeat for the other, they share a common desire to stay alive. In this respect, a cease-fire without victory would reward both sides, and peace would let all soldiers return home to their families.

This example is typical of many situations of political interdependence. The rewards of both partners in an interdependent system vary together positively in some respects but negatively in others. Some rewards for one also reward the other, but other rewards for him may penalize his partner. On the other hand, if something penalized both partners it would again join them in solidarity. In these situations of mixed covariance, it would be naive for any partner to act as if the other were nothing but a friend; but it would be equally naive to treat the other as nothing but an enemy or rival. Both must find patterns of *competitive cooperation* or of *cooperative competition*. Each must learn to foresee the consequences of his own actions for the actions of the other; and both must learn to coordinate their behavior.[3] Practical men have worked out such patterns of behavior through hard-won experience. Rival department stores like Macy's and Gimbel's, major league baseball clubs, large automobile manufacturers, major radio and television networks, and major political parties in constitutional democracies have been able to work out such patterns of competitive cooperation or cooperative competition. Unfortunately, we have not done very well in developing viable strategies of this type among blacks and whites in the United States; and we have done even less well in the international arena where conflicts among the great powers are most conspicuous and where the common penalties for war are most terrible.

The more we study such situations of mixed covariance, the more we realize how inadequate were the old models and theories of politics which all too often divided mankind neatly into "friends" and "enemies." But we also realize the inadequacy of the idealism that thinks that all people can become "friends" simply by ceasing to be enemies, as well as the inadequacy of the old rule of practical politics: "if you can't lick 'em, join 'em!" None of these strategies is realistic enough or good enough, but in politics better ones have yet to be adopted.

An Overview of System Levels

To say that a system is linked by covariance of rewards, and that a solidarity system is linked by positive covariance, is another way of saying that members of such a system are connected by a *community of interest*.

But the interests of a system or a subsystem are not always the same as those of the larger system of which it may be a part. Neither are they the

[3] See Thomas C. Schelling, *The Strategy of Conflict* (Oxford: Oxford University Press, 1960); Anatol Rapoport, *Fights, Games, and Debates* (Ann Arbor: University of Michigan Press, 1960); and Anatol Rapoport and Albert Chammah, *Prisoner's Dilemma: A Study in Conflict and Cooperation* (Ann Arbor: University of Michigan Press, 1965).

same as the interests of the smaller subsystems which it may comprise. To weigh and, if possible, to balance the interests of large political bodies against the divergent interests of the smaller subsystems which they include—down to the individual—has always been a central problem of politics.

To analyze such problems, we speak of *system levels*. What these levels are is indicated by three tests. The first test is the test of logical *inclusion*. Virginia is a part of the United States, but the United States is not a part of Virginia. Virginia is thus a lower-level system, and the United States a higher-level one. The second test is the test of *size*. If the larger system differs by "an order of magnitude"—that is, if it is at least twice as large— we can clearly say that the larger one is on a higher system level. Virginia has approximately four million inhabitants, the United States 201 million. The third test, related to the first two, is the *probable outcome of a conflict*. If the two systems should clash, the bigger system would, as sports writers say, "outclass" the smaller one. When the state of Arkansas in the 1950's tried to defy the judgment of the United States Supreme Court on school desegregation, the presence of federal troops in Little Rock ended the defiance within a short time, but Governor Orval Faubus of Arkansas may have felt unfairly outclassed.

A Ten-Step Scale of Politics.   In analyzing politics we may think of as many as ten system levels. These levels are shown in Figure 6.7. Organizations at each of these levels may include very roughly between two and ten times as many persons as organizations on the next lower level.

The *smallest system* in politics is the individual, comprising all the different memories, drives, and complexes carried in his body and personality. The physical and psychological subsystems within the individual are studied mainly by doctors, psychologists, and psychiatrists. They have much to do with why some individuals take part in politics while others do not, even though their outward circumstances are similar. The next largest, or *second smallest,* group is the nuclear family and other so-called "primary groups," most often comprising between two and fifteen members. These are often studied by group psychologists, sociologists, and some management experts. (Many of the latter believe that no individual can supervise closely more than six subordinates; and the psychologist George A. Miller has suggested that the human capacity for close attention and discrimination is ordinarily limited to "the magical number 7, ±2." Miller's limit is thought to apply to almost anything that we can remember distinctly, from lecture outlines to team patterns to multi-party systems.) The *third system level* corresponds to the small settlement or hamlet, or extended kin group, clan, or small tribe in developing countries, or the immediate neighborhood in cities. The membership of each such group can be counted in the hundreds. These groups are studied by cultural

Figure 6.7

A Ten-Level Political System

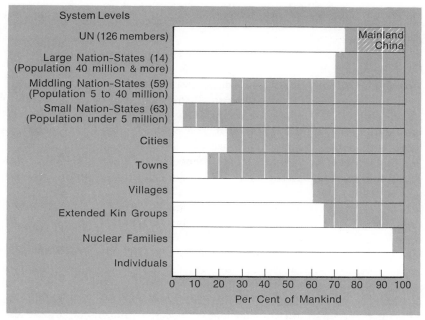

Sources: U.N. *Office of Public Information,* Membership in the United Nations, *1969; Population Reference Bureau Information Service,* World Population Data Sheets *(Washington, D.C., 1968); K. Davis,* World Urbanization, 1950–1970, *Vol. 1 (Berkeley: University of California Press, 1969).*

anthropologists, ethnologists, social psychologists, and sociologists. At the *fourth level,* we find thousands of people, aggregated in large villages and small towns, middle-sized factories and other business enterprises with about 500 employees (which approximates two thousand people including dependents), small colleges, and the like. Here sociologists have a field day, and some political scientists get a piece of the action.

Where Politics Becomes Impersonal.   At all larger system levels, intimate face-to-face knowledge of all participants in a system is no longer possible. Relationships now become more indirect. Psychologically, they are often more superficial, but their effects may be very powerful. Seeing a candidate on television, or reading a commentator's discussion of his personality, is not the same as knowing him well from many evenings at his home, the local tavern, or the neighborhood clubhouse. The *fifth level* comprises units of tens of thousands of people in such units as towns and small cities, counties and districts, large tribes, large factories and firms, and the large universities. Here authority tends to become more formal. Rules of behavior are often written down, and many tasks of management and administration are carried out by full-time specialists working according to increasingly elaborate rules. What we call *bureaucratization* is thus in part a function of the level of political system to which an organization corresponds. This level is studied less by psychologists than by sociologists, management experts, and to some extent political scientists.

The *sixth level* deals with hundreds of thousands of people. It includes big cities, more populous districts, large counties, large tribes, and many fairly large organizations. (Nearly a dozen small states in the United States, such as Vermont or Nevada, and some small sovereign states such as Iceland, Luxembourg, and Guyana, are on this level in terms of numbers, but their institutions correspond to those of higher system levels.) Concerning this level, there is still a good deal of work done by sociologists, and there are a few psychologists and anthropologists active in the field, but most of the research here is conducted by political scientists and to some extent by economists.

Units on the *seventh level* count their members in the millions. Here we encounter thirty-five of the fifty states in the American union and roughly one-half of the approximately 140 sovereign nations of the world. At this level we also find all but two of the world's fifty largest metropolitan areas.[4] Organizations at this and at all higher system levels are primarily the province of political scientists and economists, although important contributions are being made by a small number of social psychologists, sociologists, and cultural anthropologists. A sizable minority of large sovereign nations (about fifty at the start of the 1970s), as well as four states in the American union (California, New York, Pennsylvania, and Illinois) and two of the largest metropolitan areas (Tokyo and New York), form the *eighth level* and count their populations in the tens of millions. Here we are clearly in the realm of politics and economics on a national and quasi-national scale.

Giant States and World Affairs.   The *ninth level* brings us to the largest powers and to much of international politics. Here the numbers of people within each unit run in the hundreds of millions. Only seven giant nation-states have populations of this size but these seven comprise nearly 60 per cent of the world's population and income. In the population rank order of 1966 these are: China, India, the Soviet Union, the United States, Pakistan, Indonesia, and Japan (see Figure 6.8). No metropolitan area and no private business organization is even remotely in the running for entry into this category. But a few religious organizations, notably the Roman Catholic Church, have constituencies of this size. By contrast, practically all major international alliance systems, such as NATO and the Warsaw Pact, are of this order of magnitude.

[4] *World Almanac and Book of Facts* (New York: Doubleday, 1969), p. 651. The years for the estimates of urban areas vary between 1958 and 1968.

Figure 6.8

The World's Chief Nation-States

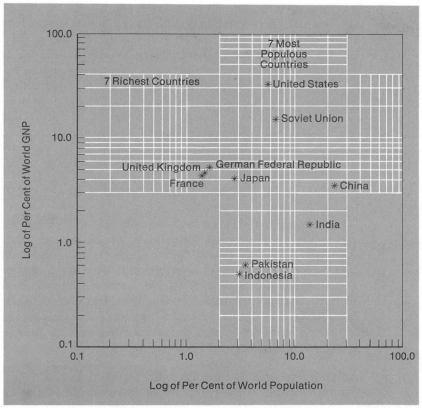

Source: *Economic Bureau, U.S. Arms Control and Disarmament Agency,* World Military Expenditures and Related Data, 1966, *Research Report 68–52, 1968.*

The *tenth level* includes organizations which deal with more than a billion people. The principal organization at this level is the United Nations, together with the specialized organizations affiliated with the UN. These include the World Health Organization (WHO), the International Labor Organization (ILO), the Food and Agricultural Organization (FAO), and many more. Paradoxically, though world peace and world order are most important to the survival of mankind, the actual organizations, manpower, budgets, and legal powers are much weaker at this level than the corresponding facilities at the nation-state level. While national governments allocate about 30 per cent of the gross national product of mankind, world organizations control less than 1 per cent.

System Levels and the Individual

In politics as in mathematics, the whole may be greater than the sum of its parts. Systems may have different characteristics than the components or *subsystems* they comprise. It is certainly possible to organize sane motorists into the pattern of a crazy traffic jam. The drivers are not out of their minds; rather it is the traffic system that has gone haywire. Likewise, it is possible to take small, petty, mean, cowardly, unimaginative bureaucrats, who are not particularly bloodthirsty—only eager to do exactly what they have been ordered to do—and organize these men into tiny links of a huge machine that will send millions of men, women, and children to their deaths. In this way, a large number of petty Nazi bureaucrats were organized to send millions of Jewish men, women, and children to extermination camps. When afterwards one of the top bureaucrats of death, Adolf Eichmann, at his trial in Israel, pleaded mere "obedience to orders," the philosopher Hannah Arendt was appalled by "the banality of evil" which his case epitomized.

Modern large states lend themselves to organizing people into vast bodies which can be much stronger, much more knowledgeable, much more persistent, and, as in the case of Nazi Germany, sometimes much more evil than the individuals who compose them. But the size or system level of an organization is not necessarily related to its capacity for evil. A hospital is more tireless and persistent in saving lives than even the most dedicated doctor on its staff. Perhaps mankind can learn to make political systems that increase its power for good at least as much as it has devised political systems that have increased its power for evil.

Moral Responsibility and System Levels.   A recurrent problem in the politics of all countries is the moral responsibility of individuals for taking part in large organizations that do things which they as individuals would not do. On the level of a village, Friedrich Dürrenmatt's play *The Visit* raised the question of the responsibility of individuals for the cruelties committed by a village as an operating system. On the level of a much larger system, the state, some Russian intellectuals have raised the question of individual responsibility for the cruelties committed under the Stalin regime and for the continuing acts of Soviet repression.

Similar questions have arisen in other major countries of the Western world. "To throw a baby into the fire," said an Englishman recently, "is a crime. To throw fire on a baby is a military operation." When students demonstrated on American university campuses against recruiters for the Dow Chemical Company, spokesmen for the company replied that it bore no responsibility for the use of one of its products, napalm, in throwing fire on settlements in Vietnam and burning to death many civilians, including women and children. It was not the company's business, the spokesmen asserted, to question the policies of the government. Dow was merely supplying a weapon. It was the government's responsibility to determine how, when, and if that weapon should be used.

In the late 1960s, a number of American voters were inclined to agree with the company's viewpoint, but a considerable number of their younger contemporaries were inclined to disagree. In the end, Americans may have to decide whether it is enough for a citizen to carry out unquestioningly whatever orders his government may give, or whether he should pursue a more active interest in what his government does—in the actual means, methods, and results of its policies. Such a decision may take years to reach. But whatever they decide will have a profound effect not only on the policies but also on the very nature of the United States and on the character of the American people.

In short, individuals and small groups are often merely small cogs in the large machines of bigger interest groups or national governments. To what extent do these cogs retain the capability of understanding what the machine is actually doing? How far does their responsibility go for the acts of the machine? The answers to these questions will decide how much governments of the future will display the blindness and moral insensitivity of still bigger and bigger machines, and how much they will resemble the behavior of sentient, self-conscious communities of human beings. The thing to remember is that our biggest machines are not only man-made; they are also composed of men. Thus there is a moral interdependence between individuals and the large organizations they compose. Our most fateful decisions, therefore, will not be technological but political. They will deal with changes in our patterns of communication, obedience, criticism, and responsibility among people.

A Scale of Political Values. Scholars frequently forget that the individual is at the basis of all large systems. One of the reasons for this oversight is the arbitrary division of organizations into small and large system levels. Students of political science will note the break in the scholarly interest in a system that comes at the seventh system level, the unit size of approximately one million people. Microeconomics deals with the decisions made by individual firms and small groups. Above the level of one million, macroeconomics replaces microeconomics and deals with problems of national economies and problems of the world economy. Similarly, *micropolitics* deals with the political behavior of individuals, small groups of voters, and the affairs of small communities. Above the level of one million, *macropolitics* replaces micropolitics and deals with the political behavior of large interest groups, cities, states, and nations, and the affairs of the world. Moreover, whereas the systems below the seventh level are of interest to almost all social scientists, large-scale organizations containing a million or more people are studied more by political scientists and economists—and after the event by historians—than by the specialists in all the other behavioral sciences.

This is the prevailing situation, but it is not an ideal one. It hampers our knowledge. Scholars studying small-scale processes often take too little account of the large-scale changes that influence profoundly the background conditions for all the matters they study. And the students of large-scale processes often pay too little attention to the methods and findings of behavioral scientists concerned with the small-scale processes which can modify profoundly the outcome of large-scale events.

For centuries, political leaders have called upon individuals to sacrifice themselves for the presumed good of the state, the party, or some other large-scale organization or cause. In contrast, they have rarely called upon a state to sacrifice itself for its people. Yet it is a fundamental characteristic of human organizations that the smallest components—individuals—are more complex and in a certain sense more important than the large organizations which they form. The best thinkers of mankind always have recognized this and have refused to treat human beings as disposable or expendable. Theorists of democracy, from Pericles to John Stuart Mill, have seen the test of a good government in the quality of the individuals that grow up under it. This test is still relevant today.

Political Structures and Political Functions

Up to this point we have been talking about systems as structures. The *structure* of any situation or organization consists of those of its aspects which change relatively slowly, and whose change can be modified or accelerated only at considerable cost. The rocks and mountains in a landscape, and the skeleton of a human body, are structures. Likewise the size and level of a political system are structures, for, ordinarily, there is no quick or easy way to change them. (Our definition of structure is worth remembering when people speak of "structural" changes in colleges, cities, or nations. Regardless of their merits, such changes require much time, or great efforts and costs, or possibly all of these.)

In contrast to slow-changing structures, those aspects of a situation or organization which change relatively quickly and easily are called *processes* or functions. The movement of winds and water in the mountains are processes, and so is breathing in the human body. When we wish to stress the effects of one process upon other processes or upon structures we speak of its *function*. Thus wind and water may have the function of leveling mountains by erosion, and breathing the function of maintaining life in the human body.

A single structure may support many different processes or functions. The human skeleton and the general structure of the human body sustain the play of muscles, the circulation of blood, and the movement of impulses through the nervous system. The government of a city sustains the regulation of traffic, the functioning of public schools, the administration of welfare, and a host of other tasks. The multiplicity of functions of the modern nation-state is still larger. Most structures are thus multifunctional.

The same function, however, may be fulfilled by more than one type of structure. Railroad service may be provided by private companies as in the United States or by the nation-state as in Switzerland or Britain. Elementary public schools can be run by the national government, as in France, or by the state governments, as in the German Federal Republic, or by cities, municipalities, or local school districts, as in the United States. To the extent that different structures can fulfill the same function, and can thus be substituted for each other, we say that they are *functionally equivalent.*

Political structures are first of all governments, from the local level all the way up through the international level. Political structures also include those organizations specifically designed to influence governments in regard to many matters, such as political parties. In the United States political parties range over many system levels, from the local political club to the municipal, state, and national party organizations. Similar but more tightly knit hierarchies are found in the major parties of Britain, Germany, and Italy, and, with a much lesser degree of party regularity and discipline, in France. Other organizations, though not primarily political, may have large political interests, as do labor unions, employer organizations, and other interest groups, as noted in Chapter 3. For organizations of this latter kind political activity is obviously only one among the many tasks they perform; it is one among their several functions.

The same is true, however, of all the major systems discussed in our ten-step model. The most important organizations at each level are multipurpose systems: the individual, the family, the small community, the city, the state, the nation, and mankind. All these are social systems (even the individual, as we saw, may be thought of as a society of the components of his personality). Politics is only one of their functions. If political activity fits well into the context of their other functions, it will derive strength from them, both for itself and for the social system as a whole. If politics fits in badly it may become *dysfunctional.* It will then tend to weaken the system and ultimately to weaken and destroy itself.

The Political System as a Component of the Social System

Functions of a Social System.   All social systems have a certain number of basic functions in common. According to the sociologist Talcott Parsons, the basic functions of every social system are four. First, it must *maintain* its own basic patterns, particularly those of its own governing and control, so that the next day or the next year finds the social system still recognizable and in charge of its own actions. Second, it must *adapt* itself to changing conditions in both its physical environment in nature and its human environment in terms of other systems. Third, it must *integrate* its different tasks and functions. Fourth, if it has specific goals beyond mere adaptation, integration, and the maintenance of its patterns, it must move to *attain* its goals. Accordingly, pattern maintenance, adaptation, integration, and goal attainment are its basic tasks. From Parsons's approach we can derive a way of looking at politics and the subsystems of society in the context of these basic functions.[5]

Pattern maintenance is a task that can be carried on by many actors, but some structural (or multipurpose) subsystems spend much more of their time and resources on this task than on any other. The main subsystems devoted to pattern maintenance in Western society are *families* and *households*. They maintain the bodies of their members by cooking their meals and giving them a place to sleep. More subtly, they maintain the motivation of their members by a process of mutual support and encouragement. Finally, it is they who maintain the culture of the society by transmitting it to children, sometimes with some interesting variations and with some unexpected results.

The main *adaptive* subsystem of the society is the *economy*. Economic activities enable us to transform our somewhat inhospitable natural environment into one in which people can survive and from which they can draw sustenance and resources. The economy is reinforced in this function by the technological and scientific subsystem. At more primitive levels, science and technology are not separate from the efforts of farmers and craftsmen. As societies become more complex, science and technology become full-time occupations carried on by specialized institutions. Even here, however, they are effective only if their findings are eventually applied in economic life. The basic adaptive function of the economy holds true equally for societies characterized by a large element of private enterprise and for societies characterized by the predominance of central planning.

The *integrative* subsystem of every society consists mainly in its *culture*, or cultural sector, including education, religion, philosophy, and art. Education not only has the task of reproducing yesterday's culture in the young people of today and the older people of tomorrow; it also has the task of making the different elements of society somewhat more compatible with each other. Religion and philosophy have the same task to an even greater degree. Every one of the world's great religions asks people whether their pursuit of short-run values or goals is compatible with their long-run interests. Thus religion and philosophy teach the long-run nature of the

[5] See Talcott Parsons, *The Social System* (Glencoe, Ill.: Free Press, 1951). The responsibility for the application of this general approach in the present book is, of course, my own.

universe, the long-run values of mankind, and, perhaps, the long-run purpose for which mankind itself exists. And in their own way, artists either integrate different elements or aspects of the world or, in the case of the artists of despair or protest, tell us in some powerful way about some lack of integration which may need our attention.

Finally, the typical *goal-attaining subsystem* of society is the government, or more generally, the *political sector*. It is the government that organizes the society for the pursuit of whatever goals the society may have chosen. Pursuing a goal involves forming an image of it, which we may call an *intention,* and then finding the means to implement the intention, or a course toward the goal. It was the Spanish government in the fifteenth century that organized Spain first for the reconquest of the Peninsula, then for the expulsion of the Moors from Granada, and still later for the conquest of the New World. In our own time, the governmental sector has organized Americans for a variety of purposes including resolving the race problem, maintaining full employment, making higher education available to an ever-larger part of young people, and putting an American on the moon.

Interchanges Among Subsystems. Each of these classic subsystems of society has interchanges with all of the others and depends on all of them. Members of households, for example, perform labor in the economy and eventually receive consumer goods from that subsystem. In most advanced societies this is not done directly by barter but by a generalized medium of exchange. The man working in the economy gets paid in money. His wife spends his wages in the supermarket to get in return the goods and services for the household. And this exchange between work inputs, on the one hand, and goods and services, on the other hand, is mediated by money, a generalized and abstract medium which is accepted as a currency by both sides.

Something similar goes on between the household sector and the government. The population usually makes specific demands upon the government. The government, in turn, reaches decisions which serve to coordinate people's expectations and are often backed with the promise of enforcement. In the early states of a political relationship, specific demands are exchanged for specific decisions. This is political logrolling, but as time goes on the government may take on a generalized role of responsibility. The government says to the population: "We are in charge. If you need something done that you cannot do yourselves, the government is here to do it." If individuals find that governmental decisions are acceptable to them and that living under the government is rewarding, they are likely to develop a generalized loyalty. They no longer give their support to specific decisions. Instead they give to the government a general loyalty in exchange for the government's general assumption of responsibility.

Just as money is the generalized medium of economic interchanges, so *power* serves as the generalized medium of interchange between the government and its people.[6] Power thus functions as the currency of politics. Just as money is worth no more than the things it can buy, so power is worth no more than the teamwork it can procure. Economics is really not about money but about wealth; and politics is really not about power but about the changing ways people find to work and live together. A government uses its power to enforce some of the decisions the people want enforced, but in reality the power of the government comes from the support of the population. A government that is not supported by its people is in a precarious position. The less popular a government is, the less likely it is to endure. If a government is popular at home, but seems alien to the poeple of a distant country, its power to control the latter will be precarious as well.

Of course, where populations are apathetic, ignorant, unarmed, or powerless, minority governments based on small bodies of armed men have long maintained themselves in power. Thus colonial rule has endured longest in the world's most backward colonies, such as Portuguese Angola and Mozambique in Africa. However, the more educated, active, and capable a population becomes, the harder it is to neglect it in politics, and the harder it becomes to rule it against its will. Everywhere in the world, industrialization and modernization have increased the interests, communication levels, needs, knowledge, demands, and capabilities of populations. These changes may well be irreversible. Since they have made all countries in the world harder to govern against the will of their populations, a politician's lot is now a less happy one than it may have been fifty or a hundred years ago. And since all countries are now even harder to govern from a distance, the job of a would-be ruler is hopeless.

Goal Change and Self-Transformation

The four classic subsystems are found, according to Parsons, in all social systems of which we have knowledge. But the four functions which these subsystems perform deal mainly with keeping societies as they are and do not tell us enough about the way societies change. Thus Parsons seems to suggest that all social systems have an inclination to behave in accordance with the way they are set up. We know, however, that many social systems in the world have changed, some of them very thoroughly indeed.

It is important, therefore, to ask what are the basic functions in systems in which change is a major part of their behavior. There are two such functions (see Table 6.1). The first is *change of goals*. Systems not only pursue old goals, they may also from time to time abandon old goals and

---

[6] Other aspects of power are discussed in Chapters 2 and 7.

Table 6.1

Ways to Basic Change in Social Systems

		Political Method	
		Reform	Revolutionary
Substantive Change	Goal Change	Britain gives up Empire Britain shifts to Welfare state, 1945–	France quits Algeria (but Fifth Republic preserves continuity at home), 1958–62
	Self-Transformation	Britain's Reform Bills, 1832–1867 Japan, 1868 Turkey, 1920– US, 1933–	US, 1776–1830 France, 1789–1830 Russia, 1917– China, 1911– Mexico, 1912–1940 Algeria, 1954–62 Cuba, 1959–

replace them by new ones. Societies that cannot change goals either fossilize or perish. Sparta and ancient Rome largely refused to change their goals and thus became extinct. Modern societies, on the other hand, have changed their goals again and again.

All major powers in the world have gone through periods of major goal change. England in the Middle Ages had as a major policy goal the maintenance of power on the European continent. Its rulers kept garrisons at Bordeaux, Calais, and other strategic places. In the sixteenth century England gave up all military footholds on the continent and turned her attention to sea power and to colonial empire. Four centuries later, Britain's goals changed again. In 1947 England conceded independence to India and dropped her pursuit of empire to concentrate her efforts on the modernization of technology and the improvement of human life within the British Isles.

Similar examples of goal changes can be found in the histories of other nations. Switzerland and Sweden at certain times in their history were great military powers with major foreign policy ambitions. At later stages they substituted for these schemes the goals of internal progress and peace. The United States pursued as a major goal for many decades isolation from the politics of Europe. During World War I and after the late 1930s American goals changed to worldwide intervention and involvement. The 1970s may find the United States once again engaged in redefining its goals, this time perhaps with greater emphasis on domestic affairs and space exploration. It is not enough, therefore, to consider only a country's current goals or interests; one must also ask how long will they last? When, how, and under what conditions will they change?

The other basic function of a social system is *self-transformation*. A system may transform a good part of its own structure which ordinarily is slow to change. Every one of us has gone through at least some self-transformation as we moved from infancy to childhood and again from childhood through the storms of adolescence to adulthood. Countries also transform themselves, sometimes violently, sometimes gradually. In either case, they end up not only with different goals but also with different basic structures and patterns of behavior than before. Even so, important elements of their identity may remain unchanged.

In political systems, violent self-transformation involving a large part of society is called *revolution,* as distinct from *coups d'etat* or palace revolutions, which merely change the people in power or a few laws, without changing the fundamentals of social living. Daniel Boorstin's brilliant book, *The Genius of American Politics,* emphasizes the ways in which colonial America and present-day America are alike. But no less important, as Charles Beard and other historians point out, are the many ways in which America after the Revolution was radically different from America before the Revolution. A period of revolution occurred in Britain during the fifty-year interval between Oliver Cromwell in the 1650s and the Act of Toleration in 1690. A similar period occurred in France in the forty years between the storming of the Bastille in 1789 and the acceptance of the formerly subversive colors, red, white, and blue, as the national colors of France in 1830. Revolutions in Mexico, in China, and in Russia are other examples. Each of these has usually involved its society in roughly a half-century of self-transformation.

In nonviolent cases, we may speak of *reform.* In many of these respects England transformed herself during the period of the great reform bills between 1832 and 1884, and again during the time of the new wave of social reforms between 1945 and the 1960s. In the United States, the year 1933 may well have ushered in a period of reform legislation which, with some interruptions, has been going on until the present and which may not yet have ended.

A modern adaptation of Parsons's system would probably include these basic functions of political and social change. Goal change and self-transformation are always closely related to the problem of the *integration* of society. A social system changes its goals or its inner structure because some elements or functions within it are no longer compatible with other elements or functions. That is to say, every problem of goal change and self-transformation begins with a severe strain on the integrative system. Because a system can no longer live with itself or with its environment, it then begins to change its goals or transform its structure. Goal change and self-transformation are, therefore, more complex and more elaborate aspects of the basic function of integration. If we include them in the integrative subsystem in more highly developed societies, the remarkable economy and simplicity of the Parsonian scheme becomes still more useful for analyzing the basic problems of political systems.

A Second Look at the Political System

Thus far we have looked upon politics in the context of multipurpose systems. We saw that families, villages, cities, nations, and the world all have their political aspects, but they deal with more than merely politics. It is time now to look at specifically political systems at various system levels and to examine the concept of the political system somewhat more thoroughly.

A *political system* is a particular kind of system. It maintains coordinated expectations among the people who live under it, and coordinates a good deal of their actual behavior by means of their cooperation and compliance habits which are reinforced by rewards and penalties.

Since human beings tend to learn more from rewards than penalties, this implies that most political systems must contain at least a significant probability of some rewards for those who accept their rules and regulations. The less rewarding a political community or a government is to those living under it, the less likely it is to endure. Habits of cooperation are reinforced not only by the specific rewards or penalties offered by the government, but also by the general rewards implied in living within the political community. American governments have not often given specific rewards to their citizens beyond such items as congressional medals, presidential citations, and occasional veterans' bonuses. But the American economy has produced a living standard so markedly higher than many other countries, and American life has been so much freer and more permissive, that immigrants from dozens of places and many different backgrounds have found themselves more closely tied to and eventually integrated into the multifarious American political community.

Political systems are thus based on other social systems. Usually a political system is based on a territorial community. Thus a nation-state is often based on a country. And a country may contain one or more peoples. Thus a political system usually has an ethnic, as well as a territorial, base.

A third concept often associated with political systems—in addition to the concept of a country and the concept of a people—is that of a *citizenry* or *body politic* or *polity*. Here we speak of persons who have acquired a common set of political behaviors and civic loyalties. A person we call a *fellow citizen* in the true sense of the term, is one whom we trust and by whom we are willing to let ourselves be outvoted. Those whom we do not trust and by whom it would be intolerable to be outvoted, we consider as *aliens* in effect, even though they may have a legal right to vote.

Finally, we may speak of a *state* as an organized body of men, some of them armed and some of them at desks and other instruments of administration, all engaged in the business of government. The classic definition of a state used to emphasize its responsibilities for deterring enemies from without and repressing disorders from within. Liberal followers of Adam

Smith and radical followers of Karl Marx agreed: the main task of the state was the exercise of force. Adherents of *laissez-faire* liberalism pictured the state as a night watchman who stood by while the "invisible hand" of the market ran the economy. Marxists viewed it as a committee to look after the interests of the bourgeoisie as a whole. Engels and Lenin considered the state primarily a body of armed men, weapons, and prisons.

The actual development of the modern state has taken a somewhat different direction. Today, in every modern industrial country, more than one-half of the resources and activities of the government tend to be devoted to civilian services and facilities that involve functions other than the exercise of force. In the United States, government at all levels—municipal, state, and national—spends, as we know about 30 per cent of the gross national product; and at least 18 per cent or more of the United States gross national product is spent by American governments at all levels for activities not related to force, such as public education, public health, traffic and transport, science and research, and a host of other services. The same is true of most other highly developed countries.

It is the coincidence of these four types of systems—the country, the people, the body politic, and the state—which makes the modern nation-state such a powerful instrument for so many different kinds of action. In districts and countries where this coincidence is weak, the nation-state is likely to be weak. Where the coincidence is strong, the nation-state is likely to be strong.

One property of political systems, perhaps the most remarkable of all, has yet to be mentioned. This is the ability of political systems, like that of many other social systems, to steer themselves. It is this capacity for self-steering, for autonomy, that makes governments and political communities vital and effective, and it is this capacity that we shall discuss in the next chapter.

Key Terms and Concepts

political system	interest
side effects	system levels
threshold	ten-step scale of politics
cohesion	subsystem
covariance	micropolitics
interdependent	macropolitics
components	structure
transaction	process
relative frequency of transactions	function
boundaries	multifunctional
boundary line	functionally equivalent
boundary zone	political structure
covariance of rewards	dysfunctional

positive reward

negative reward

positive covariance

solidarity system

integration

negative covariance

conflict system

mixed covariance

four functions of a social system

intention

two functions of a changing social system

revolution

coup d'etat

reform

body politic

fellow citizen

alien

Additional Readings

Almond, G. A. and S. B. Powell. *Comparative Politics: A Developmental Approach.* Boston: Little, Brown, 1966.

Deutsch, K.   *The Nerves of Government.* Rev. ed. New York: The Free Press, 1966.

Easton, D. *The Political System.* New York: Knopf, 1953.

——————. *Framework for Political Analysis.* Englewood Cliffs, N.J.: Prentice-Hall, 1965.

——————. *Systems Analysis of Political Life.* New York: Wiley, 1965.

Parsons, T.   *The Social System.*   Glencoe, Ill.: Free Press, 1951.

Self-Government: How a Political System Steers Itself

In general usage, the word *self-government* has two meanings. Sometimes it refers to a political unit that governs itself in all respects, including its relations to the outside world. But sometimes it may refer to any unit that decides about its internal matters by its own processes, even though its external affairs are managed by some larger political system. In this latter sense, New York City is self-governing in many of its local affairs, even though it is certainly not wholly independent. And sometimes the word self-government is used ambiguously, straddling the two meanings; or it is made to refer to a matter of degree, of more or less self-government, rather than to an all-or-nothing quality. Politicians have found these ambiguities of usage convenient, permitting them to use the same word to build support by promising different things to different people.

Chapter 7

The Behavior of Self-Governing Bodies

The difference between self-government and political dependence resembles the difference between driving an automobile and being towed. A car with its own steering wheel and driver can go in many directions; a towed car goes where the towing truck takes it. Similarly, a piece of driftwood must float with the current; a motorboat can move across it or against it. Together with their human operators, or sometimes with their automatic piloting devices, automobiles, motorboats, airplanes, and some types of guided missiles and space vehicles, manned or unmanned, all are examples of *self-steering systems.* Ordinarily their course cannot be predicted from knowing only their environment. To know where they will go, we must also know something about what is going on inside them.

Self-Rule and the Environment.   Much the same is true of political systems, large or small. For if we can predict completely what a group, a party, a city, or a nation will do, without knowing anything about its inner processes—if we can predict its behavior completely from knowing its environment—then this system is entirely dependent on something outside itself and is therefore not self-governing. In contrast, to the extent that a political system's behavior is determined by structures and processes inside itself—whatever these may be—we call such a system *independent.*

Self-government can exist at different system levels, as shown in Table 7.1. In the case of a self-governing country or nation, we say it is *sovereign,* that is, it obeys no outside command and it recognizes no law higher than its own. When such a country obeys international law or an international treaty, it does so voluntarily for reasons of prudence or morality. But it is possible for a country to be dependent in international affairs but still have effective autonomy in domestic matters. (*Autonomy* as defined by Rousseau is "obedience to the law which we prescribe for ourselves.") Thus the island of Antigua in the Caribbean is wholly dependent upon Britain in its foreign policy, but politics within the island are largely in the hands of its 68,000 people. Real political arrangements can be much more complex than the simple distinctions shown in Table 7.1. Near Antigua, the much larger Commonwealth of Puerto Rico is associated with the United States by a special arrangement which gives the islanders no vote in American policy but subjects them to the United States draft, gives them a special tax status, permits unlimited migration to the United States, and leaves the internal affairs of the island to Puerto Rico's own political processes.

Subsystems within a self-governing system may not necessarily be self-governing or autonomous. A nation-state could be sovereign in international affairs and yet dominate most groups and individuals within it. It could deny any significant autonomy to its subsystems, such as its regions, provinces, or cities, or to political parties, labor unions, and other interest groups. At the end of the 1960's, this was the case in many dictatorships, such as in Spain under Franco, Greece under her military rulers, many Latin American regimes, and the Communist countries, to varying degrees, from Yugoslavia to China.

Self-Rule and the Past.   There is more to self-government, however, than mere independence from outside domination. The course of a high-velocity rifle bullet over short distances is practically independent of much of its environment; no wind is likely to deflect it. But once fired, its course is almost completely dependent on the bullet's momentum, and thus on its past. It has no freedom. It is enslaved to its own weight, speed, and direction, and hence to what happened to it earlier, when the gun was pointed and the trigger pulled.

Table 7.1

Self-Government at Different System Levels

	Effective Self-Government[1]	
	Yes	*No*
Nation in Foreign Affairs	US USSR Chinese People's Republic France German Federal Republic	Czechoslovakia East Germany Dominican Republic
Nation in Domestic Affairs	Canada, 1867–1898 Commonwealth of Puerto Rico	India, 1857–1947
State or Province	Any of the 50 states in the US	Any French département Any state in Brazil, 1964–
City	Hamburg in German Federal Republic	Washington, D.C. until 1968
Interest Group	Any labor union, or business organization, or student organization in the US	Any labor, industrial, or student organization in the USSR

*(left axis label: System Level)*

[1]Test: Not subject to superiors, or free to oppose them.

Larger systems, too, can be imprisoned by their past. A car going at sixty miles per hour cannot stop in less than 200 feet, no matter how hard the driver may step on the brakes. A large ocean liner like the "Queen Elizabeth" takes about one-and-a-half miles to come to a stop from full speed ahead, after its engines have been reversed.

Human organizations may have a kind of momentum of their own. How long does it take to stop a traditional political or social practice in a local community, after it has become clearly out-dated? How long does it take to change a major national policy? How long does it take to stop a war? Political systems evidently also can be prisoners of their past, as well as of their environment.

Real self-steering differs both from the past-determined path of a bullet and from the environment-determined path of driftwood. The behavior of a self-steering system cannot be predicted wholly from its environment or from its past. Self-steering consists in combining the effects of the past of a system with those of its present, and the effects of its environment with those of its own inner structure and processes. But just how is this done?

The Feedback Cycle, Steering, and Goal-Seeking

The Processing of Information and the Feedback Cycle.   Self-steering in any system requires first of all an intake of information from the outside world. In the simplest case, the information comes in directly; more often there are special subsystems called *receptors*. In the human body, these are eyes, ears, and other sense organs. In an airplane or ship, they may include radio receivers and radar sets. In a government, receptors may be foreign service officers sending in reports from abroad, or they may be organizations, polling groups, the press, or public hearings which tell the government what the voters think. Regardless of its original source, information comes in through receptors.

Eventually information results in an output of action or behavior by the system which receives it. Usually, this behavior it carried on by specialized *effectors*. In the human organism, these are arms, legs, muscles, teeth, the tongue, and vocal cords. In an airplane, they are engines, the rudder, and control surfaces, and in a warplane, rockets, guns, and bomb release mechanisms. In a government, effectors are officials, bureaucrats, the army, the navy, Social Security administrators, tax collectors, or whoever else performs services for the government.

The important thing about any self-steering system is this: its effectors send back new information about the results of their actions. This new information is added to the information already in the system, and it is used to correct the output in the next cycle. Results from this corrected output are again fed back, cycle after cycle. Each such cycle of output, feedback, and corrected output is called a *feedback cycle*. All goal seeking, all steered or controlled behavior, depends on feedback cycles.

Feedback is a process which requires a structure to carry it. It is based on a return flow of information, but every flow of information needs a *channel* by which it is transmitted. In every feedback process, information flows in a loop; and the channels carrying it must form a *circuit*. In electronic devices, these circuits may consist of wires, or invisible beams. In politics, they may consist in standardized procedures or informal habits of reporting and listening. Thus in dealing with a bureaucracy, we usually are told to "go through channels." A more informal feedback circuit consists in the habit of congressmen and senators of sending news of their speeches and votes to the voters in their districts or states, by whom they want to be re-elected, and of listening to their responses as a guide for their future actions.

Amplifying Feedback Processes.   Feedback, however, can be of two kinds—amplifying or negative, with important differences in their operation and results. *Amplifying feedback* adds a signal to preceding behavior which says, "Do more of it; increase the behavior." If the amplifying feedback signals add about the same proportion to the output in every cycle, the effect is comparable to compound interest, or sometimes to the explosion of a stick of dynamite. Both are described by the same type of exponential curve. The graph of amplifying feedback seems to grow slowly and then takes off and seems to go through the roof (see Figure 7.1).

For instance, let us assume that countries A and B each has a hundred missiles or some other expensive pieces of military hardware and that they are engaged in an arms race with each other. A government official or a political candidate in country A says, "We must have clear cut superiority over country B." The government of A then agrees, "Yes, we do need clear cut superiority," which to its joint chiefs of staff may mean 10 per cent more, or a total of 110 missiles. But the joint chiefs of country B are just as patriotic. They must now have clear cut superiority for *their* country, and 10 per cent more than 110 is 121. Country A rejoins by seeking 133 and B responds with 147. Unless this attempted outdoing of each other ends, the graph will soar. If we fit the differential equations which describe this process to the arms budgets of the major powers before World War I, we get a remarkably good match. From 1914 to 1918, however, the process described by these equations put a considerable number of people into cemeteries.

An amplifying feedback process, if continued with a constant rate of increments, is likely to run out of control. If the increments decline, however, if, for instance, fuel, manpower, or resources dwindle, the process becomes exhausted after a while. Instead of an exponential curve, a logistic curve which is S-shaped is formed, and the output flattens out (see Figure 7.2).

The amplifying feedback principle is worth knowing because it is the basic pattern of *escalation*. It occurs not only in international politics but also in domestic politics. Suppose that scandalous neglect of the poor and of racial minorities in a city eventually causes a riot. The National Guard is called up, shoots into the crowd, and there are thirty-four dead, as in the

Figures 7.1 & 7.2

Exponential Curve

Logistic Curve

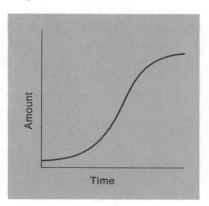

Watts riot in Los Angeles. As a result of amplifying feedback, great resentment spreads among the ghetto dwellers, which, in turn, results in clandestine attacks, more arson and rioting, more violence against the police, more armed men, more armored trucks patrolling the streets, more outbreaks of violence, more heavy-handed repression, and therefore, a spiral of bloodshed on both sides. Ultimately, it is discovered that this has to be stopped. Efforts are then made to improve the situation and end the bloodshed and the misery on both sides. Unfortunately, we know very little about how to prevent the escalation of violence or hatred, even of the verbal kind. But perhaps by spotting amplifying feedback processes early, we may someday be able to stop the growth of hostility, or at least bring it under control before it gets out of hand.

Negative Feedback Processes.   In *negative feedback* the signal reporting the results of a previous action says, "Oppose this action; change it or modify it." Negative feedback is in essence critical. It says "no" to those in charge of the preceding operation. A negative feedback system is at the heart of all controlled situations. A thermostat is a negative feedback system. The thermometer reports the temperature of the room; the setting of the control determines the desired level. If it is set at 68 degrees, for example, and the temperature falls to 65, the furnace will turn on, the registers will open, and hot air will come into the room. When the temperature reaches 68 or 69, the furnace will shut off. In effect, the 68-degree temperature had been made a *goal state* for the system. The goal state of any system is that relation of the system to its environment in which its inner imbalance or *disequilibrium* is at a minimum. In negative feedback, whenever the system departs from its goal state, the preceding operation is opposed or reversed.

A control system of this sort maintains a steady state. Processes which tend to maintain some particular state of affairs are called *homeostatic*. In the human body, for instance, a homeostatic or negative feedback system makes sure we do not have too much carbon dioxide in our blood. Every time the CO_2 concentration in our blood gets too high, the system turns on the breathing mechanism and we breathe. A similar, slower working system makes us hungry when we have too little blood sugar, and makes us feel sated when we have enough. In the body politic, a similar conservative or homeostatic feedback system exists to induce the Council of Economic Advisors in the American government to recommend the manipulating of credit rates in such a way that unemployment is not less than 2 and not more than 4 per cent of the work force. However, the idea of using one over-all feedback circuit on the whole employment level of the economy may turn out to be an oversimplification, for it may ignore the significance of pockets of unemployment in ghettoes and depressed areas. Nevertheless, the basic principle of maintaining a certain state of affairs, by reversing any behavior leading away from it, has been tested thoroughly. It is as applicable to a government or to politics as to the nerves in an organism.

Critical Aspects of Steering: Load, Lag, Gain, and Lead.   Negative feedback systems can, of course, also be used to make an object home on a moving target. A greyhound racing after a rabbit is homing on a moving target. The rabbit may rapidly change its course whereas the greyhound, who runs faster but is heavier, has more difficulty in controlling its own momentum. Thus, although the greyhound is faster, many rabbits survive by imposing a greater load on the steering system of the greyhound than that system can handle. This leads to a concept of power that is fundamentally different from the traditional one. The greyhound surpasses the rabbit in sharpness of teeth, strength of body, weight, and speed, but cannot match him in cybernetic capacity—the capacity for self-steering.

So the rabbit frequently changes course, imposing a load on the steering system of the greyhound. Generally, the *load* on a steering system is the amount of behavior change per unit of time that is demanded by the changes in the system's course of target. The interval between the moment the rabbit turns and the greyhound notices it and slows down his own body in order to turn himself is the *lag* in his response. The extent to which the greyhound corrects his action is his *gain,* that is, the change which is accomplished by the response to a new input signal. But if the gain is too large, the greyhound will overcorrect and overshoot his target. Unlike a duck hunter, the greyhound ordinarily does not lead his target. Duck hunters and antiaircraft artillery, on the contrary, both lead their targets, by aiming at the target's probable future position, instead of at its present one. Thus, the amount of *lead* is the amount of time by which a steering system can predict and respond to the future state of a target, within an acceptably small margin of error.

These four measures of performance—load, lag, gain, and lead—are relevant to politics, as well. They apply to all negative feedback processes, and hence to all self-steering systems. They can be used, with appropriate qualifications, to study and evaluate the performance of electronic control devices, business organizations, and governments. To return to the slum problem, sensitive observers often can see that life is becoming intolerable for certain people under certain conditions. In the past, they have sent out warnings of trouble but sometimes, as in Chicago, it has taken bloody riots in the streets for a city government to authorize turning on the fire hydrants during a heat wave so that slum children could enjoy a shower. A little more intelligence would have cut down this *lag.* Indeed, it should be possible for governments to *lead,* to know when it will get hot and, thus, when the hydrants should be turned on.

But governments tend to *lag,* and the greater the lag, the greater is the temptation to use heavy-handed overraction—and repression, in particular—as a way of *gain.* Unfortunately, overreaction may merely result in replacing one error by an equal or bigger error in the opposite direction. When a dictatorship first purges left deviationists and then, with the same elephantine thoroughness, purges right deviationists only to reverse itself once more to purge left deviations again, it is behaving much like a novice driver who notices too late that he is heading for a ditch and, overcorrecting, is forced to yank the steering wheel in the opposite direction. Governments are perfectly capable of oversteering, and frequently they are deficient in the ability to lead events, to foresee the action that will be needed.

The Nature of Goals and Goal-Seeking.   Negative feedback systems are usually goal-seeking systems. A goal-seeking system that is in internal disequilibrium is likely to change; when it is in equilibrium, it is likely to be at rest. So long as it is in disequilibrium, and therefore changing, it is also likely to change in its relation to the outside world. If its new relationships to the environment preserve the system's inner disequilibrium, changes will continue; in effect, the system will act as though it were searching for still other relationships. If, however, in some new relationship the system's internal disequilibrium is reduced, its drive to change will be reduced. If in some particular relationship to the environment the system's inner disequilibrium is brought to a minimum, then the system will tend to remain in this relation: it will have reached a goal. Systems that behave in this manner—as negative feedback systems ordinarily do— are called *goal-seeking* systems. If negative feedback signals tell a system to change or reverse any behavior that moves it farther away from a goal situation—while confirming or reinforcing any behavior moving it closer to a goal situation—we have a *goal-seeking* system in the proper sense of the term.

Goals or goal states, as we have seen, are those relationships between a goal-seeking system and its environment in which the system's inner disequilibrium is minimal. If more than one such relationship has this effect for a system, then the system has several goals. A *goal* is thus not a thing but a relation of a system to its environment. When such a goal relation has already been attained by a system, and has only to be preserved against disturbances, we speak of a *homeostatic* system. When the goal situation is distant, or the target is moving, we ordinarily speak of goal-seeking in its narrower sense. The word *purpose* applies when a more distant goal is approached by a longer and more complex course around obstacles. Purposeful behavior requires the steadfast pursuit of a goal through a sequence of changing moves. In all these cases, the basic relation is the same.

Goal-seeking and homeostatic behavior turn up almost everywhere in life. If we have set our thermostat at 68 degrees, the disequilibrium in the heat control system will be at a minimum when the room is at 68 degrees. A hungry greyhound will be at a relative equilibrium when he has caught the rabbit and eaten it. Governments may be under disequilibria owing to their internal political setup, but they may reduce these disequilibria by conquering a colony or a border province or by acquiring a favorable political or economic treaty. Thus governments tend to pursue foreign policies which are likely—or expected—to relieve domestic tensions and the pressures of rival interest groups. In other words, what governments seek as political goals are in essence responses to internal disequilibria.

Environment and the Nature of Decision-Making

Two Kinds of Environment.   Any self-steering system has two kinds of environment. The first is obvious; it is the world outside the system. The second should be no less obvious but is often overlooked; it is the environment within the system. The inner world, and its effects on the disequilibrium of the system, can influence decisively what the system does. What a person does depends not only on the world around him but also on the state of his body and mind. An automobile driver must take into account not only the condition of the road but also the state of his brakes and engine.

The existence of two separate environments, both of which a system must take account of, has a significant effect on decision-making. If a system could pay attention to its outside environment alone or its internal environment alone, it might have very few decisions to make. Decisions become frequent and important wherever information from one kind of environment must be confronted with information from the other.

Something like this has been happening to our universities: important current information about donors and alumni, about local, state, and national governments, and about the local community have been confronted with urgent current information about internal problems of the university, and particularly about the needs and feelings of students and faculty. In many such cases, current messages from both environments have called for decisions. (Often the addition of messages from the past, recalled from memory, introduces a third element into the decision problem. This matter will be discussed later in this chapter.)

Decision-Making on the National Level.   For a national government, too, there are two kinds of feedback of current information. There is an external feedback about foreign policy and an internal feedback about what goes on inside the country. The latter is usually more important. Domestic politics tend to outweigh foreign policy in most countries most of the time, particularly in the modern age of mass politics. It is a commonplace of political experience that politicians ignorant of foreign policy who make gross mistakes in foreign affairs can get re-elected if they correctly gauge the realities of domestic politics. Today most government policies are domestically determined more often than internationally determined, although most political decisions are a mixture of the two.

When all the information comes in from the different streams of current intake, a decision must be made by the government. The more diverse intake streams of information a system has, the freer it is in making decisions. In this sense, the replacing of the four intelligence agencies which existed under Franklin D. Roosevelt by a single one, the CIA, impoverished the decision-making latitude of the President of the United States. It reduced his degree of freedom and increased his risks of error. The task of reconciling different and conflicting streams of information is one of the most high-level tasks of government. By delegating this responsibility to a lower level of authority, this action may have resulted in a weakening of the country's intelligence and decision-making capabilities, as seen in the abortive invasion of Cuba's Bay of Pigs in 1961 and in the war in Vietnam. Having subordinate officials reconcile or "consolidate" contradictory streams of information from different sources often may look like efficient preparation for decision-making. But their work may prejudge the decision; indeed, they, in effect, may make the decision, without their superiors being fully aware of it.

Decision Points and Decision Areas. To a superficial observer, a decision point is something in the environment which forces a decision, like a fork in the road or a soda fountain menu. On closer inspection it turns out that a *decision point* is a point where two different streams of feedback information are confronted. Since information is carried in channels—whether they are copper wires, electronic beams, nerves, or human chains of reporting and command—a decision point is the meeting place of at least two channels. Where several channels meet, and many decisions have to be made, we may speak of a *decision area*. The judge—or the jury—stands at a decision point in a lawsuit. The court is a decision area for many lawsuits. The United States Congress is another kind of decision area; and the presidency is still another. President Harry Truman dramatized this fact when he put a sign on his own desk which read: "The buck stops here."

Decision points and decision areas are junctions in the flow of information where organizations—and especially governments—are vulnerable to damage and exposed to influence for good or ill. Knocking out a crucial junction may paralyze a government. Filling, infiltrating, or occupying it with one's own friends or adherents may give a leader or a group influence and power out of proportion to its numbers. Such considerations played a part in the "court-packing" controversies of 1937 and 1969 about the composition of the Supreme Court of the United States. Conversely, the incumbents of a decision area can be rendered powerless if the information streams leading to their junction are cut off or if they are rechanneled so as to bypass them. Finally, the incumbents of a decision area also may become powerless when one stream of information becomes so predominant over all others that there is nothing left to decide. In this case, the incumbents of the formal decision area can make only gestures of agreement; they are reduced to being rubber stamps.

From Memory to Autonomy

Among the most important junctions in the flow of information are those where messages from the present meet with information recalled from the past. As a function, *memory* is the storing and recall of past information. As a tangible structure, memory consists of those parts of a self-steering system where past information is stored, together with the channels and facilities for its recall. Any large computer must have such a memory to store the information required for its calculations. The facilities for such storage may include magnetic cores, tapes, discs, or drums. These are supplemented by channels and devices to search the stored information, pick out items for recall, and apply the recalled data to decisions about current operations.

In the human body, information is stored in the brain; it is recalled and applied with the help of other parts of the brain and the nervous system. The human personality resembles a long single run on the thinking and storage facilities of our nervous system. But unlike a computer a human mind cannot be "cleared" or emptied of the past. To the day we die, some of our past will stay with us and will make each of us the unique individual he is.

Selfhood and Autonomy. In this sense, memory is the source of selfhood and identity. To have a *self* means to have a memory, together with facilities for intake, output, and decision, and the feedback circuits linking them.

An ethnic or cultural group of people can be said to acquire a "self" when it acquires a common memory and a common set of channels of social communication that links them into a self-steering system. At first, such a self is often cultural, based on common memories, communication habits, and ease of understanding. It often becomes a *political self,* however, when it is applied to political actions and decisions. The Irish people in the nineteenth century, when they followed the slogan *Sinn Fein* ("we ourselves"), and the American Negro people when they proclaimed in the 1960's the slogans "Black Power" and "Black is Beautiful," directed their movement toward this kind of political selfhood and identity.

Identity is then the recognition and awareness of one's own memory and of one's self. It is the ability to remember that one can remember. "This is I, myself," says the individual. "This is us, ourselves," say, less grammatically, the members of a group that is attaining a sense of its identity. And from this sense of group identity it is only a short step to the assertion of political preferences and the taking of political actions. Often these eventually culminate in demands for political self-government and self-determination.

In terms of action, memory is the source of our autonomy. To be *autonomous* means to be able to apply information from the past to a decision in the present. Without memory, without an effective past, there can be no autonomy. Not every feedback system, therefore, that already is self-steering will necessarily have full autonomy. To have full autonomy a system must have a memory; it must have stored information from the past which can be recalled and fed back into the decisions of the present. If a system has such a memory, if it is truly autonomous, then even the most exhaustive knowledge of its environment will not predict with complete accuracy what it will do next, since it might act in terms of its memories as well as in terms of its current intake.

Here is the fundamental error in the otherwise great and liberating theories of John Locke and his followers. Locke believed that the mind of a child was like a blank piece of paper. The child's associations and environment would become associations in his experiences; these experiences would then become associations in his memory; and his future action would be governed by the associations of his past as recorded in memory. The social scientists of the eighteenth century were quick to draw the conclusion that complete control of a human being's environment would in time completely control the content of his mind and therefore his behavior.

The eighteenth-century writers of the Enlightenment were optimists. They believed that governments on the whole would be reasonable and benevolent. Princes, they thought, could be educated, and even despots could be made enlightened. If these rulers could control the environment of their subjects and thus shape their minds, the results were likely to be good. Two-and-a-half centuries later, knowledge of totalitarian governments and of the horrors of World War II seemed to support the opposite view. Some writers, such as George Orwell, expressed the belief that there was much evil in all men, and that evil had freer rein among men in power. Governments, therefore, were likely to be both dishonest and cruel, and the more power they had over the environment and the minds of their subjects, the worse the results would be. Orwell's imagined world of *1984* is a world of horror. Watched by the ever-present television cameras of "Big Brother," men's environment and every action are totally government controlled. At the end of the novel, the hero has become a walking robot. He believes what government tells him to believe, fears what he is told to fear, and hates what he is told to hate. In both the optimism of the Enlightenment thinkers and the pessimism of George Orwell we find the same view that men's thoughts can be determined from the outside: control of the environment controls the intake and the memories of men; hence it controls their personality and thus their future behavior.

In its one-sided form, this "environmentalist" theory is demonstrably false. A man's behavior is strongly influenced not only by what he learns from his environment, but also by the autonomous processes and combinations inside his mind, and particularly inside his memory.

Dissociation and Recombination: Elements of Human Freedom.

The important point about the human memory is that it is dissociative and combinatorial. The ability to *dissociate*—to separate pieces of information and to sort them out—is essential for critical thinking; the ability to *combine* them into new patterns is essential for creativity. Human beings are capable of breaking into pieces the patterns which they perceive in their environment. The most obvious example was their ability to see a bird and, by detaching its wings in their imagination and putting them on the body of a man, to conceive of human flight, something radically new, thousands of years before the flight of an airplane. By dissociating what he sees and learns and hears, and then recombining it in an almost infinite variety of ways, man achieves degrees of freedom no creature with a less deep memory can match. Even if a dictator completely controlled everything his subjects saw and heard, he could not control the many ways they might piece together inside their minds the things which they had seen. If the dictator shot every man in the world who expressed a certain idea, he could not be sure that a bright sixteen-year-old might not put the idea together again. It is impossible to fix the human mind in an individual, or in a group, by controlling that individual's or group's environment, for there is an ineradicable element of combinatorial freedom in the human mind and in human society.

Dissociation and recombination occur in the memory, usually below the level of our awareness. Not all memories are recalled and not all of them prevail, but those that are recalled can have a great effect on the decision area of a human being or of a government. We interpret riots at home, or new foreign-policy crises in the Near East, in the light not only of what we remember but also of how we remember it, and in the light of combinatorial new ideas. In this sense, societies are autonomous, as well as the individuals of which they are composed; and the collective memory of societies—as embodied in their history, literature, language, and general culture—is often decisive for their autonomous behavior.

Governments, too, have memories, and these often are decisive for their actions. In foreign affairs, many of the effective memories of a government are in the files of its foreign office or state department, and in the minds of its senior officials. What the files record, and what these men remember, about the past actions of a foreign government or statesman may make all the difference to how they respond to current messages from them. Different elements from a government's memory also may be combined into a new policy. What many American scientists remembered about the effects of radioactive fallout on the bones of children was combined in 1963 with what American military and diplomatic experts knew about military strategy and international relations. A similar intellectual and political effort was made in the Soviet Union. The result was a new departure in world politics: the Partial Test Ban Treaty of 1963, banning all nuclear explosions in the open air, and signed by the United States, the Soviet Union, and about eighty other countries.[1]

Memories of voters, or of people in local communities, may make a major difference to how they respond to later political challenges. In Spain, there are small peasant proprietors in the province of Navarra in the Pyrenees, as well as in the Basque provinces on the Bay of Biscay. But in Navarra, loyalties to the Spanish monarchy have lived on for generations, while the Basque provinces have not only more industrial workers but also long memories of local self-government and of an equalitarian and almost republican political tradition. At the outbreak of the Spanish Civil War in 1936, most of the men of Navarra joined Colonel Francisco Franco—the later Generalissimo—in his insurrection against the Spanish Republic, while the Basques, together with the majority of the Spanish people, supported the Republican side.[2] Historical memories thus had a major influence upon the political alignments of important parts of the Spanish people at a crucial moment in world history.

Will: The Hardening of Decisions

Ordinarily, there is a good deal of change and variation in the current information which a self-steering system takes in from the outside world, as well as in the current information it receives from within itself. Similarly, there may be much change in the stream of past information, recalled from memory. Since complex decisions are produced by the combination of current information recalled from the past, such decisions are apt to vary frequently with the changes in the information streams from which they are produced. Decisions thus often may change faster than they can be carried out.

[1] France and China refused to accept this treaty and produced in the 1960's a small number of nuclear test explosions in the open air; but the amount of fallout thus produced was much smaller than that which would have occurred if there had been no test ban treaty and the major nuclear powers had continued open air testing. There seems little doubt that by 1970 the partial test ban treaty saved the lives and health of many children around the world. The test ban treaty thus is an example of an innovation in world politics that seems to have worked well.

[2] Franco won after three years, thanks to massive aid from Hilter and Mussolini, which dwarfed all aid given to the Republic by Russia and other countries.

To be acted on, a decision must be held long enough to take effect. This is accomplished by the screening out of information that might change the decision, or change it too soon. *Information screens* or filters are thus essential for the fuction of a complex self-steering system, such as the political system of a country. In order to get anything done, there comes a moment when a society must stop taking more and more and more information into account and make a decision. After it has been made, the decision must hold. Sticking to a decision means rejecting information that is incompatible with it. The decision-makers make a decision in the light of all the information available until the moment the policy is set. They then stop considering information contrary to this decision. Political *will*—the capacity to subordinate post-decision information to pre-decision information—is an essential aspect of any sustained political action.

This capacity, however, is a two-edged weapon. Will is the capacity not to learn. Although will is needed to get things done, it is a danger of the first order, for it is the temporary and deliberate cognitive impoverishment of an acting organization or organism. The more a government is likely to stress will, the more a statesman speaks of "a test of will" (as former Secretary of State Dean Rusk called the Vietnam War), or the more a political movement proclaims itself a "triumph of will" (as the Nazis did in the 1930s), the more the system is apt to be deficient in cognitive performance. The more a government or a political system becomes completely oriented toward will, the more likely it is to suffer a cognitive catastrophe.

We can picture will as a system of screens (see Figure 7.3). Certain information is not taken in from the receptors. Certain information is not recalled from memory. In the individual, this is called Freudian repression. Some countries censor their history books; other countries just select what they care to remember and censor their memories without being fully aware of doing so. For instance, American history books imply that the United States never lost a war; they play down the fact that the War of 1812 failed in its major objective—the conquest of Canada. Every nation has such blind spots in its memory. But if these blind spots become too large, or too serious, they may deprive the nation of much needed information; they may prevent the timely correction of mistakes; and they may let government and nation move blindly toward disaster.

One form of screening the intake of information is to control the flow of messages and persons across a nation's boundaries. Boundary control by a government may have large effects. It may enable the government for a time to stop or slow the growth of those opposition movements—and of many other initiatives toward innovation—which might clash with established policies or be troublesome to control. But if necessary amounts of such resources as information, manpower, or equipment cannot be found at home, some import of them may be needed from abroad. And boundary control works to inhibit such imports.

Figure 7.3

A Functional Diagram of Information Flow in a Political System

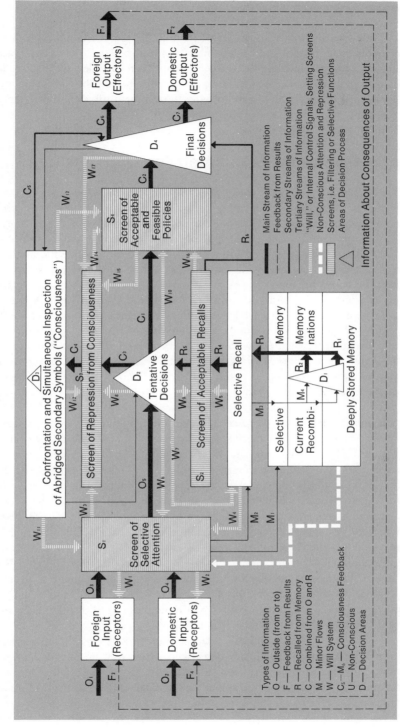

Source: Adapted and redrawn with permission of The Macmillan Company from Nerves of Government by Karl W. Deutsch. Copyright © 1966 by The Free Press, a division of The Macmillan Company. Copyright © 1963 by The Free Press of Glencoe, a division of The Macmillan Company.

Tight control at the boundaries thus makes governments more secure over the short run, at the price of making their societies more conservative, sluggish, and backward over the long run. Open societies, with a free flow of transactions over their borders, are harder to rule but they are more likely to innovate, adapt, and grow, and are thus ultimately more likely to survive.

Consciousness: Self-Monitoring for Coordination

A complex system may have to try to compare what goes on in its receptors, screens, and decision areas, and then try to assemble highly abbreviated excerpts of all this information at one place for simultaneous inspection, coordination, and decision. The situation room in the White House is such a place. The situation room is where highly condensed and abstracted information from many parts of the world is put before the President and his top advisors. Another such place was the plotting room for the defense of London during the Battle of Britain in 1940. A big map as large as the room pictured the south of England. Little wooden toy-like replicas showed every German plane coming in and every British fighter plane available. Soldiers with long rakes moved these replicas over the map, and the general in charge of the air defense of London could see at a glance what was going on and could thus make the best decision for deployment of British planes.

This is consciousness. *Consciousness* means the processing of highly simplified and condensed summaries of second-order messages (that is, messages about first-order messages) for simultaneous inspection and decision (see Figure 7.3). A society that lacks consciousness lacks complete control of itself. But like will, consciousness has its own costs and risks. Its most serious cost probably is delay. It takes time to monitor the first-order messages going through a system, to abstract them into shorter second-order messages, and to assemble them in one place for side-by-side inspection and decision. When quick action is needed, the risks of such delays must be weighed against the risks of error from insufficient information, inspection, and coordination. Consciousness also requires tangible facilities, such as monitoring circuits and display screens. In governmental, military, or business organizations, it requires human monitors, abstractors, and other personnel, often together with briefing rooms and display facilities. It thus requires costs in money and resources.

Together, the costs and delays can be crippling. A centipede was immobilized, according to a story, when asked which foot he planned to move next: the creature became lost in thought. Governments, no less than centipedes, can become entangled in their own complexity. Moreover, political decisions can be slowed down as more people become aware of them. More individuals and agencies may try to get into the act, more interest groups may insist on being heard, more logrolling politicians with veto power may demand a price for allowing the project to go through. No wonder that it is a rule of practical politics to arouse as little attention as possible about any plan that has enough support to pass.

Added to these costs are special risks of error. A society that has consciousness risks three things. First, it runs the risk of a false consciousness. At the end of World War II, Adolph Hitler in his command bunker in Berlin was ordering German divisions to advance that had ceased to exist. The symbols were still on the map, but the divisions no longer were in existence. Second, a society runs the risk of an incorrect estimate. Something that is mildly important may be overrepresented; something significant may be underrepresented. The history of the American Negro has been underrepresented in the awareness of American historians for many years, much as the needs and aspirations of black Americans have long been underrepresented in our politics. This is one of the many deficiencies that now are crying out for remedy.

Third, condensation and simplification are fraught with dangers of their own. The U. S. State Department gets about a thousand cables a day. Each week it gets several hundred messages and reports, averaging ten to twenty pages, in the diplomatic pouches. No Secretary of State or any other human being could read all this without going out of his mind. Condensation is thus indispensable. Highly abbreviated one-page summaries are drawn up by lower-level officials from every longer report and put on top. Cables of half a page are summarized in a sentence. These summary slips then go to one official who quickly scans all of them. He summarizes the summaries. By the time the world situation is condensed into what can be discussed with the Secretary of State or the President in a one-hour briefing session, it has been fantastically simplified, and sometimes dangerously oversimplified.

In every large political system, all politics must pass between the twin dangers of being blinded by superficiality and being drowned in detail. What is true of the consciousness of the State Department about world politics or the Air Force about airplane and missile dispositions, or the Navy as to where its own ships and those of other countries are, is equally true of our knowledge of our cities, our economy, our domestic politics, and our educational situation. Thus societies must have consciousness, but they must be critical toward their consciousness lest they become prisoners of their own illusions.

Self-Government in Perspective

Self-government at its core is based on self-steering; at its boundaries it is founded on relative independence from the outside world. The legal doctrine of *sovereignty* stresses the latter aspect in its extreme form: a state is held to be sovereign if it obeys no laws or commands from outside itself, except those it accepts voluntarily by its own internal decision processes. This legal concept of sovereignty says little, however, about the ability of a government, a nation, a city, or any other organization to control its own affairs.

To control its own affairs, a government or any other organization must first be able to direct its own behavior. All self-direction—and hence self-government—is a process of steering. It must combine several streams of information: past information as to what its goal or target is; current outside information as to where the goal or target is; and internal information as to where the system itself is in relation to its goal. All these streams of information are based on cycles of feedback. These report back to the system the results of its own previous behavior. If this behavior has brought the system closer to its goal, it is continued; if not, it is reversed or modified, until the goal is reached.

Self-government implies the ability to set goals and to keep to them; to make decisions and keep them stable long enough for action; and hence to screen out or suppress post-decision information that might jeopardize stability. This is the function of the will, which is a subsystem of information filters performing this service.

In complex systems, the coordination of many subsystems and decisions is facilitated by internal monitoring. The voluminous primary messages moving through the system are abstracted and condensed into much shorter secondary ones which are then presented for simultaneous inspection and decision. This process corresponds in its essentials to what we call consciousness.

All these processes have their particular costs and risks. Together, however, they make it possible for individuals, small groups, and large nations to govern their own actions, and thus to win a greater share in controlling their own fate.

Key Terms and Concepts

self-government	lead
independent	disequilibrium
sovereign	goal-seeking system
autonomy	goal
receptors	purpose
effectors	decision point
self-steering	decision area
feedback cycle	memory
amplifying feedback	self
escalation	political self
negative feedback	identity
goal state	autonomous

homeostatic process	dissociative
load	combinatorial
lag	will
gain	consciousness
	sovereignty

Additional Readings

Hoffman, S. *Gulliver's Troubles.* New York: McGraw-Hill, 1968.

Kennedy, R. *Thirteen Days.* New York: Norton, 1969.

Orwell, G. *1984.* New York: Harcourt, Brace, 1949.

Weiner, N. *Human Use of Human Beings.* Boston: Houghton Mifflin, 1950.

Wildavsky, A. "The Empty-head Blues: Black Rebellion and White Reaction."
The Public Interest, Vol. 11, No. 1 (1968), pp. 3–16.

The Process and
Machinery of Government

The two preceding chapters have presented an abstract model of the political system. They have focused on the system's main functions—how a system keeps itself together and how it steers itself—and on the general processes by which these tasks are attained. It is now time to turn our attention to the specific processes and machinery by which the work of government and politics gets done.*

Politics and government, we may recall, refer to a single complex of activities from different but overlapping perspectives. Politics stresses competing demands and the allocation of values—that is, of valued outcomes, resources, and opportunities—among them. Government emphasizes steering and control. Politics deals with Harold Lasswell's classic question: "Who Gets What, When, How?" Government deals with the question: "Who controls what, when, and how?" One distinction between politics and government is this distinction between getting and controlling.

Chapter 8

Politics and government interact, necessarily and closely; and both need specific institutions, organizations, channels, and procedures in order to operate. It is these specific arrangements, and some of the main similarities and differences among them in different countries, that we shall study in the present chapter. Through this study we can find out what is subject to political and governmental decisions, who makes them, how they are made, how they are put into effect, in what ways they are limited, and what opportunities they offer.

Decisions and Their Limits

One of the most difficult and most important features of all politics is how one makes decisions—and more particularly, decisions on policy. In any organization there is always some mystery to the decision-making process.

* For some of the material in this chapter I am indebted to Professor Carl J. Friedrich.

This is as true of big commercial companies as of universities, governments, and other kinds of organizations. And yet, because of the importance of decision-making, many organizations establish elaborate rules, which seem to tell us how decisions are supposed to be made. In fact, many of these rules are observed mostly in the abstract and frequently not at all. For example, if you buy shares of stock in an American company, you will be invited to the annual stockholders' meeting at which the stockholders are supposed to reach basic policy decisions. Actually, they do nothing of the kind. If somebody should have the temerity to suggest a policy decision, the stockholders are informed that management opposes the proposal; and, as you might expect, an overwhelming majority of stockholders roundly defeat it. Of course, most of the people making this decision are in no way aware of its significance, nor do they really care so long as management is earning 7 per cent on the stock. Something similar is characteristic of all kinds of organizations: so long as things seem to go well, most people are happy to "let George do it"—to let someone else make the decisions.

Many people have the illusion that something important is accomplished in the change of a rule about decision-making. The curious thing is that these decision-making processes have an inner dynamism with which we cannot cope effectively by formal rule-making. Robert Kennedy's book, *Thirteen Days*, a memoir of the Cuban missile crisis of October 1962, is a revealing case study of a particular type of decision-making process. It describes step by step how President Kennedy arrived at a series of decisions which were precipitated by the Soviet Union's attempt in the summer of 1962 to install intermediate range ballistic missiles (IRBMs) in Cuba. The Soviets may have intended their action as a move to deter another United States supported invasion of Cuba, similar to the one that had failed at the Bay of Pigs in April 1961; or they might have wanted to match the positioning of similar United States missiles since the 1950s in Turkey, near Soviet territory, and at a somewhat greater distance in southern Italy. Another possibility is that the Soviets might simply have wanted a bargaining card to trade for some United States concession, such as an American promise not to attack Cuba again. Or they might really have thought that their intermediate missiles in Cuba might change the strategic balance of power in the world.

We will not know what the true purpose of the Soviet move was, or indeed whether it had a single purpose, until the Soviet archives are opened. But we know the impression which their move made on the American government and public. Most Americans interpreted it as a direct threat against various countries in this hemisphere, particularly the United States. As President Kennedy saw it, American domestic politics thus left him very little choice about how to interpret the Soviet move. It left him very little *decision latitude*. A majority of his advisers considered the installation of Soviet missiles in Cuba a possible change in the world's balance of power. A small minority denied this; they thought these missiles would make little or no difference and saw no need for action. But as President Kennedy later said, if he had not acted in some way, "I would have been impeached."

The account of another White House adviser, Theodore Sorensen's *Decision-Making in the White House*, provides an interesting supplement to Robert Kennedy's story. Both Robert Kennedy and Sorensen suggest that the very word "decision" often is deceptive. Sorensen says at the very beginning, "The President is in his decisions very much affected by basic forces and factors which will shape his decisions." He adds, "The President may ignore these forces or factors, he may even be unaware of them, but he cannot escape them. He may choose to decide in solitude, but he does not decide in a vacuum." In other words, you may think you are deciding something, but actually it is being decided by forces and factors over which you have no control but which must be taken into account if you want to make a good decision. If you ignore them you are likely to make a bad decision which will not accomplish any of the things you want.

Thirteen Days is a most exciting and dramatic illustration of this point. In those thirteen days in October 1962 some very important decisions were made. At one stage there was an intense debate over whether to respond to the threat of the installation of the missiles in Cuba with a relatively mild measure, such as a blockade, or with military force. Robert Kennedy strongly opposed a massive surprise attack by a large nation on a very small nation because he believed that the immorality of such an action was contrary to America's traditions and ideals. Secretary of Defense Robert S. McNamara later wrote in his introduction to *Thirteen Days*: "The air and ground strikes favored by so many would have brought death to thousands of innocent Cuban civilians and to thousands of U. S. military personnel." The expected number of Cuban civilian casualties alone was put at 25,000. Thus the conscience and moral tradition of the American people was one of the forces acting upon President Kennedy's decision. In addition, President Kennedy decided in favor of the milder measure rather than military attack for still another reason: the latter might have precipitated a nuclear confrontation and possible nuclear war between the United States and the Soviet Union.

Once the decision for the blockade was made, Secretary General of the United Nations U Thant appealed to Nikita Khrushchev, who then was Chairman of the Supreme Soviet, to order all ships from the Soviet Union en route to Cuba not to proceed until some adjustment had been reached between the United States and the Soviet Union. Khrushchev responded to this appeal and thus avoided a particularly dangerous confrontation. On both sides, in the United States and in the Soviet Union, crucial decisions led to the course that eventually emerged. Large-scale loss of life was avoided, and all three governments remained in power.

In the first stage of the crisis, President Kennedy's decision latitude was small. He could not choose to wait. Had he done nothing, he would have risked a deterioration in the international power and prestige of the United States, and in any case, serious political troubles with Congress and the public. At the same time, he could not do very much. If he had chosen to attack Cuba, he could not have prevented Soviet retaliation against Berlin and the risk of World War III. At a later stage, President Kennedy's decision latitude increased. Within the limits of his decision to blockade Cuba, he had a range of options as to the manner of carrying it out. These limits were wide enough for him to act forcefully and yet to remain at all times in control of his own actions. They permitted him to reach his main objective, the removal of the missiles, and yet preserve peace.

Soviet Chairman Nikita Khrushchev also had to face his own limits of decision-making. He could not choose to defend Cuba locally with any prospect of success against a full-scale American attack, since neither the U.S.S.R. nor Cuba had enough forces on the spot. He could decide at most to apply counter-pressure elsewhere, such as on Berlin, and risk all-out war with the United States. Or he could choose to respect the American blockade and to negotiate. Once he decided on the last course, his options improved. In exchange for removing the missiles, he obtained an informal American pledge not to attack Cuba; in addition, the aging American IRBMs were removed from Italy and Turkey, in tardy fulfillment of an order given by President Kennedy long before the crisis.

In the handling of the Cuban missile crisis, both Kennedy and Khrushchev were true statesmen. For a part of the art of statesmanship consists in recognizing the limits to decision-making at a particular time and place, and in making the most of the opportunities within those limits.

Decisions are often broken into sequences. First a decision is made about the general preferences, purposes, or goals in regard to some class of problems. This is called a *policy* decision. Later decisions deal with the means and methods of carrying out the policy. The difference between policy and its execution resembles that between strategy and tactics. *Strategy* consists in setting a long-run series of goals or targets; *tactics* consists in choosing and applying the short-run means to attain them. Generally, strategy looks farther ahead into the future and involves setting a larger class of goals, whereas tactics denotes choosing a more limited class of intermediate steps within the larger class.

Policy also often implies the setting of a relatively distant goal or purpose which may have to be approached by a zigzag course of short-run moves around several intervening obstacles. Since these moves seem to contradict each other, much like in the tacking of a sailboat into a tricky harbor entrance, the notion of "policy" sometimes connotes a devious sequence of actions aimed at a single goal. So does the word "purpose." As we recall, it refers to pursuing a goal through a circuitous sequence of steps around obstacles. The French, Shakespeare wrote in *Henry V,* "with pale policy seeks to divert the English purposes."

In modern politics, policy is a very controversial word. Before World War II, people did not talk much about "policy." During the time from John Locke to the beginning of the twentieth century, people talked about "legislation." When Locke divided power among several authorities, he was primarily concerned about the power of legislative decision, not the power of policy-making. He wanted each legislative decision to be made very carefully, when the time came to make it. He did not concern himself with setting policy as a general guide for the future conduct of the government. Nowadays people demand just that. They have become increasingly preoccupied with policy. Those in public life are very keen about being involved in policy-making. This has become the really important task of government; legislation is looked down upon as a technical matter. The concern of important people is to decide policy. They then leave it to lawyers to work out the technicalities of the legislation involved.

At this point, the interests of the "important people" meet with those of the man in the street. He, too, knows little about technicalities of legislation, and he is impatient about them. But he knows what he likes and often knows what he wants. He can make clear which goal or outcome he prefers. He can express his support for a policy, or his opposition to it; and he can vote for a candidate or party who appears to stand for the policies he likes.

But something else is characteristic of policies besides their generally accepted importance. Policy decisions involve particular objectives, and the more important the objectives are, the more important the decisions are. The security of the United States is an extremely important objective. Consequently, any decision involving the security of the United States is an important decision. But somebody could raise the question, what *is* the security of the United States? Wherein does it consist? Some Americans might think themselves secure if nobody could shoot them without being shot at in return. Unfortunately, it is not as simple as that. When a government seeks security in national armaments, other nations are provoked to arm, which can lead to the dangers of an arms race. As Henry Kissinger, an advisor to President Nixon, is said to have remarked about security through superior armament: Absolute security for any one nation is absolute insecurity for any other.

The definition of objectives, or goals, is a critical stage in policy-making. Goal definition has all kinds of ramifications. Much of the present student unrest all over the world stems from different views as to the goal of university education. There is a difference of opinion among many students and among many students and members of the faculty and administration. Some see a university's main task as the education of undergraduates. Others see it as service to the community, or to its poorest members. Still others see it as the discovery and application of new knowledge; and still others see it as providing its graduates with hunting licenses for better-paying jobs. Deciding on the goals of a university is typically a policy matter, because agreement on policy means that we have decided on our goal.

The goal of President Kennedy during the Cuban missile crisis was above everything else to avoid an all-out war. (Giving in to the Soviet Union, he thought, would not accomplish this. It would only bring a more warlike American administration to power and invite further Soviet aggressiveness.) Robert Kennedy wrote of his brother: "The thought that disturbed him the most, and that made the prospect of war much more fearful than it would otherwise have been, was the specter of the death of the children of this country and all the world—the young people who had no role, who had no say, who knew nothing even of the confrontation, but whose lives would be snuffed out like everyone else's." A little further on in *Thirteen Days* he repeats this and says, "It was this that troubled him most, that gave him such pain." Then comes the crucial point—how to make certain that the Soviet Union would not misunderstand the goals of the United States, and the United States the goals of the Soviet Union: "And it was then that he and Secretary Rusk decided that I should visit with Ambassador Dobrynin and personally convey the President's great concern." Robert Kennedy in effect was to say to Dobrynin: Look, you know you are really playing with fire and you are marching right into a war— an uncontrollable conflagration—with the United States. Is that what you really want? Dobrynin then came back the next day after having communicated with Moscow and in effect answered: This is not what we want; we want some other things; our goals have been misunderstood. An understanding of the significance of this conversation is very important for the understanding of the meaning of policy.

Policy, in short, means goal-setting or goal definition. It is a decision as to what one's goals should be. One reason why discussions about foreign policy are usually so unenlightening and futile is its lack of definition. If you ask people, "What do you mean when you say you are displeased with foreign policy?" you usually do not get a specific answer because they do not really know what they are displeased about. The reason is not that they are stupid. Rather, the term "foreign policy" is not a clearly defined proposition.

What does foreign policy really mean for a country like the United States? If you say, "I am displeased with its foreign policy," you may mean "I am displeased with the goal definition of a particular aspect of its foreign policy." Many people meant by such an assertion that the proclamations of Secretary Rusk and President Johnson on Vietnam contained a goal definition with which they totally disagreed. They in effect said, "We do not want to turn the Vietnamese into little Americans. If that is your goal, we do not like it, and hence we do not like your policy." Other people, however, said: "We accept this goal provided it can be reached at a price that does not reduce our chances to reach other and more important goals."

As a rule, it is very difficult to say what is the goal of American foreign policy, or indeed of the foreign policy of any modern democratic nation. The reason that Richelieu and Bismarck and Napoleon in their day were able to make such "good" foreign policy was because they had perfectly simple, clear-cut, aggressive imperialist goals. Moreover, no other groups in their countries were strong enough to assert other goals for the state that might be partly or wholly incompatible with the acknowledged ones. Richelieu told Louis XIII in 1625, "We must smash the power of Habsburg." The King agreed. No one else with real power objected. All Richelieu had to do was to direct his efforts at smashing the power of the Habsburg dynasty. Unfortunately or luckily, in a democracy nobody can decide to seek such clear-cut, simple, and aggressive goals for foreign policy (quite apart from whether they can be carried out in today's world). All sorts of people in a democracy have different kinds of needs and orientations and, hence, different preferences as to national goals; each will try to make his definition prevail, and many have enough power to compel at least some consideration. Thus by the very nature of the democratic process, long-range foreign policy will only rarely be real policy, since usually it will lack an agreed-upon, clearly defined goal. More modest short-range goals sometimes command easier agreement, because different groups may interpret them as steps toward different long-range policies and support them for different reasons. Of course, we can proclaim general formulas like "peace" or "security," but those are not goals that define operations.

Something similar holds for domestic policy. Only if widespread agreement can be reached on well-defined, specific goals—such as nearly full employment, or speeding the end of race discrimination in housing, education, or employment, and only if such goals are realistic, will domestic policies have a chance to succeed. Here again, some groups, for example, may support fairer treatment for black people because they expect it to increase the general role of government in promoting social justice. Others may support the same policy in the hope that it will advance "black capitalism" and strengthen the private enterprise system. For a considerable time, both groups may be able to cooperate and bring about a significant reduction in discrimination. But at some later time, they may quarrel decisively about this matter—or else the main problems of policy may change.

Deliberation: Deciding About Ends and Means

The Deliberative Process.   Deliberation goes on in any political organization, even a dictatorship, but it is at the heart of democratic politics.

Deliberation is the chief process by which policy is determined. It is a continuous process of debate. Like any genuine debate, deliberation not only lets each participant promote his own views and interests, but also permits him to adjust his own view of reality and even to change his values as a result of this process. All policy decisions involve *deliberation,* which is directed toward the same two distinct ends as policy. First, as we have seen, deliberation and policy seek to set common ends or goals. Second, all policy debates and deliberations concern the choice of *means* to achieve the defined goal.

These twin aspects of deliberation and policy are illustrated by the debate over Social Security in the United States. In the 1930s the United States held an extensive debate over what is now known as Social Security, the term itself a testimonial to the great skill of Franklin D. Roosevelt as an inventor of catchwords. Until that time the concept had always been talked about as "old age pensions" or "public assistance," that is, in terms that were hostile to the traditional imagery of Americans. Why should any red-blooded American need any help from the government to provide for his old age? Indeed, why should anyone admit to being old or to having lost his job? By defining as his goal the achievement of "Social Security" through a government-run administration, Roosevelt was able to broaden the support for his policy. Once the decision had been made about the goal to be achieved—government provision of Social Security—the debate then focused on the means to be used to achieve the desired end, on how the government was to set up old-age insurance, unemployment insurance, and other related security arrangements. Through the years, the system of providing Social Security set up under Roosevelt has been revised, modified, and improved, under both major political parties.

Thus the graph of this process of deliberation is a jagged line. First, before a goal is determined, nothing happens, then there is a great outburst of activity to set the general goal, then again for a time nothing happens, and so on, until not only the general policy but its practical implementation is set. The deliberation goes on all the time, but at certain key points, it crystallizes into a decision, and then immediately after a decision has been made the deliberation begins again. People come along and say, "Did we make the right decision? Look—this is a consequence we didn't anticipate. What are we going to do about it?" For example, in connection with Social Security, something ultimately had to be done—a new decision had to be made—about the enormous financial reserves which soon piled up in the hands of the Social Security Administration because nobody had foreseen that these large accumulations of money would affect the economy. Thus, in the short run, "to deliberate" means "to stop and think," but in the long run we can never stop thinking. The deliberative process is continuous, with ups and downs and culminating points where crucial decisions occur. It is a process that goes on and on, unceasingly.

Procedures Safeguarding Deliberation.   Because of its importance and continuity, it has always been felt that political deliberation should be carefully institutionalized. An *institution* is an orderly and more or less formal collection of human habits and roles—that is, of interlocking expectations of behavior—which results in a stable organization or practice whose performance can be predicted with some reliability. Governments, universities, hospitals, law courts, planning boards, and business firms are such organizations; voting, marriage, property, and law are such practices. To *institutionalize* a practice, process, or service is to change it from a poorly organized and informal activity into a highly organized and formal one.

Attempts to institutionalize the practice of political deliberation have led to the development of the elaborate codes of parliamentary procedure which pervade the Congress of the United States, the House of Commons, and the other parliaments of Europe. This is one of the areas in politics in which Western man has been most significantly innovative. *Jefferson's Manual of Parliamentary Practice* and *Robert's Rules of Order,* although they might look rather dull now, represent the accretion and culmination of a long struggle to cope with the intense practical problems of deliberation and decision-making.

The history of parliamentary government is in a sense the history of parliamentary procedure. In England such procedure is particularly impressive because the British have been especially alert to its importance and have been remarkably inventive in connection with it. A whole range of procedures which we now consider matters of course, such as referral to a committee, putting a motion, and amending a motion, were developed in the course of the last 700 years. One reason why democratic schemes of government sometimes do not function in emergent nations is that they have not developed these habits of parliamentary procedure. The frequent failures of parliamentary government in continental Europe have been due in some part also to a lack of sound procedural rules for getting at the work of deliberation in parliamentary bodies.

The word "parliament" comes from the French *parler,* which means "to talk." Theorists in Europe sometimes have said of European parliaments, "Parliamentary government is government by talk." A German theorist called it, *"Das ewige Gespräch,"* the eternal dialogue. Holders of such views forget that English parliamentary procedure developed continually not in terms of talk, but in terms of how to reach decisions. It is important to understand that in decision-making through deliberation, one cannot wait indefinitely. The business of government must get on. The English House of Commons until the last century afforded unlimited protection for all people who wanted to talk, including protection for holders of minority opinions, and was able to get its business done. But then the Irish Independence Movement produced a group of Members of Parliament who were not at all interested in arriving at any decision. They wished to sabotage decisions, to prevent them from being reached. Accordingly, they drew on the technique of deliberately wasting time, the *filibuster*, which the United States Senate had originated in 1825 and has since perfected.[1] What could Parliament do? It was supposed to reach a decision, yet certain Members utilized the rules of procedure not to get the job done, but to prevent it from being done. At the crucial point, the Speaker of the House of Commons, its chairman, made a decision, as he could because of an old tradition in English procedure. He exercised his right to recognize. He decided not to recognize any more speakers from the Irish contingent, and that was the end of legislative filibustering in England. Only in England would this have been appreciated as being the decisive political step it actually was. This step, of course, has since developed into a variety of rules for ending debate and bringing the matter to a vote, the so-called rules of closure or *cloture* which operate in all parliaments and which play an important part in getting things done.[2]

On the other hand, the decision-making process works best without extreme limitations of time. Robert Kennedy pointed out the crucial role that time plays in decision-making in *Thirteen Days* under the heading, "Some of the Things We Learned." The Kennedy group learned that "if we had to make a decision in twenty-four hours, I believe the course that we ultimately would have taken would have been quite different and filled with far greater risk." The alternative of taking military action was the more obvious way to respond to the threat. Thus if the group had had only twenty-four hours it would have supported military action. But having time to talk and to deliberate, they could consider a wider range of consequences and options. This made it possible for them to arrive at a better decision. Group experiments, simulating the making of major decisions, confirm this view. The greater the pressures of time, and the more simple-minded the participants, the more extreme and warlike the decisions are likely to be. Similar experiences from real life are summed up in the proverb: "Decide in haste, repent at leisure."

[1] The custom of filibustering began in the United States Senate in 1825, when John Randolph of Virginia began making long speeches which John C. Calhoun refused to rule out of order. By custom, it had always been the chair's privilege to limit debate, previous to 1825. By 1872 filibustering had itself become a custom, to the extent that Vice-President Schuyler Colfax ruled that the chair could not restrain a senator from remarks the senator considered pertinent. The practice is definitely American by invention as well as by extent of use. A filibustering senator will speak at inordinate length—for days if necessary—until his strength gives out or until he is relieved by another filibustering colleague. The method is impractical for a single individual, but can be quite effective for a dozen senators of adequate endurance.

[2] The real basis of the filibuster is the tolerance of the majority whose members usually refrain from voting *cloture*—that is, for ending the debate and bringing the matter to a vote. Until 1967 the rules of the Senate provided that cloture could be voted only by two-thirds majority of all members of the Senate, that is, sixty-seven votes. Since then the requirement has been lowered to a two-thirds majority of those senators present and voting—generally a much smaller number. Efforts to change the majority needed for cloture to three-fifths, or even to a bare majority, have continued, thus far without results.

Another thing which Robert Kennedy said he learned was the importance of keeping such deliberations entirely secret. If the deliberations had been publicized, he said, the final decision would have been hastily made, and would have entailed far greater risks. Very often the need for secrecy while deliberating is forgotten by those who believe that publicity is always a good thing. Publicity can be an obstacle and can lead to bad decisions. When you publicize discussions, some politicians or officials will no longer stick to the job at hand but will play to the galleries. They will talk with a view to what is going to be said in print rather than to its pertinence to the discussion. For this reason, in most parliaments today deliberations have been transferred from the publicized general debate to committees which can bar publicity. Very few people realize that the British Parliament deliberated entirely in secret until the nineteenth century, not because of disdain for the general public, but because Parliament still saw itself as essentially opposed to the monarchy and believed that the King and his councillors should not know who had said what in Parliament. As Parliament became stronger, this need for secrecy declined, but secrecy still has its uses in modern deliberative processes.

The Representation of Special Interests and the Deliberative Process.   According to some classic theories, deliberation should be carried out by wise men impartially pondering the common good. No selfish thoughts or special interests are supposed to distract them. In practice, however, few politicians are that wise, or unselfish, or free from links to special interests. Indeed, if they were any or all of these, they would not be representative of most of the people they are supposed to represent.

In the United States, most people believe in representative government and also in government by deliberation. They rarely notice the tension between these two concepts. Calling a legislator the *representative* of his constituents may seem one of four different things. First, he may be a true *sample* of his voters in his opinions, personality, and circumstances. Without any special instructions from them, and knowing neither more nor less than they, he may represent perfectly their passions, prejudices, and experiences. The ancient Athenians sometimes chose representatives of this kind by casting lots among the voters, and even today some old-line American politicians, representing relatively homogeneous constituencies, try to look and sound like perfect samples of the folks back home.

Second, a representative may simply be a *messenger* or deputy carrying out the instructions of his constituents. He will then vote exactly as they have told him to; his own knowledge or judgment on the matter will be irrelevant. Ex-President John Quincy Adams in the 1820s indignantly refused to serve in the United States Senate as this kind of "messenger boy" for his constituents—who elected him just the same. Third, a representative may serve his constituents much as a doctor or lawyer serves his patients or clients. He may act as a *trustee* for their best interests, but use his own superior knowledge and experience to judge what their true interests are and how they should be served. Edmund Burke insisted on this role in his famous letter to his constituents in Bristol: "Your representative owes you, not his industry only, but his judgment; and he betrays, instead of serves you, if he sacrifices it to your opinion." Burke, too, was elected. Finally, if his constituency includes a wide variety of groups and interests, the representative's role may be that of a *broker*. Ever mindful of the need to be re-elected, he will then arrange coalitions and compromises among his constituents, carry out whatever consensus emerges, and keep a shrewd eye on his most influential or financially powerful supporters.

A real representative must be a mixture of all four of these roles. Unlike a doctor or lawyer, he has much greater power to bind by his decisions those whom he represents. They cannot easily or quickly recall him or change the laws he has passed. They will feel safer therefore if his habits and interests are similar to theirs—or at least seem to be so—and if he is willing to carry out their will whenever they express it clearly and explicitly. They will be pleased, however, if he can engineer a higher degree of consensus among them, and if he uses his superior competence to serve their interests and to make their will prevail.

But only one of these four views of the role of a representative—that of a trustee or professional counselor—is compatible with the idea of government by deliberation. The other three concepts of a representative—as a sample, messenger, or broker—are not. The actual process of representative government, therefore, and in particular of legislation, resembles a bubbling stew of occasional calm deliberation and frequent struggles among interests.

In a viable democratic state, the many special interests of different groups will overlap to such a degree that the notion of a common good will have real meaning for all or most of them. Conversely, groups whose diverging interests are so large that they dwarf the few interests they have in common cannot be kept together in a well-functioning democracy. This is one of the reasons that the United States was pulled apart in the decades before the Civil War. The divergent interests of slavery vs. free labor, free trade vs. protection, debtor vs. creditor, cotton and tobacco growing vs. industry, and the competition between rival transcontinental railroad projects—all these causes for quarrels between North and South outgrew the social and political bonds between the sections while leaving intact the unity of each. Every President between 1852 and 1860 was weak because there was no strong coalition to support him.

Similarly, when Frenchmen in the late 1930s became badly divided between the leftist coalition led by Léon Blum and the rightist groups who later united behind Pierre Laval and Marshal Pétain, many conservatives were quoted as saying: "Rather Hitler than Blum." When in 1939 the left coalition split again, France was ready to fall before the first Nazi armored column that entered the country in the following year.

These are not only matters of history. They could happen again in any country, including the United States. The American people could become deeply divided between conservatives and radicals, blacks and whites, affluent suburbanites and impoverished slum dwellers, militarists and pacifists, Protestants and Catholics, old stock Americans and those of more recent immigrant descent, the hip and the square, the young and the old. None of these cleavages coincides exactly with any other. Between them, they could split and cross-divide the American people so thoroughly that no common political will could be formed. In that event, no coalition could be organized strong enough to bring about reforms, and nothing could be done to maintain the paralyzed political system.

It takes not only the skill of political leaders but also a genuine community of interests to ensure a happy political outcome. Where interests overlap sufficiently, their pursuit is compatible with true deliberation and compromise in the framework of representative government. In such cases, the decisions arrived at are likely to have the authority of law.

One Product of Deliberation: Law.   A *law* is a general rule, deciding not a single case but a whole class of cases. Under the English and American tradition, a vote of a legislature to penalize a specifically named individual—a "bill of attainder"—cannot be a law. In the United States, it is forbidden by the Constitution (Article I, Section 9, Paragraph 3). The main tasks of law are three: to make the operations of government predictable, technically consistent with each other, and morally legitimate—that is, consistent with the main value patterns of the community.

Not every general rule, therefore, is a law. Even though it is general, it may not be enforced by the government or, more importantly, complied with by the people or by even the government's own officials. In any of these cases, the effects of the operations of the government cannot be reliably predicted. The rule then will be obeyed sometimes, and sometimes not; and no one will know which to expect. Thus the Volstead Act of 1920, prohibiting the sale of alcoholic beverages, was disobeyed by a large part of the American people, and by many government officials, while other officials tried to enforce it unsuccessfully. The legal restrictions imposed on those who use electronic surveillance devices such as wire-tapping also have been disregarded frequently by law enforcement officials, including those within the federal government, sometimes with the approval of cabinet officers and even of the White House. On the other hand, most of the laws in the world's highly developed countries are complied with and enforced to a remarkably high degree. In the 1950s and 1960s, the United States collected more than half of its revenue by means of a federal income tax on individuals and corporations, for which only one individual tax return out of twenty had to be checked each year.

Effective laws limit the actions of the government itself, so that people can know what the government will and will not do. In contrast to governments dependent on the whims of absolute princes, or of modern dictators, constitutional governments are meant to be "governments of laws, not of men."

To ensure predictable and lawful rule, a whole array of political machinery has been created. The role of the lawmaker in most countries has been made a specialized full-time job. Legislators are subject to election and re-election so that they must win and retain the confidence of the voters of their constituency. In most advanced countries, national legislators are adequately paid so as to keep legislative office from being a monopoly for those rich enough to afford it, or for those subsidized by special economic interests.

The laws which legislators make must pass through a repeated process of deliberation. In the United States, Britain, France, the German Federal Republic, and even in the Soviet Union, the national legislatures are divided into two chambers, with most of the proposed legislation being scrutinized by each. (In the Soviet Union, as we shall see in this chapter, most of the scrutinizing occurs within the top echelons of the Communist Party.) In addition, in most countries, proposed laws are first submitted as drafts, then discussed and amended in committees of each legislative chamber, then debated, possibly amended, and finally voted on by each full legislative body. In many countries, this final vote has to be repeated. In the British House of Commons and the German Bundestag, bills are required to pass three separate readings; and in the United States House of Representatives, money bills must pass once as an *authorization* for the government to spend the money, and a second time as an *appropriation,* allocating to the government the actual money to be spent—often in a less generous amount. Before final passage, the different versions of a bill passed by the two chambers have to be reconciled; in the United States, this is done by joint *conference committees* of the United States Senate and House of Representatives. Finally, in many countries the bill still must receive the signature of the chief executive, or else it must be passed once again over his veto by a larger legislative majority. Only then is the bill ready for promulgation to the public, usually in print—which is the last step in the making of a law.

Separation of Powers. The elaborate machinery of the law-making process is meant to ensure that laws will be considered and formulated carefully, and that the bulk of the population—as well as the major interest groups in the country—will recognize the laws passed as legitimate. Inevitably, this process consumes a great deal of time, except in war or other rare emergencies, when legislatures may quickly pass laws delegating sweeping powers to the executive. In constitutional governments of the Western type, however, such delegation of emergency powers is exceptional.

The separation of the deliberative process—the legislative as well as the judicial—from the carrying out of laws has remained the basic rule. This is the famous *separation of powers:* the principle according to which the legislative, judiciary, and executive powers are to be separate and independent from each other so as to provide a system of checks and balances that limits the powers of the government and safeguards the rights of individuals. Under this arrangement, the legislative power deliberates and decides about the making of general laws; the judiciary power—that is, the courts—deliberates and decides about applying these general laws to particular cases; and the executive power gives effect to the decisions of the two other branches.

This doctrine is well designed to protect individuals from the police, civilians from the military, and property owners from expropriation and the tax collector. It encourages governments to wait rather than to act, and to do less rather than more. It was formulated in the eighteenth century by Montesquieu and other theorists of the Enlightenment who sought to protect the rights of relatively rich or self-sufficient individuals against absolutist rule, at the risk of making government slower, and sometimes weaker. Poorer people who urgently needed the help of government often preferred quick public action at some risk to their liberties. The best balance between liberty and speed is thus a matter of group interest as well as of political design.

Separation of powers has been put into practice most thoroughly in the Constitution of the United States. It has been used less in Britain, where the Prime Minister is merely the leader of the House of Commons, dependent on its confidence; and where the Cabinet is in effect a committee of the House. Each branch of the American government is limited in its lawful powers. In Britain, by contrast, as legal scholar John Austin saw it, there was not a thing between heaven and earth Parliament could not do. In the German Federal Republic, there is a greater separation of the three powers of government than in Britain, but less than in the United States. And the Fifth Republic of France concentrates a large proportion of power in the hands of the President as chief executive.

The Merging of Powers: The Soviet System.　Under the Soviet system of government, the principle of separation of powers has been explicitly rejected. According to Lenin, the Soviet state was to be the instrument of a social revolution, directed by a highly disciplined party of professional revolutionaries who could foresee in part the course of future history. This revolution was to get its power from the backing of Russia's industrial working class and the much larger mass of Russia's poor and "middling" peasants. In Marxian theory the result of this coalition of workers and peasants was to be a "dictatorship of the proletariat," that is, "the dictatorship of the vast majority in the interest of the vast majority." In practice, it implied the predominance of the workers over the peasants, and very soon the predominance of the Communist Party, many of whose leaders were intellectuals, over the working class. Within a decade after the Communists' seizure of power in Russia in 1917, the Soviet regime had become in effect the dictatorship of a small group of party leaders and officials over the bulk of the Communist Party membership and the Russian people. The circle of persons exercising decisive power in Russia thus had become much smaller than Marx and even Lenin had envisaged. But the manner in which power was wielded was close to Lenin's conception in at least one respect. "Dictatorship," he had written, "is a rule based directly on force and unrestricted by any law."

In setting up the government of the U.S.S.R., Lenin adopted the institution of councils, or *soviets*, of deputies of workers, peasants, and the local population. Such soviets had sprung up spontaneously in the unsuccessful revolution of 1905, and they had reappeared in greater strength in the revolutionary turmoil of 1917. Some soviets were formed for large factories or other economic enterprises; other soviets were formed for city blocks or neighborhoods, and for villages and rural districts. Deputies for each soviet were often elected publicly in meetings of fellow workers in factories or in meetings of their neighbors in local units. These local soviets in turn elected higher councils of deputies for larger cities and regions. This ladder of indirect elections eventually culminated in an All-Union Soviet which was formally the highest organ of the Soviet government. The whole procedure lent itself very well to the leadership and eventual domination by the Communist Party. The hierarchy of councils served as a multistage amplifier, or as the Communists called it, a "transmission belt," by which a few tens of thousands, and later hundreds of thousands, of Communists could govern a country which in 1917 numbered 150 million people.

This view of government excluded a separation of powers. Each soviet was not only to deliberate about what was to be done within its area of control but was also to carry out whatever acts its members agreed upon. It thus was to be both a legislative and an executive body. The courts, of course, likewise were to be an instrument of soviet power with no independence for judges. "All powers to the soviets!" ran the 1917 revolutionary slogan. When power shifted from the soviets to the Communist Party, legislative and executive tasks remained merged.

In the half-century that followed, the Soviet Union turned into a modern industrial country, with increasing specialization of political, administrative, and judicial roles, and with growing pressures towards some separation of its governmental powers. Since the mid-1950s the demands for greater respect for judicial independence and "socialist legality" have been increasing. The limits and prospects of these trends will be discussed in Chapter 11, but they suggest in any case that the existence of some degree of separation of powers may not be a mere "middle-class prejudice" but may fit some of the needs of any highly advanced society.

Cabinet Solidarity and Democratic Centralism.

To some extent, however, there are in most political systems some bodies which both deliberate and execute. The British Cabinet deliberates about policy but then it must carry it out. Hence its members are free to oppose a policy before it has been decided on, and to advocate another course of action.

But once the decision has been made, all Cabinet members are obliged to support it in public, even if they had opposed it earlier. If any member should be unwilling to do this, he must leave the Cabinet. The Cabinet and the National Security Council in the United States have a similar practice.

The Communist Party in the Soviet Union, as well as Communist parties in other countries, extend this obligation to all members. They may debate freely a proposed policy, at least in theory, before a decision has been made on it. After the decision, however, they must support the official policy that has been set, even if it runs counter to their own judgment. In Communist parlance, this practice is called *democratic centralism*. British writers speak of *cabinet solidarity*. To the more limited practices in the United States, people apply such looser terms as "party regularity," or "loyalty" to the administration and the President.

In all cases, the practice derives from the union of deliberation and execution in the same body. (Members of a legislature—or of the electorate—usually are free to continue criticizing a majority decision and to agitate for its reversal.) It clearly makes it easier to get things done, but it exacts a price. Those who opposed the decision now must support it, perhaps against their own convictions; and since they may no longer criticize it, a mistaken decision is less likely to be corrected or reversed.

If problems are very urgent, and weakness is a greater danger than error, then cabinet solidarity or "democratic centralism" may seem preferable. If problems are less urgent, if resources of wealth and power are abundant, and if the risks of error are great and its likely consequences serious, then separation of powers with its continuing opportunities for debate and reconsideration might seem preferable. In the short run, therefore, American institutions may not fit the needs of poor countries which face as their most critical task an increase in the power of the government to deal with urgent social and economic problems. But in the long run, increasing wealth as well as the increasing costs of large errors in a highly politicized and technological society may make the separation of powers desirable for a larger number of countries.

Decision-Making by the Judiciary.   Another important aspect of the concept of separation of powers relates to the deliberations and decisions carried on by the judiciary in most countries. The courts have developed an elaborate procedural law or custom about how to arrive at decisions. In most countries, the rule of secrecy in the deliberations of the judiciary, after hearing arguments in open court, has always been observed. If Americans were to insist that what the Supreme Court justices say to each other be made public—or what jurors say to each other in the jury room—the outcry from the legal fraternity would be loud and clear. Most lawyers and judges would argue that it would not be possible to arrive at good decisions in this way. Hence, how judges or juries arrive at their decisions is much less well known than how presidents or legislative bodies arrive at theirs.

Anyone who talks about deliberating on decisions and policy must not limit himself to the executive and legislative branches but should bear in mind that in free societies the judiciary is also involved in the deliberative act. The deliberative process of judges to some extent is organized within the open court. The so-called *adversary procedure* by which lawyers present their cases is an organization of deliberation. Each lawyer cites the cases and data that support his position. Then the court (or the judges) withdraws into private chambers and tries to sort out the arguments for the purpose of eventually arriving at its decision. This is the process that Justice Benjamin Cardozo emphasized in his book, *The Judicial Process,* which undertook to analyze how judges arrive at their decisions.

In the United States, the substance of judicial decisions can be far-reaching indeed. Back in 1803, the case of *Marbury vs. Madison* established the right of the Supreme Court to review the actions of Congress and the executive branch. In 1810 the case of *Fletcher vs. Peck* extended *judicial review* to the acts of legislatures, and in 1819 the *Dartmouth College* case put contracts anywhere in the country under federal protection. Since that time, the United States has always been a machinery for the production of "judge-made law" to supplement and correct or balance the laws made by Congress, the state legislatures, and the rule-making power of administrative agencies.

Judicial review offers an additional opportunity for redress to citizens whose needs and rights as individuals or members of minority groups have found no adequate response in the legislative process. In *Plessy vs. Ferguson* in 1897, the Supreme Court established the "separate but equal" doctrine, according to which separate public schools for Negro children were legal but had to be equal—in theory at least—to schools for white children, in the equipment, teaching staffs, and educational opportunities they offered. More than half a century later, in *Brown vs. Board of Education of Topeka* in 1954, the Supreme Court decided that there was in fact no possible equality for Negro children in segregated schools. Segregation by race, the Court held, in itself was doing an injury to children; and it had to be ended in all public schools "with all deliberate speed." Fifteen years later, in 1969, perhaps 90 per cent or more of black children in the five states of the Deep South of the United States were still attending segregated schools, as compared to the virtually 100 per cent in 1954 when the Court first issued its decision. In October 1969 the Supreme Court under a new Chief Justice, Warren E. Burger, broke with the doctrine of "deliberate speed." Dual school systems—that is, segregated ones—were to be terminated "at once" in public education everywhere in the United States. Local authorities were to put into operation "immediately" unitary public school systems "within which no person is to be effectively excluded from any school because of race or color." Enforcement of this order, or its failure, will be a test of American government in the 1970s.

Though the direct impact of the Court on actual practice was slow and limited, its impact on the climate of American thought and on the long-term trends of politics was profound. In 1957, 86 per cent of southern white voters in a poll said that school integration would never come. Six years later, in 1963, only 46 per cent still clung to this thought. In nationwide polls, 67 per cent of voters in 1962 said they could not accept a Negro as President of the United States. Seven years later, in 1969, only 34 per cent still held to this view. A series of Supreme Court decisions, supported by the mass media, by important political groups, by the efforts of black Americans themselves, and by the spontaneous responses of millions of young people, had transformed race discrimination from a majority prejudice into a minority one. The main direction of American thought had been set on a new course of speed and urgency; and the new setting seemed to be irreversible.

Federalism: A Political Invention

Unitary vs. Confederal Governments.   Every government has two major tasks which may be in competition with each other. The first of these is to concentrate most of the forces and resources of its population on a single common goal or the pursuit of several such goals. *Common goals* may be the winning of independence, victory in war, the purchase of a large territory, the rapid industrialization of the country, the fending off of some major external or internal threat against the integrity of the system or some valued institution, or, on the contrary, the making of some desired major political, social, educational, or economic change. In all such cases the government has to mobilize, unify, and apply the power of the people. It must organize them so that they can form a common will which they are collectively capable of carrying out.

An equally important task of every government is to respond to the needs of its population. The more diverse the population is, the more different will be the needs and wishes of various groups and regions. The more powerful we wish a government to be in order to do the things on which most people agree, that is, in order to achieve common goals, the more unified and centralized the government should be and the larger the population and geographic area under its direct control. Such a centralized government is known as a *unitary* form of government. But the more we want the government to respond quickly and adequately to the needs of many different groups and localities, the more decentralized and localized it has to be, the more it must be a *confederal* form of government. The Swiss Confederation, a government of many diverse ethnic and political elements, was almost totally decentralized for over 500 years. Each canton, or self-governing region, was a small sovereign state well suited to respond to the needs of its inhabitants, or at least to the needs of the most influential among them. In contrast, although respected for their success in unifying power, the great centralized monarchies from ancient Rome to eighteenth-century Britain, France, Russia, and Prussia were deficient in the ability to respond to diverse popular needs.

When the American colonies declared their independence, their leaders were familiar with both types of government, unitary and confederal. They knew the large monarchies of their time; they knew the small republics such as Venice; they knew the Confederation of the Swiss. But they needed a government that would combine the strength of both types of government, and in due course they invented it. They started out in 1776 with an alliance; seven years later they turned it into a confederation, somewhat like that of the Swiss but with stronger provisions for common interests and actions; and still later in 1787 they started drafting a federal constitution. This constitution was ratified in 1791 and to this day has remained in essence the basic United States charter of government.

Federal Unions vs. Confederacies.   A federal union of states differs from a *confederacy* in four main respects. First, a federal government is relatively strong in regard to organization, personnel, budget, and jurisdiction. Ordinarily, it is stronger in all these respects than the government of any of its constituent states. In a confederacy, the common institutions are weak or nearly nonexistent in some or all of these respects. They are much weaker than the corresponding institutions of the major states that make up the confederacy.

In the second place, while federal governments act directly upon individuals in all matters within the scope of the national government, the government of a confederacy ordinarily deals with individuals only indirectly, through the state governments and their administrations. A federal government can collect taxes, raise armies, and enforce its own decisions, but a confederacy depends for all these matters on what the states will do for it, or what resources the states will give it.

In the third place, states often may secede from a confederacy, if their own governments or voters so desire, whereas such secession is not permitted in a federal union. In the Soviet Union, the major republics have in theory the right to secede. The actual structure and distribution of power, however, which resembles that of a federation or even of a unitary state, has made secession impractical, and few, if any, Soviet citizens appear to mind.

Fourth and finally, within the sphere of federal jurisdiction, the laws of a federal union usually prevail over those of the states, and the state governments are expected to obey them and carry them out. In a confederacy, however, a law or decision of the confederal authorities becomes valid in a state only if the state government endorses it, or at least does not exercise its right to veto its application within the state. (The latter doctrine is known as *nullification*, since it holds that each state can "nullify" at will within its own territory any federal law of which it disapproves. This doctrine was advocated mainly between 1798 and 1830 by some southern leaders in the United States and was finally buried by the outcome of the Civil War.)

All four differences make it likely that, among countries comparable in size and in military and economic power, a confederacy will be much weaker than a federation. In the American Civil War, some southern states withheld at critical moments needed troops, weapons, and supplies from the Confederate Army. The leaders of these states believed so thoroughly in states' rights that they were more concerned with upholding this doctrine than with preventing the defeat of their own confederacy and the victory of the North.

If a country is too large and diverse to accept a unitary government, and if it needs more effective power and performance than a confederacy can produce, then federal union seems to be the most effective form of government so far discovered. If people in the various states are not ready politically, socially, culturally, or economically to accept a federal union, then a confederation may be the best that can be organized and made to work for the time being, and it may prepare the way for federation at a later stage.

The Dual Nature of Federalist Government.   *Federalism* consists in putting every individual under two governments at one and the same time. So far as the individual is concerned, these governments coincide in domain but differ in scope. Each of them has a claim to the individual's obedience in some respects but not in others. One of these governments, the national or *federal*, governs the entire country. The other, the *state* in the United States and India, the *province* in Canada, the *union republic* in the Soviet Union, the *canton* in Switzerland, and the *Lands (Länder)* in the German Federal Republic, usually governs only a relatively small part of the country. Thus each of the two most populous states in the United States—California and New York—has less than 10 per cent of the total population. Together, however, the several states of the Union include most of the country's population with only a small part living in federal districts or territories. (Nowadays the states make up most of the geographic area of the United States, but there have been times in American history when the thinly populated federal territories contained more square miles than the states.)

Some of these other small political units may include a larger part of their country's national population than do their counterparts in the

United States. The provinces of Quebec and Ontario each includes more than one-quarter of the Canadian population; the Lands of North Rhine-Westphalia includes nearly one-third of the population of West Germany; and the Russian Soviet Federal Socialist Republic (RSFSR)—itself a federation—includes more than one-half the population of the Soviet Union.

Throughout the national territory, the scope of the federal or national government includes jurisdiction in foreign affairs and other matters assigned to it by the country's constitution or through subsequent usage. In the United States these matters include national defense, interstate commerce and transport, protection of contracts, and several more; the states have primary jurisdiction over civil and criminal law, public order and the police power, education, and—a peculiarity of the United States—the conditions for voting in both state and federal elections.

In some areas, federal and state jurisdictions overlap. In the United States, both levy taxes, but the state governments are restrained by the practical fact that if their taxes become too heavy the richer taxpayers and business firms may move into another state. This has been one of the reasons for the migration of the textile industry from New England to the South. It explains why many New York business executives prefer to live in Connecticut or New Jersey and why some Californians establish legal residence in Nevada. It also explains why some national corporations maintain headquarters in Delaware. In contrast to state taxes, federal taxes cannot be easily avoided in this manner; any large sums needed for public purposes must be raised by the federal government on a nationwide scale. When taxpayer organizations cry "states' rights," they are in reality trying to keep the government from effectively collecting large amounts of tax money and are thus opposing the domestic programs for which these funds are required.

The Assignment of Residual Powers.   No constitution and no tradition can provide for every specific situation. Which government, federal or state, has the *residual powers*—that is, the responsibility and legal power—for dealing with those tasks that have not been assigned to either?

In Canada and India, following British tradition, such residual powers are reserved to the national government. In the Soviet Union, of course, the powers of the national government are overwhelming. For this reason, some writers doubt that these governments should be called "federal" in the strictest sense since the balance between the nation and the smaller political units seems to be heavily weighted in the national government's favor.

In the United States the ratifiers of the *Tenth Amendment* of the Constitution (Article X of the Bill of Rights) tried explicitly to reserve these powers to the states: "The powers not delegated to the United States by the

Constitution, nor prohibited by it to the states," they said, "are reserved to the states respectively, or to the people." In the Preamble to the Constitution, however, the framers had listed among the purposes for which the federal union and its government were being founded the promotion of the "general welfare" of the people of the United States. From the days of Alexander Hamilton to those of Franklin D. Roosevelt and the present, national statesmen and federal courts have held that this *general welfare clause* in the Constitution empowers the federal government to deal with a wide variety of tasks of which the Founding Fathers never even dreamed. The constitutions of Switzerland and of West Germany in their own ways achieve a similar balance between the powers of the federal government and those of the states.

The "Sovereign Equality" of States and Nations.   Another mark of federalism is the far-reaching degree of equality among the smaller political units composing a federal system. All the states, large and small, are legally equal. In some federal systems the states also have equal representation in one house of the national legislature as in the United States Senate or, in somewhat different form, in the Soviet of Nationalities in the Soviet Union. Such equal representation of states implies, of course, an overrepresentation of the voters of the smallest states. As most Americans know and many city dwellers lament, the 320,000 people of Wyoming, as well as the 450,000 people of Nevada, have as many senators in the United States Senate as the nearly 20 million people of California or New York. If all the senators from all the small states should vote together, less than one-fifth of the American people would command a majority of the Senate. Similar problems exist elsewhere. Switzerland follows the same principle of equal representation for large and small cantons, though some small units are defined as "half-cantons." The German Federal Republic compromises; it gives the larger Länder a somewhat larger representation in the federal council, but still overrepresents the smaller ones.

In genuine federal systems, the national government cannot legally abolish any state or remove its officers or judges. Neither can any state or group of states abolish the federal government or secede from it. (This last point was disputed in the United States from 1771 to 1861, but was settled by the Civil War. In Switzerland it was also settled by civil war—a minor one in 1847.) A federal constitution can be amended only by the nation as a whole, acting through a substantial majority and by procedures which each constitution provides.

In emergencies, a federal government may determine that some state government has become temporarily incapable of functioning and may take measures to appoint officers for the duration of the incapacity. It may also send federal marshals or troops into a state in order to enforce federal laws or court decisions, as the United States did in the 1950s in Little

Rock, Arkansas and Tuscaloosa, Alabama. In a genuinely federal system, however, all such actions are subject to review by independent courts. These safeguards contrast with the practice of some Latin American republics which have federal "paper" constitutions but where the national government and army intervene freely in the affairs of the states.

The element of equality distinguishes the powers of states in a federal system from the important but lesser powers of local and city governments within the states. In day-to-day administration, the governments of towns, cities, counties, villages, and districts form a third layer of government, which is by no means equal to the other layers. To a greater or lesser degree, these local units are the creatures of the states in the United States, the cantons in Switzerland, or the Länder in West Germany. In the United States, a state can revoke or amend the charter of a city; acting through its legislature of a state constitutional convention, it can merge cities or counties, or abolish them. In other federal systems, local governments are similarly subject to decisions by the states, and in unitary states, they are ruled by the national government. Nowhere in modern countries do local governments enjoy to any significant degree sovereign equality with the other layers of government.

If the proof of a pudding is in the eating, the proof of federalism is in administrative practice and in spending money. Although many taxes have to be collected nationally for reasons discussed earlier, in any system of "living federalism," a large part of the money collected as taxes has to be spent in states and localities by governments closer and more responsive to local needs than the national government. National budgets and bureaucracies have grown spectacularly with the increase in the scope of government; however state and local personnel and budgets have not declined either. They have grown along with those of the national government, albeit sometimes more slowly. State and local governments are now spending a smaller slice of the political pie than formerly. In the United States between 1900 and the 1960s their share declined from nearly 70 per cent to only 40 per cent; the comparable Swiss figures are 75 per cent and 50 per cent respectively. But the whole political pie is now much bigger. Gross national products have increased and so has the share of the public sector in them. State and local governments are therefore likely to play a large and vigorous role for many years to come in most of the world's existing federal systems. And such systems are quite likely to spread.

Getting Things Done: Executive Responsibility and Party Government

In his memoirs, Winston Churchill recalled a remark he made to Stalin and Roosevelt during the conference at Teheran. They had to remember, he told them, that they could go home and whatever they had agreed to at

Teheran would stand, whereas if he brought back anything unacceptable to Parliament he could be overthrown on the day of his return to Britain. What Churchill sought to indicate to Stalin and Roosevelt was that he was directly responsible to the majority in the House of Commons and therefore was not quite as free as they to yield on points that might be controversial. In a way this was a true remark; and it does represent a conventional view of the difference between the British government, on the one hand, and the American and Soviet governments on the other. But in another way, at least as far as Roosevelt was concerned, it was not quite accurate. Fundamentally, there are two kinds of political power—closely controlled and relatively uncontrolled—and there are two kinds of executives, those with wide powers of decision and those with narrow powers only.

Executive Discretion.   The word "executive" suggests by its derivation that someone executes what has been decided either by him or by others, but more particularly by others. The things to be executed are primarily laws that need to be enforced. In the language of the United States Constitution (Article II, Section 3), the chief executive "shall take care that the laws be faithfully executed." From this point of view, executives have little choice but to carry out the general commands of lawmaking and voters.

In government, as in business, however, executives have a good deal of *discretion*, that is, a range of choice, about what they put into effect. In business corporations or universities, executives execute what they as directors or trustees first have decided upon as policy. This practice to some extent also holds true for governments. Although government officials are formally called upon to execute what others have decided, they actually propose a great deal of what is decided and then execute if afterwards. Where others have chosen a policy for the executives to carry out, the latter may choose to delay or not to act at all, citing various reasons for procrastination. Moreover, executing a decision inevitably runs into difficulties and problems which require some changes in the original policy or rule. There is thus some range of discretion, large or small, which must be granted any executive. The range of discretion given to him goes far in determining the extent of his power before he decides. *Responsibility* then determines the rewards or penalties he is likely to receive for having decided as he did (see Table 8.1).

Responsibility and Power.   Power that is subject to control is different from power not subject to such restrictions. In a famous dictum, a distinguished nineteenth-century British liberal, Lord Acton, said, "All power tends to corrupt and absolute power corrupts absolutely." But in a very real sense power is hardly ever absolute. Even the power of Stalin

Table 8.1

Executive Discretion and Responsibility

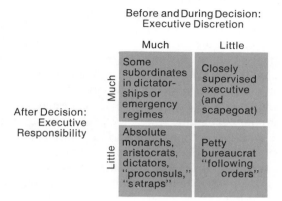

		Before and During Decision: Executive Discretion	
		Much	Little
After Decision: Executive Responsibility	Much	Some subordinates in dictatorships or emergency regimes	Closely supervised executive (and scapegoat)
	Little	Absolute monarchs, aristocrats, dictators, "proconsuls," "satraps"	Petty bureaucrat "following orders"

and Hitler, while very great, was not absolute. All executives, and all rulers, even in dictatorships, are limited by what their subjects and subordinates can do, and by what they will stand for. As these capabilities and compliance habits change, the ruler's power changes with them.

To be *responsible* is to be controlled by someone else; those to whom an actor is responsible are his controllers. In the language of our model of a political system in Chapter 7, responsibility depends on a circuit of communication channels, and responsible behavior is a feedback process. To say that an individual or group which holds power is responsible to some other person or group is to say several things all at once. First, it means that there is a channel of communication through which signals about the behavior of the responsible actor are transmitted to his controllers, that is, to those to whom he is responsible. Second, it means that his controllers are receiving and interpreting these signals, checking them against their own memories as to which of his actions or omissions they will reward or penalize, and within what limits. Third, it means that his controllers have a channel through which they actually can apply these rewards or penalties to the actor whom they control, and that they are able and motivated to do so.

Thus, in most situations descretion does not mean arbitrary power. Although it seems to be the nature of discretion to leave it to the individual to decide what he is to do, the executive who has been granted some discretion does not have leave to do whatever he pleases. In theory, he is bound by the goal that has been defined. (If he acts for reasons irrelevant to the goal, we may condemn his action as *arbitrary* or capricious.) In practice, he is bound by the persons and organizations to whom he must report: by their capacity to keep informed of his actions; by their ability to reward or punish him for his conduct, or to remove him from office; and by their memories and motivations to use their powers to make their supervision of him and sanctions of his action effective.

Although no executive power is unlimited, not all rulers know the limits of their power, nor do they all know the persons and groups upon whom these limits depend. It is this knowledge which makes the difference between responsible and *irresponsible power*. A political actor may in fact be responsible to someone else without knowing it. We then say that he acts irresponsibly, but that in the end his responsibility may be brought home to him, perhaps quite painfully. A hot rod driver may career irresponsibly through traffic until forcibly reminded of his responsibility to other drivers and to his family by a policeman or an accident. After the Japanese attacked Pearl Harbor, President Franklin D. Roosevelt said that the warlords of Japan had "started this war but the massed angry forces of humanity will finish it." The famous words of Louis XV of France, "After us, the deluge," are a supreme example of political irresponsibility; his successor, Louis XVI, paid for it with his head. Some of our present-day advocates of preventive nuclear war, too, do not seem to have progressed much beyond the level of the Bourbons.

To act responsibly means to act with the knowledge that one is going to be held accountable for one's actions, and to know in what ways and to whom, one is accountable. A power holder may be responsible to some group or individual outside his immediate establishment; for example, a United States President is responsible to Congress, and also to the people. Or a power holder may be responsible to insiders, the superiors in his own organization. Thus officials within the federal executive establishment ordinarily are responsible in the United States to the President. There may also be a pattern of responsibility beyond the boundaries of a power holder's national establishment—a responsibility which Adolf Hitler and others like him did not understand.

Party Government and Power.   We may now return to the remark of Churchill to Roosevelt and Stalin. There is indeed a difference between executive responsibility to Congress in American government and executive responsibility in a so-called parliamentary government. The *theory of parliamentary government* says that at any time the prime minister or cabinet, or any individual minister, may be confronted with a vote of "no confidence" and be obliged to resign. In other words, the ministers are responsible to the parliament. This theory was most thoroughly put into practice in Britain and France throughout much of the nineteenth century. The parliaments of this period consisted of freewheeling individuals, legislators who had to obey only their conscience or their special interests. All this changed with the growth of the *party system*. Responsibility shifted from the parliament as a body to the majority party within it. This happened not only in England but also in other countries.

Between 1919 and 1933 the Weimar Republic was run somewhat like the governments of Britain and France. The government had to resign when a majority in the parliament expressed its lack of confidence. Since the Weimar Republic had a great many parties, with changing coalitions, this system led to the frequent fall of cabinets, much as it did in France. Often quite disparate elements in the parliament would get together and pass a vote of "no confidence," not because they were agreed on anything positive but merely because they were opposed to the incumbent cabinet and Chancellor (or prime minister). Many people in Germany attributed the fall of the Weimar Repubic to this arrangement.

After World War II, many Germans were anxious to get something better. Therefore they invented in 1949 a rather ingenious device. An article in the basic law introduced a *constructive vote of "no confidence"* which provided that a parliamentary vote of lack of confidence in a government could be entertained only if coupled with the election of a new Chancellor. The result of this provision was that during the next twenty years there were no votes of lack of confidence, because the deputies opposed to the old government could not agree on a new one to take its place.

Nevertheless, although the provision for a constructive vote of "no confidence" has not become operative, its existence—that is, the threat of its being used—has brought about changes in Germany's government. When the party of which West German Chancellor Ludwig Erhard was supposed to be the leader lost confidence in him, Erhard resigned because he realized that it was only a matter of days until his party would get together with one of the opposition parties in the choice of a new Chancellor. Erhard's successor, Georg Kiesinger, then governed for two years with a coalition of the kind that Erhard had been unwilling to entertain, namely a coalition between the Christian Democrats and the Social Democrats.

There has also been a curious transformation as a result of the development of the party system in the United States. In one way, the development in the United States has been exactly the opposite of that in Britain. In Britain, the major parties are highly disciplined; legislators from the same party usually vote together. In the United States, legislators cross party lines quite often in voting for or against some proposed law. In another way, developments in the two countries have become more alike. Thus, the British Prime Minister has come to depend more and more on the support of the majority party rather than the support of Parliament, and, owing to the looseness of the American party system, the President has come to depend more and more upon the support of a working majority coalition in Congress rather than on the support of a majority of his party. Thus, in a sense, the United States now has more of a parliamentary government than it ever has had, perhaps even more than in

Britain. How has this come about? It has originated in the fact that the American Constitution requires the Congress, and more particularly, the House, to grant money for the affairs of government. More and more, policy decisions and their execution depend on these grants. And the increasing costliness of government has produced the increasing dependence of the government upon maintaining majority congressional support.

Yet there is still at least one major difference between American and parliamentary government. In the United States, the government need not resign when it loses the support of Congress. Lyndon Johnson, in announcing on March 31, 1968 his decision not to seek re-election, several months before the nominating conventions were to be held, in effect resigned his office as of January 20, 1969. Even if Johnson had said, "Since I have lost the effective control of Congress and the support I need, I can no longer carry on," even if he had resigned as of April 1, this would not have meant that the government would have been taken over by another party or party combination. It would have only meant that the government would have been taken over by the Vice-President and carried on by him.

In recent years in the Soviet Union, maintaining the support of top Communist Party leaders has been the major limitation on executive power. This curtailment of executive power is a reaction to the period between 1934 and 1953 when Stalin was so strongly entrenched that no one, in effect, seemed to be able to call him to responsibility. The success of his policies of forced high-speed industrialization and the victorious outcome of World War II gave him a measure of continuing popular support; his relentless use of police repression and mass propaganda did the rest. His successors, however, never gained such power. Each of them remained to some extent responsible to the majority of the Politburo and the other top level committees of the Communist Party. Without their support, no Soviet leader after Stalin has been able to remain in office—as Chairman Nikita Khrushchev discovered when he was deprived of power in November 1964. To what extent the Communist Party and the Soviet leaders collectively are held responsible to the people of their country is another question. It seems certain that their power is not unlimited, but their poeple—even those strata which count in politics—seem far from controlling them closely or effectively on day-to-day matters.

Staff and Line: The Importance of Administration

Parties are organized to demand what things should be done. Executives are put into office to decide how they should be done. But it is the men on the spot, the administrators, who must do them.

No policy can be put into effect without administration. But the administrative machinery can continue to function by routine—and often does—

even where there is no carefully thought-out policy. Only in the long run do decisions about consistency and policy become inevitable.

Even the business of thinking about policy needs to be administered. The type of administration that serves this task is called *staff*. Officers or officials on the staff of an organization—private or public, civilian or military—collect and process current information and past memories which are relevant for the decisions to be made. On the basis of all this information the staff then advises the *line executive* who makes the actual decision.

The Structure of Administration.   Most administrative services in government or economic life are organized as hierarchies or chains of command. In such pyramids or chains, small numbers of superiors give orders to larger numbers of subordinates who in turn give more detailed orders to still larger numbers of their own subordinates, and so on "down the line." This *one-way downward flow of commands* continues through link after link of the chain or layer after layer of the administrative pyramid, down to the lowest clerk in the last local office, who then carries out his instructions in dealing with the public. In perfect bureaucracies of this kind the "man in the street" runs a great risk of being treated as the lowest of the low.

As commands flow down the line, responsibility is demanded from above. Each subordinate is responsible to his superior who is expected to supervise his performance and usually has means to reward or punish him for it. However, in this generally *one-way upward flow of responsibility*, it is unusual for superiors to be made responsible to their subordinates. In this sense, armies, political bureaucracies, priestly hierarchies, and business organizations are all quite different from democracies where lines of command are circular—from the government to the people and back again from the people to the government. In a democracy responsibility is often mutual and ultimately it must be to the people—provided that they do not forget their own responsibility to mankind and to the future. A key problem of modern administration is to reconcile the built-in tendency of every line organization towards one-way chains of command with the essentially *two-way circular process of democracy*.

In coping with this problem, the line executive may be aided by his staff. The staff may include not only specialists in various matters of substance, such as transportation, finance, safety, and the like, but also specialists in listening to subordinates, to clients, and to people. Through such a staff their needs and responses can be brought effectively to the executive's attention. From the days of Franklin D. Roosevelt to those of Richard M. Nixon, this has been one of the many tasks of the growing staff of presidential advisers. Similar tasks have developed among the staffs of state governors and other executives at lower levels in the United States, as well as among the the staffs of prime ministers and other political executives in Western Europe, and albeit more informally, in the Soviet Union and other Communist-ruled countries.

Policy at the Mercy of Administrators.   Administration can make or break a policy. Bureaucrats can go through the motions of carrying out a policy or law while actually sabotaging it. In the eighteenth century, such enlightened despots as Catherine II of Russia and Joseph II of Austria tried to abolish a large part of the institution of serfdom in their countries. But the land-owning noblemen who controlled the administration of their governments took care that the policies remained ineffective. In the 1930s, many generals of the Spanish army pretended to obey the Republican government while preparing the uprising of Colonel Francisco Franco which eventually overthrew the Republic. In the United States, laws have long specified equal rights for black voters and educational opportunities for black children, but local registrars, school boards, and other administrative agencies have long prevented the practice of many of these rights.

If a policy is to work, or if a leader or party is to have real power, it must have the support of a body of administrative personnel that is loyal and competent enough to give effect to its orders. But while policies, leaders, and parties change, bureaucrats remain. Bureaucracy may be an unmoving anvil that wears out many hammers of reform. If a new policy is to be implemented, can the old bureaucracy be expected to administer it?

This question has provoked four main competing answers. The first answer is provided by the concept of a *civil service*. This notion goes back to the time of European monarchies, when government officials were supposed to be primarily loyal to the king and not to any policy, party, or special interest group. Civil servants were expected to be equally loyal and competent in serving any minister or policy the king commanded. Later this loyalty of civil servants became oriented not to the king but to the Crown, that is to say, the state, for even kings come and go or make mistakes. Civil servants then were expected to be loyal to the interests of the state and its constitution, if need be against the errors of kings and cabinets. Under this tradition, a Labour government or a Conservative government will expect to be served equally well by the nonpartisan professionals of the British civil service.

Recruitment and promotion of such professional civil servants are usually carried on by means of some *merit system* in accordance with supposedly objective standards of training and performance. In practice, however, such standards often favor members of particular social classes or particular ethnic, racial, or religious groups. As Sir Dennis Brogan has put it: "The British Civil Service is open to rich and poor alike—like the Ritz Hotel." Certainly thus far no fully "objective" standards for the hiring and promotion of government personnel have been discovered.

A strikingly different theory developed in the United States in the nineteenth century. In the days of President Andrew Jackson, government offices were a matter not for specialists and experts but for ordinary men. Any right thinking—and right voting—man was good enough to fill an office after his party had won the election, for "to the victor belong the spoils." This *spoils system* permitted the victorious party to fill administrative posts with its own adherents who were expected to carry out its policy, if it had one, and in any case to be grateful to the party for getting them their jobs. Such officeholders, of course, were not politically neutral but intensely partisan. Benjamin Franklin's old practice of filling postmasterships with political supporters thus was extended for a time to most of the American government. Few other countries went as far, but a part of the practice lingers on in the machine politics of many American cities.

A third notion of administration is a *class theory*, as elaborated by Marx, Engels, and, particularly, Lenin. As they saw it, professional bureaucrats would serve different masters or policies equally well so long as these remained within the same ruling class and social system. As soon, however, as a new policy or government went radically beyond the old class limits, the old bureaucracy could not be expected to serve it loyally. (In fact, democratic socialist governments in Britain, Sweden, Norway, and Denmark experienced no crippling difficulties with their civil servants.) According to Lenin, however, Socialist or Communist governments, on coming to power, would need to dismiss most of the old officials and replace them by new ones recruited from the working class and its allies. Even this new bureaucracy would have to be watched closely and purged often, in order to prevent it from becoming a new middle class. Finally, the Communists would have to reorganize the whole machinery of government, making it so simple that eventually, as Lenin put it, "any cook could rule the state." The practical experience of the Soviet Union and other Communist countries shows that Communist bureaucracies have a way of becoming large and persistent. Dissident Communists have complained bitterly of the rise of a "new class" of Communist bureaucrats and managers.[3] Clearly, the administrative machinery of Communist countries thus far has not become so simple, nor their cooks so sophisticated, for Lenin's words to be fulfilled.

The fourth answer to the question of administrative competence and loyalty is a *compromise* between the merit and spoils system, a compromise which has been gradually emerging in the United States. Currently somewhat more than 1,500 top positions in the federal government are defined as "policy-making" or political. Their incumbents are expected to resign whenever the administration changes. The new President then may fill these positions with his own men, either to insure the faithful execution of his policies or as spoils to reward some of his supporters. The bulk of

[3] See Milovan Djilas, *The New Class* (New York: Praeger, 1957).

federal jobs—more than two million—has been put under the protection of civil service laws and regulations. Accordingly, their incumbents are to be promoted by merit and are only to be discharged for cause and under carefully safeguarded proceedings. During World War II and in the heyday of the cold war, some of the safeguards were weakened seriously. A large number of security regulations and requirements made it possible for many officials to be denied "security clearance" and to be discharged from office on the basis of anonymous accusations and with no chance to face their accusers.[4] The recurrent purges of administrative personnel, so characteristic of Communist dictatorships, thus found a minor but disquieting counterpart in the United States.

Despite these tensions the American administrative machinery has on the whole worked well. Since World War II it has carried out a greatly expanded range of responsibilities and policies. Compared to its size and the vast sums of money it has handled, the federal bureaucracy has remained remarkably free from corruption. It has been efficient in many of its tasks, both old and new, ranging from road building to rural electrification and to putting a man on the moon. Despite the ominous powers given to the security system, it has not turned the country into a police state. Congressional and popular defense of civil liberties has provided an effective counterweight.

America's administrative machinery has been least successful where it has had to change major habits and practices among the American people, such as in race relations, poverty, and the crisis of the cities. Here neither line nor staff has been able to provide a substitute for the needed reorientation of the will of the American people. Individuals and small groups can urge this *reordering of national priorities* or goals, but only the people can bring it about. Only they can decide which things they want done first. They must decide on the kind and size of the new jobs to be done, and on the machinery with which to do them. As this reorientation develops and popular support increases for new policies, it will be an important task for citizens to see to it that the administrative machinery of the American government—in the nation, the states, and the cities—will prove adequate to its new tasks.

---

[4] For a good study of the legal implications, see Ralph S. Brown, *Loyalty and Security: Employment Tests in the United States* (New Haven: Yale University Press, 1958).

Key Terms and Concepts

decision latitude
policy
strategy
tactics
deliberation
institution
institutionalize
filibuster
cloture
representative
law
separation of powers
democratic centralism
adversary procedure
judicial review
unitary government
confederacy
federal union
nullification
federalism

states' rights
residual powers
Tenth Amendment
general welfare clause
discretion
responsibility
arbitrary act
responsible power
irresponsible power
theory of parliamentary government
constructive vote of "no confidence"
staff
line executive
one-way downward flow of commands
one-way upward flow of responsibility
two-way circular process of democracy
civil service
merit system
spoils system
reordering of national priorities

Additional Readings

Friedrich, C. J. *Constitutional Government and Democracy.* 4th ed. Waltham, Mass.: Blaisdell Publishing Co., 1968

Huntington, S. P. *Political Order in Changing Societies.* New Haven: Yale University Press, 1968. Chapters 1 and 2.

Merton, R. K. *et al.* (eds.) *Reader in Bureaucracy.* New York: The Free Press, 1965.

Neumann, S. (ed.) *Modern Political Parties: Approaches to Comparative Politics.* Chicago: University of Chicago Press, 1955.

Neustadt, R. E. *Presidential Power.* New York: Wiley, 1960.

Schubert, G. A. *The Judicial Mind.* Evanston, Ill.: Northwestern University Press, 1965.

The Performance of
Political Systems

Some people adapt their attitudes toward political change simply according to their prejudices, as they have learned them from others or as they may fit the needs of their own personality. "Every boy and every gal that's born into this world alive," in the words of a song in *Iolanthe* by Gilbert and Sullivan, "is either a little liberal or else a little conservative." Some people are born conformists. They are simply in favor of the existing political order, whatever that may be. In a small town in the American Midwest, they would cheer for the American Legion; in a small town in Russia, they would be for the Communist Party. If they had been born in a New Guinea tribe, they would be loyal headhunters or cannibals. Other people are dissenters by nature, such as the nineteenth-century immigrant from Ireland who, arriving in America on election day, got off the ship and went straight to the polling place. Asked whether he knew anything about the candidates or issues, he replied: "No, I don't. But I want to vote against the government." A Philadelphia taxi driver in the 1960's said the same thing: "I pay no attention to politics but I always vote against the gang that's in."

In our time, politics is such a serious matter that neither unthinking conformism nor blind nonconformism will suffice. In order to decide intelligently whether a political system needs changing, and in what respects, we must know how it performs. We must know whether it produces the outcomes we want, and how well it does in producing them.

If we know how to analyze the workings of political systems and the machinery of government, we may feel less naive and uncritical about politics. We also may feel less helpless and bewildered by the actions of the governments under which we live. Systems theory and systems analysis may make us less inclined to search for demons and villains in political life, and to see it as a simple crusade of good against evil. Our questions

Chapter 9

may then become more pointed toward reality, and more likely to lead us to effective action.

The Uses of Systems Theory

Some years ago a student radical (who has since become an expert labor lawyer in the complicated field of workman's compensation) asked, "Who really determines American foreign policy?" The question was a little like that of the small boy who asks, "Where in the refrigerator is the little man who turns on the light when you open the refrigerator door?" Or the questions of primitive peoples: "Where is the god within the hurricane? Where is the spirit within the earthquake?" In effect, most such questions are attempts to personify the workings of systems.

A hurricane is a revolving disk of air, one mile high and 500 miles across, which is fed by streams of air in two dimensions and by the rising of air in a third dimension all the way to the stratosphere. It is a complicated but understandable system of storms which is part of a larger system of storm tracks. An earthquake is a system. And so is a war. Systems analysis thus may help us to see that the great catastrophes in history as well as in nature are properties of systems.

Systems do not always work for human good. Quite the contrary, the outcome of a system may be pernicious and destructive. Systems can be traps. They have a logic of their own, which goes even beyond the interests of the individuals whom they may temporarily reward. Many slaveowners, for example, benefited from the social system of slavery. Hence, they learned to believe in it and to defend it. They persisted in acting in accordance with this system even when it led to economic stagnation and civil war, the destruction of their homes, the loss of their property, and the death of their children.[1]

Whether we speak of the catastrophes of nature or of man, the workings of a machine, or the slower changes in human politics, it is important to see that many developments in each of these cases are produced by systems. As we saw in Chapter 6, a *system* is a collection of recognizable units or components which hang together and vary together, in a manner regular enough to be described. Political systems consist of political units and are connected mainly by political processes. We can try to analyze each system to see how it works, how its outcomes are produced, and how it can be changed. With the help of systems analysis, we can try to separate the properties of systems from individual interests, group interests, and the shares of persons in making decisions.

[1] For detailed accounts, see William C. Dodd, *The Cotton Kingdom* (New Haven: Yale University Press, 1919); and Eugene D. Genovese, *The Political Economy of Slavery* (New York: Pantheon, 1965).

The political systems analyst uses his skill to understand how wide must be the *decision latitude* of an individual, office, organization, or a government, so that it can make a real difference to the outcome. He also tries to recognize when and where the momentum of a system is so great that officeholders become rubber stamps or "dependent variables," making very little difference to the outcome. For it is always important to know whether you can change the outcome of a system by appealing to the judgment of an individual, or by replacing one officeholder with another, or only by changing some or most of the structure of the system. The political analyst also tries to learn who would help make the change, who is interested in it, how to build a coalition big enough and motivated enough to produce the change, and how to aim one's resources with sufficient precision to bring about the change desired.

The Concept of Performance

A systems analyst is aided in his work by the concept of performance. Performance tests occur everywhere. Automobile firms take part in races to test the design and performance of their cars, and to improve them in the light of experience. But automobile races are tests not only of machines but also of drivers. A first-rate driver may win even with a less than first-rate car. In addition, every race also involves track or road conditions, weather, chance, and luck. Performance, in government as in automobiles, is thus determined jointly by systems, the individuals who operate them, and the environment in which they must function.

Effectiveness and Efficiency.   *Performance* is the name we give to any outcome which is desired but improbable without an effort to produce it. Performance achieves some result which otherwise would not occur. If an outcome is certain, no one has to act to bring it about. No human being or organization has to perform anything to make the sun rise. By contrast, a room that is cold in winter may be warmed by the performance of a stove. Any performance is measured by the outcome attained as against the costs and other adverse conditions which make its attainment unlikely. Performance thus includes two dimensions: *effectiveness*—making an unlikely outcome more likely to happen—and *efficiency*—the ratio between change in the probability of the outcome and the costs incurred in producing it. The effectiveness of an automobile may be measured by the speed it can attain, and its efficiency by its consumption of gasoline. (Another kind of effectiveness might be the automobile's freedom from the need for repairs in over 100,000 miles of normal use; the corresponding efficiency would be measured against the higher cost for stronger and better original parts.)

A similar distinction between effectiveness and efficiency applies to the performance of governments and entire political systems. We ask not only how likely is a government or political system to attain some value we are interested in, but also at what price. The American government of the 1920s gave free rein to private business enterprise, with a minimum of government intervention. The enormous cost became evident in the 1930s when ten million people were made unemployed for years by the greatest of depressions. Semi-developed Russia was transformed into a modern industrial state by Stalin's iron-fisted methods, at vast cost in human suffering.

Emergency Politics: Pursuit of a Single Value.   Performance is measured, first of all, by specific values. If there is a single overwhelming goal, the primary emphasis will be on *effectiveness* in reaching it. A leader of a political movement, a party, or a government may ask what headway is being made toward this particular goal. He may then give this goal priority over all others. Even democracies do so in time of war. After the attack on Pearl Harbor there was overwhelming agreement in the United States that the war against Nazi Germany and imperial Japan had to be won. Everything else for a time became subordinate to this goal. Similarly, when the Nazis invaded Russia, and Stalin's dictatorship was at war with Germany, Winston Churchill promptly offered Stalin an alliance. He was asked in the House of Commons how he could justify allying Britain with such an immoral dictatorship as Stalin's. Mr. Churchill replied that if the Hitler government should invade hell, His Majesty's government would offer the devil a treaty of alliance. This, incidentally, was a paraphrase of the statement by Lenin a generation earlier that the Bolsheviks would enter an alliance "with the devil and his grandmother" if it would bring about the victory of the Russian Revolution. With victory in war or revolution as the only primary goal, the best system of government is that which appears most likely to win.

If there is more than one major value, however, the question of cost and efficiency cannot be ignored. If justice and other conceptions of the national interest are as important or more important to people than the military effort, if a large part of the people do not believe in the justice of a war or in the war's being in the national interest, then the issue of priorities arises. Thus in the late 1960s, many Americans said, "Carrying on this war is not our paramount goal. Vietnam is not the most important problem facing the United States. It is more urgent to improve our own society right here at home."

In the long run no single goal, no matter how just or admirable, can be pursued completely. The methods of emergency thinking and *emergency government*—the argument that one would do anything, override any scruples, make any arrangements, pay any price to get a goal—are psychologically and organizationally tolerable only for limited amounts of time. The pursuit of one overwhelming goal year after year will change and distort the personalities of individuals, the behaviors of small groups, and the structure of a government. It can even destroy the moral fabric of society. If it is justifiable to use any means to achieve a desired end, if violence or concealment is acceptable, as in a wartime crisis, then why not use the technique of the "Big Lie"? If you want followers, why not gain them by deception? If someone disputes your leadership, or disagrees with your goal or your methods, why not jail him, or assassinate his character?

In every large emergency, people are tempted to set aside the basic rights of individuals and groups, such as free speech, freedom of assembly, or due process of law. In the late 1960s, General Lewis B. Hershey, then Director of Selective Service in the United States, ordered active protestors against the draft to be inducted forthwith into the army. His involuntary retirement followed. If basic rights are set aside briefly, the damage is limited. If emergency rule violates them for a longer time, the damage to constitutional government will be severe, and may prove fatal.

Multiple Goals and Open-Ended Values. Over any longer period of time it is vitally important for people to learn to restore to their governments the capacity to pursue many goals without neglecting any of them. A good political system is able to balance different values, to accept the possibility of error and to correct it, and to accept the likelihood that there are many questions to which the exact answer is not yet known. The poet Bertolt Brecht, a life-long believer in communism, once said to his Communist readers, "Shouldn't we ask our friends to make a list of all those questions to which they do not yet know an answer?" Brecht was reminding them of a general truth, valid for all ideologies. It is important to keep open the frontier to the unknown so that we know where we must still seek for answers. *Multiple goal-seeking* capacities and research capabilities must be included, therefore, among essential performance criteria for any government or political system that is to endure.

It was in this frame of mind that Thomas Jefferson worked on the draft of the American Declaration of Independence. At one stage, the draft document spoke of men's "unalienable rights" and went on: "These rights are life, liberty, and property." Jefferson then changed the text. He crossed out "These rights are" and substituted "Among these rights are," making clear that men's unalienable rights were not necessarily limited to any particular number. He also struck out the word "property" and substituted "the pursuit of happiness." Some scholars think he did so believing that in future centuries people might be less concerned with property but would always search for happiness. In any case, "happiness" included much more than property, and it was more open to the changing needs of future generations. Thus amended, the Declaration was signed and published, giving shape to the spirit of the new nation. It became one of America's greatest documents and a testimony to the open-ended nature of the American dream.

The Budget: First Tests of Performance

"For warfare, three things are needed," wrote the Austrian General Monte-cucculi in the seventeenth century: "money, money, and once again, money." Much the same is true for government. To get anything done anywhere, a government is likely to need money in the amount required at the time and place it is needed. The ability of a government to raise money, and then to spend it wisely, is a major test of its performance. If a government has to do several things, it must plan to have money available for all of them and it must plan how to get it. A summary of these plans is called the *budget*. Every modern national government needs a budget, and so does each of its administrative subdivisions. What a government plans for in its budget will reveal its values. How well it plans and executes its budget is a first test of its performance.

Anyone who knows how to read a budget can know the goals of a government. If a government plans to build many highways, its budget for road construction will be large. If a city plans to increase opportunities and facilities for education, its education budget will increase. If a national government decides to acquire expensive new weapons, its defense budget will rise—and so may those of other nations. *Budgetary analysis* is the art and skill of reading a budget so carefully that the analyst can tell for what purposes the government's financial resources will be spent, and usually also how its spending pattern will have changed from those of the previous years. Budgetary analysis thus may serve as a test of both political intentions and performance.

Revenue Budgets and the Art of Collecting Taxes. What holds for public expenditures also holds for public *revenues*—the way the government expects to get the money which it plans to spend. The revenue budget—the income side of a budget—will reveal which groups the government is willing to burden more heavily and which ones will be let off more lightly. Governments favoring the rich at the expense of the poor tend to use poll taxes which are collected in equal amounts per head of population or, as in past decades in the United States, per head of voters. Governments that are solicitous of special groups—such as mothers, churches, universities, or oil producers—may grant them special tax exemptions or allowances. Governments that want to collect revenue in accordance with ability to pay tend to use *progressive taxes*. These taxes, such as corporate and individual income taxes in most modern countries, progress to higher tax rates as the taxpayer's income increases. *Regressive taxes* have the opposite effect: a uniform sales tax on bread tends to fall most heavily on the poor. Poll taxes usually are regressive in their impact, too.

The revenue side of a budget will also reveal much about the capabilities of a government or an entire political system. The less income a government gets the less it can do. Generally the art of collecting taxes, as J. B. Colbert once said, resembles the art of plucking a goose: it consists in getting the largest amount of feathers with the fewest squawks. The tax system of a country thus depends in part on which groups can squawk loudest and most effectively. Politicians anticipating the reactions of such groups—on whose support they may depend—tax them lightly, if at all. This is what happens in many underdeveloped countries. Extremely underdeveloped countries collect most of their revenue at their borders, generally at ports of entry. Tariffs and export taxes—and foreign grants and loans—tend to be the major sources of income for their governments. Somewhat more highly developed countries collect much of their income through *indirect taxes* on trade within their borders, and sometimes through excises at the boundaries of their cities. Highly developed countries collect most of their revenue through *direct taxes* on individuals, households, and business enterprises. (The Soviet Union raises most of its tax revenue through a combination of *turnover* and profit transfer taxes at the factory level.) Progressive direct income taxes tend to be more just and humane— and they bring in more money. The ability to use taxes effectively is thus an additional test of government performance.

Deficit Financing. Governments have another potential source of income besides taxes, loans, and what they earn from public services. They can deliberately spend more money than they take in, and unlike housewives and business firms they can get away with it. For governments can create money—and most of them do—and they can compel anyone in the country to accept this money as "legal tender" for paying taxes or settling debts. In spending a billion dollars more than it has collected, a government may either borrow the money and pay interest on it or it may print it or create it in other ways. The last two practices are known as *deficit financing.*

If a government prints or otherwise creates it, the purchasing power of the remaining money in the country will be somewhat diluted. When this happens there may be some *inflation*—more money purchasing the same amount of goods. Inflation acts like an indirect tax that falls unequally on different groups. People hurt by inflation—housewives, consumers, creditors, white-collar workers, civil servants, the military, pensioners, and others living on fixed incomes—may turn against the government. In contrast, debtors, farmers, manufacturers, and skilled union labor will be little troubled or may even be quite satisfied with the government's policy. Whether the government then stays in power will depend less on the amount of the inflation and more on the strength and attitudes of these contending interest groups. Inflation may not necessarily occur, however. If there are unemployed men and resources within the country, the new money created by the government may stimulate demand and induce the production of additional goods and services which might counter the inflation wholly or in part. The government, of course, will get its money whether there are idle resources in the country or not, but if there are unemployed resources, deficit financing may actually promote employment and prosperity. How skillfully a government foresees the effects of its financial policies, and how well it controls its own actions, constitutes another test of its performance.

Budgetary Planning and Control.   Ordinarily budgets are prepared for one year ahead. In the case of large public expenditures or investments, however, some countries use capital budgets or development budgets which are planned for several years ahead. The five-year plans of the Soviet Union and other countries are the most elaborate form of such budgeting, comprising much of the country's national economy. The art of *budget forecasting* aims at predicting how much money each of a government's several activities will receive in next year's budget or in the budgets of other future years. A rough rule of thumb seems to be that most items in a large government budget will not differ by more than 10 per cent from the sums budgeted in the preceding year. Changes of more than 10 per cent, either upward or downward, are no longer matters of routine; they are likely to require relatively substantial political decisions.

A budget is not only a tool of action but also of control. It enables a government to control its own actions, by making sure that subordinate offices and agencies spend their budgetary allocations on the purposes intended, and that the amounts spent stay within budgetary limits. Most countries assign this control function to special national accounting offices or comptrollers general. The United States also has a Bureau of the Budget which controls the requests of the various agencies for future appropriations to make certain that they are compatible with each other, with government policy, and with expected income.

The budget can be a tool for controlling the government from outside. Whoever controls the budget can control most of what a government can do. Countries whose budgets are controlled by foreign powers or creditors are not fully sovereign. In sovereign countries, on the other hand, legislatures or the people can use the budget to control executive power. When the British Parliament in the seventeenth century gained full control of this *power of the purse*, it wrested effective power from the Crown. Even in the twentieth century, the day on which the British Chancellor of the Exchequer presents the government's annually proposed budget to Parliament for its approval remains one of the high points in British political life.

In the United States, the double process of authorization and appropriation of each major budgetary item is intended to strengthen Congressional control over the executive. It is partly counteracted by the skill of some executive departments in concealing their specific expenditures under vague budgetary headings and in exceeding budgetary estimates. Sometimes, under systems of direct democracy, as in some Swiss cantons, certain budgetary items must be approved directly by the voters.

In the muted contest between the controllers and the controlled in any country, there is no substitute for the vigilance of informed legislators and voters. In all modern countries, the need for some executive discretion must be balanced against the need for some political control of the bureaucracy through the budget. How well this balance is maintained is yet another test of performance. But all such budgetary tests do not tell what quality of life a government buys for its people. Here we must ask not how much money is collected and spent but what qualitative and quantitative results the combination of money and politics produces.

Some Qualitative Tests of Performance

The performance of government relates to both the present and the future. It must aim at *attaining* as much as possible of each of the many values which people now desire, and it must keep the pursuit of all these values as *compatible* as possible. But it must also preserve and enhance the capacity to seek *new* values in the future and to attain these, too. Serving these three tasks, governments must often work for subtle configurations of values which are not easily spelled out, but which people can sometimes recognize by intuition. People then speak of the quality of a political system or of the *quality of life* in a society. We all know some simple tests for this kind of quality: how breathable the air still is, how well the garbage gets collected, how safe it is to walk home after dark, how many children are properly fed and how many go hungry, how many sick are well attended and how many are not attended at all, how many people lead meaningful lives and how many lead "lives of quiet desperation."

The Quality of Leaders.   A more profound test of the quality of a political system was stressed by Pericles in ancient Greece and by John Stuart Mill in nineteenth-century England. It consists in the kinds of individuals who grow up under it, and in the kind of persons it elevates to leadership. Clearly, in all countries the personalities of leaders will vary as they succeed one another in the course of time. But the personalities and actions of Britain's Prime Ministers and cabinet ministers since 1945, such as Winston Churchill, Clement Attlee, Anthony Eden, Harold Macmillan, and Harold Wilson, say something about the quality of British politics since World War II. Similarly the personalities and acts of Adolf Hitler, Joseph Goebbels, Hermann Goering, Heinrich Himmler, Ernst Kaltenbrunner, Franz Hoess, and Adolf Eichmann say something about the quality of the Nazi political system.

A look at the personalities of American leaders reminds us of the great variety of political life in the United States. American leaders have included men of vast accomplishment and great humanity like Franklin D. Roosevelt and Dwight D. Eisenhower. They have included leaders of great promise cut off before their time, like Martin Luther King, and John and Robert Kennedy; and they have included many men of lesser stature, each stubbornly doing his best as he saw it. A longer view of American history would give us a similar picture. The roster of Presidents is composed of great leaders like Washington, Jefferson, Jackson, and Lincoln, as well as of lesser men like Martin Van Buren, James Buchanan, Chester A. Arthur, and Calvin Coolidge. But in nearly two centuries the American political system has never yet elevated to high office any man who was outstandingly criminal, cruel, or insanely ambitious.

The Quality of Ordinary People.   Another test for the quality of a political system is in the types of personality and behavior it produces among ordinary men and women. How numerous are the drunks, drug addicts, and suicides? How many murders are committed? How frequent are other crimes of callousness or cruelty? Some of the answers can be found in the crime statistics of each country. Others can be found in its surveys of social attitudes and mental health (see Table 9.1).

But the quality of life under a political system does not depend only on crime and acts legally defined as antisocial. How many persons suffer from race discrimination and how many people practice it? How many "authoritarian personalities" do we find, how many petty tyrants of the office or the breakfast table? What is the most frequently found personality type among the people—the *"modal personality"*[2]—which accounts for so much of what is called "national character"?

And the quality of life is determined as much or more by the presence of good things as by the absence of bad ones. How many people volunteer to help those in need? How many will help their neighbors, shelter refugees, answer an appeal for blood donations? How many acts of interracial decency do we find? In how many cities can people leave their coins on unwatched newspaper piles without the money being stolen? In how many homes are the doors left unlocked? How many jurors and judges treat the accused as innocent until proven guilty? And how many taxpayers are honest in filling out their tax returns?

Every reader may apply this list of questions to the community in which he lives. American readers may find that their country is seriously vulnerable to homicide, carelessness, intermittent corruption, and the destruc-

[2] For a discussion of modal personality and national character, refer to A. Inkeles and D. Levinson, "National Character: The Study of Modal Personality and Sociocultural Systems," in Gardner Lindzey, ed., *Handbook of Experimental Psychology,* 2nd. ed. (Reading, Mass.: Addison-Wesley Publishers, 1969), Vol. 4, pp. 418–506.

tive overuse of stimulants. They will also find evidence of remarkable generosity and openness, respect for people, and confidence and trust in them.

Political Culture: The Sum of Qualities.   Taken together, all these qualitative aspects of a political system add up to the political culture underlying a country or a people. The notion of "culture" is used here similar to the way it is used by anthropologists. The *culture* of a people means the collection of all its traditions and habits, particularly those transmitted by parents to children and by children to each other. It includes their common stock of images and perceptions of the world in which they live. It thus includes their views of what is practical and possible, and what is not; what is beautiful and what is ugly; what is good and what is bad; what is right and what is wrong. Culture functions like a traffic code for behavior. It tells people where to go ahead and where to stop, and where and how to make detours.

Culture has implications for political behavior. All cultures, say the anthropologists Florence Kluckhohn and Fred Strodtbeck, can be compared in terms of a few basic questions.[3] Three of these are most relevant for us here. (1) Does a culture teach men mainly to submit to their environment, to work along with it, or to master it? (2) Is it oriented chiefly toward the past, the present, or the future? (3) Does it see human relations primarily as *lineal*, that is, in terms of fathers and sons, superiors and subordinates, or as *collateral*, that is, in terms of brothers and sisters, equals and colleagues?

People who are used to submitting to their environment will easily submit to rulers, foreign or native, and may feel frightened and bewildered when faced with the task of ruling themselves. People accustomed to working along with their environment in constant two-way communication also may favor compromise and decisions by unanimity, even at the cost of much delay; they may dislike quick decisions by majority rule. (This trait, common among many of the emerging peoples in Asia and Africa, often has exasperated Western economic development experts.) People taught to master nature will resort more readily to power and manipulation. They will seek quick decisions overriding all doubts and obstacles, disregarding the needs of dissenting opinions, minorities, and the less obvious consequences of their actions. Such masters of nature will win many triumphs in technology and politics, but in their rush ahead they may leave a trail of neglected vital problems such as eroded soil, polluted air, careless wars, and ill-treated minorities. Those who have learned to work *with* nature—learning from her as often as imposing their will on her—may learn from their dialogue with nature the art of working through dialogues with their fellow men.

[3] See Florence R. Kluckhohn et al., *Variations in Value Orientations* (New York: Harper & Row, 1961).

Likewise, people's basic view of the relative importance of the past, the present, and the future will shape their attitudes toward economic growth, political reform, and to the needs of old and young. A culture looking more to the past than to either the present or the future may be better in preserving monuments than in accelerating innovations. It may enact laws for old-age pensions many years before expanding large-scale public higher education for the young. Britain passed legislation for old-age pensions in 1908, but legislation for greatly expanded public higher education only after 1960. A culture looking to the future, such as that of the United States, passed these kinds of legislation in reverse order: land grant colleges came in the 1860s and Social Security in 1935.

Finally, if a people tends to regard its members as equals, as Americans and many Frenchmen do, its politics will be fairly different from that of a people who tend to divide its members into superiors and subordinates, as Japanese, Germans, and, to a lesser extent, Englishmen have done during many periods of their history.

Political culture is related to the *frequency* and *probability* of various kinds of political behavior and not to their rigid determination. England has had its great forward-looking reformers, Germany and Japan have had their democrats, the United States has produced its share of conservatives and conservationists. Nonetheless, the different political cultures of these countries can be seen in the record of their past behavior and will not soon disappear completely from their future actions.

The Nature of Authority

The culture of a country is the basis for the concept of authority prevailing in its politics. In some countries and ages, political leadership is attained through ascription, such as by noble birth. At other times and places, leadership must be won by achievement, as in public service, war, or electoral contests. Englishmen get their authority from who they are and what they are. They *stand* for election and *sit* for their exams. Americans get their authority from what they do. They *run* for office and *take* exams. One concept of authority is static and bound by status and *ascription*—what people are labeled to be—the other is dynamic and oriented to *achievement*—what people actually accomplish. As Britain transforms itself to meet the modern age its image of authority, too, will grow more dynamic—but it may be an uphill struggle.

Behind these differences, the concept of authority has a common meaning in all countries. *Authority* means first of all the credibility of a source of communication: its messages will be believed almost regardless of their content. If a scholar has become an "authority," his views will be believed even when the evidence for them is weak. "The authority of a scientist can be measured," wrote a disillusioned colleague, "by the number of years for which he can retard progress in his field." (Real science, of course, is antiauthoritarian in its essence. The youngest instructor or student can contradict the most senior professor when the evidence is on his side. When Charles II of England joined Britain's first organization of scientists—the Royal Society—the awkward problem arose of how any other scientist could presume to contradict the scientific theories of His Majesty. The Royal Society thereupon put into its seal *nullius in verba*—"on the words of no man." Its members thus decided to believe not in authority but facts.

In political and military matters, too, men often pay more attention to who is talking than to what is said. This tends to save much time and effort since no one person can test the evidence for everything he hears. But this easy acceptance of authority can lead to catastrophic error. Many civilians have believed the word of some general who told them that the war in prospect would be short and easy. The bombed-out cities of Germany and Japan and the military cemeteries of many other countries bear witness that authority can err. In politics, voters often have trusted the authority of leaders who assured them of the safety or success of some financial or economic policy, or who asserted on the contrary that some reform could not possibly work. President Hoover predicted that grass would grow in the streets of American cities if Franklin D. Roosevelt's New Deal policies were adopted. But the voters were in revolt against Mr. Hoover's authority which had been discredited by previous unsuccessful predictions. The New Deal program won, with Mr. Hoover making very little hay from his pronouncement.

Why do people so often believe an authoritative voice without testing what it says? Convenience is not the only reason. A deeper motive is emotional. As children we all had to learn to trust authority. Our fathers and mothers had to tell us of many dangers too serious to be tested by our own bodies. When they told us about reality we had to take their word about it. In the same years we learned to love our parents and to identify with them. Thus most of us made a three-way association in our minds that was deep and lasting. We learned to associate the commands of our parents with reality and both command and reality with someone we loved. In later life the commands or instructions of a teacher or superior may remind us of the voice of our parents—most often of our father on whom we may have wanted to model ourselves. This kind of childhood experience is normal in many societies. People who have had it can easily obey the commands of their superiors and government and feel happy about it. They may gladly volunteer to do more than is asked of them. Glad to obey, they may also be glad to command. When they themselves become parents or are promoted in business or to political or military office, they will speak with the voice of authority and expect to be obeyed.

Authority in this sense is *internalized*, that is, it has become part of the innermost feelings and the self-image of each individual. If such an individual should violate the commands of what he takes to be authority he can do so only at the price of psychic conflict. He will feel pangs of conscience, as they used to be called, or experience "neurotic guilt feelings," as a more fashionable phrase would put it. An active conscience, like a sense of pain, may seem an inconvenience to many of us. How simple would life be if our bodies could feel no pain and our minds no inhibitions and scruples! But the person who cannot feel pain is a cripple. He lacks an essential warning device for his body. He may continue to hold something hot rather than drop it immediately and is therefore more susceptible to burns and the infections following from them. A person who lacks all internalized sense of authority and all conscience is a social cripple. He lacks an essential warning system that would keep him from damaging himself and others, as well as his community. Under many political systems he may become a criminal, or else a tyrant. If he stays clear of the law and rises to power in the system, the hidden damage he does may be greater still.

All individuals and all political systems thus need some sense of authority. But authority must not be accepted blindly, uncritically, or without limits. Much of what is called *conscience* is whatever we were taught before the age of six. It is in part a matter of accident in our biography, a matter of the family and country in which we grew up. (In Mark Twain's novel, southern-born Huckleberry Finn had a bad conscience when he helped his black friend Jim escape from slavery.) But *legitimate authority* has also an objective character. It implies the promise that its commands will remain compatible with other values which we personally hold, and with the needs of the persons and communities which we hold dear. Such a promise may be true or false. It is our responsibility to test it against facts and to make sure that we do not follow false authorities no matter how long established or how recently in fashion.

To say that authority must be tested against fact is to say that it must be tested by performance. For authority is both the product of a political system and a condition for its future functioning. The way a political system has performed in the past goes far to determine what authority it has among its people; but the kind of authority a system has at any one time will have great effects on what it can do in the future. The performance of political systems can thus be tested by the authority relationships which they create and by the loyalties which they evoke. These authority relationships and loyalties, in turn, will determine some of the capacities of these systems for future performance.

The effectiveness of authority can be measured by the frequency and dependability with which it is obeyed in the absence of supervision or coercion. Conscience, said a Greek philosopher, is what controls our acts when nobody is watching. Wherever data are available on a population's rate of compliance with the laws or commands of a government we learn something about authority. When authority disintegrates, compliance will decline. The ratio of prisoners to casualties among combat troops is a rough-and-ready indicator of their loyalty. In World War I both the German-speaking and the Hungarian regiments of the Austro-Hungarian army were very loyal to the Empire. On the average it took one casualty among them to induce another soldier to surrender. The Slavic regiments in the same army had little sympathy for the Empire and its war. For every casualty among them, more than three others let themselves be taken prisoner. In the war in Vietnam, figures published by the United States Department of Defense show many more desertions than fatalities among South Vietnamese troops, but among the Vietcong they have shown persistently many more fatalities than prisoners or desertions. It is obviously difficult to compile accurate figures for a guerilla war, but the language of these Vietnam data over several years is too clear to be ignored. The actual rates of compliance or obedience, by soldiers as well as by civilians, are a kind of voting-by-action on the commands of those trying to rule them.

The Test of Human Rights

Authority and loyalty determine what the state may demand of its people; *human rights* sum up what people may legitimately demand of their state. Authority and loyalty define one's duties toward the government; and if one does one's duties, one should not expect to be thanked for it. (It is only for courage "above and beyond the call of duty" that members of the United States armed forces receive the Congressional Medal of Honor.) The same applies to rights. Whatever is yours by right is not a privilege or a gift. You should get it without owing thanks to anyone, and you may take it if need be.

Through the centuries many writers, from Cicero and St. Augustine to St. Thomas Aquinas and to the great liberals like John Locke and John Stuart Mill, have held that certain rights are *natural*. By this they have meant that these rights are inborn. Any younger brother or sister seems to demand quite naturally equal rights with an elder sibling. But "nature" is a difficult concept to apply. The more that scientists have discovered about nature the less freely have philosophers been able to use it in their theories. Some rights which were considered natural in the past, such as the right of revenge or the right to own slaves or large estates of land, have turned out not to be rights at all in other times and places, and societies function fairly well without them.

Nevertheless, we may ascribe to the concept of natural rights an operational meaning. Natural behavior is probable behavior. It is likely to occur whenever it is not prevented by "artificial" obstacles, that is, by obstacles which are less probable and which can be maintained only by special efforts or arrangements. *Natural rights* are rights which people are likely to claim whenever not specifically restrained from doing so, and likely to claim again as soon as the restraint ceases. Whether a particular right is a natural right in this sense—one that is claimed spontaneously at many times and places—is a question of fact. And it is a task of political scientists to look at the facts and to see whether and to what extent this is the case.

Insofar as any human right is natural in this sense, it cannot be sold or signed away. By definition, people will automatically claim it again as soon as no one stops them; and they will claim it anyway if they are strong enough. From this point of view, no one can legally sign away his right to live. Neither can anyone sign away his right to be free. Nor can such rights be lost by "prescription"—that is, by long usage, habit, or the passage of time. They are "imprescriptible," in the language of eighteenth-century lawyers, or "unalienable" in the language of the Declaration of Independence.[4]

In the two centuries since the American and French Revolutions, the demand for human rights has spread around the world. England has had a Bill of Rights since 1674, dealing mostly with legal procedures that safeguard individuals against the abuse of power by the government. In the United States a Bill of Rights forms the first ten amendments to the Constitution. In the German Federal Republic, similar rights are embodied in the country's Basic Law. The constitutions of most countries, including that of the Soviet Union, contain some provisions of this kind. It is a task of political scientists to observe and report how well such rights are respected in practice.

Many of the early lists of human rights are *negative* in character. They state what the government *may not* do to the individual. It may not mutilate or torture him, or kill or imprison him without due legal process, or deny him equal protection of the law. It may not stifle his freedom of speech or stop him from worshipping according to conscience, or force him to worship against his will. The limits and margins of these rights vary with time and place, but their core is the same in many countries.

In our own century a demand for *positive* human rights has been added. It is not enough to treat all men equally before the law. The right to life, it is now argued, implies the right to food and shelter, and in more recent views, the right to medical help when needed. Freedom of speech implies the freedom to read; it implies the right to knowledge and education. Generally the absence of restraint is useless without the presence of opportunity and the knowledge and capacity to act.

All human rights and freedoms thus have their positive aspects; and where these are not automatically supplied by social and economic life,

---

[4]Not all political thinkers have shared this view. Burke, the great conservative, thought that all rights were artificial, made only by convention and experience. Natural rights, he once suggested testily, were nonsense; natural and imprescriptible rights, nonsense on stilts.

men are turning increasingly to their governments for them. President Franklin D. Roosevelt expressed this new perception of freedom in 1941 when he spoke of the "Four Freedoms" which were to be established everywhere in the world: freedom of religion, freedom of speech, freedom from want, and freedom from fear. The first two are primarily negative, demanding restraints from governments. But freedom from want—which has not yet been achieved even in the United States three decades later— requires a vast positive effort of both production and distribution within each country and among countries as well. Freedom from fear may require the most complex action. It implies nothing less than the abolition of war—and in the long run, the end of all tyranny and persecution. And the abolition of war requires the peaceful management of conflicts. It requires, therefore, a great deal of positive coordination of the behavior of governments and nations, of which the United Nations is only a beginning.

President Roosevelt later gave a more detailed list of positive human rights. In his message to Congress in January 1945, he called for a "Second Bill of Rights" for the American people. As a whole, such a bill has yet to be passed. The full employment legislation and the medicare and medicaid bills in the United States are steps in this direction. President Nixon's proposal for a guaranteed minimum income is another. Similar principles and practices have been adopted in many Western European countries. Long catalogues of positive rights are also found in the constitutions of the Soviet Union and other Communist countries.

But it is one thing to promise human rights and another to deliver them. In a later section of this chapter we shall see how the performance of government in many of these matters can be measured. First, however, we must ask another set of questions. *Who* is to implement these rights? Is it to be the central government alone who will do these things for its people? Or can the people do them for themselves, by joining together in their localities and neighborhoods and in a multitude of groups and self-governing associations?

The Ability to Form Self-Governing Groups.   Whether a political system enables its population to form many self-governing associations is another test of its performance. The more capacity and opportunity it produces for the formation of such groups, the better will be its performance for its people. But the capacity of the people to form such groups, and to govern themselves in conducting the affairs of these groups, is in itself an important condition for the performance of a political system. Indeed this capacity may be one of the most important aspects of the political culture of a country. Thus, when the Japanese political theorist Masao Maruyama wanted to understand the political changes in his own country, he developed a scheme for comparing political systems of dif-

Figure 9.1

Maruyama's Typology of Political Systems

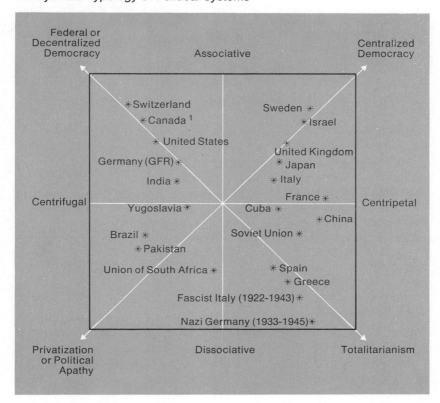

[1]On paper, the Canadian Constitution gives more powers to the central government than does the American. In practice, French-speaking Quebec has more effective "states rights" than Alabama or Mississippi.

ferent periods and countries in terms of their capacity to form self-governing associations[5] (see Figure 9.1).

Maruyama proposed two ways of comparing different political systems. First, he would determine whether they were centrifugal or centripetal. The decentralized or *centrifugal system* attempts to allocate power outward to regions and not inward to a single center of decision-making, whereas the centralized or *centripetal system* tends to draw power together to a single center. Second, he would determine whether they were associationist or dissociationist. An *associationist* society contains traditions and skills for forming autonomous, small, self-governing groups on matters of substan-

[5] Masao Maruyama, "Patterns of Individuation and the Case of Japan: A Conceptual Scheme," in Marius B. Jansen, ed., *Changing Japanese Attitudes toward Modernization* (Princeton: Princeton University Press, 1965), pp. 489–531.

tive relevance. Such groups include local governments, labor unions, cooperatives, churches, and the like. A *dissociationist* society reveals the opposite pattern of behavior. Here individuals think that in all important matters they cannot trust other individuals very much, and on the whole they withdraw from permanent, direct, self-government.

It is important to note that not all nations in which people join organizations are associationist. Joining powerless associations has no political effect. What counts is how important these associations are, how seriously people take their self-government within their groups, and how tenaciously they will defend it. If the organizations joined deal mainly with trivial affairs, then there is no associationism in that society. The German people in the 1920s and early 1930s, for example, were remarkably rich in numbers of organizations. They joined everything in sight: stamp collection clubs, garden clubs, rabbit breeders' clubs, and similar *Vereine*, of all kinds. But when it came to really important matters, they deferred to authority and reorganized their associations in line with Nazi policies.

Maruyama suggests that a highly associationist, centripetal political system permits a particular type of *centralized democracy*. In the United Kingdom, for instance, a great deal of government is carried on by all sorts of voluntary associations. We may think of British local government, of the trade unions or cooperative societies, or of the British clubs which organize a good part of the elite of Britain's political parties, whether Conservative, Liberal, or Labour. One might even include among the many British voluntary associations the Englishman's local castle, the neighborhood pub. In addition to encouraging voluntary organizations, Britain tends to give most power to Parliament as a single center of decision-making. Thus the United Kingdom rates high on both the associationist and centripetal scales.

The United States, on the other hand, is markedly more centrifugal, with its distribution of power between the federal government and the states, its interest in states' rights, and its continuing allocation of a little more than one-third of the government sector to spending by states and municipalities. At the same time, it is strongly associationist. Switzerland is even more associationist and more centrifugal than the United States. Maruyama calls this combination "individualism." We might call it pluralism. *Pluralistic individualism* might be an even better term.

Another type of government is heavily centripetal, giving all power to a central decision-maker, but dissociationist in that its subjects or citizens do not trust each other. This pattern is characteristic of *totalitarian* regimes. Such a government resembles a wheel with strong spokes but no rim. People do not trust each other, but they trust the central government, a government where voluntary and spontaneous groups (except those run by the government) are strongly discouraged. Nazi Germany (1933–45) and Fascist Italy (1922–43) are telling examples.

At some stages in its history the Soviet Union fitted into such a scheme, but even then the fit was a poor one. The Soviet Union's collective farms, labor unions, cooperatives, and various local and factory councils all brought about a considerable increase in associationist skills in Russia. It is fairly certain that a Russian of today, or even of the 1920s and 1930s, is a member of many more organizations in which he has more of a share at least in minor decisions than was his father and grandfather in the days of the Czar. On the other hand, these organizations usually are not free to differ in fundamental policy from the national government. Their members do not get much experience in discussing or deciding fundamental matters. The U.S.S.R. is also still dissociationist in part. Its citizens are always exhorted to look for "bourgeois remnants," deviationists, agents of counterrevolution, and similar foes of their society. And the more one looks for all these wicked people, the less one can trust one's neighbor, since, after all, he might be an agent of capitalism in disguise.

To some extent the People's Republic of China fits a pattern similar to that of the Soviet Union. Many Chinese now take more part in decision-making and in the administering of villages, communes, factories, and cooperatives than ever before. Yet they are told in many ways to be "vigilant," which means, in effect, to distrust each other. A recent document from a Chinese Communist Party Congress denounced the Communist president of Communist China as a "scab." Apparently a really loyal Communist Chinese cannot trust anyone else, not even the president of his country. Almost anyone, with the possible exception of Mao Tse-tung, might be revealed as a "deviationist" in the course of the next campaign. Such suspicion leads to real difficulties in building lasting trust or lasting cooperation among individuals in a political system that again and again teaches each man to look upon his neighbor as a potential traitor, heretic, or enemy.

Finally, a country may be both centrifugal and dissociationist, with people trusting neither their government nor one another. This somewhat dismal state of affairs fits what Maruyama calls the pattern of *privatization*. Edward Banfield has found this pattern in a south Italian village. In his book, *The Moral Basis of a Backward Society*, he speaks of the "amoral familism" dominating the life of a Calabrian village and relates how it was impossible for this village to organize a cooperative ambulance service to the nearest hospital not too many miles away. It could not be done because every villager was convinced that all other villagers would steal the gasoline from the vehicle. When it was proposed that the village priest should have charge of the gasoline, the villagers pointed out that he might steal it too. As a result, people who needed emergency medical care continued to suffer and die without a chance of getting to the hospital in time.

Maruyama points out that none of these patterns are eternal. Japan, he finds, during the last century has passed through all of them. So, to some extent, has Germany. In appraising the political performance of other

Table 9.1

Some Indicators of the Quality of Life

	GNP per Capita (1966)	Infant Mortality in First Year per 1000 Live Births (1966)	Suicides per 100,000 Population	Homicides and Operations of War per 100,000 Population	Students of Higher Education per 100,000 Inhabitants
US	3,796	23.7	10.9 (1966)	6.0 (1966)	2,840 (1965)
USSR	1,531	26.1	n.a.	n.a.	1,674 (1965)
UK	1,924	19.6[1]	England and Wales 10.4 Northern Ireland 5.5(1966)[2] Scotland 8.0	England and Wales 0.7 Northern Ireland 0.6(1966)[2] Scotland 1.1	England and Wales 480 (1965) Northern Ireland 525 (1965) Scotland 531 (1965)
France	2,052	21.7[1]	15.0 (1965)	0.8 (1965)	1,042 (1965)
GFR	1,990	23.5	20.0 (1965)	1.3 (1965)	632 (1965)

n.a. = not available

[1]Provisional.

[2]Data tabulated by year of registration rather than occurrence.

Sources: United States Arms Control and Disarmament Agency Economic Bureau, *Research Report 68-52; World Military Expenditures 1966-67 (1968);* United Nations Demographic Yearbook, *1967; and* UNESCO Statistical Yearbook, *1967.*

countries, we may ask where they are now in terms of centralized power and of self-governing associations, and where they seem to be going.

The Effectiveness of Government: Some Quantitative Indicators

In sum, the efforts of the national government, the effects of laws, the functioning of administration, the services of state and local governments, the activities of voluntary groups and associations, and the behavior of individuals all add up to the general performance of a political system.

We may also ask more specifically how well does a government or political system perform in attaining particular values? If a system promises life to its people, what does it deliver in terms of life expectancy? If it promises enlightenment, how does it perform with respect to primary and secondary school enrollment and higher education? For every major set of values, we can find some measurable indicators of this kind and test the performance of the country's political system against them (see Table 9.1). Of course, such performance also involves the effects of the country's social and economic systems, but it is the political system through which these other aspects of life can be preserved or changed. If the conditions of life are bad and a political system lacks the power or motivation to change them, this would be a fact worth knowing. If conditions are good and getting better, a political system would deserve much of the credit—and in practice would be likely to get it from many of the people living under it.

Life Expectancy.   Perhaps the first value of politics is the value of life—the value which both John Locke and the Declaration of Independence put first among the rights of men. If we consider the life expectancy for women (which is higher than that for men), we find that in this respect, the best performance by any political system in the world nowadays is turned in by the government of Sweden which provides for its population a life expectancy of seventy-five years. It is followed in a tight group by all the world's advanced countries, both Communist and non-Communist: with about seventy-four years for France and Britain, seventy-three years for the United States, Canada, and Australia, seventy-two years for Czechoslovakia, the Soviet Union, and West Germany; seventy-one years for East Germany, and seventy years for Italy and Japan. The American life expectancy of seventy-three years is an average of seventy-five years for whites and about sixty-five years for Negroes. (It still costs one-tenth of one's life to be born black in the United States; and this bitter statistic is worth repeating until this deadly aspect of race discrimination is gone.) Among the world's poor countries the average falls to thirty-two years for India and to twenty-six years for some of the sub-Saharan African states; some of the countries with still worse life expectancies cagily do not publish statistics. We do know, however, that in some African countries in recent years every second baby born has died before it has reached the age of two.[6]

Where statistics of infant mortality are available, they offer the chance to further substantiate data on life expectancy, and on the incidence of human grief and pain. Of every 1,000 children born in a country, only 17 die in their first year in the Netherlands or Sweden, only 21 in Switzerland, and only 24 in Britain. In the United States the number of such children who die is 26, in France 27, in Czechoslovakia 31, in West Germany 34, and in the Soviet Union and Belgium 35. In Italy it is higher still with a death toll of 49 per 1,000 children. In Poland it is 75, in Mexico 78, in Chile 128, and in India it is a staggering 225, nearly one-quarter of all live births.[6]

The protection of life is the first performance requirement of governments because whether people live or die is a political question. If we leave living and dying to the ballot of the dollar bill and to the forces of the market, the poor and their children will die like flies. There is no way in which any modern country can keep the mass of its people alive except by public, civic action. No country in the world that has introduced socialized medicine in some form has ever given it up. The ledger now contains about thirty countries in the world with comprehensive low-cost public medical care.[7] The concept of a government's responsibility for the health of its people began with conservatives like Bismarck in Germany and liberals like Lloyd George in England, but now cuts across all ideologies. Public health services have become important parts of the responsibility of government.

Wealth and Economic Growth.   A second value desired by people almost everywhere is *wealth*. Except for a few saints or philosophers, most people do not like to be poor. At the end of the 1960s the gross national product of the United States was about $800 billion, or about $4,000 per capita, that is, for each individual in the population. At the other extreme of the scale, poor countries such as India, Pakistan, Tanganyika, Burma, Ethiopia, the Mongolian People's Republic, and Nepal all had per capita incomes well below $100. Among the world's advanced countries the United States has no close rival in per capita income. Canada at the end of the 1960s had less than $3,000; Switzerland and Sweden less than $2,300; West Germany about $2,000; France, the Soviet Union, and East Germany about $1,800; and Britain, about $1,700.

[6]These figures apply to the start of the 1960s, but the situation was much the same at their close.

[7]About thirty countries have subsidized or nationalized medicine (or a nationwide state insurance program) which absorbs at least 80 per cent of the cost of treatment and which covers the great majority of their population. At least another forty-five countries have assumed some of the burden of public medical care.

Per capita income figures do not mean that the individual consumers in these countries have these amounts to spend. Only two-thirds of these sums were available for private consumption in France and Britain in the 1950s; a little less in the United States, Canada, Switzerland, and Sweden; 60 per cent in East Germany and Japan, 59 per cent in West Germany, and only 56 per cent in the Soviet Union. The rest of the gross national product in these countries was spent on capital formation in private or public enterprises, on national defense, and on other government expenditures. In very poor countries much less is available for public purposes. In such countries as Nigeria, the Philippines, and Chile over 80 per cent of the gross national product goes to private consumption, and their people are still poor.

The higher the per capita income of a country, the more its people can do, either privately as individuals or collectively through public institutions. Very rich countries can allow themselves a great deal of waste and error and still not be too badly off. Poor countries must spend their financial resources more carefully if they are to buy for their people a tolerable amount of other values. Thus, Britain, with less than half the per capita income of the United States, still secures for its people the same life expectancy as the United States does for Americans.

People want to know not only how rich they are at any one moment but also whether they are going to get richer. Therefore, another performance test which most people consider important is that of *economic growth*. The normal performance for governments is a growth in gross national product of 4 per cent per year. This is the median rate for the whole world—and since the world's population grows at about 2 per cent a year, this means that per capita income should grow at about 2 per cent a year. In countries with prosperous economies and vigorous governments, per capita growth rates of 6 and 7 per cent a year can be attained, as they often have been achieved in Japan, West Germany, Israel, and the Soviet Union. In countries where things go badly, per capita growth rates can sink to 1 or 2 per cent or less. Such stagnating countries included in the 1950s Ireland, Thailand, Indonesia, Chile, India, Pakistan, Argentina, and Syria. The United States grew at a 5 per cent average in the 1960s but only at 1.3 per cent in the 1950s. (America's years on the golf course during the Eisenhower era were characterized by one of the lowest growth rates in the world at the time.) Of course, averages can be computed for long periods of time. If we count the long-range growth of the United States since the 1890s, per capita income has grown at 3 per cent a year, which means it has doubled every twenty-three years. Russia has grown at about the same rate over the same period, despite the devastations of revolution, civil war, and two world wars. Both the performances of the United States and of Russia are clearly better than the average performance of the rest of the world.

The Extent of Inequality.   But whether income grows or not is not the whole story. There is an anecdote about a man eating a roast chicken in a room and a hungry man looking on. A statistician looking in through the window reported that "on the average" there was half a chicken per capita in that room. That did not help the hungry man. Thus we also want to know how equally or unequally the benefits of life are distributed within a country.

As we noted in Chapter 4, the best method for reporting this, and for measuring this performance in regard to equality, is the so-called *Lorenz Curve* (see Figure 4.6). If everybody received exactly the same amount of income, 10 per cent of the population would get 10 per cent of the income, 20 per cent would get 20 per cent of the income, and the line connecting all these groups of people would be absolutely straight. The more unequal the distribution of income, the smaller is the share of the poorest group and the higher the share of the richest, and the more steeply curved becomes the line of income distribution. The more bent the bow is on the Lorenz diagram, the greater may be the tension in a society.

In reasonably decently governed countries the top 10 per cent tend to get approximately 20 to 30 per cent of the income, and this is usually borne without great social unrest. Israel distributes 24 per cent of its income among the top 10 per cent of receivers, Sweden 27 to 29 per cent, England about 30 per cent, and the United States 31 per cent. In India the figure rises to 36 per cent; in Puerto Rico it is 40 per cent. In Guatemala or Mexico it exceeds 47 per cent, and in Bolivia the figure is a state secret or unknown, but obviously the inequality there is grim.

If we take the area under the curve, double it, call the sides of the square one, and subtract the area under the double curve from the area of the square we get the *Gini Index* of inequality (see Figure 4.7). This index shows how unequally anything is distributed—voting rights, representation, income, and many other things. As yet there is no experience of any large society with a Gini Index of below 20 per cent. It would be interesting to know what such a society would be like. In the meantime, it is worth noting that the more advanced and richer countries have less inequality. Countries with more inequality, as shown by a higher Gini Index, also have less economic growth. For our time at least, the old view that great inequality is essential to progress has turned out to be a myth.

The Gini Index of inequality may indicate a society where the poor are relatively well off but the middle class has been shortchanged. Or it may describe a society where the middle strata do fairly well but the poor are treated very badly. The United States, on the whole, has an income distribution that distributes prosperity well in the middle groups. The third, fourth, fifth, and sixth deciles (a decile is one-tenth of the ranked total of cases) of income receivers, and probably also the seventh decile, still are well off in the United States. Human misery begins in the eighth decile; the last 20 per cent of Americans are miserably treated, and the last 10 per cent, which include of course many people from broken homes and families, live in conditions which no self-respecting northwest European country would tolerate. Thus in providing for its poor the United States is behind many countries in the world because of the scandalous conditions which it tolerates.

A country can do something about inequality if it wants to, and if its people know how income is distributed and on whom suffering is inflicted. We can therefore judge the performance of a political system not only by the quality of life it provides for its people but by the specific figures that measure it; and specifying those figures, we can begin to see whether things are getting better or worse, and whether some particular political changes make a difference.

The Relevance of Facts and Figures. We could present a much longer list of indicators (see Table 9.2). Some of these might be indicators of performance in regard to values shared by most political systems in the world, such as literacy and mass education. Others might be indicators of performance in regard to matters highly valued by some nations but much less by others, such as the concentration of political power, the growth of big cities, the size of the state, or the nation's military strength. A recent study of the Swiss political system used more than forty indicators of performance. The task of this book, however, is only to introduce the

Table 9.2

Some Quantitative Tests for the Performance of Political Systems

Test or Criterion	Quantitative Indicator (per 1000 population)
1. Quality of leaders	How many criminal acts? How many people in prison?
2. Quality of common people	Life expectancy, Gini Index, number of suicides, number of homicides.
3. Provision of rights	What guarantees exist? How much freedom to speak, read, publish? Are the guarantees positive or negative? To what extent are they respected in practice?
4. Opportunity to form self-governing associations	How many and how important self-governing associations or major informal groups? How much mutual trust? How many persons report sense of belonging and of political effectiveness? How many have right to oppose government on specific issues? On general policy?
5. Protection for minorities	How many children taught in mother tongue? How many people belong to minority religions or philosophies protected by law? How many cases or complaints of group discrimination? How great a difference among the occupations and values attained by different racial or ethnic groups?

reader to various methods of political analysis. It will suffice to present only a limited number of examples of empirical and quantitative research data if the ways in which these data are used are explained fully.

Facts and figures can tell us what the world is like, and to what extent it is being changed by the actions of others or ourselves. If we say we are against the dying of children this is as helpful as saying that we are for home, God, and mother, and against the man-eating shark. However, if we can say that child mortality in Mississippi has been cut by one-third, then we have said something meaningful. We have said that there now exists a visible number of children who would not have survived otherwise. Our general sentiments of value and good will are taking on the cutting edge of specific fact. If such facts are lacking, sentiments and values are likely to stay impotent and empty, just as facts without values are likely to remain meaningless. Values and facts, qualities and quantities, must be put together, if political analysis and action are to be effective.

Quantity and Quality: Political System Performance as a Whole

The measurement of quantities and the transformation of the quality of life are two aspects of one and the same reality, of a single social process. When we ask what something *resembles,* we refer to its quality. When we ask *how often* have we recognized it, we refer to its quantity.

We can now recognize that much of what happens in politics and government is the result of the workings of a political system rather than the plottings of a few villains or conspirators. We can gauge the effectiveness of such a system by the extent to which it is likely to attain its main goals, and we estimate its efficiency by the ratio of its successes to their costs. Such judgments are easily made in political emergencies, when a single goal or value predominates; they are more difficult to make in normal situations where goals are multiple and open-ended.

Quantitative tests for government performance begin with the budget. Qualitative tests begin with the quality of leaders and of ordinary people, as well as of the political culture and authority, as produced by the system. A key test of such qualities is the ability of a people to form self-governing groups dealing with matters of genuine importance.

The results of political performance become visible through a host of quantitative indicators about the life of the people. These include life expectancy, infant mortality, per capita gross national product, economic growth, literacy and access to education, voting rights and actual political participation, and the extent of inequality in regard to these and other values. Together with indicators of political violence, executive stability, and popular compliance with the laws, these indicators can tell us much about how well a political system works.

But they do not tell us enough. There is more to the performance of a political system as a whole than a mere sum of quantitative tests. It is this something more to which we refer when we speak of the "quality of life."

Quality of life means a chance at fulfilling one's possibilities, one's ability to grow. On the one hand, it means acting out what we are and have right now, but it also means the possibility of reaching beyond what we have and are at any one moment. As the philosopher Nietzsche once said, "Man is a transition and a perdition." We are reaching beyond what we are because we can become more. And this openness is one of the essential aspects of the quality of being human.

Quality of life also involves whether people have to be afraid of each other or can trust and count on each other. Political systems that destroy trust, and political movements that deny all trust, produce political paralysis. Without a minimum of mutual trust, people cannot cooperate and cannot control their fate.

The fate of man is man. We are each other's fate; and if we can do something about getting control not only of our own lives but of our larger environment, and if we know what to do with that control, we can improve the quality of our lives and our own quality as persons and as a community. This can only be done if competence and compassion are united. Competence without compassion could turn us into hangmen, whether we know it or not. And compassion without competence could turn us into well-meaning quacks. Where illness is serious a quack is a menace. The difference between medicine and quackery is defined by the test of facts. We had better not offer ourselves as surgeons for appendicitis if we do not know where the appendix is.

Key Terms and Concepts

system	lineal human relations
performance	collateral human relations
effectiveness	ascription
efficiency	achievement
emergency government	authority
budget	internalization
budgetary analysis	human rights
revenue	natural rights
progressive tax	Maruyama scheme
regressive tax	centrifugal
indirect tax	centripetal
direct tax	associationist
turnover tax	dissociationist
deficit financing	pluralistic individualism
inflation	privatization
budget forecasting	Lorenz Curve

power of the purse   Gini Index
modal personality   decile
culture   quality of life

Additional Readings

Almond, G. A. and S. B. Powell. *Comparative Politics: A Developmental Approach.* Boston: Little, Brown, 1966. Chapter 8.

Aristotle. *Politics.* Books II and IV.

Banfield, E. *The Moral Basis of a Backward Society.* New York: The Free Press, 1958.

Bauer, R. A., A. Inkeles, and C. Kluckhohn. *How the Soviet System Works.* New York: Vintage Books, 1956.

Brzezinski, Z. and S. P. Huntington. *Political Power: USA/USSR.* New York: Viking Press, 1963. "Conclusion."

Maruyama, M. "Patterns of Individuation and the Case of Japan: A Conceptual Scheme." M. B. Jansen (ed.) *Changing Japanese Attitudes Toward Modernization.* Princeton: Princeton University Press, 1965, pp. 459–531.

Pitkin, H. F. *The Concept of Representation.* Berkeley: University of California Press, 1967.

Five Modern Countries

Part Two

The United States

Nobody really understands the United States—neither foreigners nor its own people. Winston Churchill once spoke of Russia as "a riddle wrapped in a mystery inside an enigma." Much the same might be said about the United States by any harassed Kremlin specialist in American research. If American "Kremlinologists" find it hard to forecast the Soviet Union's moves, Russian "Pentagonologists" or "Washingtonologists" find it equally difficult to forecast United States behavior.

Chapter 10

Government by Design

A few background characteristics stand out. The United States is the first of the world's new nations. Born of an anticolonial revolution, it faced many of the problems of nation-building which the world's emerging nations are encountering today. But since 1791 the United States also has been the oldest, steadily functioning constitutional political system in the world. In contrast to the United States, every other political system has undergone more radical changes in recent times. This includes Sweden, Norway, Denmark, and Switzerland, whose written constitutions all date from the first half of the nineteenth century; and it is certainly true of all other large countries. Compared with the rest of the world then, the changes in the American political system have been moderate; and the continuity of its tradition has been remarkable. This has not always been a blessing: the United States was the last modern country in the world to abolish slavery. But for good or ill, the historic facts of early anticolonialism and political traditionalism very likely have contributed to the traits of impatience and conservatism so evident in American politics.[1]

[1] For two books, each exploring a different aspect of this paradox, see Seymour Martin Lipset, *The First New Nation* (New York: Basic Books, 1963); and Daniel Boorstin, *The Genius of American Politics* (Chicago: University of Chicago Press, 1953).

Second, in terms of economic capability, the United States is the largest political system in the world. It has one-third of the gross national product of the world, together with nearly as large a share of the world's capital equipment. The United States also has on a per capita basis the highest average living standard in the world. In manpower and in area, the United States is the world's fourth largest political system. Only three countries—the Soviet Union, Canada, and China—are bigger in area, and only three countries—China, India, and the Soviet Union—are larger in population.

In less than two centuries, the American political system has succeeded in organizing a country on the scale of a continent. Only religious ideologies have done comparable jobs of organization on such a vast scale and they did so much earlier in history. The Confucian philosophy helped unite Chinese culture, Hindu religion kept India together, and Byzantine Christianity was the basis of the Russian state. The United States is the child of the only secular ideology that has *created* a huge country and kept it intact. Varieties of communism have taken over large existing countries such as Russia and China, but the United States started off with a bundle of colonies with three million people and parlayed this population into a country of over 200 million—close to what Benjamin Franklin predicted at its start.

At present, the United States is perhaps the largest country in the world in capabilities for good and evil, insights and errors. It did more than any other country in relieving famines after World Wars I and II, and again in the 1950s and 1960s. Its economic aid under the Marshall Plan in 1948–52 was crucial in the reconstruction of Western Europe. Its technological contributions—from Edison's electric light and the Wright brothers' airplane to nuclear energy and the landings on the moon—have changed the world. But its errors have been more devastating, shattering, and damaging than those of any other country because they have had more power behind them.

To be sure, the United States was not meant to commit errors but to be the world's first truly rational government. Its political system was shaped by the ideas of applied social scientists who were familiar with the social science of their time. Franklin, Jefferson, Hamilton, James Wilson, and especially Madison, all were men who had studied carefully what was then called "the science of government."[2] These founders of the Republic were men who were deliberately trying to set up the United States as a piece of social engineering. They designed the American political system with several tasks in mind. It was designed for expansion across a continent, and in the minds of at least some, for further expansion across

[2] The reading lists of these men have recently become available. See Douglas Adair and Walton Hale Hamilton, *The Power to Govern: The Constitution, Then and Now* (New York: Norton, 1937).

the oceans. It was also designed to attract capital from abroad and from within the country and to promote its investment in advanced technologies. And it was meant to give its inhabitants a better opportunity for spontaneity, freedom, and self-expression than could be found anywhere else.

People by Development

Unlike its political institutions, the American *people,* of course, was not produced by anyone's design. It was formed by history and by the decisions of millions of immigrants. The American colonists were molded into a new people by their common experience in the New World, the growing communication among the colonies, the distance from Europe, and finally by their growing revolutionary movement. They learned to think of themselves as Americans, and of the colonies as one country, before the first shots were fired at Lexington and Concord.[3]

Americans became recognizable as a people as they became more and more associated with certain distinctive traits. One of the persistent characteristics of the American people has been its great geographic mobility. About one-third of Americans live outside the state of their birth; and there is reason to believe the proportion has been this high since the Revolution. This figure is much higher than the exchange of population among the states of Western Europe. Even within Germany, as late as 1870 only 5 per cent of the inhabitants of Bavaria came from outside of Bavaria. Benjamin Franklin commented on the ability of Americans, thanks to a plentiful supply of land, to move freely to take up farming or other work in new locations. This mobility put a limit on what anyone could do to people. If local government or conditions of work became oppressive, they could pick up their possessions—which for most of them were sparse enough to be mobile—and move on. Mobility dispersed them, first along the Eastern seaboard and then across the continent, but this constant flow of migrants kept Americans uniform in culture. In the late eighteenth century, British travelers reported that the speech of the American people was almost identical over a thousand miles distance, in contrast to the speech of the English rural population which differed by dialect every hundred miles.

Another shared characteristic of the American people was a relatively high degree of literacy, uncommon in eighteenth-century Europe, and yet to be reached by many developing countries. A third was the high degree of political participation, in rural areas as well as in towns. A fourth trait was the habit of self-government and the widespread ability to form and

[3] For the growing use of the words "American" and "Americans" in the colonial press, see Richard L. Merritt, *Symbols of American Community, 1735-1775* (New Haven: Yale University Press, 1966).

maintain self-governing groups for a variety of political, economic, and social purposes.

Two final common conditions, in part underlying the others, were the facts that most farmers owned their land and that they did not feel bound by tradition in choosing their methods of tillage. As a result, American farmers were more independent, innovative, and prosperous. Unlike their European counterparts, they owned guns and horses; they wore felt hats and leather boots; they were free to hunt and fish; and most of them never had been subject to large landowners or noblemen. In short, they were not *peasants.* Their mobility, and their resources, gave them far greater capabilities to escape oppression or frustration, or to resist them successfully. Thus the Constitution did not *give* freedom to the American people. Rather, it helped them to make more effective use of the freedom which was already woven into the fabric of their lives. This point is often forgotten by those who would transplant political institutions and constitutions from one society to another.

If American farmers were far more free than the peasants of Europe, the black people in America were slaves, with neither freedom nor mobility. But the model of free farmers and free workers was set for everybody, and once the slaves were liberated, their descendants sooner or later would insist on claiming the same freedom in full measure.

When the Constitution was framed, it was designed to fit the needs of this particular people, as it emerged from one-and-a-half centuries of colonial history and a decade of revolution. But once the Constitution had been ratified, its design influenced the further development of the nation.

Federalism and the Separation of Powers

A Successful Federal Union.   One of the primary characteristics of this design for the government of the United States was its basic pattern of *federalism* which was then a radically new idea in its application on a continental scale. (Prior to the United States, the only successful large republic had been that of ancient Rome, which was not federal. Since Rome, only small republics, like Venice, had flourished. So had small confederations, like Switzerland, and the small-scale federal institutions of the Dutch.)

This federal design combined a legislative Congress, representing the diversity of the states, and a single chief executive—an "elective monarch," as he has been called—to direct the power of the nation. In such a federal union, as discussed in Chapter 8, every person is subject at one and the same time to two governments which are partly independent of each other. The federal government and the government in each state are separated in scope—in *what* they are supposed to govern—but united in domain, that is, in *whom* they are governing. Thus far, under this arrangement, no small region or group, nor any individual, has been able to dictate to the rest.

Some theorists have claimed that government is based on two monopolies: the monopoly of violence and the monopoly of legitimacy. The American experience casts doubt on this view. During its formative decades, the United States was relatively decentralized. For many decades after the ratification of the Constitution, there was no federal monopoly of violence, and indeed no federal monopoly of legitimacy. In part, this was due to a physical fact—the army of the United States federal government in the 1790s had 1,500 soldiers strung out over almost as many miles along the Indian frontier. The state militia of a single state such as New York, on the other hand, had 20,000 men. Thus the federal government in the early years of the Republic had no way of coercing the states. Only if the states backed the federal government could the federal government make its will prevail.

The American system also offered remarkable freedom to opposition. Americans refused to believe that anything was right merely because the government said so. Some Americans even held that rebellion was legitimate. Jefferson said of Shay's Rebellion that it might be necessary for the United States to have such an uprising every twenty-five years. These views did not prevent him from being elected President of the United States.

In its essence then, the American federal system has always tended to permit searching criticism of basic practices and institutions by the people, as well as by their elected representatives. Again it was Jefferson, this time after his tenure of office, who said of slavery, "I tremble for my country when I reflect that God is just." Serious criticism of one's own country is as old as the Republic. Through freedom of criticism, the United States has remained cohesive, and its federal system has remained strong; and both have become more so in the course of time. The argument that criticism is divisive, or that dissent weakens national unity, thus runs counter to the mainstream of American experience.

America's federalist scheme has been imitated widely, but not always with the same degree of success as in America. Federalism worked as a political system in the United States for a combination of two basic reasons. First, as we noted, Americans early became a single people and identified themselves as such. Being highly mobile, they perceived of their needs and interests as shared, more often than not, and thus were willing to commit themselves to supporting a national government. Second, and equally important, America had a long tradition of independent and self-governing states. If either of these factors had existed alone, federalism might not have succeeded. The existence of both of them in combination helped provide the workable balance between local and national government that is the essence of federalism.

A System of Checks and Balances. Another characteristic of American government is that it is based on a *separation of powers,* that is, a sharp separation of legislative power from that of the executive, and of judicial power—the power of judges and courts—from both. This was a recent concept of eighteenth-century theorists like Montesquieu, but the United States was unique in the thoroughness with which it put it into practice. To ensure the independence of all three branches of government, and at the same time to ensure that these three branches made up one coherent government, a system of *checks and balances* was developed (see Figure 10.1).

Pluralism vs. Populism. American government is also characterized by an informal separation of powers, called by some political scientists, *pluralism:* a plurality of competing interest groups and a diversity of rival interests—regional, social, economic, religious, and psychological. As James Madison pointed out in the "Tenth Federalist Letter," no special interest commands a majority in the United States: no one religion, no one economic interest, and no one region. Madison was confident that this fact would prevent the rise of tyrannical popular majorities for a long time. In the short run, he thought, there could be a tyrannical popular majority, but even that would be difficult to achieve and it would soon vanish. The view that the will of a popular majority should prevail in all matters, including science, art, and morals, and that neither experts nor minorities ought to have any valid claims against it, became known in nineteenth-century American politics as *populism.* The quick decline of populism in the 1890s and McCarthyism in the 1950s (the demagogic and intolerant kind named after Senator Joseph McCarthy of Wisconsin) can be taken as examples of Madison's wisdom.

Pluralism, however, is not an unmixed blessing. In its early stages, half the interest groups of a political system may be unorganized while the other half run the show. In that case, pluralism helps the strong but can be merciless against the weak. Later, when everybody is organized, the political system may become immobile, unless its leaders play a brilliant role in discovering workable policies and organizing broad coalitions to carry them out. But such statesmanship happens rarely. If it does not happen, then the immobility-emergency syndrome discussed in Chapter 3 will set in, and people will start looking for emergencies—foreign, military, or other—to force quick action.

However, for nearly two centuries, separation of powers among the legislative, executive, and judicial branches has worked remarkably well. For the stronger and better organized groups, at least, it has provided a framework within which their different interests could be expressed and brought together into acceptable programs for action.

Figure 10.1

The Separation of Powers: A Simplified Sketch

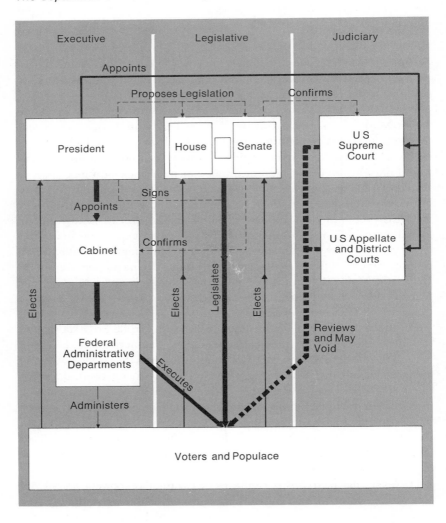

Two-Track Legislation for the Nation

Another political invention has given America's national legislature its distinctive cast. This invention deals with the relation of large and small states and their representation in Congress. The legislature was organized into two chambers. In one, the House of Representatives, equal representation was given to the people. In the other, the Senate, equal representation was given to the states. England had long had a two-chamber legislature comprised of its House of Lords and its House of Commons, but the use of the two-chamber system to accommodate the interests of large and small states in a federal union of continental dimensions was an American invention.

Representing the People by Numbers: The House. In the House of Representatives, the people are represented by one representative for every equal number of inhabitants as fixed by law—originally one for every 30,000, now one for almost every 500,000.[4] The representatives— or congressmen—are chosen directly by the people for two-year terms. They are elected from congressional districts, all intended to be equal in population. To ensure this equality, congressional districts are supposed to be readjusted, both among and within states, after each decennial census. The manner of adjustment within each state, like the qualifications for voting, is left to the state's legislature, while allocation of districts among states is entrusted to Congress. All these provisions were intended to ensure equal representation of the people in the House of Representatives.

In practice the representation in the House has turned out to be much less equal. Although congressional districts are supposed to be readjusted every ten years, at the start of the 1960s there were some state legislatures which had neglected this duty for as long as half a century. Many legislators from rural districts were benefiting from this neglect because they did not have to share power with representatives of the faster growing urban areas. In the eighteenth and nineteenth centuries, a similar neglect to provide adequate representation for the rapidly growing cities of Britain led there to the evils of the *"rotten boroughs"*—thinly populated rural districts overrepresented in Parliament. These were abolished by Britain's Reform Bill of 1832, although Britain today is still far from achieving absolutely equal representation for all its people. In the United States, major efforts to provide just apportionment of congressional districts

---

[4] Until the abolition of slavery in 1865, only free persons were counted fully; each slave, though without vote, was to be counted according to Article I, Section 2, Paragraph 3 of the Constitution, as three-fifths of a person, for the benefit of the state where he was held in bondage. Nowadays representation is by the number of people who live in a state, even if they are not registered to vote. Southern states have increased their seats in the House by counting many Negroes to whom nevertheless they denied the right to vote.

gained momentum only in the 1960s and then with the aid of the courts. By that time, it was charged that rural voters in some sparsely settled Illinois districts had nine times the voting power of citizens in some of Chicago's crowded precincts. Moreover, the new suburbs on the edge of many big cities had long remained underrepresented in Congress.

By the end of the 1960s, the doctrine of *"one man one vote"* had been established by decision of the United States Supreme Court, and the courts were beginning to demand that redistricting plans, in order to be constitutional, had to provide for districts that would vary by no more than 10 per cent in their number of voters. This principle was also applied by the courts to state legislatures, with far-reaching implications for the distribution of political power within the states and, indirectly, throughout much of the country. These developments promised to wipe out the last elements of representation by wealth or ownership of land.[5] At the start of the 1970s the full effects of redistricting—or *legislative reapportionment*—in accordance with the "one man one vote" principle were yet to come. Meanwhile, during the 1950s and 1960s the overrepresentation of rural districts had helped to make the House more conservative than the Senate—contrary to what the Founding Fathers had expected.

The two-year term for representatives may have had a similar effect. Intended to keep each congressman close to his constituents, this provision has involved many congressmen in contested districts in expensive and almost permanent campaigns for re-election, giving them little time for what was to have been their first responsibility, legislating for the people. This same provision, of course, gives disproportionate influence to those of their colleagues who are virtually unopposed in their rural districts or in urban districts dominated by a single ethnic group or political machine. Legislators from such safe one-party districts get re-elected time after time; and through the congressional custom of *seniority* (which allocates committee chairmanships to legislators with the longest continuous term of service) they dominate the important committees of the House and thereby much of the legislative business (see Table 10.1). These conditions have condemned many urban voters in contested districts to a feeling of powerlessness. Even if they succeed in electing a congressman of their choice, he rarely, if ever, seems to get anywhere in Congress. Although voters can change their congressman every two years, it would take them ten to twenty years to get their representative to head an important House committee. In 1968 Shirley Chisholm, the first Negro woman elected to Congress, represented a crowded urban area in Brooklyn but was promptly assigned to the House Committee on Agriculture; her refusal to accept brought her a change of assignment—to the Veterans Affairs Committee.

[5] Conservative opponents of thoroughgoing equality among voters have backed a constitutional amendment proposed by Senator Everett McKinley Dirksen of Illinois which would explicitly permit the allocation of districts, and in effect the weighting of votes, by standards other than the equality of voters.

Table 10.1

Democratic Congressmen, January 1964 (in percentages)

| | North | | South | |
	Rural	Urban	Rural	Urban
All Democratic Congressmen (255)	21%	42%	29%	9%
Major Committee Chairmanships Held by Democrats	18%	29%	53%	0%
"Safe" Seats Occupied by Democrats	7%	30%	52%	11%

Source: R. E. Wolfinger and J. Heifetz, "Safe Seats, Seniority, and Power in Congress," American Political Science Review, 59 (1965), pp. 337–349.

Representing the People by States: The Senate. If one branch of Congress was intended to represent the people in all regions of the country more or less equally as individuals, the other branch was designed to represent them unequally as individuals but equally as states. For this reason the small states of the Union, inferior to the large ones in population and effective political power, have the same representation in the Senate as their large neighbors: two senators for each.

Those small states which are virtually one-party states, such as Mississippi, Arkansas, and, until recently, Maine and Vermont, can gain disproportionate influence in the Senate through the seniority system that in time tends to put their senators at the head of major Senate committees. The effects of the seniority system, still accepted by many senators from industrial or urban states, make it harder for a senator from New York or California to head a key committee. However, this power of seniority may be declining. As two-party competition spreads to formerly one-party states, senators from two-party states may be gaining in influence.

The framers of the Constitution expected the Senate to serve as a counterweight to the House. They believed that senators would be older, more conservative, and more representative of the established elites of their states—those whom an eighteenth-century writer called "the rich, the well-born, and the wise." As we shall see, this is not quite what eventually happened.

Senators are elected for a term of six years, so as to have a greater measure of stability and independence for their term of service. At every congressional election, every two years, only one-third of the Senate faces re-election in contrast to all the members of the House. This is to protect the composition of the Senate from quick changes in the mood of the voters.

Originally, the Senators were elected indirectly by the legislatures of their states. But in 1912 the Seventeenth Amendment to the Constitution changed this to direct election by majority vote of those voters who "have the qualifications requisite for electors of the most numerous branch of the state legislatures." The effect of this change has varied somewhat by regions. In most northern and western states the registered voters make up a large part of the adult population, though, as we have seen, by no means all of them. In some southern states, owing to various discriminatory practices against Negroes and the poor, less than half the adult population have been registered to vote, and less than one-fourth of them have actually voted. Yet, the sharp increase in Negro registration in the South after the Voting Rights Act of 1965 suggests the beginnings of a change.

Since the Senate is supposed to represent the states equally, regardless of population, it has been particularly sensitive to regional, or sectional, differences and more distrustful of simple national majorities. The still continuing practice of the filibuster—or its threat—and the long struggle for workable rules of *cloture* confirm this built-in bias (see Chapter 8, footnotes 1 and 2, for a discussion of the filibuster and cloture).

Despite the conservative role intended for it by the Founding Fathers, the Senate in many matters has become more liberal than the House. Senators must be elected by the voters of an entire state, so the unequal apportionment of voting districts has no effect on them. Voters from urban and industrial areas within each state thus have their full share of influence on the election of their senators. It is also much more difficult for any political machine, ethnic group, or special interest group to dominate an entire state, compared with the relative ease with which such groups can hold sway over a congressional district. There are, to be sure, a few senators with well-known concerns for the interests of cotton or tobacco growers, dairy farmers, aircraft manufacturers, or defense contractors, but they make up a relatively limited part of the Senate, and even seniority cannot put them in charge of *all* Senate committees.

To get re-elected, therefore, most senators must be responsive to both rural and urban interests in their states, to many different ethnic groups and economic interests, and to the independent voters who may hold the balance in many two-party states. These conditions often favor the selection of more statesmenlike candidates, and the six-year term gives them a better opportunity to build a record of accomplishment. Although many legislators in the House as well as in the Senate have done their best to serve the public good as they saw it, the prestige of senators has usually been higher, perhaps with good reason.

The Modern Congress at Work

The Constituents of Congress: Congressmen and Senators.   A brilliant conservative theorist of American politics, Willmoore Kendall, once remarked that many an American voter, when stepping into the polling booth, develops a split personality. First, he thinks of himself as far-sighted and generous. He considers the problems of the nation as a whole, both in domestic matters and world affairs, and likes to think about American world leadership. Willing to accept some American responsibilities toward mankind, he then casts his vote for the presidential candidate most likely to represent these aspirations. As soon as he has done this, says Kendall, our voter turns around and asks himself: what about *my* district, *my* locality, *my* special economic interest, and *my* ethnic group? All the grand, costly, national and international policies go out the window. Now he seeks the most distrustful, tightfisted, narrow-minded, intensely parochial candidate he can find—and in this mood picks his representative to Congress. Once his President and congressman reach Washington, they must try to work out the conflicts which the voter failed to resolve in his own mind.

Kendall's sketch may be overdrawn but there is some truth in it. Congressional and presidential candidates of the same party rarely receive the same number of votes from a particular district. In districts where one party is strong enough to win at least 65 per cent of the vote for congressman, the victorious legislator tends to run ahead of the presidential candidate of his party. In all other districts, on the average, the opposite tendency prevails; the congressman, more often than not running behind the presidential ticket, tends to benefit from the pulling power of his leader's coattails. Once elected, however, the entire Congress, as Lewis Froman has shown, is likely to approve less than one-half of the President's proposals.

Once in Congress, legislators try to represent their constituency as well as their own convictions. The votes of each representative are shaped by what his constituency is like and by what he himself is like; by what the voters in his constituency think and by what he thinks they think; by the events that impinge on both the voters and their representative; by the legislative system which offers him specific choices; and by his perceptions of these options. These seven conditions and the way they shape the votes cast by a legislator are shown in Figure 10.2.

The House and Senate work in strikingly different ways. With its 435 members, the House is larger, more impersonal and formal in its proceedings, and more hierarchically organized. It is governed by more rigid rules, but is geared to quicker action. Power in the House is more unevenly distributed, and apprentice periods for freshmen legislators are longer. With shorter terms and smaller and less important constituencies, House members carry less prestige. Because they more often represent local and small town interests, their politics tend to be more conservative.

The 100 members of the Senate run their smaller chamber in a less formal manner. The Senate is less hierarchical, its rules more flexible, its actions slower, and its politics more personal. Power in the Senate is more evenly distributed; apprentice periods for new members are shorter. Often the Senate has been called a "club." With longer terms and larger and more important constituencies—entire states—senators carry more pres-

Figure 10.2

Why Congressmen Vote as They Do

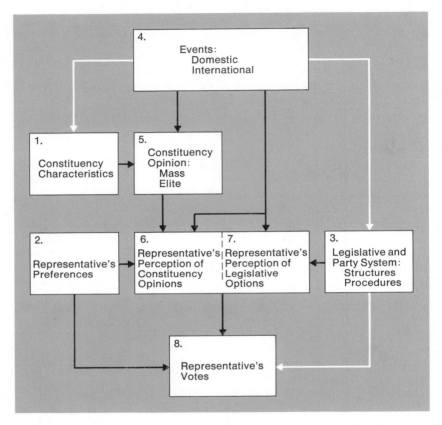

tige. Representing statewide interests, they are often politically more liberal.

Even within their chambers senators are likely to be more powerful than congressmen. In 1964, as Froman also has shown, four out of five Senate Democrats held at least one committee or subcommittee chairmanship, while in the House only two out of five Democrats held such positions.[6] When the Republicans are in power, similar proportions tend to apply to them. In either case, the power that comes from holding a chairmanship—to expedite, delay, or sidetrack legislation—is twice as accessible to senators.

The Work of Congress: Passing Legislation.   For both branches of Congress the workload has grown. The first Congress (in 1790-92) passed

---

[6] Senate committee chairmen are appointed by the meeting—called a *caucus*—of all senators of the majority party, in accordance with seniority. The caucus of the minority party chooses the "ranking" minority member of each committee in the same manner. Nearly the same procedures prevail in the House.

one law for every five of the few days it was in session; in the 1960s Congress met much longer and worked much faster: it passed about nine times as many laws, or nearly two laws per day. In such a crowded calendar, a bill's chances of becoming law are uncertain. Its hopes of passage depend first of all on its substance—the interests at stake. It is more likely to pass if more members support it, if their support is more intense, if its supporters are influential, and particularly if support comes from congressional leaders and the President. Its chances further improve if its supporters are strategically located, such as on the committee or subcommittee to which the bill is assigned, or on the Rules Committee which determines which committee will be assigned the bill. Finally, the bill is more likely to succeed if its opponents are few, lukewarm, lacking in influence, and poorly located.

Most bills are neither so popular in Congress as to be certain to breeze through nor so unpopular as to be hopeless. Proponents of such uncertain bills must win additional support for their proposals and they do so by bargaining. Some of this bargaining may occur without overt negotiation. Legislators seem to go ahead and act but in fact take into account what they anticipate will be the reaction of their colleagues. In other cases there is more direct negotiation, explicit or implied.

The simplest technique is *"logrolling."* Legislator A votes for Legislator B's project expecting or arranging that B will reciprocate. He expects B to be an "honest politician"—that is, one who never fails to repay favors. Sometimes logrolling may extend over time. A legislator will vote for a colleague's project in return for an invisible legislative I.O.U. to be cashed in at some future date. A raft of well-rolled logs is found in the omnibus Rivers and Harbors Bills, which comprise a large number of separate and independent projects, each one dear to a particular legislator but all of them as a package appealing to a sufficient number to ensure the support of a majority of legislators.

Sometimes logrolling involves large interest groups. In 1964, when the House passed a Cotton Bill, the Senate tacked on a wheat section. When the Cotton-Wheat Bill was returned to the House and still needed additional support for passage, the rural Democrats supporting it made a deal with urban Democrats who wanted a Food Stamp plan. As part of the bargain, the Food Stamp Bill had to be reported to the floor of the House first, but eventually both bills became law.

Another form of bargaining is the making of *compromises*. The proponents of a bill settle for less than they had originally demanded and they modify the bill to meet opponents halfway. Compromises may end up exactly halfway between different positions, or at some other highly visible or "prominent" solution acceptable to both sides; or else a compromise may give much to one side and little to the other, reflecting perhaps their unequal power or bargaining skills.

Finally, bargaining may involve *side payments*—advantages distinct from the content of the bill. Positive side payments to a legislator may consist of federal judgeships, postmasterships, or other patronage appointments being placed under his control in exchange for his support of legislation important to the President. Other side payments may come from within Congress, such as desirable committee assignments or subcommittee chairmanships. Still other side payments may come from outside the government from the national party or from special interest groups. These may include campaign contributions, well-paid speaking engagements, and the like. Influential legislators have reported annual income from such sources in excess of $100,000.

Outside pressures on Congress—such as from voters, interest groups, or the executive branch—clash or mesh in a changing balance with *inside influences* from congressional leaders or ordinary members. Inside influences tend to prevail and inside strategies are more likely to succeed, according to Nelson Polsby, when (1) the pending decision can be made a matter of procedure rather than substance; (2) one side has much greater inside strength while both are evenly matched outside; and (3) the members are shielded from surveillance by outsiders. When these conditions are reversed, outside forces are likely to predominate, together with the strategies designed to marshal them.

Miniature Legislatures: The Congressional Committees. Congressional committees resemble small cross-sections of Congress. They often are selected in a biased manner favoring some groups in Congress at the expense of others. Nonetheless, their contribution is indispensable. They permit bargaining, compromising, and log rolling with a minimum of publicity, until a workable majority coalition emerges. After a bill is reported out of committee, other members of Congress know more readily how to vote on it; they can pick up cues from committee members who are familiar with the measure and who have outlooks and interests similar to their own. A bill that passes in committee has a good chance to pass on the floor. Without the work of the committees a larger percentage of legislation would be defeated. While making legislation more acceptable to their fellow legislators, the committees tend to make it also less ideological, as abstract and sweeping provisions are whittled down and specific points are changed or added. Finally, by involving diverse interest groups outside Congress through formal hearings or informal communications, committee work makes the ultimate legislation more acceptable to the country.

The House Committee on Appropriations performs a particularly important task: it deals with money. Its decisions shape the federal budget and in the course of time much of the national government. In voting on the budgets of federal agencies, most of the increases or other budgetary changes it makes are marginal; and the over-all pattern of its decisions is balanced and conservative. Within this pattern, says Richard Fenno, most increases go to those agencies which have much support in the House outside the Committee and in the country at large, or have in the course of

time won the confidence of the Committee. A very few agencies, such as
the Federal Bureau of Investigation, meet all three tests. The Appropriations
Committee is greatly trusted by the House; from 1947 to 1962, by
Fenno's count, 90 per cent of its recommendations were accepted.

Representation in the committees is heavily weighted on the rural and
conservative side. Rural congressmen made up half of the House Democrats in 1964, but held nearly three-quarters of the House's major
committee chairmanships. Rural congressmen from the South contributed
less than 30 per cent of the House strength but had more than one-half the
chairmanships. Significantly, southern representation among major committee chairmanships corresponded almost exactly to the proportion of
southern "safe" seats in the House (see Table 10.1). On the important
House Rules Committee, the giving of half the Democratic seats to
southerners has become traditional. Limited steps to liberalize the House
Rules Committee were taken in 1961 and 1965, but a more conservative
Congress elected in 1966 repealed one of these.

In *roll-call votes* (where each legislator present publicly records his vote by
name), a Democratic President can count within the House committees on
an average support of 73 per cent from his own party and 37 per cent from
Republican committee members. The same holds true for Senate committees. For a Republican President in a Congress dominated by Democrats the proportions might be reversed if he did not shape his program
to attract more bipartisan support.

The Favored Elements in Congress. In matters of procedure
Congress is dominated by two parties. Democrats and Republicans
compete to organize the Congress to determine its majority and minority,
its committee chairmanships, and within each party the committee assignments. But on matters of substance many writers have seen four parties at
work in Congress: northern Democrats, mostly urban and liberal; southern
Democrats, mostly rural and conservative; liberal Republicans, mostly
from northeastern cities, suburbs, and rural areas; and conservative
Republicans, mostly from the rural Midwest, suburban California, and
parts of the urban South. None of these four has a majority in Congress.
On many issues an informal coalition of conservative Republicans and
southern Democrats has commanded a majority. (No such coalition
formed in the 1964–66 Congress which passed a program of social legislation much of which had been held up in previous decades.) A still more
detailed division would add two more groups to the four listed: middle-of-
the-road Democrats and middle-of-the-road Republicans. These two are
minorities but they are likely to be needed in helping majorities to form
and thus their influence is often great.

All told, Congress has come a long way from the days when Ralph
Waldo Emerson called it "a standing insurrection." In its operations it is
slow, conservative, and compromising in domestic matters. It is replete

with lawyers, farmers, and businessmen. Of some of its members it must be said that their prejudices seem more rigid than their ethics. In foreign affairs Congress following World War II drifted into the habit of backing a vast expansion of foreign involvement and military expenditure with little supervision or criticism, reserving its distrust mainly for the Foreign Economic Aid program which is now allocated but $2 billion (one quarter of one per cent of the GNP) or about one-tenth of its share in 1949.

Despite these shortcomings, Congress has enacted a vast program of legislation since 1933—one which has in many ways transformed the country. It has continued this work of transformation in the 1960s and it is likely to go on doing so in the decades ahead. Congress remains one of the broadest and most essential channels of communication between the American people and their government; it is an essential instrument for translating communications into agreement and agreement into action.

Legislative Representation and State Politics.   On the state level as on the national level, bicameral legislatures are the rule. (Only Nebraska now has a single-chamber legislature.) In the states, too, the twentieth-century trend has been toward direct election of both chambers.

Unlike politics on the national level, state politics have been characterized more often by unequal districts, or districts of bizarre shape, deliberately drawn to favor one party at the expense of the other. The first such district was drawn in the early years of the Republic with the advice of Mr. Elbridge Gerry of Massachusetts; it was elongated like a salamander and Gerry's opponents called it a new monster, the *gerrymander,* thus adding both a noun and verb to the language of politics. Together with restrictive residence requirements and other voter registration laws and practices, these conditions have favored the domination of many states by political machines well entrenched at the state, county, and municipal levels. In recent years, industrialization, mass migration, and the growing participation of large numbers of people in politics have put mounting pressure on these ancient practices. Struggles over voter registration, equal representation, legislative reapportionment, and breaking or limiting the power of state political machines now loom large in American politics and may continue to do so for some time.

The struggle for political control on the state level has been a persistent factor in American government, for state politics are critical to the working of the federal system. There are four basic ways by which they affect the federal system. First, they indirectly control the nomination and election of all United States senators and thus the composition of one branch of the federal legislature. Secondly, the major political parties in the nation are actually little more than federations of state party organizations. The state organizations of each party control more manpower and resources than each party's national committee. Each national party therefore critically depends on influence and patronage within each state. Control of national parties is often won or lost at the state level. Without control of jobs and favors at the state level, a party cannot hold together much of its organization. With such control, a party can survive for many years out of national office.

Thirdly, the party organization in each state often plays a decisive part in the nomination and election of candidates for the United States House of Representatives. And finally, state politics, state parties, and sometimes state primaries, often determine the nomination of major party candidates for President of the United States. In this respect, the party machine in each state tends to be more important than the party voters. In 1968 both Republicans and Democrats nominated presidential candidates who seemed to be more popular with the regular party organizations than with the mass of voters. Thus state politics frequently exercise a direct influence on the composition of Congress and an indirect but powerful influence on the selection of the Chief Executive of the United States.

The Presidency and Executive Power

The most demanding job in federal government is the presidency of the United States. It is always wearing, often thankless, and sometimes deadly. Abraham Lincoln once remarked that his position reminded him of the man who commented, while being ridden out of town on a rail, "If it were not for the honor of the thing, I would rather walk." For more than a century there has been a bitter reality behind Lincoln's quip. The presidency has killed many of its incumbents, four by assassination—Lincoln, Garfield, McKinley, Kennedy—and others, such as Wilson and Franklin D. Roosevelt, by strain and overwork (see Figure 10.3). When it has not killed them, the presidency has certainly worn them down (see Figure 10.4).

Yet the office has never wanted for occupants; there has never been a need to put a "To let" sign on the White House lawn. The presidency has always been the most powerful office within the United States, and with the coming of nuclear weapons, it has become one of the most powerful on earth. Today the President of the United States could be both his nation's chief executive and executioner: he shares with the rulers of the Soviet Union the power to destroy civilization and to kill most of mankind. At the same time, with the coming of the welfare state and of international economic aid, the United States presidency has become crucially involved with a growing range of human needs. Its potentialities for good, too, are vast and are still growing.

In the past, some American Presidents have chosen not to use their full powers. They have been passive in office. When the writer Dorothy Parker was told that President Calvin Coolidge had died, she asked: "How could they tell?" But just as the passive presidents of the 1850s—Fillmore, Pierce, and Buchanan—were followed by the Civil War, the passive Presidents of the 1920s—Harding, Coolidge, and Hoover—were followed

Figure 10.3
Woodrow Wilson

1913

1920

Source: Bettmann Archive.

Figure 10.4

Lyndon B. Johnson

1963

1968

Source: Wide World Photos.

by the Great Depression. Again, during the 1950s, many voters wanted President Eisenhower to preside over a relaxed nation and a passive government, and some of the things left undone in those years may have borne bitter fruit in the unemployed young, the neglected minorities, and the urban riots and crises of the 1960s. The presidency is the primary place from which unified leadership can be offered to the American people, and its opportunities cannot be neglected without high cost to the country.

The President's Election. The American President and Vice-President are elected for a four-year term, and the President is limited to two terms in office. Both are elected by all the people, and in their election the people's votes have more nearly equal weight than in the election of any other branch of government.

Even here, however, the weighting of votes is not completely equal. As a matter of form, the President is elected indirectly by an *Electoral College.* Each state has a number of electors equal to the sum of its senators and congressmen; and its state legislature may provide for the appointment or election of these electors in any manner it sees fit. This arrangement favors somewhat the smaller states, since even the smallest ones must have at least two senators and one congressman, and thus cannot have less than three votes in the Electoral College. Nonetheless, in 1968 the massive electoral votes of the seven most populous states—California, New York, Pennsylvania, Illinois, Ohio, Texas, and Michigan—accounted for 210 votes out of a total of 538 electors. These states have been decisive in past elections, and they are likely to continue to be decisive in the future.

Despite the intentions of the Founding Fathers, the election of the President has in effect become the result of a popular vote, and most voters so perceive it. Electors are usually *pledged* to vote for a particular candidate; most voters neither know nor care who the electors are but vote for a slate of electors because these electors promise to cast their ballots for the candidate whom the voters favor. In some states, however, it is legally possible for a slate of electors to present itself *unpledged* to the voters, perhaps with the promise to strike the best bargain in the Electoral College in regard to some issue of particular importance to the voters of that state. Electors pledged to the candidate of a minority party might play a similar role if no major party candidate were able to command a majority of electoral votes. It is also legally possible for an elector to break his pledge to his voters and cast his ballot for another candidate. The Constitution provides no remedy against such a breach of party discipline or of faith to the voters, but in 1969 proposals for an appropriate constitutional amendment were underway.

The President is the only officer of the United States government elected from a nationwide constituency. He is expected therefore to act as President of all the people. And in practice the presidency is that branch of the government which is most responsive to urban and industrial voters and to the needs of ethnic, religious, or racial minorities. The mechanism ensuring this responsiveness rests in the present composition of the Electoral College and the crucial role of the seven largest states within it. These seven are highly urban and industrial; each includes a high concentration of minorities; and the votes of each state must be cast as a unit. A presidential candidate therefore must win or lose each state as a whole; and for winning he depends heavily on the urban, industrial, and minority group voters within it.

This winner-take-all provision for the electoral votes of each state represents in one sense an injustice against the voters of the losing party. Their votes are not counted, and they might well prefer some scheme of proportional representation among the electors of their state. But in another sense the winner-take-all arrangement is a countervailing injustice. It balances the overweighting of the small states, and of the rural areas and old stock elements in the population; as we have seen, this overweighting characterizes the way in which the House of Representatives and, to a lesser extent, the Senate are elected.

In the late 1960s, various proposals for reforming the procedure for presidential elections were discussed. There seemed to be widespread agreement that the Electoral College should be replaced by the direct vote of the people, but there was disagreement whether to retain majority rule within each state or whether to replace it by some scheme of proportional representation. If the latter device were adopted, voters from urban and industrial areas and from minority groups might find their influence drastically reduced. Lacking any compensating change in other aspects of political representation, such voters might then feel permanently underrepresented in the American political system and become alienated from it. Under the present arrangement, voters disappointed with their representation in Congress often still look to the presidency for redress.

Since the President is an essential part of the system, he must be promptly replaced in case of death or disability. Detailed rules for the succession to the presidency have been worked out to guarantee a rapid and peaceful transfer of power. If the President dies in office he is succeeded by the Vice-President. After the assassination of President Kennedy, the transfer of his office to Vice-President Lyndon B. Johnson was accomplished within an hour. If both the President and the Vice-President should die, the Speaker of the House would become President; after him, the succession would go to the President *pro tempore* of the Senate, and then to the Secretary of State, the Secretary of the Treasury, and the rest of the Cabinet. There are also specific provisions for succession in case of the President's illness or incapacity. These seem unique, and they contrast strikingly with the practice of dictatorships. They also appear as reasonably safe as can be expected. Even in the age of nuclear weapons, where one large hydrogen bomb could wipe out Washington, D.C., it seems unlikely that all these persons could be killed at once. Some continuity in the office of chief executive thus seems to be as well assured as anything else in the American political system under conditions of modern weaponry.

The President's Many Roles.   Once elected, the President must fulfill many different roles which may be only partly compatible with each other. In military matters, he is *Commander-in-Chief* of a 3.5 million peacetime defense force, and of the entire nation in times of war. In recent years, the increasing power of modern weapons systems has made him responsible for more destructive power than any man should have. The same modern technology has made the President potentially more helpless. On the eve of an all-out war he would have to depend on radar echoes and other types of electronic information, hard to interpret and subject to error. He would have to make decisions under extreme constraints of time, and he would then have to live on the bullseye of a target, with Washington and the White House exposed to the thermonuclear weapons of an enemy. He might have to use a large part of the few minutes available to him for decision just to get himself and his family moved to some presumably safer shelter; and any orders he might give to American aircraft and missiles might soon prove impossible to recall. The military technology which has so vastly increased the President's power also has tended to make him its prisoner.

In regard to conventional weapons and troop commitments, the President has a wider range of discretion. According to the Constitution, only Congress can declare war. But tradition has long permitted American Presidents to commit troops and ships—and more recently aircraft—to smaller "police actions" on their own authority. Such precedents reach from Jefferson's sending a few ships against Algerian pirates to numerous skirmishes on the Indian frontier of the United States and to various interventions by the United States marines in the Caribbean and Mexico during the first two decades of the twentieth century. In recent years these "police actions" have tended to become much bigger in such places as Korea, Lebanon, the Dominican Republic, and Vietnam. They have involved not only professional soldiers and volunteers, as in earlier "police actions," but also large numbers of drafted citizen soldiers, including many reluctant or unwilling ones; and the size and duration of some of these undertakings have proved increasingly difficult to control. Here again the greater powers of the President threaten to imprison him.

At home, the President is the country's *Bureaucrat-in-Chief.* As head of the executive branch of the government he is in charge of more than two million civilian employees. Many of these are now protected by civil service regulations designed to prevent their hiring and firing on political grounds. About 1,500 top-level government jobs are defined as *policy-making appointments* and are in the President's gift. The President also appoints his White House staff which has grown substantially in recent years. He also appoints members of presidential commissions to report on matters of fact or policy, and he may surround himself if he wishes with a variety of informal advisers and associates. In appointing ambassadors, federal judges, and the members of his official Cabinet who comprise the heads of the major departments of the government, he requires the *advice and consent* of the Senate. Such consent is only rarely refused to Cabinet nominees. In the 1950s the Senate discovered that an ambassador-designate did not even know the name of the head of the country to which he was to be sent, but the appointment was confirmed just the same. Generally, however, the President anticipates the probable response of the Senate in nominating such persons for appointment.

The President is also the *leader of his party* and *Dispenser-in-Chief* of federal patronage and favors. Through these powers the President can exercise not only moral but also material influence on the votes of congressmen and senators. The more responsive they are to the wishes of the President, the more receptive he may prove to the needs of their districts, states, party organizations, and personal acquaintances. Some Presidents have been more vigorous than others in reminding members of Congress of their powers. President Franklin D. Roosevelt was a master of such methods; and so, more bluntly, was Lyndon B. Johnson.

A major source of presidential power is the President's role as the *symbol of national unity* and as media *Manipulator-in-Chief.* The President makes news by anything he does, if he so chooses, and sometimes even if he does not. He often can define a situation as he wishes, and thus predetermine much of the response of American opinion. After taking over the presidency in 1963 Lyndon Johnson chose to define the fighting in South Vietnam as a case of simple foreign aggression by the North Vietnamese, and in August 1964 he defined an ambiguous incident in the Gulf of Tonkin as an attack on the United States Navy. These definitions went far to prepare Congress and the voters to accept the escalation of the American commitment in South Vietnam from 16,000 "advisors" in late 1963 to over 540,000 troops in late 1968. By contrast the Johnson decision *not* to define the capture of the American electronic intelligence ship *Pueblo* by the North Koreans in 1968 as an act of war kept public opinion relatively quiet and permitted the government to obtain the return of the ship and its crew through negotiation. The President's power to define issues and direct public attention is scarcely less in domestic affairs. Presidential support and leadership, or their lack, have decided the success or failure of many a civil rights or social welfare program.

Despite all these assets, the President's powers are severely limited. He cannot allocate any major amounts of money without congressional support. Even some of his major official appointments depend, as we have seen, on senatorial good will. Beyond Congress, the President depends on the courts which may declare his acts unconstitutional—even though they usually are reluctant to do so. Yet the Supreme Court did exactly this when it threw out some of the early acts of Franklin D. Roosevelt's New Deal. Major executive acts, such as President Harry S Truman's seizure of the strike-bound steel industry in 1952, likewise may be subject to court scrutiny. Beyond the courts, the President depends on the voluntary cooperation of his officials and the people. Only if the great majority of these comply can he enforce his decisions on the rest.

In regard to these many elements, the President often must act as a *political broker,* striving to put together a coalition which is like-minded enough to agree and strong enough to act. As a rule, a President can be no stronger than the coalition behind him. But even if backed by all elements of the American political system, the President is not all-powerful in world politics. The actions of many foreign nations are outside his control. Neither has he unlimited power over nature and technology. Inescapably, the President is human and fallible—and so is the American people. One test of greatness for both consists in the ability to recognize these limitations.

Federal Powers and the Judiciary

Federal powers, characteristic of the American system, are very great over credit, commerce, and contracts. These powers were crucial for the integration of the United States into one country. The first large step in the development of federal power was taken by the states under the Articles of Confederation with the *full faith and credit clause.* Under this clause, each state had to give full faith and credit to the public acts, records, and judicial proceedings of every other state. The Constitution now embodies this principle but it shifts the main integrative task to federal institutions.

A major channel of federal influence is the institution of *judicial review*— the right and duty of the courts to decide whether any law or act is valid under the Constitution. It does not appear in the Constitution but grew up as an interpretation of it. In no other country in the world has the Supreme Court as much power and as much respect as in the United States. The Court has functioned in a very important way, beginning in 1800 with Chief Justice John Marshall's opinion in the famous case of *Marbury vs. Madison.* Ever since, the courts have had the right to review the executive acts of the federal and state governments, and the laws of the national and state legislatures.

The power of the judiciary to determine the constitutionality of legislation and executive acts has five major consequences. First, the courts settle many serious political conflicts peacefully. Second, they are one of the chief instruments of balance in the American political system, by limiting the power of the other branches of government, and by protecting individuals and minorities. Third, they often slow down change until it becomes acceptable to a larger majority of the people. Fourth, they sometimes accelerate change, or they bring about immediate changes which the other branches of government have failed to produce. Fifth, the courts offer in all these respects an additional channel of communication between the people and their government, and a long-term feedback circuit through which the American political system can steer itself.

The courts contribute an important check and balance by their practice of judging acts of the legislative and executive branches of government in the light of the judges' understanding of the Constitution. As Charles Evans Hughes said before he himself became Chief Justice, "The Constitution is what the judges say it is." Though the Constitution looks like a simple document, it is often not at all clear how it should be applied to the many complex problems that have arisen since its enactment. The judges' latitude in interpreting it is great indeed, and their decisions, in particular those of the Supreme Court, have become an important part of "judge-made" law. Because most Americans habitually respect and obey their courts, and the lower courts accept the overriding decisions of the higher courts, the entire judiciary system has important powers over what happens in government and throughout the country.

The courts have thrown out important acts of Congress such as the National Recovery Act in the 1930s. They also have declared illegal some major acts of the President, including some taken in the name of national security. Thus the Supreme Court in the decision *ex parte Milligan* held illegal certain emergency powers assumed by the Lincoln Administration during the Civil War. A later Supreme Court took a very critical view of the compulsory internment of Americans of Japanese descent during World War II. In both cases, the Court acted, however, only after the emergency had passed; and the compensation finally paid to the illegally and unjustly interned Japanese-Americans for their lost properties amounted to about ten cents on the dollar.[7]

The courts thus cannot act quickly. In times of emergency, they are reluctant to stop the other two branches of the government from acting; and even later they cannot always insure full redress to victims of injustice. Nevertheless, they can provide at least partial redress. They can free men from prison. They can restore rights that were denied; they can clear people's names; and they can make clear what individuals and agencies of government cannot do within the law. In serving these functions, the courts protect individuals as well as the soundness of the American political process. "The brain is an organ of inhibition," said an Austrian labor leader many years ago; the Supreme Court has long been a vital part of the brain and conscience of the American Republic and its people.

As an agency of inhibition, the Supreme Court has often acted as a brake on change. On the average, a Supreme Court justice in the twentieth century has held his position for twelve years; ordinarily he cannot

[7] See Morton Grodzins, *Americans Betrayed* (Chicago: University of Chicago Press, 1949).

be removed against his will. No President has been able during a single four-year term to appoint a majority of Supreme Court justices. The justices thus often represent the memories and standards of a somewhat earlier day, and at least intermittently the view of an older generation.

For this they have often been chided. Mr. Justice Oliver Wendell Holmes criticized his colleagues for clinging too closely to nineteenth-century doctrines of government nonintervention in the labor market when they held that sweatshops and nightwork for women should not be interfered with by state governments. The Constitution, said Mr. Holmes, did not enact the prejudices of Herbert Spencer, the nineteenth-century British *laissez-faire* writer. (Later, Mr. Justice Holmes' views on this point were accepted by the Court's majority.) In the 1930s President Franklin Roosevelt complained of the "nine old men" of the Supreme Court who in his view were going too far in defending property rights and thwarting the will of the voters.

At their best, however, the courts also represent some of the more enduring values and long-term points of view. During the decades since 1945, the Supreme Court has particularly stressed the rights of individuals. It has often opposed or limited the new controls over individuals introduced by the government in the name of national security. In the face of congressional legislation and administrative practices, the Court has limited the requirements for security clearances, and it has tended to favor the traditional rights of Americans to keep their jobs, to travel abroad freely, to face their accusers, and to be held innocent until proved guilty by due process of law.

Sometimes the courts have been important instruments of change. They have struck down laws which no longer had the backing of the majority of voters but which were so intensely defended by influential minorities that no legislative majority could be found for their repeal. Since these laws no longer corresponded to the convictions of the majority, they threatened penalities for what Burke might have called "artificial crimes," yet there seemed to be no practical legislative remedy. This was the case with the legal ban on birth control information which in the early 1960s was still on the books of Connecticut and Massachusetts and made almost all local doctors and druggists into lawbreakers. When the courts finally struck down these laws as unconstitutional, no politician made any serious effort to resurrect them, and doctors and druggists could breathe more freely.

Finally, the courts function as a major communication channel both to the memories and traditions of the past and to the felt needs of the present and future. The Supreme Court, said Finley Peter Dunne's Mister Dooley, follows the election returns. In one sense this is true, but the Court often follows these returns with a time delay of one or two decades, during which it becomes clear whether these earlier returns reflected a passing mood or a genuine trend of development.

In this manner many Supreme Court justices have followed the advice of Roscoe Pound to view law as an instrument of social control and to use it as such. Some justices have been eminent lawyers, others have been highly skilled in practical affairs, often having served as governors of states, federal Cabinet members, United States Presidents (Taft), or presidential candidates (Hughes, Warren). Whatever their background, many of them have had a refreshing sense of the practical. In the early 1920s a Court majority confirmed a lower court decision which barred an immigrant grandmother, Mrs. Rosika Schwimmer, from citizenship on the grounds that as an avowed pacifist she would not "bear arms" in defense of the Constitution. Mr. Justice Holmes dissented. For three centuries, he wrote, the Quakers had been pacifists refusing to bear arms, yet they had done well by their country. Besides, he added dryly, the United States would indeed be in a perilous position if it needed the armed service of a grandmother to defend it. In later years this dissent of Mr. Holmes, too, became the Court's majority doctrine. Pacifism is not a bar to United States citizenship any longer; and the 1969 verdict of an Appeals Court, throwing out a lower court's conviction of Dr. Benjamin Spock (for allegedly having "conspired" to thwart the draft for the Vietnam War), was in the Holmes tradition.

Another problem of reconciling legal, moral, and practical considerations occurred at the time of the sitdown strikes in the late 1930s when striking auto workers occupied the factories of several major auto manufacturers. Some business and conservative interests called on the Governor of Michigan, Frank Murphy, to use military force to defend property rights and evict the strikers, regardless of the expectable bloodshed. This Governor Murphy refused to do. His refusal compelled both sides to negotiate. In time the strikes were settled; the union was recognized; the men returned to work; and in due course, Governor Murphy was appointed to the Supreme Court. Some lawyers said that the Court henceforth would offer "justice tempered with Murphy," but the balance between property rights and human rights, between strict law and the politically practical, has remained among the Court's significant concerns—as such cases as *Baker vs. Carr* in favor of legislative reapportionment have demonstrated.

In one respect the role of the judiciary is unique. Both legislation and administration are processes designed primarily to deal with human beings in large numbers. Inevitably, they are most often concerned with *mass* legislation and *mass* administration. The courts alone are primarily designed to deal with *individuals* and with specific cases. It is this we have in mind when we say that every man ought to have a right to "his day in court"—the day when the legal and political system is focused on him and his problems as an individual. This function of the courts has often been obscured in practice by the enormous costs and delays of court procedures. Carrying a case through the trial court, the higher courts, and the Supreme Court usually costs upwards of $10,000. "A poor man has a chanst in coort . . ." said Mr. Dooley more than half a century ago. "He has the same chanst there that he has outside. He has a splendid poor man's chanst."

In recent years, the Supreme Court has handed down several decisions that are beginning to make a difference to a poor man's chances. Indigent defendants in federal felony trials have won the right to a free lawyer, and in *Gideon vs. Wainwright* the Court extended this right to the state courts, where most of the actual felony trials are held. A suspect in police custody has long had the right to ask for a lawyer if he can pay for him, or if he can get him free. In *Escobedo vs. Illinois* the Court ruled that the police must honor such a request for consultation; and in *Miranda vs. Arizona* it said that before being questioned in police custody an individual must be told of his right to keep silent and to have a lawyer (free, if he is poor), and he must be warned that anything he says may be used against him—a warning customary in federal practice and long-standing in Britain. Together these decisions give the same protection of legal rights to the innocent suspect and the ignorant lawbreaker as the professional criminal and the large-scale operator of crime have had for many years. The effects on actual police practice have thus far been moderate. Nonetheless these decisions have been charged with hampering the work of the police and thus endangering the victims of future crimes. In making its rulings the Court has had to decide between these conflicting viewpoints and values— the rights of individual citizens as against the convenience of administration and the fears of the community—and it has decided in favor of the individual.

In the long run such Court decisions require the backing of the people if they are to be effective. But these decisions show that the Court may sometimes try to lead opinion rather than, as is so often thought, merely follow it. Leading or following, the judiciary helps to decide whither the American people and their government will go next; and the size and importance of its contribution to this self-steering process make the American political system different from all others in the world.

The Underlying Premise: Economic Abundance

American politics has been based on a belief in optimism, spontaneity, harmony of interests, readiness to experiment, and willingness to compromise. Why did these beliefs prevail and why did the political system succeed? Perhaps most important, the American political system was superimposed from the beginning upon a highly prosperous economy. For a long time, this economy was nearly automatic. At the start of the Republic, there was no dogmatic taboo against government acting in economic matters, but most of the expansion of the frontier was done by individuals, not government. Most of the nation's farming, manufacturing, mining, and transport was undertaken spontaneously by individuals seeking profit, and was guided automatically by the market mechanism.

In most markets people vote not with ballots but with dollar bills or their equivalent. In the United States the distribution of income is such that the top 10 per cent of income receivers hold 30 per cent of the income, the second 10 per cent hold about 15 per cent, and the third 10 per cent have at least 10 per cent or more (see Figures 4.6 and 10.5). That is to say, 30 per cent of the American people have more than 50 per cent of the dollar votes in the market. One must never forget that in voting with dollars there is a differential franchise which makes a permanent minority of over two-thirds of the American people. But in voting with ballots these two-thirds have a better chance of making their needs known and their voices heard.

The American economy worked as well as it did because the country was unusually well supplied with highly skilled personnel. From the beginning, American settlers had many more skilled craftsmen among them than did Latin American settlers from Spain, or settlers in Canada or Australia.

Secondly, immigrants to the United States between 1775 and 1875 came with more capital. The average covered wagon with which pioneers—many of them foreign born—crossed the prairies in the mid-nineteenth century contained in current prices about $5,000 worth of axes, rifles, blankets, ammunition, and other things. New capital was found and new labor kept arriving through immigration from Europe. Most of the new arrivals were of prime working age, whereas the babies and the aged stayed in the Old World. The cost of raising babies until they were husky twenty-year-olds was borne by the European economies. The *dependency burden* stayed in Europe, the working potential came to America. In this sense, throughout the nineteenth century the rest of the world subsidized the United States—perhaps to a larger degree than the United States has subsidized the rest of the world in the twentieth.

Added to this voluntary subsidy by adult immigration was a grim involuntary subsidy. The import of Negro slaves until 1808 transported net labor power from Africa to the United States. It left the terrible cost of this traffic mainly in Africa and took some of the economic growth of the country out of the bones of the slaves.

Additional capital, too, was accumulated in the outside world and then imported here. Alexander Hamilton's policies specifically aimed at making capital import attractive to foreign investors. But the United States not only attracted more capital than other countries, it squandered less. Both American and foreign observers in the nineteenth century often commented on American wastefulness and corruption. They overlooked that the proportionate cost of all such scandals was much less than the regular cost of maintaining monarchies, aristocracies, and large standing armies as the European powers did. The large amounts European nations spent on the splendor of monarchs, and on cannons and barracks, Americans spent on factories, fields, and mines. The United States had the smallest standing military force among nineteenth-century powers, and the highest rate of economic growth.

Figure 10.5

Income Distribution in the United States, 1968

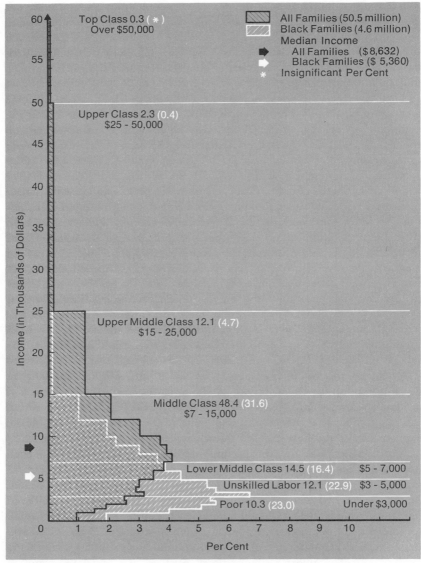

Source: *U.S. Bureau of the Census,* Current Population Reports, *Series P-60, No. 63, 1969.*

The result of this uniquely productive, uniquely prosperous, and invisibly subsidized economy with its vast resources of land, labor, and capital was a steady growth of living standards. At the time of the American Revolution the American people used more iron per capita than any other country in the world. They were using more tonnage of shipping than any other country in the world as well. The American living standard was ahead of Europe as early as the 1840s and 1850s. It has never lagged.

This prosperity—fostered by the presence of the frontier until 1890, by business growth until 1929, and by the revival of business growth in the years following the war prosperity of World War II—produced a popular belief in private enterprise. The American economy was characterized by what the economist Gunnar Myrdal has called a *spread effect.* Since there was so much capital and so much managerial talent available, these factors of production often spread into the less developed regions. This effect is the opposite of the *backwash effect* in areas where skilled manpower, management, and capital are rare and where economic growth elsewhere leads to a draining of these resources out of the poorer regions and into richer ones. Appalachia, Mississippi, West Virginia, and South and North Dakota long were examples of such regions and states where wealth flowed out rather than in. But in most other states the American economy pumped wealth in rather than out, and the exceptions—the poor regions, neighborhoods, and strata—were frequently forgotten.

Although most Americans enjoyed the fruits of their economic practices, they had a hard time finding a precise name for them. Since economic activities within a country are interdependent in many ways, it seemed natural to think of them as forming an economic system. An economic system, however, is far more complex than the simple labels—"capitalism" and "socialism"—which nineteenth-century economic thought made current. *Capitalism* is the name for a system in which factories and land are privately owned and where economic development is directed by the automatic working of supply and demand in the market. *Socialism,* by contrast, is a system in which land and factories are owned publicly, either by the state or by large cooperatives, and economic development is directed by plan. The American economy from the beginnings of the Republic has been mixed. It was clearly much more capitalist than socialist, but from the Erie Canal to the Panama Canal and from the original land grants to the railroads and to the current vast public activities in education and research, the government's share has never been negligible.

Since capitalist elements clearly predominated, however, and since most Americans approved of the results, businessmen were proud until 1929 to call themselves capitalists and the United States a capitalist system. In 1929 the national treasurer of the Democratic Party, John J. Raskob, listed his occupation in *Who's Who* as "capitalist." The Great Depression, with its mass unemployment, then made capitalism unpopular. Whether or not businessmen privately thought of themselves as "capitalists," their public relations advisers preferred the words "business" or "private enterprise" or "management" to the term "capitalism." Radicals used the words "capitalist" and "capitalism" with enthusiasm for persons and practices they did not like. Many moderates began to shun these words as potentially misleading or divisive. Only in the 1960s did use of the terms revive in the United States. Conservative leaders like Barry Goldwater, and a few writers like William F. Buckley, Jr. and Ayn Rand, stressed them again, and at the same time their use became much more widespread among social critics from the left half of the political spectrum.

At present, both conservatives and their critics think of "capitalism" not only in terms of an economic system but also in terms of a social class and of the power which it is supposed to have, or ought to have, within the political system. Some political scientists have taken part in this debate, but other political scientists have preferred the use of the term *elite* as permitting a more discriminating and precise analysis. Many of them agree, however, that at the heart of the debate stand two important questions: Which groups in the United States have the most power? And how is the unequal distribution of power related to the economic system?

Locations of Power

Where does the power lie in the United States? Some people think that it is concentrated in the hands of a small group, perhaps even an anonymous one. Others think that power is widely dispersed among the people, or that in a democracy it ought to be. Our concern is with the actual *distribution of power* in the United States, which lies somewhere between. Though this distribution is highly unequal, it is by no means fully concentrated in any one group—and it is subject to continuing change.

In order to study this distribution more closely, one might make a distinction between *general purpose elites* and *special elites*. The former have influence in regard to many matters; the latter have influence in some narrower field.

The Core of the American Establishment.   Probably the greatest single concentration of influence and power for general purposes in the United States is in the credit, banking, and investment communities. Since money is needed for many purposes, those who control its flow will have power in many matters, if they choose to exercise it. The sociologist Robert Lamb proposed that one could find the leading families of any small American town by looking up the names of the board of the local bank twenty-five years earlier. Insofar as these families had not left town, they would be the leading families today.

On the whole, the banking-financial community—which is fairly broad, reaching from the small-town banker all the way to the president of the Chase Manhattan Bank—has the greatest amount of influence. Studies of congressional mail show that a letter from a small-town banker weighs more with his congressman than a letter from most other people.

Also at the core of the establishment is the top political leadership of the country. This includes the leaders of both major parties, in or out of office. The political scientist Ralph Huitt recounts how an ambitious graduate of Yale and the Harvard Business School went to work for the Wall Street firm of J. P. Morgan and Company. After a time he concluded that the decisions were no longer made by financiers but by politicians. Accordingly, he moved to the Midwest and in due course became Senator William O. Proxmire of Wisconsin.

The interchange between bankers and the government is extensive. Andrew Mellon as Secretary of the Treasury under Hoover, Douglas Dillon in the Kennedy and Johnson years, and the executives of Dillon, Reed and Company and other investment houses in New York as major officers in the Defense and State Departments after World War II, all reflect the close ties between the investment interests and the federal government.

A second large group influential in government is manufacturing and advertising. A list of the ten biggest industrial corporations in the United States in rank order of their advertising budget was published some years ago. Included in this list was General Motors in first place, Procter and Gamble, and the Ford Motor Company. At the time when these firms were among the ten top advertisers in the United States, the American Secretaries of Defense were Charles Wilson originally of General Motors, Neal McElroy of Procter and Gamble, and Robert S. McNamara of Ford.

The law firms are another major link in connecting the financial community, the industrial community, and the government. Such firms as Sullivan and Cromwell, in which the late Secretary of State John Foster Dulles was a partner, is a good example. President Nixon's law firm is another; his law partner, John Mitchell, ran his presidential campaign and then became his Attorney General.

Since 1942 the military establishment has become a major force. A United States senator recently pointed out that two thousand high-ranking former military officers are now occupying high-level executive posts in American industry, usually in firms that had and continue to have contracts with the Defense Department. The late General Douglas MacArthur was board chairman of Remington Rand. General Omar Bradley is on the board of Bulova Watch Company. The list of eminent military alumni is long. It should be remembered that good generals are competent executives, that business firms are perfectly willing to hire good executives where they can get them, and that generals know very well what kind of goods the armed forces are likely to buy.

There has also been an interchange of military and financial judgment. For instance, in World War II, an investment banker, Robert Lovett, was

Undersecretary of Defense in charge of bombing strategy. The selection of targets for investment and the selection of targets for strategic bombing are intellectually analogous processes. In each case one is trying to find key facilities, in one to buy, in the other to destroy, but in both the same type of judgment is involved.

Then there are the information and communication services—the advertising and public relations complexes on Madison Avenue; the mass media empires, such as the Henry Luce papers and the Scripps-Howard and Hearst chains. In recent years, the major television and radio networks—NBC, CBS, and ABC—have outgrown the newspaper chains in importance. Still more important are the great news agencies, Associated Press (AP) and United Press International (UPI), which supply news to newspapers and newsmagazines, as well as to radio and television.

Putting these five groups together—banking, large industry, the military complex, law firms, and fringe services such as advertising and mass media—we get the core of the *establishment*. Somewhat more dependent at the fringes are the foundations and major private and public universities.

The Power of Special Interests.   The establishment interests must be distinguished from special interests; the five groups named above are so diversified that they are interested in many things, not only in one. General Motors and Du Pont are involved in dozens of products in dozens of lines. Rarely will they exert all-out pressure on one particular law because their interests are so diversified. One division of General Motors or of Du Pont may want a protective tariff for its specialty, but another division, making a product for export, may want free trade.

Special interests have much clearer configurations. First of all, there is the aircraft and electronic industries. The military effectiveness of strategic bombing was discredited after World War II by the strategic bombing survey, after the Korean War by the failure of the air force to stop the flow of ammunitions to the Korean front, and it has been once again discredited in Vietnam. But the belief in air power does not stop since the aircraft industry continues to sustain it. Just as smoking does not disappear with a report from the Surgeon General, but is more related to the persistence of popular habits and to the advertising budget of the tobacco industry, so the belief in air power is related in part to the persistence of military traditions and popular habits of thought, as well as to the public relations budgets of the aircraft and electronics industries. Their large social and economic interests will continue to have an input into the political and communication systems of the United States.

The oil companies form another obvious major interest group. The old oil interests of Standard Oil have now merged with the general financial community, through such institutions as the Rockefeller interests and the Chase Manhattan Bank. More recent special oil interests, such as those formed by some Texas oil men, are on the fringes. They are more inclined to express their grievances against the Eastern establishment through support of raucous, super-patriotic groups and to suspect all of Wall Street as "unpatriotic."

The mineral interests in the southeastern states and the copper and tin interests in overseas operations are also special interest groups, with strong views on Latin American affairs. Cotton, tobacco, and sugar interests are located mainly in the southern states. Large-scale farming is more prominent in the Midwest and in California. Control of the import of bananas from Central America, and of sugar from Cuba and the Caribbean, together with the plantations producing these commodities, long has been concentrated in Boston and New York. There are declining interest groups, such as the railroads, and rising interest groups, such as road building, heavy construction, and urban redevelopment—all of which have very close ties to local political parties and to state and local governments. Building and road contractors are usually involved in politics. The electronics industry is growing, and so is the research industry; they have many common ties and form a rising interest group.

Labor unions also form a powerful complex of interest groups. On some issues they are united. Unions of all types tend to support a federal minimum wage, and higher wages in general. On other issues, such as the maintenance of a restrictive apprentice system which can almost close a trade to newcomers and thus tends to work to the disadvantage of black people and other minorities, only some highly skilled craft unions will commit their efforts. In contrast, proposed laws against race discrimination are more likely to be supported by industrial unions, comprising both skilled and unskilled workers, such as the United Automobile Workers of America.

Special interest groups tend to use their power only in regard to matters of specific concern to them. On these matters, they may form shifting coalitions; and for their particular objectives, they usually get fairly good service from the political system.

Social Strata and Their Power.   Below the interest groups are the social strata. The middle class, or what can be called the middle class in the United States, has been steadily growing. Today the United States probably has the broadest middle class in the world. Depending on how one defines it (and whether one includes what is called the *lower* middle class to which nobody wants to belong but which always turns up in the statistics), the American middle class goes down from the 95th to at least the 60th percentile of income, and possibly to the 40th percentile. This group overlaps in part with the clerical and service occupations, the white-collar occupations which also have grown. Most mass media cater to the tastes and views of the middle class. Politicians bow to its mores and values; those who do not rarely are elected to national office. Almost the only ones who sometimes purposely offend it are its children—but often with the opposite political results from those intended. Though the middle class is generally respected in matters of form, it may fail to get its way on some large matters of substance, such as ending an unpopular war or keeping America's central cities habitable. Nevertheless, while most of the political coalitions among interest groups change from issue to issue, they remain within a general middle-class setting. Civil rights legislation in the 1960s was put through by a coalition of liberals, conservatives, labor groups, businessmen, intellectuals, and others who felt an injustice being done. Last but not least was the pressure of the Negroes themselves. This pressure, too, was motivated in no small part by the desire of black Americans to win access to middle-class living standards on equal terms.

Labor as a social stratum is less powerful. As a rule, it can prevail politically only in coalition with other groups. Production-line labor has not grown for twenty years. The skilled workers, insofar as they are union men, are now in the middle third of the income distribution in the United States. Unskilled and nonunion labor are well below this level. Farmers have been reduced to 5 per cent of the work force; less than 2 per cent produce major food surpluses; the remaining 3 per cent are subsistence farmers. Then come the forgotten Americans, the 20 per cent who are poor and the 10 per cent who are very poor.

This inequality in income, status, and power is greater in the United States than in any other highly advanced industrial country. Some of the poor are black in the cities, but at present at least half and possibly more than half of the very poor are not black. There is poverty in Appalachia, and there is poverty in the hillbilly neighborhoods of Chicago as well. There is a second group, which is less poor but still forgotten: the hard-working whites at the fringe of poverty and at the edge of respectability. These are tense and worried people who resent the increase in attention given to the poor. A third forgotten group is the mobile disfranchised. These are the professional people, the students, and in part the young—all those who for one reason or another do not make it into the ranks of stable, organized interest groups and registered voters. They number many millions. Together, these three groups get far less political influence and consideration than their needs and their numbers should entitle them to.

This unequal distribution of power—from the core establishment to the most disadvantaged—will not change quickly, but it *is* changing, and larger changes are on their way. The question remains whether these changes can add up in time to a transformation of the American political system.

The Elements of Change

To discover something about the future of American politics, we must study both the processes of change, and of resistance to change, at work. Many of these processes occur on a large scale, beyond the power of any individual or small group to speed or slow them. Nonetheless, these processes are important for the limits and opportunities they pose for the actions of individuals and groups. A man who wants to sail a boat may not be able to create the wind and the current, but if he knows how to navigate he can make use of them, and if he has an engine in the boat he can do even more. But he still must know the speed and direction of the current and the storm.

Currents of Change in American Society. Two major elements of change in America are the continuing shifts in occupation and residence. In 1940, 20 per cent of the American people were in agriculture; today there are less than 5 per cent. Yet more than 40 per cent of congressmen still list rural or small town addresses, and a majority of the heads of the important congressional committees, such as the Appropriations Committee in the House, come from small towns and rural neighborhoods. The nation therefore stands at the threshold of a structural change in its representative system. There is now a more than 95 per cent nonagricultural majority in a country which is still partly represented—or misrepresented—by a heavily agriculturally oriented and overweighted Congress.

The second shift is from rural residence to urban. Only about 20 per cent of the American people still live in rural areas; four-fifths live in cities, towns, and suburbs. Indeed more than half the American people live in large cities over 50,000. These metropoles would be the most endangered targets in a nuclear war. Yet their representatives have little influence on foreign policy. In the meantime the majority of small town legislators believe in "deterrence" and legislate accordingly.

Another shift going on now is that from the central city into the suburbs. Currently this is favored by the tax system which still puts part of the national welfare burden for migrants and other needy groups on the taxpayers in the central cities.

A fourth shift in process is from the rural South into southern cities. This has had a definite effect on southern politics. Observers in the North and West tend to believe that American youth is moving in a liberal, humanitarian direction. They do not see the quasi-South African or Rhodesian-type movement into the cities of some rural and young ex-rural southern whites which may be producing a more militant racial conservatism in southern cities. This trend resulted in 1968 in a vote for George Wallace in southern cities amounting to 20 per cent—and over 30 per cent among the South's young people. Other southern whites have remained in the countryside but have been shifting to greater political participation and greater use of mass media. In the future then some southerners may become more tolerant, others more racist; but few will stay indifferent.

In addition, there is the large movement from the rural black South into the central cities of the North. The mechanization of cotton-picking and other changes have driven black people from the countryside, and low southern relief rates have driven them north. Gradually, this shift may slow down as the pool of black rural southerners declines, but this slowdown may be balanced by the rise in black births in the northern cities and the entry of black youths into adulthood. Together, these changes are causing a revolution in northern city politics.

There are two further shifts. From grade school to high school and college, a radical change is underway in the educational level of the American people. And in the highly filtered news media there is a great shift from newspapers, which simply do not print what they do not think is fit to print, to television, where the pictures on the camera let through a great deal of information which was not intended to be seen. In many ways television is a more simultaneous medium. It is more difficult to censor, and to some extent we get more total involvement and more total immersion by seeing something on television. This creates new opportunities for criticism and independent thought.

The Resistances to Change.   Resistances to change come from many sources. Some are habitual, for the habits of millions of people are hard to change. Other resistances are based on age groups. There are twice as many voters in the United States over fifty years of age than under thirty, and older voters are more reluctant to accept change. At the end of the 1960s, on many issues American voters over fifty years of age were more conservative by twenty percentage points than voters under thirty.

Resistance also comes from some special interest groups. In the late 1960s there was a food stamp scandal. Food stamps were being manipulated in the interests of the farmers who wanted to sell their produce, and not in the interests of the hungry children who needed adequate food. Reformers urged transfer of the program from the Department of Agriculture, which serves only the producers, to the Department of Health, Education, and Welfare, which presumably has a greater interest in children. Many changes of this kind are technically possible, but they require the substantial weakening or removal of some conservative bulwarks. The overrepresentation of rural areas, small towns, and voters who never move are all such bulwarks, as are the electoral underrepresentation of the young, the educated, and the mobile. Still other obstacles are the congressional systems of committees and seniority.

Opportunities for Change.   To some extent the mass media are sensitive to needs for change, and to communications from individuals. Partisans of change can help to increase the popularity of those persons and programs that promote newer attitudes. Any individual can write to newspapers and broadcasting stations, although the man who always writes is often discounted, whereas the many who occasionally write are much listened to. Individuals can gain even more influence by founding groups that have cohesion, political know-how, and the capacity to form coalitions. Coalitions get more results than does mere rhetoric.

But can the American political system change far enough and fast enough to cope with the mounting problems that confront it? At a slower pace it has always been changing since the first days of the Republic. In some periods in some sectors it has changed very rapidly. The entire population has become more politicized and this process is continuing. Today Americans of South and East European ancestry are just as active in politics and as insistent on their rights as old-stock Americans have ever been. Millions of black Americans, too, have become aroused to political concern and participation, and so have many of the poor of all races. Large professions whose members used to think themselves too genteel to join a labor union, such as teachers, newspapermen, actors, and radio and television personnel are all becoming unionized in many cities. So are the poorest and most often forgotten groups of labor such as the hospital orderlies and garbage collectors. Also awakened to political participation are large parts of another previously passive group—the young.

As more Americans have become politically active, the political system has accepted a wider range of responsibilities. Medical care for those over sixty-five is no longer disputed in principle. It is now law and the discussion turns on the best ways to make it work. Public aid to low-rent housing and to students seeking higher education have become accepted principles. Broader voter registration and the fairer apportionment of legislative districts are now under way. The abolition of race segregation in public schools has become national policy and the law of the land, and beginnings have been made to put these into practice. In some of the big cities a search has started for methods of decentralization that will give different ethnic groups and neighborhoods a greater share in the decisions affecting their lives and the education of their children. City politics may be rediscovering in some respects the principle of "concurrent majorities" which John C. Calhoun proposed more than a century ago for the politics of the nation. If accepted, this principle would mean that decisions directly affecting a black urban region such as Harlem in New York City would require majority support in Harlem as well as in New York City as a whole. There have been many political inventions and innovations in the American past; there may be more in the future.

The American political system has the capacities for change if its people have the will to use them. There is a gap between the interests that are already organized and the potential ones that are not. The great majority of the American society has nothing to gain from perpetuating poverty or war. It is passionately interested in its own survival and that of its children. But these majority interests have yet to be organized. There is a vast opportunity for discovering and developing strategies of coalition-building and of action to this end. If reformers can recover the commitment, the dedication, and the intellectual and political skill to keep people of good will working with each other instead of against each other, then the most powerful country in the world can turn itself around and move in the direction selected by its Founding Fathers.

One part of such a reorientation and renewal of American politics would be a rethinking of United States foreign policy. No nation can go on indefinitely thinking itself omnipotent and invincible, least of all in today's world. If its people are told that their country "never lost a war," they may suspect that some historical evidence has been stretched a little. Or else they may think that earlier governments were wise enough not to involve the nation in wars that could not be won or were not worth winning. Championship sports teams know that "you can't win them all." Sooner or later every nation learns the same. History knows no nation that was never defeated, but it knows the vital difference between those nations that survived their defeats and learned from them, and those that failed to do so.

As every nation must learn to survive its setbacks in world politics, it also must learn to cooperate effectively with allies. The United States did so with spectacular success in two world wars, and in the great reconstruction of Western Europe after World War II under the Marshall Plan. Since that time, however, the sheer size of the population and economy of the United States has often tended to dwarf the interests of America's allies, unless these allies were able to find strong American domestic interest groups to speak for them. During the first decade after World War II, the impoverished nations of Western Europe were glad to follow American policies, particularly so long as these coincided with their own needs for European reconstruction. In the 1960s, however, such newly and more prosperous nations as France, West Germany, and Britain demanded more independence for themselves, and more consideration for their views. They wanted less Western involvement in Asian wars and more American attention to European needs. Whether the United States government and electorate will be able to preserve and renew a meaningful Western alliance in the 1970s under these new conditions, only time can tell.

In the meantime, the domestic experience of the United States has much to offer the rest of the world. The American social and political habits which emphasize equality and mobility, respect for all kinds of work including manual labor, and interest in discovery and practical solutions all could be of real help to many societies whose politics have remained bound by more rigid barriers of class and status, tradition, or ideology. And other nations may secretly admire the American optimism that undertakes impossible technical tasks, such as a voyage to the moon, and completes them not only successfully but on schedule.

Foreign nations may be less enthusiastic about the American unconcern in practice for the conservation of natural and human resources. They know that Americans easily discard old things rather than mend them, that they like to use throwaway packages and containers. They fear that this habit may carry over into an American inclination to have throwaway cities and perhaps even throwaway people. They note that Americans are quick to use things and people, and sometimes foreign countries, without knowing them well. And they are worried by the occasional American propensity to see foreign people as so many dominoes blindly falling with each push of power. Foreigners watching pictures of American race riots on their television screens may feel in no particular hurry to imitate American politics or institutions. In times such as these, the United States perhaps needs more constructive innovators working at home and less political propagandists sent abroad. It needs to advance its ideas in the world arena more by example than by attempts at persuasion. If the example is good enough, other nations will find their own ways to respond to it.

Key Terms and Concepts

government by design
federalism
separation of powers
checks and balances
pluralism
populism
"rotten boroughs"
"one man one vote"
legislative reapportionment
seniority
Seventeenth Amendment
caucus
logrolling
side payments
roll-call votes
gerrymander
Electoral College

policy-making appointments
full faith and credit clause
judicial review
Marbury vs. Madison
ex parte Milligan
Baker vs. Carr
Gideon vs. Wainwright
Escobedo vs. Illinois
Miranda vs. Arizona
dependency burden
spread effect
backwash effect
capitalism
socialism
distribution of power
general purpose elites
special elites

Additional Readings

Bailey, K. *Congress Makes a Law*. New York: Columbia University Press, 1950.

Boorstin, D. *The Genius of American Politics*. Chicago: University of Chicago Press, 1953.

Drury, A. *Advise and Consent*. New York: Doubleday, 1959.

Fenno, R. *The Power of the Purse: Appropriations Politics in Congress*. Boston: Little, Brown, 1966.

Froman, L.A., Jr. *The Congressional Process: Strategies, Rules, and Procedures*. Boston: Little, Brown, 1967.

Lipset, S. M. *The First New Nation: The United States in Historical and Comparative Perspective*. New York: Doubleday (Anchor), 1967.

McCloskey, R. G. *The American Supreme Court.* Chicago: University of Chicago Press, 1960.

Neustadt, R. *Presidential Power.* New York: Wiley, 1960.

Polsby, N. W. "Two Strategies of Influence: Choosing a Majority Leader, 1962." R. L. Peabody and N. W. Polsby (eds.) *New Perspectives on the House of Representatives.* Chicago: Rand McNally, 1963, pp. 237-270.

Riker, W. H. *Federalism: Origin, Operations, Significance.* Boston: Little, Brown, 1964.

Schattschneider, E. E. *Party Government.* New York: Holt, Rinehart, 1942.

Schubert, G. *Constitutional Polity.* Boston: Boston University Press, 1969.

The Soviet Union

Most studies of the Soviet Union available to Western readers resemble descriptions of hell as written by fairminded theologians. It is particularly hard for Westerners to understand that most Russians are loyal to their government and will fight to defend it against foreign attack. Russians have a similar difficulty in understanding political loyalties in the West. But anyone who thought that either Americans or Russians would not defend their government against any direct attack would be deluding himself. The Japanese military discovered this when they attacked the United States at Pearl Harbor. So did Hitler when he attacked the Soviet Union.

Chapter 11

Two Expanding Peoples—Two Ideas of Government

Like the United States, the Soviet Union has been shaped by a unique combination of vast historical development and deliberate political design. The United States is the product of an outpouring of largely English-speaking (followed by non-English-speaking) people westward across rivers and mountains and then across a continent and onward to Hawaii and Alaska. This had made Scottish- and Irish-Americans, Pennsylvania Dutch, Louisiana French, Minnesota Swedes, Slavic- and Italian-Americans, Spanish- and Indian-Americans, Jews, Puerto Ricans, and black Americans all members of the American people. The Soviet Union, now a nation of 240 million, is the product of an eastward outpouring of Slavic-speaking peoples, mainly Russians and Ukrainians, across the land mass of Eurasia all the way to Vladivostok and Sakhalin Island. To an even greater extent than the United States, the Soviet Union emerged from its expansion as a *multilingual* country. Russians now account for only about 55 per cent of the Soviet people, while twenty-one major minorities compose another 40 per cent and more than a hundred ethnic splinter groups make up the rest. Yet both of these large countries—the United States and the

Soviet Union—grew out of a revolution and out of a deliberate political design at a decisive stage in its history.

A Common Dream.   Out of each revolution came a political system engineered by theorists who had tried to master what they held to be the social science of their day. These theorists were desperately determined to make their blueprints practical. The purpose of each design was no less than the liberation of man and the creation of the political conditions for his happiness. Now, nearly two hundred years after the event, we can see the good and bad that has come out of the vision of the American revolutionary theorists: the triumphs, the disappointments, and the hopes deferred but perhaps not quite forsaken. It is difficult to realize that the Soviet system was also created by theorists with no less idealistic a vision— even though Lenin and his Bolshevik comrades would have bridled with indignation at the very word "idealism" which they considered bourgeois.

The word *"idealism"* has many meanings, among which three stand out. In common speech, "idealism" first means a selfless aspiration to make things better, particularly for others; here it is opposed to the common speech meaning of "materialism" as a preoccupation with tangible rewards, often with overtones of selfishness. Second, also in common speech, "idealism" sometimes means an inclination to see things as better or more perfect than they actually are; here it is opposed to a common speech meaning of "realism." A third meaning pertains to the philosophy of knowledge. Here "idealism" means the doctrine that thoughts, abstract forms, or ideas are more real and enduring than tangible things and events, and that man's inner life is more real than the world around him. It was this third, philosophic, meaning of "idealism" that Marx and Lenin opposed. They contrasted it with philosophic *"materialism"* which taught that the outside world was real, independent of the wishes of observers. Putting ideas first, they believed, was to stand knowledge on its head. Only by putting its feet on the ground and seeing the world as it was, they argued, could it be changed for the better.

Philosophic "materialists," of course, may be quite capable of unselfish—or "idealistic"—behavior. Lenin, the revolutionary, and Krasin, the economic planner, Stalin and Trotsky, Radek and Bukharin, even perhaps Khrushchev and Kosygin, all had their vision of a better social order. Each attempted to transform his vision of the "good society" into reality for a vast, poor, and backward country in order to implement man's happiness there. But if the underlying visions and aspirations were similar in Russia and in the United States, there were nevertheless profound differences between these nations' attempts to realize their dreams, and between the outcomes each attempt produced.

Two Revolutions and Their Differences. The American Revolution had five characteristics which distinguished it from the Russian. It began with a vision of *plenty*. Not only were the three million colonists of the 1770s and 1780s at the edge of a rich continent, on a per capita basis they also had the richest capital equipment in the world. Thus, in that sense, the Americans were already at the time of their revolution the most advanced people in the world.

Second, the American people at the time of the revolution had had a long tradition of local *self-government*, of spontaneous organizations in small, self-governing groups, such as church congregations, town meetings, and committees of correspondence. By the end of the eighteenth century the English-speaking world had had at least a century-old tradition of local self-government, and of agreements voluntarily arrived at.

Third, the American revolutionaries envisioned the possibility of harmony or at least of a workable *compatibility of interests* within the country. Divergent interests would be accommodated not through factionalism or violence, but through accepted and legal channels of government. These ideas later found expression in James Madison's "Tenth Federalist Paper." On the whole they also felt that if America stayed out of international entanglements after winning its independence and remained reasonably well defended, no foreign countries would have a major motive to harm the United States. Such thinking pervades George Washington's Farewell Address.

A fourth basic characteristic was the American trust in the *spontaneity* of individuals. Setting men free to pursue their happiness, as the Declaration of Independence put it, implies having automatic trust in their knowing what will be good for themselves. Both before and since the Revolution the mainstream of American culture has trusted the spontaneity of men and women.

Finally, from the American Revolution onward, there has been an American tradition of *moderation*. This might now be called into question by some, but there seems to be a fair chance that it will endure. Extremist episodes always have been short-lived. In major emergencies the American people have tended to move toward the middle, whereas some of the European populations, such as those of Russia and Germany, have tended to move toward the extremes. Comparing the extreme German responses to the Great Depression of the 1930s with the American responses shows the American tradition of moderation, which is sometimes frustrating and irritating but which has stood the country in good stead.

In contrast to the American experience, the Russian tradition began with *scarcity*, in a poor country, with many people and little capital. At the time of the Russian Revolution, of all the poor peasantries of Europe, the peasants of Russia had long been among the poorest. The Revolution occurred at the end of the bloody First World War which had exhausted the country and ruined its economy. Food was scarce in the big cities before the first shots of the Revolution were fired. And scarcity remained a critical factor even after the end of the Revolution. A Soviet teamster at the building of the Dnieper River Dam in the late 1920s exhorted his helper to take good care of the horses. "You can always make a man," he said, "but just try to make a horse." Twenty years and two five-year plans after the Russian Revolution, only half as many pairs of shoes were being made each year as there were Russians, amounting thus to one shoe per Russian. This was seen by many Russians as an improvement: in the days of the Czar, the normal winter footwear of 100 million peasants was burlap rags tied around their feet.[1]

Violent conflict, like scarcity, had long been a basic assumption of Russian politics, and the Russian Revolution merely reinforced it. Revolutionary Russia saw itself in the position of a besieged fortress. And indeed from its start in 1917 the new Soviet government faced foreign conflict. Fourteen foreign countries made war on the Soviet government in the first four years of its existence. They did so ineffectively and half-heartedly, but they still killed many people, and the intervention prolonged the Russian civil war to 1921. The situation of the Bolsheviks resembled that of the embattled Jacobins in the French Revolution of 1793, who were besieged by more than a half-dozen European monarchies and who resorted to a terrorist dictatorship to save the Republic. A similar mood of desperate determination was characteristic of the Russian Revolution. In contrast, the American Revolution had strong foreign allies: France, Spain, and the Netherlands.

Whereas the leaders of the American Revolution believed in spontaneity, the experiences of the Russian revolutionaries led them to a different conclusion. Prior to the revolution, Lenin and the members of his conspiratorial Bolshevik party had had an almost full-time job dodging the Czarist secret police. The leaders who emerged from these struggles believed in *discipline,* direction, and organization. The Soviet leaders distrusted spontaneity and do so to this day.

Finally, where the American tradition stressed moderation, the Russian tradition stressed desperate *ruthlessness.* In order to get things done any means were acceptable. Lenin said he would make an alliance "with the devil and his grandmother" if it would help the Revolution. It is tempting for Westerners to sit back and criticize the tactics of the Russian revolutionaries. Living where and when the Soviet leaders did, they regarded ruthlessness as the only realistic way of completing their revolution. But we should not forget that even when a price seems inevitable it still has to be paid. Bertholt Brecht, the pro-Communist German poet, said that even righteous indignation will make one's voice hoarse. And the Soviet people and their government have paid with more than hoarseness of voice.

[1] Towards the end of the 1960s, the U.S.S.R. produced annually 560 million pairs of leather shoes, or 2.4 pairs per person.

The Basic Theory: Marx

Essentials of Marxism.   The originator of the theory which was taken over by Lenin and the Bolsheviks in Russia was Karl Marx. Marx's theory was rooted in a profoundly pessimistic evaluation of the nineteenth-century private enterprise system, based mainly on the experience of England (where Marx spent much of his adult life) in the first half of that century. As we have seen in Chapter 5, Marx assumed that the conditions which he had seen were not unique characteristics of a particular society at a specific point in time, but general tendencies of an entire economic system. Among these tendencies, as he saw them, were increasing wars and depressions, increasing oppression, the increasing misery of working people, and the increasing alienation of people who were being treated more and more like things or commodities. Marx assumed that the only response to this experience would be a struggle among economic classes out of which the industrial wage earners would eventually emerge as the most numerous, and eventually the dominant, class. Indeed the middle classes would disappear; the children and grandchildren of the peasants and artisans would overwhelmingly end up as factory workers or unemployed wage earners, with only a tiny minority becoming property owners. These workers would become increasingly dissatisfied and radicalized. Factory work would teach them organization and discipline. They would learn to form unions and fight for higher wages. Communists would teach them class consciousness and the need for revolution. The resulting class struggle, Marx asserted, would determine the future course of history.

Marx believed in stages of historical development. After the stages of primitive communism and of feudalism, there would be a stage of private enterprise in which middle-class capitalist rule would replace the power of the nobles and the landowners. Only after this stage had reached its height would social revolution and socialism follow. Marx believed that socialism would be an outgrowth of capitalism, that socialism would grow under the surface within the husk of the private enterprise society, so that one would have only to remove the shell and the full-blown industrialized socialist economy would emerge near completion.

At this point in time the working class would be united, Marx believed. Workers would on the whole accept the Marxist ideology, and since they would be united, enlightened, and in the vast majority, they would exercise a dictatorship over the remaining few former members of the owning classes. This new regime somehow would not be a dictatorship over the workers themselves, because there would be so many of them and they would all know what they wanted. They would be able to be dictators and yet act spontaneously. It would be the rule of the many over the few.

Two economic stages would follow capitalism. The first, which Lenin later called *socialism* (Marx just called it a lower stage of communism), would be an economy of scarcity, where land, machines, and means of production would be owned collectively, but where the society would still be poor. In this society everybody would work according to his ability and be paid according to his performance. Those who worked more or did more complicated or more urgently needed work would be paid better regardless of their needs or those of their families. The society of socialism, therefore, would be unjust, and the state machinery would still have to be used to defend the higher incomes of what we now would call the *meritocracy,* the more productive or more skilled workers, technicians, and managers.

Marx's Vision of the Future.   This early stage—socialism—would have only one purpose: to put itself out of business. It would amass more and more wealth, more and more capital, and more and more machines until in the end production would become plentiful. The symptoms of the transition to the age of plenty would be clear to see, Marx thought: the differences between worker and intellectual, and between town and countryside, would disappear.[2]

Marx expected a society of plenty to emerge ultimately. Within such a society the government of men would be replaced by the administration of things. Marx's notion was that a great deal of the productive equipment of mankind would eventually become semiautomatic or automatic. It would have to be maintained, but the business of government would be replaced by the business of maintenance.

Thus, sitting in the library of the British Museum behind his bristling beard, Marx envisioned a society of freedom and generosity for all men. In the middle of a long economic discussion in the third volume of *Das Kapital* there is a revealing throw-away sentence in which he speaks of "that full development of all human capacities and powers which is an end in itself." This is what Marx wanted to live for: the full realization of human capabilities, the end of the subordination of human beings to the division of labor, a new age of the all-sided development of individuals. After the revolution, all this would depend on economic growth. Only after men had made the transition from poverty to plenty would they move "out of the realm of necessity into the realm of freedom." Only then would the prehistory of mankind end and the real history of man, the interesting history, begin.

[2] It is ironic to think that these predictions have been most nearly fulfilled in the world's least Marxist country, the United States. Whether you call a television repairman a worker or an intellectual is a moot question; he is likely to be a skilled and intelligent man. And whether you call a suburb a "town" or a "countryside" is again debatable. Contrary to Marx's theory, these blurrings of age-old categories in the United States have been the result of industry, not of revolution.

Some of His Predictions—and the Facts.   Marx assumed the existence of a high degree of technological determinism. To Marx, as we saw in Chapter 5, a hand mill meant a society of landlords and serfs; a steam mill meant capitalists and wage workers. His assumption has turned out to be partly false, for modern machines have served a variety of social systems. Henry Ford's tractors have worked on Russian collective farms as well as on American private enterprise farms.

Second, Marx foresaw automatic growth of all the elements for a socialist economy under the capitalist surface. This has not materialized. Countries which have wanted public planning agencies and skills have had to create them by deliberate political effort.

Third, he thought that the advanced countries, and particularly their urban and industrial sectors, would be the most likely areas for Communist success. He had blistering phrases of contempt for peasants and for what he called "the idiocy of rural life." The best thing Marx might have said about peasants was that their children or grandchildren might someday become honest, upstanding proletarians. Here reality has differed from this prediction in a crucial way. Communist revolutions have triumphed thus far only in semideveloped or underdeveloped countries, and then only with the help of peasant uprisings.

Fourth, Marx predicted that the proletariat—the wage-earning factory workers—would become the vast majority. Again this has not been the case. In the United States, for instance, production-line jobs have not increased in numbers since the end of World War II. The main increase in the work force has been in services and clerical work, not in manual labor. The same is true of all other highly industrialized countries, including those ruled by Communists. Some dissident Communist writers, such as the Yugoslav Milovan Djilas, have attacked this growth of bureaucracy and management as heralding the rise of a "new class." Some Communist regimes have tried to slow the trend, or at least play it down in their published statistics, or they may define as a "proletarian element" any government or Party official who was once a worker, even many years ago. None of this necessarily proves the rise of a new hereditary class of privileged persons but rather the pressure of modern technology which requires fewer people in manual work and more in handling information.

Finally, Marx expected the workers in the highly industrialized countries to move spontaneously toward revolution and proletarian dictatorship. All efforts at reform and real wage increases would fail in the end, he thought; history would drum revolution into the heads of most workers. This too has not happened. The majority of factory workers in the advanced countries have benefitted from reforms and higher living standards; and most often they have become attached to labor unions committed to further reforms, further wage increases, and constitutional government.

The Modified Theory: Lenin

Marx's most important follower in Russia was twelve years old when the theorist died. His name at birth was Vladimir Ilyich Ulyanov. He came from a family of professionals, with some petty nobles among his ancestors. He earned a law degree and might have become a civil servant. But in 1887 his older brother was hanged by the Czarist authorities for conspiracy against the monarch. This act of deterrence proved counterproductive for the Czar. Young Ulyanov, at sixteen, became a revolutionist and within a decade turned to Marxism, seeking in the social conditions of his country an explosive more powerful than dynamite. Years later, in 1912, a large strike in the gold fields at the Lena River was smashed by Czarist forces who killed about 200 workers. From then on, Ulyanov called himself *Lenin,* "the man from the Lena River," who like a ghost of the slain would come back to claim the Czar.

Lenin's Theoretical Contributions.   Marx's assumptions were partly modified and changed in several ways by Lenin. First, Lenin believed in *uneven development* among the countries of the world. Some countries would become highly industrialized while others would stay far behind. Modern technology would increase the political choices open to a society rather than completely determining the outcome through economic influence alone.

Second, Lenin, like Marx, thought there was an automatic tendency in most societies toward weakening the power of landowners and replacing it by the power of industrialists and businessmen. This is what he called the *bourgeois revolution.* Unlike Marx, however, he expected far less support for this revolution from the bourgeois proper—the big and middling businessmen—except in colonial and semi-colonial countries, where a native business class might struggle against foreign rulers or competitors. Major support for a bourgeois revolution would come from the peasants, Lenin believed, particularly tenants and landless laborers, who would revolt to make themselves owners of the land they tilled. Also unlike Marx, Lenin no longer maintained that the tendency toward socialism would be automatic.

Third, Lenin felt that the countries particularly well-suited for a revolution were those which formed the *weakest links* in the chain of capitalist countries. They had to be backward enough to keep the workers poor and disgruntled but advanced enough to keep them numerous and concentrated at strategic centers. In these countries, Lenin predicted, bourgeois revolutions would break out but they would remain weak and incomplete; out of them, however, proletarian revolutions would emerge and finish the job. The best bets for such combined revolutions in Lenin's view were Russia, China, and Spain.

Lenin saw two alternatives. Once revolution had triumphed in one country, it either would spread quickly throughout the whole world, in which case Lenin would preside over a *world revolution,* or else one or a few countries would have to establish their own Communist regimes, and try to establish *socialism in one country* (as Stalin later called it). These regimes would then hold out as long as needed, even for decades or for generations, until the rest of the world would accept the new doctrine. Sooner or later, revolutions in colonial countries would destroy imperialism and much of the capitalist world market, making capitalism in Western Europe un-workable. This is the thought behind Lenin's reported remark that the way to Paris might lead through Peking. Such expectations were behind Lenin's New Economic Policy in 1921, in which he made major conces-sions to private enterprise among the peasants while tightening authori-tarian control over the Russian Communist Party at the Tenth Congress.

Fourth, Lenin assumed that *peasant-worker alliances* would be extremely important, whereas Marx had relegated the peasants to the fringes of his intellectual universe. Lenin believed there would be peasant revolutions against landowners in all developing countries, and that the art of Com-munist revolution would consist in synchronizing the strikes and uprisings of disgruntled urban workers with the uprisings of disgruntled peasants. (Later Mao Tse-tung in China went one step further by putting the major weight of revolution on the peasantry.) Lenin assumed that the peasant revolution would result in the minority rule of workers, allied with the peasants but exercising power over them. The Communist Party in each country, in turn, would lead the working class. It was to be the *vanguard* of the workers, thinking and acting today in the way most workers act tomorrow. (In theory, it would *not* become, therefore, a permanent *elite,* different from the workers. Maintaining this principle to any extent in practice has been one of the continuing and acknowledged problems of the Soviet regime, as we shall see later.) In Lenin's views, the resulting "proletar-ian dictatorship" would no longer be spontaneous; it would deliberately direct further economic development. In effect, it would be a dictatorship of the Communist Party, but it would have to be skillful enough to retain enough popular support among the peasants and workers to stay in power.

Fifth, Lenin made a more radical psychological break with the existing order than had his ideological forerunners. Lenin was thoroughly alien-ated both from his government's bureaucracy and from Western Eu-rope. Both Marx and Engels were the most radical revolutionists of their day, but they felt very much at home in Western Europe. In contrast, Lenin—who spent many years in the West—in many ways remained a stranger in the Western world. Yet Lenin put great stress on maintaining close contacts with the workers anywhere; and it is recorded that in Russia, unlike many other radicals, he spent considerable time listening to peasants and plain people.

This psychological distance from the mainstream of Western tradition had something to do with Lenin's fifth basic contribution to Communist theory, his *distrust of spontaneity.* When left to their own initiative, Lenin thought, workers would always try to behave like the American Federation of Labor, getting higher wages but not really questioning who was running the economy or whether their wages came from a war contract. It was the intellectuals, the Bolsheviks, the revolutionaries, who had to supply the sense of historical mission. But only individuals fully committed to this mission could do so, and they had to devote their lives to it. Such intense commitment had occurred also in the West briefly and exceptionally, during the revolutionary period of Cromwell in England and of Robespierre in France. In Russia, however, this style of leadership proved more lasting and significant.

Lenin's distrust of spontaneity had a practical side as well. A spontaneous, loose, liberal organization, such as a Western-type political party, Lenin held, would be a sitting duck for the police forces of the Czar, the most elaborate secret police organization of the time. Dodging the police would be a full-time job, and being a revolutionary, a profession.

As a result of these ideas, Lenin developed a concept of a tightly disciplined, small party of full-time professional revolutionists. The Czarist regime, like other anti-Communist dictatorships, unwittingly aided this development. By denying alternative employment to intellectuals who opposed it, it turned additional numbers of them into such professional revolutionists. Party members of the Leninist kind were much less likely to express themselves spontaneously, but might develop a sense of common pride and dedication.

Lenin's Tactical Contributions.   The quarrel between the two concepts of a party—the loose and the tight—came to a head in 1903 at a Congress of Russia's Social Democratic (SD) Party held in Brussels and London. Lenin's followers were defeated on this issue. But the withdrawal of some members of the SD Party during the Congress enabled Lenin's minority to become a majority at the end of the Congress when elections were held for the central committee. From the Russian word for majority, they were henceforth called *Bolsheviks;* the "minority," their more Western-minded opponents, became known as *Mensheviks.* Until 1952, the full name of the ruling party of the Soviet Union was Communist Party of the Soviet Union (Bolsheviks)—CPSU(B).

In order to keep his small party disciplined, doctrinally pure, and uncontaminated by the capitalist environment, Lenin insisted on authoritarianism both in matters of party strategy and in terms of doctrine. At the same time, he exhibited a mastery of coalition tactics and tactical retreats, and topped it all off with a ceaseless demand for what he called "Bolshevik tenacity." In some ways one might compare the social organization that Lenin built with an organization developed for entirely different purposes by Saint Ignatius of Loyola in the sixteenth century. Jesuit fathers were taught to be masters of compromise, masters of adjustment, masters of practicality, and yet to have the utmost devotion to both the general teachings of the Church and the specific authority of the head of the Jesuit order. This combination of external flexibility with intense internal commitment was something which the Jesuits had successfully incorporated into their religious organization. Lenin tried to do something similar in the name of a secular doctrine.

Lenin died in 1924. He lived long enough to see that his hopes for world revolution would have to be deferred and that for some time his followers would have to hold out in a single country. But should they concentrate their efforts on internal development or on foreign revolutions? This unresolved question in Lenin's thought surfaced as a fateful quarrel among his successors.

The Stalinist Years

Trotsky vs. Stalin. With the death of Lenin, a struggle for the control of the Communist Party and of the future of the Soviet Union began. This struggle ultimately centered on two men: Leon Trotsky and Joseph Stalin. Trotsky was a revolutionist who, far more than Lenin, saw revolution as attractive for its own sake. He believed in permanent revolution and in using military methods to accomplish it. A brilliant writer, he was better at commanding than at listening. Trotsky was a highly effective organizer of the Red Army during the period of civil war, and as late as 1920 he advocated organizing all of Russian industry on the Red army model.

Trotsky was much more cosmopolitan than either Lenin or Stalin. He was more at home in the West emotionally and intellectually than in Russia. He distrusted the Russian base of the revolution; Russia, to him, was uncouth and backward. Like Marx, he regarded Germany in particular, and France and England to a lesser degree, as the predestined countries for revolution. He strove, therefore, to push revolution in the West as fast as possible. Suspicious of the Russian peasants, Trotsky wanted to tax them. He also advocated the rapid build-up of Russia's military industry. These were not policies likely to appeal to most Russian Communists, nor to most of the Russian people; and they contributed much to Trotsky's political defeat within the Russian Communist Party, to his exile in 1929 (which eventually was followed by his assassination in Mexico in 1940), and to Stalin's ultimate victory.

Stalin took the opposite tack. Born in Georgia in the Caucasus as the son of a shoemaker and a washerwoman, educated for a time on a scholarship in a seminary for Orthodox priests, he joined the Marxists at the age of nineteen and soon became a professional revolutionary. His personality has remained a riddle, even to his daughter. He was an early member of Lenin's faction and soon became an insider in its organization, in contrast to the individualist Trotsky whom the old-line Bolsheviks distrusted.

Both Stalin and Trotsky sought power. Stalin got it, partly because of his old Party connections and partly because he chose policies that suited Russia. Stalin's most important decision, and probably the prime cause of his success, was his commitment to the possibilities of the Russian base. Unlike Trotsky, he insisted from late 1924 onward that a collectivistic economy could be built in Russia, with Russian workers, few as they were, Russian industry, backward as it was, and Russian peasants, numerous as they were. After years of political maneuvering, Stalin came out strongly in support of *socialism in one country* and gave up the notion of expecting an immediate world revolution. The fact that world revolution did not take place in the 1920s also encouraged Stalin's action, since one of Lenin's options had turned out to be ineffective.

Second, Stalin wished to make a much greater attempt to industrialize Russia than Trotsky ever considered. Trotsky planned to tax the Russian peasants quickly for a relatively small-scale industrial effort. Stalin envisaged a much bigger plan, though he developed the details only later. He wanted to permit the peasants to engage in private enterprise several years longer, in order to squeeze them much more thoroughly at a later date. This would enable him to build up greater resources for the big industrial push. He therefore looked like a "rightist" (in Communist parlance) until 1927 and like a "leftist" afterwards. In actual fact, he used a fairly consistent argument—he wanted to build up a large backlog, surplus, or war chest for an internal campaign of industrialization which he knew would be very costly. Finally, more than Trotsky, Stalin believed in a type of centralized planning that would be neither militarist nor permissive but would require a new set of institutions.

Planning: The Second Russian Revolution. Once in power, Stalin began organizing the Soviet Union, and developing the new planning apparatus, on a massive scale. He decided to transform the peasantry, not just tax them, and this transformation was successfully undertaken in two five-year plans from 1927 to 1937. First, he began the *mechanization of agriculture,* largely with the help of American tractors. Second, he pushed the peasants into *collective farms.* These were farms in which the home, the household, the kitchen, and in practice the garden plot remained in private hands while the fields were held in common and the tractors were owned by the government. It was a compromise system that worked for several decades. Third, he *industrialized* the country by moving a large portion of the Russian work force from the fields into the factories. Progress was slow: when Stalin started, 80 per cent of the work force was in agriculture, but by the time he died it was down to approximately 50 per cent. Thus, about one-third of the Russian work force was transferred from agriculture into the industrial sector, but at fantastic cost.

In effect, the first two five-year plans marked a second Russian Revolution, hardly less desperate and costly than the first. As collectivization proceeded, the peasants slaughtered much of their livestock; it took over ten years to get back to pre-1927 levels. Indeed, about 5 per cent of the peasants, or approximately five million people, including the wealthier, or more tradition-minded, or more independent, resisted to the bitter end. Their defiance was ultimately broken by brutality and by deportations to Siberia. But the graves of collective farm chairmen who had been killed by the peasants in a model collective farm tell a harsh story. It was a second civil war in the countryside.

Stalin insisted on squeezing every last bit of the available grain from the collective farms. If somebody had to starve it was not going to be the cities and the workers on whom the Soviet regime depended. There followed in 1932–33 a man-made famine which cost the lives of several million peasants in the Ukraine and elsewhere in Russia. The next spring, the Soviet regime provided additional incentives for the surviving peasants to work harder, and produced a bumper crop. But a price had been paid. The famine had hit women and children, producing unimaginable suffering. It had produced a death toll comparable to the toll of the civil war.

The Stalinist defense was that until that time there had been natural famines in Russia every ten years; that everybody had said they were catastrophes about which nothing could be done; and that Stalin's ruthless policies had ended them. The fact is that, though crop failures have recurred, in no peacetime year since the mid-1930s has there been a famine in Russia. Stalin's reforms eventually left agriculture sufficiently productive to yield enough food and industry to produce enough exports to buy additional food abroad when needed.

Costs and Achievements.   The achievement of the Stalin era was, on the whole, an unprecedented success in rapid industrialization. Never before was so agrarian a country transformed into so industrial a state in so few years. Agriculture became capable of feeding the entire country even though there were many fewer people in the rural work force, and the youngest, most energetic, most able people had left the villages. In no other country did literacy spread so fast, and science and technology grow so rapidly and extensively. The nearest parallel in the non-Communist world is the industrialization of Japan in the late nineteenth and early twentieth centuries, which took longer and was also accompanied by dictatorship—and, incidentally, by very warlike, military regimes for a large part of the time. The last test of Stalin's regime was perhaps the most grueling—World War II. And, on the whole, when the test came most of the Soviet population, with its many different languages, fought for the Soviet regime, often with great heroism.

But the cost of Stalin's ruthlessness was large. A balance sheet would probably suggest that in the long run Stalin's ruthlessness saved more lives from famine than it cost. But such a method of rationalistic analysis may be a little shallow. We must also ask what this ruthlessness, this willingness to sacrifice millions for some future good, does to the minds of the people who practice it, wherever and for whatever reason. When Stalin and his followers actively accepted ruthlessness and dictatorship they became ready to go to any lengths to reach their goals. They also learned to expect hostility everywhere. As a result, they learned to fear each other. Indeed, one of the most dangerous security risks to the Soviet government has been the secret police, and a police chief's lot in Russia has not been a happy one. At least three of them, Yagoda, Yezhov, and Beria, were shot by the government. At other times, the accusations by such men sent others to their doom. Thus, in the end, the dictatorship of Stalin became a dictatorship of suspicion and paranoia.

The hidden costs of his paranoia—the inability to tell friends from enemies, reality from fantasy, and an honest difference of opinion from an attempt at sabotage and subversion—were, perhaps, even more serious. The memoirs of Stalin's daughter, Svetlana Alliluyeva, are a poignant illustration. These were losses of life and liberties far beyond the costs inherent in the policies themselves. Most of the Bolsheviks who preached ruthlessness in the name of revolution ultimately perished at the hands of other Communists who had been reared in the same creed. Stalin's purges which began after 1934 went into high gear after 1936 and 1938; and, as the Soviet government has publicly stated from 1956 on, a large number of the victims of these purges were completely innocent. They were the victims of frameups, manufactured evidence, forced confessions. In this manner, Communists killed each other in large numbers.

Solzhenitsin's *A Day in the Life of Ivan Denisovitch* is a former inmate's description of one day in the life of a labor camp in Stalin's day. These camps at their peak in 1950 had ten million people in them, and since many died there and others were released, probably over twenty million Russians got into these camps at one time or another. Nearly every second family in the Soviet Union had somebody who was touched, brushed, or hit by the Stalin terror in the years between 1934 and 1953. In the years after Stalin's death in 1953, the number of political prisoners has declined to less than 150,000, but the memory of those terrible years remains vivid among the present generation of Soviet citizens.

A Measure of Prosperity: The Post-Stalin Decades

The Stalin era laid the basis for the second largest concentration of economic power in the world. The Soviet Union today has 16 per cent of world income compared to the United States which has 33 per cent. American per capita income is about $4,000 in today's money; Soviet per capita income is around $1,800. This is below that of the German Federal Republic and France, and, according to some data, perhaps a touch ahead of England. However, it depends on whose figures you use—these are based on those of Abram Bergson of Harvard. About 1920, however, United States per capita income already was close to $1,000, while Soviet per capita income after years of foreign and civil wars was below $100. Even in 1928, Soviet per capita income was only one-fifth of that of the

United States. The American-Soviet income gap thus has shrunk from 10:1 and 5:1 to 2:1.

A per capita income of $1,800 does not mean that the Russians live or eat as well as the English. Part of their per capita income is circling the globe in the form of Sputniks and assorted space hardware. Other parts of their income are buried in hardened intercontinental missile sites in the Ural Mountains. Thus, a fair degree of Soviet income does not get to the consumers. Russian consumer standards are much lower than those of West European countries.

The Russian tendency is to concentrate efforts on *decisive sectors,* as the Russians call them. This now means space technology; earlier it was intercontinental rockets and nuclear energy; during World War II it was the tank program, and earlier still the tractor program. Coming decisive sectors may well be automation, agricultural biology, and the chemistry of fertilizers. Even if the leaders should misjudge the next decisive sector, however, Soviet industry now has a productive capacity which can survive a great deal of error and difficulties.

Nevertheless, certain critical economic problems remain as yet unsolved. First, Soviet planners have not resolved the problem of recurrent *disproportions in investment.* They invest heavily in industry which gives *increasing returns to scale*—the more you make, the cheaper you can manufacture each additional product. Agriculture and mining, in contrast, produce *diminishing returns*—the more crops or minerals you need, the poorer the soils or deposits you must go to, and ultimately the more expensive it becomes to produce each additional item. To some extent the force-feeding of capital into industry and the underinvestment in agriculture occasionally has led to bad years in which economic growth has slowed down or sometimes has even stopped. These are not cyclical depressions, as in the West, but they look like depressions and can be as serious, if not more serious. After more than four decades, Communist planning is still neither perfect nor smooth.

The second disproportion is between investment goods and *incentive goods,* that is, goods for which people are willing to work harder, such as better clothes, washing machines, and television sets. Communist ideology thinks of consumer goods as luxuries; in this belief the Communists are almost like the Puritans of the seventeenth century and Adam Smith in the eighteenth. They do not realize that many consumer goods are also incentive goods. A color television set is not a luxury, but an incentive good that makes a plumber show up on the job on the next day in order to meet the installment payments on his television set. The Russians have not yet fully discovered the tremendous power of consumer goods as incentives to further productive effort.

Moreover, the Communists have not resolved the problem of the tension between *equalitarianism* (making wages relatively equal) and *performance payments* (paying more to people who do important or good work than to people who work less or who do less important work, or who work less well). Much of the emotional appeal of socialist or Communist ideas comes from their implied promise of greater equality. Much of the motivation to work, in the Soviet Union as elsewhere, comes from material incentives, such as better pay, which are unequal for unequal work. At present, inequality among Soviet wages and salaries is not very different from such differences in the United States. On the whole, more than 90 per cent of the Soviet wage structure falls within a span between ten and one; that is, the highest paid people get about ten times as much as the lowest paid. In the United States probably 85 per cent of the wage structure falls within that span.

Neither the United States nor the Soviet Union as yet understands human *motivation* thoroughly. The American stress on material incentives perhaps slights many less tangible motives, as well as the quality of life; and the Soviet stress on exhortation and ideology underrates the incentives of consumer goods and choices, and of greater scope for individuality and spontaneity.

A Persisting Element: Government by Pyramid

In politics, as well as in economics, the Soviet system depends on the guidance of a pyramid of political authorities and on the intense efforts of millions of activists—nearly one adult out of every five—organized in the Communist Party or its youth organization, the Young Communist League, or Komsomol. All these organizations call for civic efforts, yet try to channel and control these efforts closely. Periods of somewhat greater liberality and scope for differences of opinion in politics and culture have alternated with calls for more conformity and discipline. These swings have characterized much of Soviet politics during the last two decades but they have not changed the basic structure of Soviet government.

All modern countries, in a sense, are governed by pyramids of administration and decision-making, but the Soviet system is more pyramidal than most. It consists of a multiplicity of pyramids. There is the pyramid of local and territorial government, from villages, towns, and districts all the way up to the Supreme Soviet. There is the pyramid of the Communist Party, from the primary units to the All-Union Secretariat and the Politburo (see Figure 11.1). There is a military pyramid, and another pyramid of economic planning and management. Finally, there are several lesser pyramids of mass organizations, such as trade unions, consumer cooperatives, sports organizations, youth organizations, and the like.

In the Soviet Union, all these pyramids interlock at every level. Directly or indirectly, the Soviet government reaches into every nook and cranny of social life. At the same time the system offers many opportunities for participation; it has many ties to the life of the population and many opportunities to win popular support. Last but not least, despite its multiplic-

Figure 11.1

Democratic Centralism in the Soviet Union

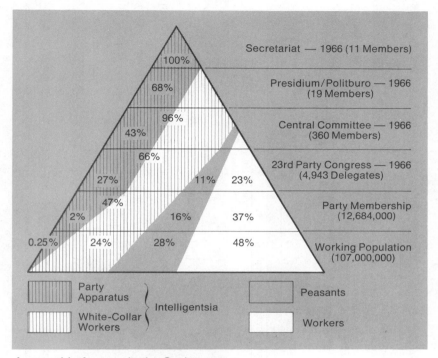

A pyramid of power in the Soviet system.

Source: V. Aspaturian, "The Soviet Union," in R. C. Macridis and R. E. Ward (eds.), Modern Political Systems: Europe, 2nd ed., © 1968. Adapted by permission of Prentice-Hall, Inc., Englewood Cliffs, N.J.

ity, complexity, and popular connections, it is well suited to centralized direction from above.

The National Government. The Soviet Union as a whole is formally governed by a *Supreme Soviet* of over 1,500 delegates. This body is so large, and meets for such a limited time each year, that its main tasks consist of confirming and ratifying legislation produced by smaller groups. The Supreme Soviet is divided into two chambers of roughly equal numbers, the *Soviet of the Union* (one deputy for every 30,000 people) and the *Soviet of Nationalities* (deputies elected by each union republic, autonomous republic, or other territorial unit based on nationality or ethnic group). In the former, voters are represented in proportion to their numbers; in the latter, similar to the United States Senate, the smaller republics, areas, and nationalities are deliberately overrepresented (see Figure 11.2).

The Supreme Soviet elects a *Presidium,* which we shall abbreviate PSS, which functions as the collective chief of state of the Soviet Union. The Chairman of this Presidium fulfills on ceremonial occasions a role

Figure 11.2

Constitutional Structure of the Soviet Union

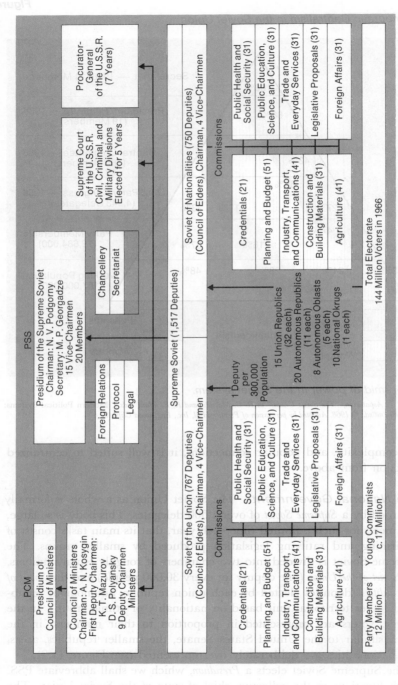

Source: V. Aspaturian, "The Soviet Union," in R. C. Macridis and R. E. Ward (eds.), *Modern Political Systems: Europe, 2nd ed.,* © 1968. Adapted by permission of Prentice-Hall, Inc., Englewood Cliffs, N.J.

analogous to that of president of the Soviet Union. Besides the Chairman, the PSS includes a secretary, fifteen vice-chairmen (one from each union republic), and twenty additional members. Between sessions of the Supreme Soviet, the Presidium exercises all the state powers of the Supreme Soviet, including legislation, as well as far-reaching executive powers.

The PSS, however, is not the government of the Soviet Union. It directly controls neither the execution and administration of policy nor the Soviet bureaucracy. These tasks fall to the *Council of Ministers* which the Constitution of the U.S.S.R. calls "the highest executive and administrative organ of state power." In the late 1960s this Council had eighty-eight members, including a chairman, eleven deputy-chairmen, and representatives of forty-seven ministries, ten state committees, and four specialized agencies, as well as fifteen union republic premiers (*ex officio*). The decrees and orders of the Council are binding throughout the Soviet Union and form the great mass of Soviet legislation. Since the Council of Ministers is much too large for efficient deliberation, its principal administrative decision-making powers are entrusted to the much smaller *Presidium of the Council of Ministers* (PCM). The Chairman of the PCM has always been a top-ranking member of the Communist Party, ranging from such early leaders as Lenin, Molotov, and Stalin to such more recent incumbents as Khrushchev and Kosygin. The office of *Chairman of the Presidium of the Council of Ministers* somewhat resembles that of prime minister in Britain or France.

Territorial Units and Ethnic Groups. Below the All-Union level, there are fifteen *union republics,* each with its own constitution, soviet, council of ministers, and prime minister. By far the largest union republic is the Russian Soviet Federal Socialist Republic (RSFSR)—itself a federation—which includes the majority of the population and land area of the Soviet Union.

Within the republics there are twenty *Autonomous Soviet Socialist Republics* (ASSR), sixteen of them within the RSFSR. Each autonomous republic is subordinate to the union republic in which it lies but enjoys a similar autonomy towards it, with its own autonomous constitution, as the union republic enjoys vis-à-vis the national government.

Below these three tiers of government—the national government of the Soviet Union, the union republic, and the autonomous republic—is a fourth layer formed by regions called *oblasts.* Some oblasts are autonomous, lacking constitutions of their own but electing deputies to the Soviet of Nationalities in the Supreme Soviet. Others are purely administrative divisions, without such autonomy. In two large union republics, RSFSR and Kazakhstan, there is an alternative regional unit called an "area" or *kray.* Altogether in 1965 there were 8 autonomous oblasts, 105 administrative oblasts, and 7 krays. Historically many of the regional units have inherited some of the tasks of the Czarist "provinces," and in addition the various autonomous units provide graduated degrees of national autonomy for ethnic minorities on a manageable territorial basis.

A fifth layer of government is formed by the districts or *rayon.* Nearly 3,500 of these were rural in early 1962, including small towns, and about 300 were urban or municipal subdivisions of large towns. By 1963 the rural districts had been reduced to 1,300, each covering a larger territory than before. The sixth and lowest tier comprises over 3,200 "settlements of an urban type," and about 41,000 rural soviets corresponding to rural villages (see Figure 11.3).

Each of these units down to the smallest village is entitled to elect a local council or soviet, there are nearly 50,000 such soviets throughout the Soviet Union. Each soviet has a limited amount of legal authority (less impressive than it looks on paper but nevertheless significant), and each also serves as an instrument for some local participation. Much of the work is delegated to the executive committee of each soviet and to a large number of local commissions; in the 1960s there were about 230,000 such commissions involving about 1.3 million Soviet deputies and another 2.3 million activists drawn from the people.

At all levels, deputies to the soviets are elected directly. However, the nomination of candidates at every level is closely controlled by the Communist Party, and there are no competing candidates. Even so, the elections as well as the work of the soviets serve to solidify the connections between the people and their government. They help the government to

Figure 11.3

Administrative Structure of the Soviet Union

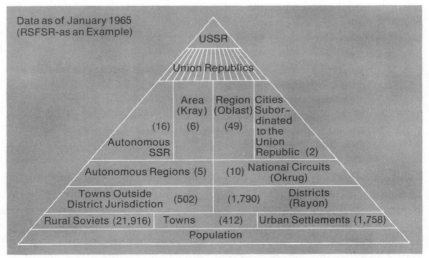

Source: Adapted from The Government and Politics of the Soviet Union, *Revised Edition, by Leonard Schapiro. Copyright © 1965, 1967 by Leonard Schapiro. Reprinted by permission of Random House, Inc.*

present its policies to the people; and, as in other countries, the experience of local government provides many opportunities for the training of local political talent and its recruitment for higher office. Unlike in many other countries, all this happens in the Soviet Union under the initiative and constant surveillance of the Communist Party.

The Party Pyramid. The Communist Party of the Soviet Union, in its organization and ideology, is itself one of the major political inventions of the twentieth century. As we saw earlier in the chapter, it grew out of a tightly-knit body of professional revolutionists, organized into small conspiratorial groups well suited to escape the persecutions of the *Okhrana,* the Czarist secret police. Each of these small groups was so self-contained that its discovery by the police was unlikely to expose other groups. These groups—sometimes called *cells* but now called *primary units*—were organized secretly where the people actually worked and lived. Most often they were formed in factories, offices, institutions, and towns, or within military units or other mass organizations; sometimes they were organized in villages or urban neighborhoods. The extent to which the Party now penetrates the different Russian social and occupational groups is shown in Table 11.1.

Though no longer secret, primary units still exist largely in this compact form. Now as in the past every Communist Party member is expected to work actively under the control of his primary unit and to report his

Table 11.1

The Composition of the Communist Party, 1966 [1]

Social Category	Total Size of Category	Percentage in Party	Percentage of Party
Executives, Administrators	1.2	76	8
Engineers	4.4	40	15
Intelligentsia	11.2	36	38
Armed Forces	3.0	29	7
Cultural, Professional, and Scientific	5.2	24	11
Women	6.9[2]	13	8
Workers	51.0	9	37
Collective Farmers	30.0	7	16
Trade, Services, Other Office Workers	14.4	4	4

[1] In millions; all figures rounded.
[2] Overlapping other categories.

Source: V. Aspaturian, "The Soviet Union," in R. C. Macridis and R. E. Ward (eds.), Modern Political Systems: Europe, *2nd ed., © 1968. Adapted by permission of Prentice-Hall, Inc., Englewood Cliffs, N.J.*

activities to it. This basic organizational design seeks to combine the personal commitment of each individual with the sustaining and motivating power of small groups in which members all know each other face to face. A modern American psychiatrist, Stanley Elkes, has called the small group "the engine of society"; the Communist Party, by its design, seeks to harness this engine to its purposes.

Since Lenin's time the number of primary units has grown, and so has Party membership—more than a hundredfold (see Figure 11.4). In 1967 there were nearly 13 million Party members in the Soviet Union—over 5 per cent of the total population, or about 10 per cent of those of voting age. Yet Party membership remains restrictive. Party members must first serve for a time as *candidates* under the supervision of a primary unit, and each candidate must be sponsored by three Party members for admission. In 1966 there were 11.7 million full Party members and 800,000 candidates. Members are dropped for failing to pay dues for three consecutive months; they may be reprimanded or expelled for inactivity or deviation from

Figure 11.4

The Growth and Social Composition of the Communist Party

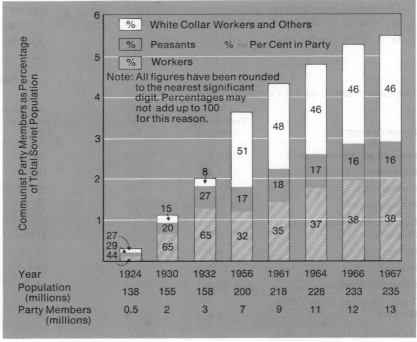

Sources: F. Lorimer, The Population of the Soviet Union: History and Prospects *(Geneva: Economic, Financial, and Transit Department, League of Nations, 1946); United Nations,* Demographic Yearbook, *1966 and 1967; T. H. Rigby,* Communist Party Membership in the U.S.S.R., 1917-1967 *(Princeton, N. J.: Princeton University Press, 1968).*

Party policy. In 1951–56, an annual average of about 100,000 members were expelled; in the more permissive period of 1956–64 this dropped to about 50,000, or less than 0.5 per cent of the total membership per year.

Communist Party members are closely supervised and are supposed to be unceasingly active—often at some cost to their families and peace of mind.[3] They gain improved chances of promotion and careers, and sometimes of power and prestige. Less tangibly, they may gain a sense of belonging to a "vocation of leadership," to a band of persons committed to a historic mission, which may give added meaning to their lives. Such commitment exacts a price. The more intensely members respond to motives of this latter kind, the more bitter will be their disputes in case of disagreement, and the more painful will it be for them to be reprimanded or expelled for disagreeing with the party line, or to support it silently against their personal convictions.

The interplay of Party practices and individual motivations has produced a Party membership which is markedly more intellectual, or at least more white-collar-oriented, more urban, better educated, higher in managers, and more predominantly Russian than the general Soviet population (see Table 11.2).

Party members were organized in 1967 into almost 340,000 primary units, averaging roughly 38 members per unit. The primary units in each locality report to local Party committees of which there were more than 26,000 in 1967, averaging 13 primary units per locality. Each local Party committee has its own secretary who forms a part of the formal "apparatus" of the Communist Party of the Soviet Union. The primary units also report to, and elect delegates to, the rayon, city, and borough (city-subdivision) Party conferences. In 1967 there were approximately 4,000 Party conferences at this level.

The next higher tier is formed by the regional Party organizations. These are Party conferences at the kray, oblast, and ethnic unit levels, which number less than 200. Each of these again is composed of elected delegates and has its own Party committee, bureau, and secretariat. The next level up consists of the Party organizations for each union republic, and for the autonomous republics within the RSFSR.

At the top of the pyramid is the single *All-Union Party Congress,* with its Central Committee, its *Politburo* of eleven full and nine candidate members, and its *Secretariat.* The latter is headed by the *General Secretary of the Communist Party* of the Soviet Union, who by virtue of his position sits atop the pyramid and is one of the most powerful men in the country (see Figure 11.5).

In theory, the constituent body of Party members or Party organizations—the primary units, Party conferences, and Party congresses respectively—should be the highest authority at its level. Though these bodies

---

[3] Some members, of course, join just to get a job and then only go through the motions needed to keep it.

Table 11.2
The Communist Party and the Soviet People, 1932 and 1967 (in percentages)

	Stalin Era, 1932			Breshnev Era, 1967		
	Share in Population (A)	*Party Members (B)*	*Over- or Under-Representation (B/A)*	*Share in Population (C)*	*Party Members (D)*	*Over- or Under-Representation (D/C)*
Peasants	78	28	0.3	25	16	0.6
Workers	14	64	4.5	46 (1959)	38	0.8
Intelligentsia	4	8	2.0	23 (1959)	46	2.0
Urban Dwellers	n.a.	n.a.	n.a.	52	78	1.5
Russians	n.a.	n.a.	n.a.	55	62	1.1
Women	n.a.	n.a.	n.a.	51	20	0.4

n.a. = Not available

Source: V. Aspaturian, "The Soviet Union," in R. C. Macridis and R. E. Ward (eds.), Modern Political Systems: Europe, 2nd ed., © 1968. Adapted by permission of Prentice-Hall, Inc., Englewood Cliffs, N.J.

Figure 11.5

The Central Organs of the Communist Party

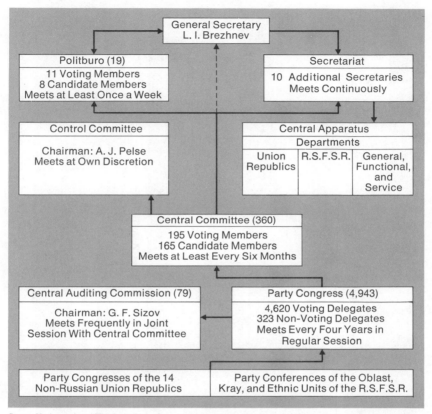

Source: V. Aspaturian, "The Soviet Union," in R. C. Macridis and R. E. Ward (eds.), Modern Political Systems: Europe, 2nd ed., © 1968. Adapted by permission of Prentice-Hall, Inc., Englewood Cliffs, N.J.

meet only rarely, they create Party committees and central committees at each level to act for them as governing bodies between sessions. These committees meet more frequently and in turn elect the bureaus or presidia to act for them between their sessions. Together the committees and bureaus at each level supervise the secretariat. At the same time, the committees and bureaus are responsible to the Party conference or congress at the next higher level, and each Party secretary or secretariat is responsible to the next higher secretariat.

In theory as well, this design is meant to balance a democratic control from below by Party members and their elected delegates with centralized supervision and direction from above in a pattern called *democratic centralism* (see Figure 11.6). This pattern supposedly permits Party members to discuss political issues freely—though usually within the Party—before

Figure 11.6

Organizational Structure of the Communist Party

Source: V. Aspaturian, "The Soviet Union," in R. C. Macridis and R. E. Ward (eds.), Modern Political Systems: Europe, 2nd ed., © 1968. Adapted by permission of Prentice-Hall, Inc., Englewood Cliffs, N.J.

a Party decision is reached, but obliges them to execute and defend both outside and within the Party any decision once made, even if they had opposed it earlier. Moreover, no Communist may deviate from a decision once made or from the *party line* once laid down, nor—since the Tenth Party Congress in 1921—may he reopen the issue for reconsideration. Finally, neither before nor after a decision may Communists organize in separate groups or factions to promote their views within the Party. These last two provisions may have been meant as emergency measures in 1921 but they still remain in force.

Practice differs from theory, however. Party secretaries alone are full-time Party officials. Their influence prevails in the bureaus whose other members have other responsibilities and cannot devote their full energies to bureau work. The secretaries also prevail in committees and the constituent bodies which meet only infrequently. Though in theory the members of the constituent body elect the members of the committees and the committees elect the members of the bureaus, in practice it is the secretaries who pick the candidates who are then duly elected to these bodies. Each Party secretary himself is not elected, but is chosen by the next higher secretary; this is the hierarchy to which he tends to look for guidance and instruction which he then transmits to his committee. As permanent links between higher and lower organizations, the secretaries form a chain of power which in effect controls the Party.[4] An old Soviet joke distinguishes three epochs of human history: the matriarchate, the patriarchate, and the secretariat. In many ways, since the days of Stalin, the dictatorship of the proletariat has turned into the dictatorship of the secretariat.

But despite its bureaucratization, the Communist Party continues to be the heart and soul of the Soviet system. The Party is the chief source of legitimacy. It is the chief formulator of political and social goals, and of the policies by which they are to be pursued. In all these ways, it is the Communist Party which makes the Soviet system work. In Russia as in all countries, the bureaucrats, policemen, and the military apply power in the execution of policy, but in no country have they shown themselves capable of formulating policy over long periods of time. They cannot create fundamental goals. In non-Communist countries, such as the United States, they depend on interest groups and on competing political parties to set these goals, whereas in the Soviet Union they depend to a crucial degree on the Communist Party alone. Not surprisingly, in every major clash between military leaders, police chiefs, or state bureaucrats, on the one hand, and Party secretaries, on the other hand, the Party secretaries thus far have always won.

[4] See Vernon Aspaturian, "The Soviet Union," in Roy Macridis and Robert Ward (eds.), *Modern Political Systems: Europe,* 2nd ed. (Englewood Cliffs, N. J.: Prentice-Hall, 1968).

Figure 11.7

Interlocking Party and State Structures in the Soviet Union

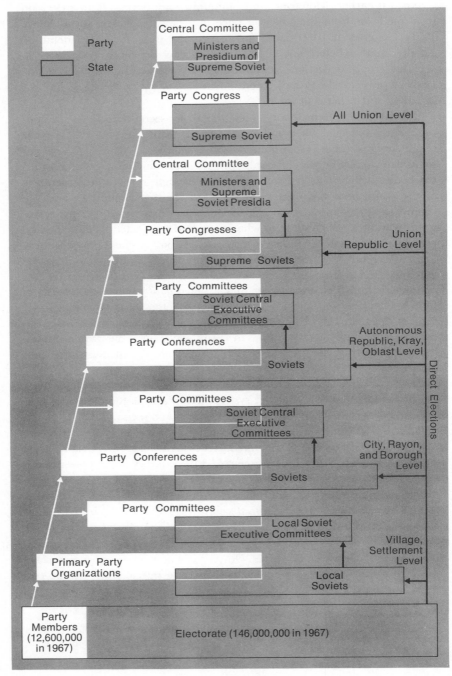

Source: V. Aspaturian, "The Soviet Union," in R. C. Macridis and R. E. Ward (eds.), Modern Political Systems: Europe, *2nd ed., © 1968. Adapted by permission of Prentice-Hall, Inc., Englewood Cliffs, N.J.*

Party and State: The Interlocking Pyramids. The Communist Party penetrates the government at every level (see Figure 11.7). The government in turn, runs the economy, nearly 90 per cent of which is government-owned, with much of the rest owned by cooperatives. The government also runs the armed forces and police, as well as the educational system, the mass media, and almost all means of support for artistic and literary life. These enormous powers of the government enhance the power of the Communist Party, and particularly the power of the Party leaders over their own members as well as over the rest of the people, which, in turn, enhances the Party's control of the state.

At the top, the All-Union Party Secretariat and the Politburo interlock closely not only with each other but also with the Presidium of the Supreme Soviet and the Presidium of the Council of Ministers. In 1967 Leonid Brezhnev, the General Secretary of the Communist Party, was also a member of its Politburo and of the Presidium of the Supreme Soviet. The Chairman of the Presidium of the Council of Ministers, Alexey Kosygin, was also a Politburo member, and so was the Chairman of the Presidium of the Supreme Soviet, N. V. Podgorny. Sometimes the names of the incumbents change, though no faster than in the United States, but the tight interlock among Party and government jobs persists.

Something similar holds true down the line. At the All-Union level, the Party Congress interlocks with the Supreme Soviet. In the union republics, the central committees of the Party interlock with the ministers and presidia of the supreme soviet of each union republic, and the party congresses interlock with the supreme soviets. There are similar interlockings at all lower levels—from the autonomous republics, *krays,* and *oblasts* all the way down to the primary Party units and the village soviets (see Figure 11.8).

Some Unresolved Political Problems

To the Soviet Communist leaders this interlocking of party and state has been a great source of strength within their own country. In international politics, however, the close linkage between a supposedly internationalist party and a national state has threatened to create almost as many liabilities as assets.

International Polycentrism. In the international arena of Communist Parties and regimes, the Russians now face a continuing problem of pluralism, or *polycentrism,* as it is called by writers on the Communist world. The Russians no longer form the only Communist country. There are now fourteen of them, and the big ones like China cannot be dictated to. Indeed, neither can the smaller ones, like Yugoslavia, Albania, or North Vietnam. Nor do French or Italian Communists always follow Russian policies, as they used to in earlier days. In Czechoslovakia in 1968, the will of the Russian Communist leadership could be made to prevail over that

Figure 11.8

Interlocked Government and Party Institutions and Personnel

Other	First Secretaries of Republics	Premiers of Republics	PSS Presidium of Supreme Soviet	PCM Presidium of Council of Ministers	Politburo	Secretariat
			Brezhnev		Brezhnev	Brezhnev (Gen'l Sec'y)
				Kosygin (Chairman)	Kosygin	
					Suslov	Suslov
			Podgorny (Chairman)		Podgorny	Kirilenko
					Kirilenko	
				Polyansky (First Deputy) (ex officio)	Polyansky	
		Voronov (R.S.F.S.R.)		Voronov	Voronov	
Shelepin (Trade Union Chairman)					Shelepin	Shelepin
	Shelest (Ukraine)		Shelest		Shelest	
	Pelshe (Latvia)				Pelshe	
				Mazurov (First Deputy)	Mazurov	
					Grishin	
	Mzhvanadze (Georgia)				Mzhvanadze	
	Rashidov (Uzbek)				Rashidov	
		Shcherbitsky (Ukraine)		Shcherbitsky (ex officio)	Shcherbitsky	
					Demichev	Demichev
					Ustinov	Ustinov
	Masherov (Byelorussia)		Masherov		Masherov	
	Kunayev (Kazakh)		Kunayev		Kunayev	
				Andropov (State Security)	Andropov	
						Ponomarev
						Kulakov
						Kapitonov
						Rudakov

Source: V. Aspaturian, "The Soviet Union," in R. C. Macridis and R. E. Ward (eds.), Modern Political Systems: Europe, 2nd ed., © 1968. Adapted by permission of Prentice-Hall, Inc., Englewood Cliffs, N.J.

of the Czech and Slovak Communists only by the physical invasion of the country by Soviet and Soviet-bloc troops. Overall, then, the Russian Communist government has lost absolute control of the international Communist world.

Though less powerful outside their country than formerly, the Soviet leaders have not become more tolerant. There is growing national diversity in the Communist world. Yet inside each country, Communists tend to claim that they are infallible and that anybody who is not with them is against them. When two Communist regimes differ in opinion, their discussion resembles that of two medieval would-be Popes. It is a discussion between two sides in which both insist on being right. For the last 500 years the Catholic Church has been most careful to avoid schismatic elections. Communism, on the other hand, has built-in schisms. Although these schisms have become increasingly evident, the Communists have not yet discovered that tolerance is not a luxury but a necessity.

A Gap in Communist Ideology. Another unresolved problem faced by all Communist countries involves the question of the property of nations. Communists agree that, in regard to means of production, individuals may not retain private property against the claims of the nation-state. But they are not clear whether a nation-state may legitimately retain the capital and land within its borders as its collective quasi-private property against the claims of poorer nations, or of any international community. Most Communists have not thought through the question of whether a Communist state owns property collectively, with the right to deny its use to poorer Communist nations. If the Russians own some empty real estate in Siberia and the Chinese are overcrowded in China, is the Russian government right in closing off all its land as the property of the Soviet Union, or is the Chinese government correct in thinking that this is a bourgeois way of behaving? The quarrels between the "haves" and "have-nots" of the Communist world pose at least as serious a problem as whether the rich free-world countries owe anything to the poor free-world countries. There is a difference, however. In the free world, people occasionally try to see the other fellow's point of view. In the Communist world, disagreement itself often is considered a deviation.

The Soviet Military-Industrial Complex. The Soviet Union shares another problem with the Western world. It, too, probably has a *military-industrial complex* of its own. A Red Army man, as a professional soldier, is as keen on getting the best modern hardware in the largest possible amounts as is any professional military man anywhere. He will probably be as skillful in lobbying and forging his connections to the political decision system as any general anywhere in the world.

But the Soviet system is not a monolith. Within the limitations set by the political system, groups vie for influence and power and their share of the nation's resources. A manager of a heavy industrial factory may want priorities in investment money for his factory, yet there is sure to be a department store manager clamoring for more consumer goods. In other words, there is a political process in Russia behind the facade of unanimity and common will, hidden but real.

Where will this political process lead? Will escalation in the conflict between East and West make Russian society more and more rigid, its military-industrial sectors more powerful, its ideology more intolerant, and intra-Communist quarrels—as well as quarrels between Communists and non-Communists—more tense and more likely to lead toward war? Or will a de-escalation of international tensions necessarily lead toward more discovery, more experimentation, and more freedom in the Soviet Union? Whether world affairs grow more tense or more relaxed depends on the actions of the West as well as those of the East European powers. But what will happen within the Soviet Union will hinge on the flexibility of the Soviet system, on its ability to accept criticism and change.

The Limited Responsiveness to Criticism

Often one hears the question, "How do individuals or small groups make their views felt in the Soviet system?" To find the answer, it becomes necessary to distinguish the channels provided by official theory and doctrine from the way things actually work.

A look at Soviet ideology shows important differences from the ideas underlying the defunct dictatorships of Nazi Germany and Fascist Italy. The word *totalitarian,* applied to all three of these regimes, only stresses what they have in common (single-party control, concentration of leadership, and the mobilization of all efforts of the population toward a single goal, with no tolerance for opposition). But it is seriously misleading because it fails to show their differences in goals (forced-speed economic growth in the U.S.S.R. vs. military conquest for the Fascists and Nazis) as well as in some of their methods. The Nazi and Fascist regimes were based on the *leadership principle:* authority flowed only from the top down. The leaders were supposed to be always right and did all the talking; the people only had to listen and, as Mussolini put it, to "believe, obey and fight." In Soviet ideology, greater stress is put on flexibility, tactical retreats, self-correction of mistakes, collective authority, and listening to the people. Soviet tradition pictures Lenin not only addressing revolutionary crowds from the top of an armored car but also patiently sitting down for hours and listening to peasants. In practice, however, Soviet listening has been highly selective.

In theory there are at least four channels through which individuals can make their views felt. First, they can write letters to the press, and the Soviet press has been quite diligent in printing such letters; however, in practice these letters are screened. The decision to print the letter is itself treated as a political decision. A letter that is compatible with current policy or that offers only minor modifications has a fair chance to get printed. A letter that says "Reverse basic policy" does not.

A similar channel is what used to be called *"Bolshevist self-criticism."* Such criticism is encouraged and permitted by doctrine; the people at small Party unit meetings and larger meetings are supposed to speak up and criticize the practices of their own unit, their own group, the management of their factory, the local government of their village or town, or the way their collective farm is being managed. They may criticize themselves, the local Party secretaries, and others. In practice, such criticism is used to prepare and mobilize opinion for changes in policy, to loosen bureaucratic rigidity, and to provide a safety valve for accumulated tensions. In general, however, criticism suggesting *how* basic policy can be better carried through is more acceptable than criticism *against* basic policy.

The Soviet Union is run to this day by people who think in the style of emergency politics, the style in which its political system was founded. They will not permit opposition to basic policies which, rightly or wrongly, they consider necessary. As a result, criticism is muzzled and limited to details of policy, to personalities, and to methods of carrying out programs. Sometimes initiatives from below are encouraged but only if they fit into the general plan. Thus, an initiative movement among central Asian farmers to dig more irrigation canals was picked up by the mass media and greatly amplified, increased, and backed. Similarly, in the 1930s the Stakhanovite movement of people who proposed improvements in production was widely publicized. This is somewhat like the kind of freedom of speech which employees have when they are permitted to drop suggestions to management into specially designated suggestion boxes. "Bolshevist self-criticism" is a relatively limited kind of freedom, to put it mildly.

A third channel is the particular units of the Party where candidates are picked. For a time, and perhaps a little more after Stalin's death, there was talk of permitting more candidates to run than there were offices so that the voters would have some degree of selection. Yet this latitude has in fact been limited to some trade union elections, and does not seem to have been applied in elections to the soviets or to Party posts. The right to nominate has not been given to the people and there is no right to organize interest groups, factions, or opinion groups within the ruling Communist Party. Nor is there any other party which has the right to contest an election. To some extent, a major link of control of the society thus inheres in the control over the nomination process and the control of personnel policy, or *cadre policy,* as the Communists call it—that is, deciding who gets promoted, appointed, or moved around. Here, too, there is only a very limited degree of freedom for the individual.

Poetry and literature provide a fourth, although indirect, channel. Strikingly enough, because free political discussion is not possible and a free political vote does not exist, some of the desire of people to express their views has moved into the channels of aesthetic judgment. If it is not permissible to say that the policy of the Party secretary is stupid, it is permissible to say that an officially approved play praising that policy is boring. Similarly, it is possible to find that certain poetry is beautiful and exciting even if it happens to stress emotions not completely provided for in the Party program. The Russian poet Yevgeny Yevtushenko pointed out that in the Russian language the words for "poet" and fighter are phonetically very similar; from this notion he developed the idea that it was the task of poets and writers in Russia to take upon themselves the role of fighting for a better expression of popular moods.

In the early 1960s, thousands of people would gather at street corners to attend a recital of poetry. Part of the explanation is that Russians like poetry. But part of it is also that poetry has become a substitute for other forms of expression which are banned. Something similar applies to movies and plays. Here again there is political control, but when the party line changes or weakens or there is a period of freer discussion, a good deal of material gets through which otherwise would not. For example, in the mid-1950s the Russian film *The Rumyantsev Case* showed a truck driver whose load of textiles was highjacked, thereby conceding that there are highjackers and robbers in the Soviet Union after forty years of Soviet government. Railroaded by the police through a trial, the man is promptly clapped into jail, whereupon his fellow workers in the factory hold a meeting, march on the police station, and protest against what has happened to their comrade. This was a film made at the height of the *de-Stalinization* campaign. This is the kind of loosening up that sometimes occurs, but since 1965, and still more since the intervention in Czechoslovakia in 1968, Soviet cultural policy has again become more oppressive—for how long, no one can tell.

The Sources of Change

In Czechoslovakia in 1968, Communist Party members in relatively high standing argued that intra-party factions should be legalized, discussions should be free, and groups defeated in one Party congress should have the right to ask for a reopening of the issue at the next Party congress. (Of course, they argued, such groups would have to offer new information or new experiences relevant to the issue and have majority support for getting it back onto the agenda.) After the Russian tanks rolled into Prague in the summer of 1968, these proposals were silenced, and some of those who had made them, or supported them, were demoted.

Nevertheless, the Czech experience shows that such lines of thought can arise under the crust of a totalitarian system and that nothing but a foreign occupation may be able to stop them—at least for a time. Hannah Arendt's theory of totalitarianism argued in the early 1950s that Communist dictatorship was like death: permanent and irreversible. Her view has been proven false. Politics, human beings, aspirations, and efforts at self-expression all exist even under Communist dictatorship. Thus, there is a degree of uncertainty and potential openness about the future even in Communist-ruled countries. Just the same, residents of the Soviet Union cannot expect many opportunities for individual political self-expression, and they must be circumspect indeed in the ways they try to make their views heard.

Yet, so far as anyone can judge, the bulk of the Soviet people continue to be loyal to a collectivistic economy. There is no mass support of any kind for giving the country back either to the Czar or to the private corporations. People have grown used to the way basic industries are being developed and they seem to like it. Despite the devastations of World War II, they have seen the steel output of their country rise from less than 10 per cent after World War I to about 80 per cent of that of the United States today. An economic system which in peacetime doubles industrial output every ten or twelve years, they reason, cannot be all bad. At such rates of growth, sooner or later some appreciable improvements will trickle down to the consumers, first in the cities and eventually in the countryside. This has already happened in the fields of basic nutrition and public health. In lengthening life expectancies and lowering infant death rates, the Soviet Union has now fully reached the level of the United States. In the meantime many of the young people continue to find careers in the expanding industrial and technological sectors of their society. Still larger numbers can derive a sense of pride from the visible accomplishments of their country, ranging from the spectacular growth of its cities (see Figure 11.9) to its continuing share in the exploration of the moon and the planets.

The very successes of Soviet industrialization in the past are now creating new kinds of problems for the future. As consumers become more affluent they will insist on a wider range of choice. They will demand a better combination of planning with a market where choices can be made.

Other problems will arise on the production side, through the growing need for innovation. Until recently, the Soviets could apply inventions and innovations developed and tested abroad at the expense of other countries. Henceforth they will need not only to apply new inventions and innovations but also to produce them by their own efforts. However, bureaucracy, dictatorship, and rigid official ideology are not conducive to the creation of new knowledge which leads to invention, or to the repeated breaking of old habits which is essential to innovation. In many ways the Soviet Union and its people were more inventive and innovative between 1917 and the mid-1930s than they have been since. Some of this intellectual slowdown may be attributable to the effects of Stalin's purges but it has long survived his death. To an increasing extent, bureaucracy, conformity, and dictatorship are hampering the future economic development of the country. For a time they will not impede the production of more pig iron, but they will curtail the introduction of new production and practices. Eminent Soviet

Figure 11.9

Urban Growth in the Soviet Union, 1920s–1960s

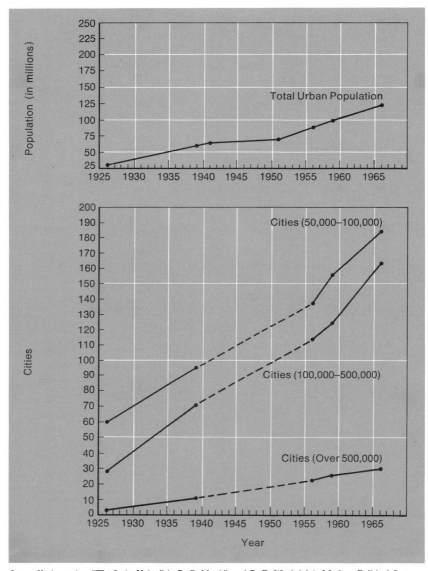

Source: V. Aspaturian, "The Soviet Union," in R. C. Macridis and R. E. Ward (eds.), Modern Political Systems: Europe, 2nd ed., © 1968. Adapted by permission of Prentice-Hall, Inc., Englewood Cliffs, N.J.

scientists like Peter Kapitsa and Victor Sakharov have repeatedly warned against these tendencies.

Similar problems are arising in the work force, in human relations, and in Soviet culture. One cannot tell people for thirty years to admire only one officially approved style in painting and poetry, while expecting them to remain resourceful and eager for change in industry and science. There will be other ideological difficulties. Increasingly the ideological image of the Soviet Union as a country of workers is clashing with the fact that its proportion of manual workers in the work force is becoming constant and seems destined to decline. As in all industrial countries, manual labor in the Soviet Union is being replaced by automation, while the clerical and professional occupations—the so-called "white-collar" personnel—are expanding, taking in perhaps another 5 per cent of the work force every decade. These groups are peripheral in Marxist theory and Soviet ideology but they are becoming central in Soviet life.

Industrialization requires mass education as well as a large expansion of higher education. The success of the Soviet government in promoting both will create in time another set of political problems. A good deal of research shows that in general people with little education prefer to be told only one side of a problem. When presented with two conflicting views, they tend to become confused and angry. This fact has contributed to the observed tendency toward an "authoritarianism of the poor" in many countries. It has also contributed to the success of the one-sided indoctrination methods of the Soviet government during the decades when a large part of its people were illiterate or had only a primary school education. Now the Soviet people are becoming a nation of high school or college graduates, particularly in the younger generation. Such better educated people tend in most countries to feel angry and insulted when presented only one side of an issue. They want to hear all sides and make their own decisions. In the years to come, a growing proportion of the Soviet people may press for far-reaching changes in the cultural and information policies of their government.

The change in generations may well bring these pressures to a head in the 1980s. Many people form their basic political ideas around the age of twenty—more broadly between fifteen and twenty-five—but these people tend to attain most power around the age of fifty-five, when they become heads of departments or organizations. The present Soviet leaders, now in their mid-fifties, formed their political ideas in the 1930s at the height of Stalin's purges but also at the time of the successes of his economic development and military preparedness policies. The Soviet leaders of the 1980s will be of the generation of the poet Yevtushenko who was born in 1933. They will have been in their early twenties when de-Stalinization was at its height and Stalin's crimes were revealed to the Soviet people. When this generation comes into control it may be more willing to cooperate with popular demands for change and liberalization.

The path to liberalization will not be straight, easy, or certain. Periods of greater permissiveness will alternate with seasons of increased repression. But life, group experiences and interests, human spontaneity and the political process will go on beneath the surface. As the Soviet people become more prosperous and confident, their needs and views will make themselves felt at unexpected points in the system.

All these considerations suggest that the Soviet Union will need first of all leaders who will seek to improve their own society and government. Beyond that, they will have to improve their ability to accept other nations—both Communist and non-Communist—as neighbors in terms of genuine cooperation and equality. The Soviet Union will have less need for missionaries to press or persuade other nations to copy current Soviet policies and institutions. To be able to say that a few more nations have adopted some type of Communist government might be a convenience for the Soviet rulers of the 1970s and 1980s, but to develop their own society, and to improve it thoroughly, will be a necessity.

Key Terms and Concepts

idealism
materialism
socialism
uneven development
bourgeois revolution
"weakest link" theory
world revolution
socialism in one country
peasant-worker alliances
vanguard vs. elite
distrust of spontaneity
Bolsheviks
Mensheviks
collective farms
decisive sectors
disproportions in investment
increasing returns to scale
diminishing returns
incentive goods
equalitarianism
performance payments
Supreme Soviet
Presidium of the Supreme
    Soviet (PSS)

Council of Ministers
Presidium of the Council of
    Ministers (PCM)
Chairman of the PCM
union republic
autonomous republic
oblast
kray
rayon
party cells (primary units)
party candidate
All-Union Party Congress
Politburo
General Secretary of the
    Communist Party
democratic centralism
party line
polycentrism
military-industrial complex
totalitarian
leadership principle
Bolshevist self-criticism
cadre policy
de-Stalinization

Additional Readings

Alliluyeva, S. *Twenty Letters to a Friend.* Tr. by P. McMillan. New York: Harper & Row, 1967.

Aspaturian, V. "The Soviet Union." R. C. Macridis and R. E. Ward (eds.) *Modern Political Systems: Europe.* 2nd ed. Englewood Cliffs, N.J.: Prentice-Hall, 1968.

Brzezinski, Z. *The Soviet Bloc.* Rev. ed. Cambridge: Harvard University Press, 1967.

Brzezinski, Z. and S. P. Huntington. *Political Power: USA/USSR.* New York: Viking Press, 1963.

Fainsod, M. *How Russia is Ruled.* Rev. ed. Cambridge: Harvard University Press, 1963.

Friedrich, C. J. (ed.) *Totalitarianism.* 2nd ed. New York: Grosset and Dunlap, 1964.

Inkeles, S. and R. Bauer. *Soviet Citizen: Daily Life in a Totalitarian Society.* New York: Atheneum, 1968.

Kassof, A. (ed.) *Prospects for Soviet Society.* New York: Praeger, 1968.

Lenin, V. I. *State and Revolution.* San Francisco: China Books, 1965.

Reed, J. *Ten Days That Shook the World.* New York: International Publishing Company, 1967.

Schapiro, L. *The Government and Politics of the Soviet Union.* Rev. ed. New York: Vintage, 1967.

Solzhenitsyn, A. *One Day in the Life of Ivan Denisovich.* Tr. by M. Hayward and R. Hingley. New York: Praeger, 1963.

Ulam, A. *The Unfinished Revolution.* New York: Random House, 1960.

Yevtushenko, Y. *A Precocious Autobiography.* Tr. by A. R. MacAndrew. New York: Dutton, 1963.

The United Kingdom

Some years ago, a popular book by a Frenchman bore the title, *The English—Are They Human?* Many foreign observers long have wondered just what the English—and since the eighteenth century, the British people—are like. Some, like Hitler's air force in World War II, found out the hard way.

A glance at English society shows that at least four different strata have long existed, like the layers of a cake. At the top there has long been an aristocratic and imperial group—the establishment. Many of its members are self-assured and relaxed about their pleasures much as their ancestors were in the unblushing days of Fielding's *Tom Jones.* Beneath the nobility but still in the establishment, there is a mixed layer of the upper middle class, including officers, professional men, and high civil servants. Inheritors of large fortunes in commerce, industry, and finance also fit into this layer, and so do well-educated white-collar workers. The diverse members of this group all have been molded into gentlemen. They were taught their excellent manners in *public schools,* which are private, and they have accepted the morals of Victorian responsibility, which is an extension of the middle-class Protestant ethic of self-control.

Below these two elite groups comes the third layer, the tradesmen. Many of these own property and employ labor, but they lack the full education and manners of gentlemen. Here we also find the more simply educated white-collar employees. Some of these hold to tighter standards of hard work and success; others try to imitate the gentility of their "betters," but still others have grown impatient and angry with upper-middle-class manners and respectability which seem stuffy and pretentious to them. Either way, most of them are likely to stay trapped in this latter stratum. For most Englishmen the abyss between gentleman and "tradesman" has remained. To them an engineer is a kind of plumber and a plumber is not a gentleman. The fourth layer consists of manual workers, both skilled and unskilled.

Chapter 12

From this society the English have produced a four-layer culture: at the top a libertarian culture of the avant-garde in the style of Virginia Woolf and the Bloomsbury set of artists and writers; next the Victorian respectability of the upper middle class; then a tight lower-middle-class respectability; and at the bottom an irrepressible working-class hedonism which is reflected in the writings of Alan Sillitoe and many others. Thus, there is no simple single English character. And the peoples of Scotland and Wales, who together with the English and the Northern Irish, form the United Kingdom and the British nation, have their own distinct characteristics. They are less class-ridden within, but more disadvantaged as a group and more ready for social or national protest. All these peoples somehow have remained cohesive around the English core; and the different kinds and strata of Englishmen have remained a single people of remarkable energy, endurance, and political resourcefulness.

The Islands That Shaped a State

More than in any other country, British politics can only be understood against a background of history. It is the history of a state that changed its major tasks five times in 900 years—and of a people that became stronger with each change.

Openness and Isolation. The English state is in some ways a unique combination of a response to given conditions and political inventiveness. The British state derived its flexibility from its geography, rich in its variety of coastlines, plains, and mountains. Geography permitted options of basic policy: the British could choose whether they wanted the state to be strong or weak, centralized or decentralized.

The Celtic culture of England and Ireland was native. Later it fused with Christianity brought by Roman missionaries. Between 500 and 800 A.D., Ireland was the most learned country in Europe. More Irishmen knew Greek at that time than did Frenchmen; and it was the Irish who sent out missionaries to civilize the Swiss. After the Celtic and Roman influence in Britain came the Saxon tribes, and still later the Scandinavian or Viking culture. The civilization and knowledge the seafaring Vikings brought from Byzantium and the Arab countries also found their way to England. In the Middle Ages, England was at one and the same time the end of the road and the crossroads of Europe, where many cultural influences met. With its long coastline and high hills and mountains, the country was suited to shelter people and ideas. Many habits could persist unchanged for centuries in mountainous seclusion, yet all the world could come by boat.

The whole tradition of the moving frontier and the savage Old Testament practice of meeting other cultures with the edge of the sword are built into British history. There were four frontiers in the British Isles—the Cornish, the Welsh, the Scottish, and the Irish. England also had a continental frontier in Europe. From the thirteenth century it held territories on the European continent. Bordeaux was under British rule for 200 years. Calais may have been to Mary, the Catholic Queen who died in 1558, what Saigon has been to some policy-makers in our day: a beachhead and guarantee of long-standing involvement and aspiration on a continent that was increasingly ungrateful and inhospitable.

From 1497 onward, starting in the days of Henry VII, England turned to sea power. In the middle of the sixteenth century, the turn was completed: upon ascending to the throne, Queen Elizabeth I gave up Calais, thereby liquidating the commitment on the continent. Beginning with a modest business partnership between the Queen of England and the pirate Sir Francis Drake, this new policy led to four centuries of dominion of the seven seas.

But before England could extend its frontiers, it first had to become united at home. At a crucial time, much of this unity was imposed by outsiders.

The Conquest That Lasted.   In the eleventh century Saxon England was economically advanced, with many towns and money in wide use. But politically weak and internally divided, it was conquered by recently Frenchified Scandinavian roughnecks. In 955 a Scandinavian with the expressive name of Hrolf the Ganger (fairly close in meaning to the modern word "gangster"), had settled with his followers in Normandy. He soon became Rollo, le Duc de Normandie. In 1066 a descendent, William the Conqueror (since he was of illegitimate birth the Saxon appellation of William "the Bastard" is technically not inaccurate), conquered England with the blessings of the Pope. The conquest was shattering and thorough, though precarious. There were a million Saxons and not very many Norsemen in the country. The result was a high degree of solidarity among the Norman rulers. They had to stand together to defend their lives and to control their Saxon subjects.

Characteristic Elements of British Government

The First Modern State.   To strengthen their solidarity and control, the Norman conquerors built up a highly centralized state with the aid of the latest administrative techniques provided by the Church. For its day, their state was very modern. In the twelfth century, the Normans established a sophisticated administration of royal taxes and spending, called the *exchequer*. This was the first modern office of the treasury in Europe outside of Italy. Out of the old Roman roads, the Normans developed a network of King's highways; the King's law applied everywhere within arrowshot of both sides of the highways. Another statute of the time specified that contracts everywhere in England could be enforced in the King's courts. This action shifted the attention of everyone interested in merchandising, trade, and money from the local powers toward the King and the central state. Thus, by the thirteenth century there were King's courts, King's highways, and the King's law (which soon became the "common law" because the King's law largely adopted customary law). In this manner the English genius combined bold innovation with deeply rooted elements of tradition. The King's courts and King's highways were new. The use of customary law linked old law to a new political system.

Centralization and solidarity were the unique gifts of Norman administration and they became two of the key aspects of British government. In the thirteenth century French nobles paid an average of 3 per cent of their income as taxes to the Crown. English nobles paid 6 per cent. As a result, the English monarchy, though ruling a less populous country, had more money than the French, and the Hundred Years' War eventually was fought on French soil. Without this superior political and financial performance, England's seapower and island position would not have kept the war from its shores, any more than they had been able to prevent the Norman conquest. From the days of the tax assessments of the thirteenth century to the rationing system of World War II, the English have made a point of obeying their laws and paying their taxes. Thanks in part to the more dependable compliance habits of its elites and of its common people, England was able to achieve more power than many larger states or kingdoms.

Soon after the Norman conquerors set up their state, they began making peace with the different elements of English society. At the time of the Conquest, William depended completely on his Normans. Thereafter he and his successors worked with several interest groups, often playing them against each other. When some of William the Conqueror's Norman barons rose against him in 1086, he promptly turned around and called out the Saxon territorial militia against them. Step by step, the Saxons were brought into the English system; and by the fourteenth century their language had come back into respectable use in the courts and in public administration.

The story of England is the story of the refusal of a people to assimilate to its conquerors. Rather things worked the other way around. The conquerors were assimilated to the people. For 300 years England was governed in French, but eventually the beer brewers and then other guilds in London brought the use of English back into the courts after 1362. By the time of Chaucer a common language had been restored, albeit one with 48 per cent of its vocabulary taken from Latin and French.

The Tradition of Enquiry.   Another key aspect of English politics from early times onward—in addition to centralization and solidarity—has been the tradition of *enquiry,* that is, the systematic asking of questions, listening to evidence, and search for facts. William the Conqueror, foreshadowing the best modern practice in government and social science, began his reign with a statistical survey. The results were recorded in his *Domesday Book* which counted every piece of real estate and every potential taxpayer as well as the population as a whole. It was an inventory of the national resources of England at the end of the twelfth century, a report that surely could have gone to a national resources planning board had one existed at the time.

The notion of enquiry lies at the heart of British political and administrative tradition. The Magna Carta in 1215 laid down as one among its major points that when a dead body was found anywhere in England, a board of enquiry had to be set up and an inquest held by a coroner. This was not an inevitable position. The conquering Norman elite might have said that, upon the finding of a dead Norman body, the next Saxon village would be burned. They could have introduced hostage systems, massacres, or other reprisals, leading to escalating hatred. Instead they chose to start specific inquests which turned out to be a more civilized and durable way of coping with murder. Magna Carta marked the rise of the tradition that every individual's life and death matters. The English poet W. H. Auden has said it is not wholly accidental that there is a detective story tradition in English-speaking countries. If a person dies in most parts of the English-speaking world, it is not something one takes for granted, as part of an Oriental fatalism or as the result of mute historic forces; it is considered a matter of human importance and thus gives rise to searching curiosity.

Parliament, too, developed from a tradition of enquiry. Arising out of the King's great council around 1240, it was based on the principle, "What touches all should be approved by all." This is still a reasonable principle of government. Hearings, consultations, and eventually giving people a widening share in decision-making are characteristic of the English tradition of government and have had a profound effect on British society. Royal Commissions of Enquiry in the nineteenth century produced the facts and recommendations that led to the legislation abolishing chattel slavery, child labor, and the exploitation of women in mines and factories. Similar commissions laid the foundations for Britain's present-day "cradle-to-grave" social security system and for the humanizing reform of British penal law. The principle of enquiry spread to other English-speaking countries. In Canada, a Royal Commission on Bilingualism and Biculturalism has opened the way for improving relations between French-speaking and English-speaking Canadians. The essential contribution of all such commissions is not advocacy but discovery. They see their task not primarily as bargaining between parties for some compromise, nor as a public relations job to arouse support for some preconceived policy, but as a probing of the facts of the problem before them in order to discover new and genuine solutions.

A Link Across Two Classes: The Gentleman.   Another part of the English tradition has been the building of human and communication bridges between groups. One of the forces helping to break the barriers between noblemen and commoners was the concept of *the gentleman*—the person who carried his gentle breeding wherever he went. Gentlemen sending their younger sons into towns to become guildsmen was typical of fifteenth-century England. Most other European nobles would rather have been found dead than have had their children join guilds of artisans or merchants. Only in England did one-third of the apprentices in the Tailors' and Skinners' Guilds in 1485 turn out to be the sons of gentlemen. In Berne and Zurich there was a touch of social equality, but in most of Europe an abyss separated commoners from noblemen. In England, in contrast, the upper middle class and the lesser nobles merged in the new elite of gentlemen.

The English *law of primogeniture* aided this development. It reserved the noble title and the family estate to the oldest son of the family. It made all other sons commoners, and these then were free to intermarry with commoners, to engage in business ventures, and to profit from the wool trade or from shipping—all of which they did.

The social, cultural, and psychological unity between the upper middle classes and the nobility took more than four centuries to develop fully. In the nineteenth century, great "public" schools were founded to mold the sons of aristocrats, successful businessmen, and some professional men into a single class of gentlemen. This class was expected to rule every major aspect of British life by its example, charm, upper-class manners and accent, and the social, political, and economic power of the "old boy" network through which the graduates of "public" schools find jobs for each other.

This far-reaching consolidation of the nobility and the upper middle class was paid for by a wider gap between "gentlemen" and "tradesmen" (or the lower middle class) than is found in many other countries. England long has been more democratic on top but more class-ridden in the middle and bottom layers of society. There one finds more deference and more resentment than in the United States. While some English voters are more responsive to the snob appeal of voting for their betters, others have long responded to the class appeal of the Labour Party with its promise to change the social system. The basis for the power of both appeals is rooted deeply in English society and history. Polite British taxi drivers still may call high-tipping passengers "governor" and "sir," and then vote for the Labour Party with its program to nationalize the coal, steel, and transport industries.

Links Across Localities and Classes: Members of Parliament.
During the reign of Queen Elizabeth I, in the mid-sixteenth century,
England abandoned the tradition of completely local representation,
which is still the formal law and usual practice in the United States. Any
constituency, borough, or shire in England became free to elect anyone as
its representative to Parliament, whether or not he was a local resident.
For Parliament, in the words of Edmund Burke, was no longer "a congress
of ambassadors from different and hostile interests . . . but . . . a deliberative assembly of one nation, with one interest, that of the whole. . . ." The
convulsions that swept through the political system of New York State in
1964 when Robert Kennedy rather quickly became a resident of New
York and then ran for senator would not have occurred in England. There
that problem was solved 400 years ago.

By the middle of the sixteenth century, about one-fifth of Parliament
comprised country districts represented by rural nobles, called knights of
the shire. Another fifth consisted of *burghers*—local citizens—from the
boroughs, and three-fifths came from urban communities which were
represented by noblemen elected by middle-class voters. This was the
political tradition which later pervaded George Washington's Virginia. A
political elite of noblemen by birth, upbringing, and education, had
enough leisure time in which to master the art of politics; and such an elite
won and retained the confidence of the English burghers—and later of the
Virginia frontiersmen. This was the tradition of building *cross-class coalitions.*

The First Great Modern Political Revolution

The Crown function, as well as the parliamentary function, was firmly
established quite apart from the existence of a given monarch by the end
of the fifteenth century. In the century before Elizabeth, in the civil wars
between the houses of Lancaster and York, the English learned to keep the
institution of the Crown functioning even without knowing who was King.
The *Crown* became the symbol of a continuing impersonal organization:
the public administration and bureaucracy, and the property, treasury,
and machinery of the state. All these somehow kept working, usually in
cooperation with Parliament, no matter what happened to the person of
the monarch. When strong absolute monarchs, like Henry VIII and
Elizabeth I, increased their power against the great nobles, these powers
soon shifted to the Crown. But inevitably, the separation of the Crown
from the monarchy weakened the power of the British king. In reaction, as
the government became increasingly able to function without him, a king
might be tempted to assert his power more, trying to balance the loss of
real power by an effort of his political will.

King James I, successor to Queen Elizabeth, succumbed to this temptation. James, perhaps a genius, was a man of tremendously high intelli-

gence but of such bad political judgment that his contemporaries called him "the wisest fool in Christendom." A strong proponent of the *divine right theory,* according to which a king ruled by the will of God and was answerable to no one else for his actions, James tried hard to block or reverse the spread of power to Parliament and the growing independence of the courts. And for twenty to thirty years he succeeded in halting the increase of Parliament's power.

James also carried out constructive reforms, some with lasting effects. He introduced the name Great Britain for England and Scotland, and he persuaded the English Parliament to vote citizenship for all Scotsmen born after 1603, and the Scot Parliament to do as much for Englishmen. Thus he laid the foundations for the British political system and people.

James's son Charles I, was less bad as a ruler than his father, but it was Charles who paid the price for both. His fate reminds one of a principle mentioned by St. Thomas Aquinas in the thirteenth century. Aquinas said that if a country has an unusually bad prince, one should not overthrow him; in the nature of things he will die sooner or later, and a less bad one is likely to succeed him and make the system work. But, said Aquinas, if the ruler is of average or better quality (as Charles proved to be), and life is nevertheless intolerable under him, then there is something wrong with the system of government itself; in that case the government must be overthrown because an improvement in the incumbent will not cure a bad system. Four centuries later, the English revolution seemed to corroborate Aquinas's views.

Charles was conscientious, goodlooking, and almost charismatic. He tried to govern England as it once had been governed but could no longer be and set off a revolution in the process. The revolution against him was led by a cross-class coalition. Country gentlemen, mainly from the shire of Cambridge and the east of England, were at first the main sources of the armies fighting him, but Parliament raised armies, too. The issue was decided by the actions of the mass of the people. A painting in the House of Commons still shows the shuttered shops in London when the City of London voted to close them all so that apprentices and journeymen could go out and take up weapons "until the city of Gloucester be relieved." Commanded by Oliver Cromwell, the armies of country gentlemen from Cambridgeshire and of Parliament—the *roundheads* or "ironsides," as they were known—swept away the royalist *cavaliers.* The King was tried and beheaded, for, as Cromwell's secretary, the poet John Milton, noted in *The Tenure of Kings and Magistrates,* kings had their office only so long as they kept their agreements with the community; otherwise they became public enemies and had to be treated as such.

Milton's doctrine was grim and perhaps more extreme than most Englishmen were completely willing to accept at the time. After Cromwell's death his generals, the "military complex" of the time, brought back a Stuart King, Charles II; Cromwell's bones were disinterred and scattered.

England, having had twenty years of Puritan dictatorship and publicly enforced morality, went to the other extreme. After the Battle of Naseby in 1645, Cromwell's soldiers had slashed the faces of women camp followers of the Royalist Army so that they should not endanger the virtue of Puritans in the future. Twenty years after that inhuman outbreak of instant righteousness, restoration comedy began to introduce plays which to this day cannot be advertised in a family newspaper without changing their titles; these plays became popular and were widely performed.

In 1688 the Stuarts were thrown out once more, and England settled down in 1690 to an Act of Toleration and parliamentary supremacy. In the military sphere, standing armies, which were considered a threat to liberty, were abolished. The British began to concentrate on building up the navy while keeping the army relatively small. A strong navy could dominate the seas but not the English people. In 1707 England and Scotland were formally united under a single Parliament, and the country formed was henceforth to be called Great Britain.

The English Revolution took more than half a century to run its full course. It made England the first great modern nation. Its first phase—the war of Parliament against the King—and the days of Cromwell are often called in England "the Great Rebellion"; its second period, the almost bloodless expulsion of the last Stuart King in 1688, is called "the Glorious Revolution." The relative importance of these events in the minds of the British seems clear: it is Oliver Cromwell's statue that now stands in front of the House of Commons, to commemorate his role as protector of Parliamentary power.

In 150 years, the reforms of absolute monarchs and two waves of revolution had merged England into Britain and made it the most modern country of the world. During this same period, kings lost power to the Crown, and the Crown lost most of it to Parliament (see Figure 12.1).

Government by Parliament

There is not a thing between heaven and earth that Parliament cannot do, said English jurist John Austin. This is largely true. Under the British system, there are no legal limits on the power of Parliament. Neither has Britain a written constitution. Nor is there a separation of powers as in the United States. Indeed, Britain has no such thing as judicial review of the acts of Parliament.

The Emerging Power of the House of Commons.   For a time, power in Britain was divided among three parties: the Lords, the Commons, and the Crown. The House of Lords and the House of Commons were the two chambers of Parliament. The House of Lords represented and were composed of the high nobility, the peers of England, as they

Figure 12.1

Parliamentary Government, c. 1600

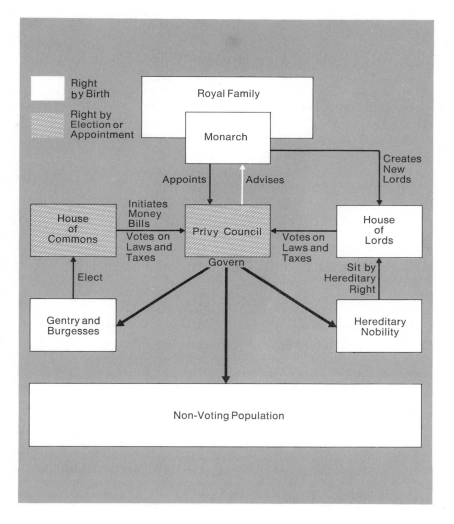

were called. These were the Barons, Viscounts, Earls, Marquises, and Dukes, each of whom took his seat by heredity as soon as he inherited his title. By contrast, the members of the House of Commons were elected, each representing one of the boroughs or shires of the kingdom (much as they now represent the 600-odd parliamentary constituencies—that is, electoral districts—of the country).[1]

In the course of time power shifted increasingly to the House of Commons. The revolutions in the seventeenth century accelerated this process, which was completed by the middle of the twentieth. The seventeenth-century revolutions destroyed many of the old families of peers. Their places were taken by new peerage created from courtiers and successful speculators by James II and his successors. As the King became increasingly obliged to choose his ministers only with the advice of the House of Commons, and then to follow the advice of these Parliament-controlled ministers in his own political actions, the House of Commons—or more exactly, the Prime Minister and his Cabinet—gradually acquired the powers of the Crown. In consequence, the House of Commons became ever more likely to prevail in any conflict with the House of Lords.

Other circumstances strengthened the hands of the Commons. Governments, as we have seen, always need more money, and from early days the Commons alone could introduce money bills. In the nineteenth century it gained exclusive control over appropriations; this was formally recognized by law in 1911. Other types of legislation had to be passed by majorities in both houses so that the Lords had, in effect, a right of veto. This right gradually eroded. The Crown could create new peers by bestowing appropriate titles on whomever it chose. The threat to create many new peers often was used to make a recalcitrant majority in the House of Lords temper its resistance to the monarch, and to the Commons majority and Cabinet advising him. Finally, in 1911 the House of Lords lost its absolute power of veto over legislation, retaining only the right to delay legislation by one year.[2] A final reason for the power of the Commons was the consent of the governed. Ordinary people became less inclined to obey the Lords, but remained willing to support the Commons.

---

[1] Until recently, no peer of England could renounce his title in order to represent a constituency in the House of Commons. For this reason Winston Churchill refused a peerage after World War II: he wanted to remain in the House of Commons.

[2] To compensate somewhat for this final loss of power, the Conservative Government after 1945 introduced the practice of having the monarch make distinguished persons peers for their own lifetime but without any hereditary title for their descendants. It was hoped that these lifetime peers would increase the quality and prestige of the House of Lords. In addition, the monarch has continued to create hereditary Lords from among meritorious commoners, including nowadays deserving trade union leaders as well as businessmen.

The ordinary rank of knight, and its title "Sir," is still bestowed by the monarch as a governmental honor on British subjects in many walks of life. It implies no peerage, is not hereditary, and does not bar its bearer from membership in the House of Commons.

The Cabinet and the Party System. The primary result of these shifts in power has been the transformation of the *Cabinet* from a council of advisers to the King chosen by the monarch and responsible to him into an instrument of the House of Commons. Today the Cabinet, the chief executive power headed by the Prime Minister, is a committee of Parliament. In theory, it is Parliament's creature. Parliament can make it or unmake it; if Parliament votes "no confidence" in the Cabinet, the Cabinet must resign. This has remained settled policy in England for several centuries. This power has been so taken for granted that no Parliament has needed to exercise its prerogative. No Cabinet has been overthrown by Parliament since 1924. When a Prime Minister discovers that he is about to lose his majority, he may step down in advance. Neville Chamberlain did so in 1940, in favor of Winston Churchill, whom all parties trusted.

In practice, the Prime Minister and his Cabinet depend on the support of their party. To function well, the British system requires political parties and *party discipline.* Parties began to emerge among the still narrow political elites from the late seventeenth century onward. The *Whigs* (who took their name from Scottish lowland opponents of the monarchy) favored increasing the power of Parliament and reducing that of the monarch. They drew their support from urban and mercantile interests and a minority of the great landed families. The *Tories* (named after bands of outlaws favoring Catholicism and the traditional monarchy) formed the court party. They stressed the claims of the hereditary nobility and the divine right of the King. Their supporters were a majority of the landed nobles and a minority of urban and commercial groups interested in monopolies and court favors. The Whigs were more inclined than the Tories to favor freer competition and more permissive government, at least for the educated and the well-to-do. Neither party advocated revolution.

In the eighteenth century both parties were deeply entangled in the inefficiency and corruption which characterized British politics at that time, and for a while the Tories were practically defunct. In the course of the nineteenth century, the revived Tories became the modern *Conservative Party,* and the Whigs became the *Liberals.* In the twentieth century, the *Labour Party* was founded, and after World War I it became one of the main pillars of the two-party system, relegating the Liberals to a minor role.

As time went one, candidates for the Commons came to depend on party support for election and re-election. They had reason, therefore, to follow the orders of their party while in Parliament. Each party organized its members in the House into a disciplined group called the *parliamentary party,* in contrast to the *national party* outside Parliament. The parliamentary party elects floor leaders, called party *whips,* to instruct members how to vote. *"Free votes,"* left to the discretion of each member, are rare.

The majority party designates the *Prime Minister,* who is then formally entrusted by the monarch with the task of forming a government. Specifically, the Prime Minister chooses the members of his Cabinet and assigns them their tasks. He may change their assignments, or drop them from the Cabinet and replace them by others. In all this, he needs the support of Parliament, and, above all, the support of his own parliamentary party. Parliament can overthrow him by an adverse vote if a majority strongly opposes his Cabinet choices or his policies, but, as we have seen, this is rare and has not taken place for decades. (The Prime Minister may even draw some of his Cabinet members from the House of Lords, provided that the House continues to back his government.)

Thus Britain is governed by a double feedback process. Parliament can give instructions to the government which exercises leadership in the House of Commons and can be overthrown by the House. But the Cabinet can also dissolve the House of Commons and can appeal over its head to the voters in a general election. The voters then elect a new Parliament and a new Cabinet may emerge as a result (see Figures 12.2 and 12.3).

The same double feedback process includes the parties. A Prime Minister ordinarily is the leader of his party both within and outside Parliament. But a parliamentary party may revolt against a Prime Minister, or a national party may induce the members of the parliamentary party to do so. When Parliament is dissolved by the Prime Minister, perhaps because no new majority can be formed, elections must be called in which the former majority is very likely to lose. Members of the House of Commons do not like to risk their seats, and hence do not overthrow governments lightly.

The British system thus has two feedback circles: a short one between Cabinet and Parliament during normal times and a long one from the Cabinet to the voters via the new House of Commons to the new Cabinet. What the United States would call the "executive branch" is one part of the process. What it calls the "legislative branch" is the other part of the process. In Britain, the two are on the same feedback cycle. Both systems, British and American, have worked well in providing constitutional and democratic government.

This comparison of the British and American governments, shows that background conditions limit the range of political choices, but that within these limits such choices do exist. Having chosen different types of political machinery, Britain and the United States have continued to face common problems: the struggle between conservatism and change and between the power of elites and broader political participation.

The Frozen Decades: 1790–1832

A nation that has its own great revolution in relatively recent memory is unlikely to feel much need for another. Grandsons and great-grandsons of revolutionaries tend to be somewhat conservative. In the second half of the

Figure 12.2

Parliamentary Government, c. 1970: The Slow Feedback Cycle

***Figure* 12.3**

    Parliamentary Government, c. 1970: Crisis: The Fast Feedback Cycle

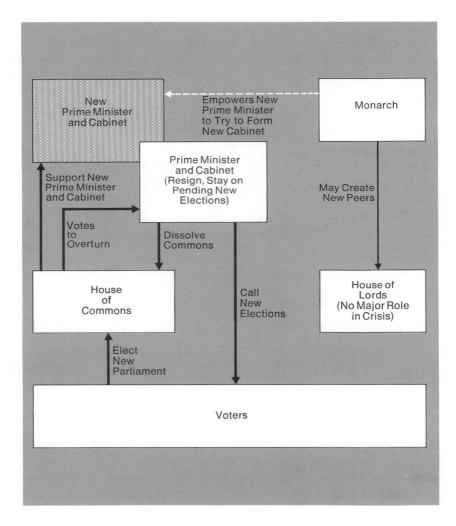

eighteenth century, British politics was just that, in contrast to the incipient revolutionary changes going on in British industry and science.

The British system failed to respond to the needs of the American colonists, although the colonists might have seceded anyway. When the French Revolution broke out so much nearer to their island, Britain for a moment was swept with the possibility of a broader middle-class and lower-class revolution of its own. But within two years, as the Revolution became more radical and violent, English public opinion switched toward opposition to the French Revolution and democratic agitation was silenced at home. This change in the public mood was accomplished in part by the deliberate political strategy of the British elites.

One of the intellectual architects of this strategy of counterrevolution was Edmund Burke. Burke emphasized that the French Revolution was godless. By exaggerating the case, he built a bridge between the privileged and established Church of England and the underprivileged Protestant sects. The latter included the Presbyterians, Methodists, and other small Protestant groups whose members had been treated as citizens of lesser right and prestige. In the name of religion, but really in the interests of a more general conservatism, differences among Protestant denominations were played down.[3]

The Great Reforms

From 1790 to 1825 the British economy and technology changed quickly, but the British political system remained almost frozen. After 1825 conservatism began to wane. The first trade unions were legalized and the first political organizations began to function in opposition to the government.

Within a relatively few years, in 1832, a *Reform Bill* was pushed through the Parliament. It had been opposed to the last moment by Napoleon's nemesis, the Duke of Wellington, who, like many military heroes, after his victory had become a conservative political leader. By 1832, the "Iron Duke" was out of a job and England was getting a new constitutional settlement through the enfranchisement of the middle class, the abolition of urban "rotten boroughs" and "pocket boroughs," and the enfranchisement of new cities such as Liverpool and Birmingham. The English working class in the towns got the vote a generation later, in 1867. The writer Thomas Carlyle compared the enfranchisement of laborers to "shooting Niagara" because he felt it was so dangerous to give working

---

[3] In Ireland this strategy was carried even further, perhaps far beyond Burke's intentions. The English royal house made a deliberate alliance with the Presbyterians of Ulster. The first Irish patriotic and revolutionary leaders had all been Protestants. Now, in the late 1790s, the Orange Order was founded in order to woo away the Protestants from the cause of Irish independence. Deliberately, members of Protestant sects were given privileges and special ties to the British establishment to divide them from the poorer Catholic Irish in the south of the island.

men the vote. He very likely felt the same way that some southern governors feel nowadays about giving a genuine vote to blacks. In 1885 the rural laborers were enfranchised. In 1918, by a somewhat unchivalrous piece of legislation, women over thirty got the vote; in 1928, the British decided to entrust the ballot also to women between twenty-one and thirty.

Changes in the right to vote went hand in hand with social change. After 1832, the first wave of labor unrest, the Chartist movement, went through England leaving in its wake the first factory inspection acts. With Tory help a labor-conservative coalition was formed at the time against liberal factory owners of the laissez-faire school of thought. This resulted in 1851 in the first limitation of working time, the ten-hour law. After 1889, the first great dock-workers' strike and the second wave of labor unrest followed, bringing with them the rise of the unskilled workers and the mass trade unions. The Independent Labour Party was founded in 1893, the Labour Party in 1900. The first avowedly Socialist government took office as a minority in 1924; the first absolute Labour majority was won in 1945, the second, in 1964.

The Post-War Decades

During the decades 1870–1920, Britain's overseas empire had been greatly enlarged. There had been much agitation for *imperialism,* the policy aimed at making the Empire even bigger. Conservatives and radicals agreed that such an empire was indispensable to private enterprise at home. From this, Conservatives concluded that empire was good, and radicals, that private enterprise should be curbed or abolished.

The Exit From Empire.   "I have not become His Majesty's First Minister to preside over the dissolution of the British Empire," growled Sir Winston Churchill during World War II. His successors, the Labour Government, did just that—and turned their policy into a success. "This," said Prime Minister Clement Attlee in 1947 to a crowded Albert Hall audience celebrating the beginning of Indian independence, "is the proudest day in British history."

During its history, the English state has served a succession of changing tasks. Its first task was to consolidate the Norman Conquest; its second to unify the British Isles into a single political and economic system. Its third task, from the sixteenth to the eighteenth century, was the conquest of the seven seas and the acquisition of beachheads from Bombay and Calcutta to Gibraltar and Halifax. The fourth task, from the mid-eighteenth through the nineteenth century, was the conquest of vast inland areas and populations in Asia and Africa and the establishment of the largest empire the world had ever seen. In 1911, when King George V of England was crowned King-Emperor of India, the sun did not set on his dominions and more than 500 million people lived under the British flag. Britain's victory in World War I added new countries and peoples in the oil-rich Near East to the lands under British control. "Wider yet and wider may thy bounds be set," ran a popular hymn of those years, "God who made thee mighty, make thee mightier yet." But during the heyday of imperial expansion, domestic economic growth was neglected. British capital was sent overseas, while equipment in many industries at home was allowed to become obsolete.

After World War II, Britain faced a radically new task. The days of empires were ending but not all imperial nations were aware of this fact. Britain's government and people met this new challenge with the same courage with which they met the Battle of Britain. They cooperated with local nationalists to organize in rapid succession the independence of India, Pakistan, Burma, and Egypt. In the next two decades there followed the independence of most of British Africa, Cyprus, Malaya, and the islands of the Caribbean.

At certain times and places the British resisted political independence, and fighting broke out between local nationalists on the one hand and British troops, and sometimes British settlers, on the other. Malaya, Kenya, and Cyprus, the British opposition to the establishment of Israel in 1948, and the short-lived Suez War in alliance with Israel and France against Egypt in 1956, all are examples of such conflicts. But if one adds up all such fighting, one still must conclude that never before in human history had so many people received their independence with so little resistance from their former rulers. Britain moved faster into the post-imperial age than did France, Belgium, the Netherlands, Portugal, and a large part of American public opinion.

The British adjustment was smoothed by the *commonwealth* concept. The term harks back to the government of England in Cromwell's day, but the word was applied widely to Britain's relations with her former colonies only from the 1920s onward. The substance of the new arrangements was developed from the nineteenth century on, at first under other names. In 1867 Britain granted to Canada the status of a dominion which implied far-reaching rights of internal self-government. Between the 1890s and the 1920s, Canada's rights of dominion were extended to include control over foreign trade, immigration, military matters, and eventually external affairs. In the same period, *dominion status* was extended to Australia, New Zealand, and the Union of South Africa. From the 1920s on, it became increasingly clear that nonwhite territories would also become self-governing, and that the Commonwealth would become an organization of equals. After World War II, this happened in the sense that the former dominions became sovereign, and the old notion of dominion status disappeared. The newly sovereign countries, such as India, Pakistan, and others, chose to accept Commonwealth membership, side by side with the former dominions.

Today, Commonwealth membership implies mainly arrangements for political consultation, financial cooperation, and the somewhat freer mobility of persons. There are also sentimental ties: some Commonwealth members have retained the British monarch as their symbolic head, although others, like India and Ghana, have become republics.

As the Commonwealth loosened and the Empire was dissolved, they became less important issues for British politics at home. The majority of British voters recognized that the Empire was impracticable to maintain at any tolerable cost. Their aspirations shifted toward building, as another popular hymn put it, a new "Jerusalem in England's green and pleasant land."

A New Start at Home.   After 1945 "the new Jerusalem" of the Labour Government began with years of stiff austerity. Many of the former sources of income from the old Empire were gone, and so were many British foreign assets which had been spent during the war. British industry had to be reconverted to peacetime production. Maintenance of equipment deferred for six war years had to be made up, and so too did the neglect of several preceding decades in mining and other industries. War damage had to be repaired in London, Coventry, Birmingham, and other cities and new housing constructed for returning soldiers and their families.

The Labour Government attacked these tasks by a great expansion of governmental powers. Mining, gas and electricity, railways and other inland transport, and the iron and steel industry were nationalized and partly re-equipped. Public control over land use was strengthened by new planning legislation which eventually led to the building of twenty-five new towns. Finally, a comprehensive national health service was created giving every person present in the British Isles—including visiting American businessmen and students—a claim to free medical care whenever needed. Together these measures did much to modernize the British economy and social structure.

The Two-Party Pendulum.   By the early 1950s voters had grown tired of austerity with its prolonged rationing and holding back of consumer goods. In this mood, they brought back Conservative Governments until the mid-1960s. These governments made greater concessions to middle-class consumers and to the private business sector. To some extent, they permitted the entire population to consume more, even at the risk of hurting Britain's competitive position in the world market. At the same time they accepted the nationalization of coal, railroads, and health services as part of their own policies and created a series of new universities. These actions made British conservatism very different from what it called "conservatism" in the United States.

After years of Conservative relaxation, voters—particularly the younger ones—once again became concerned about inequality and immobility in the country's social and economic life. In their view, members of the old "establishment" still had too many privileges while contributing too little to the modernization and welfare of the nation. Accordingly, they elected a majority Labour Government in 1964 and increased its majority in 1966.

The pendulum swings of voter support between relaxation and relying on the forces of the market under the Conservatives, on the one hand, and modernization and planning under Labour, on the other, are likely to continue. The two major parties have much common ground because of the peculiar social structure of modern Britain. By now only 3 per cent of the work force are left in agriculture, which is not enough to provide a basis for a significant party. About 75 per cent are wage or salary earners, with manual workers outnumbering white-collar employees about 2:1. No party can win without the wage and salary earners vote. Usually, two-thirds of the workers vote Labour and one-third Conservative—enough to give the "working-class Tories" more than one-half of all votes cast for the Conservative Party. Among the middle and professional classes, about seven-eighths vote Conservative, furnishing most of the rest of the Conservative votes. One out of eight middle-class voters casts his ballot for Labour. These middle-class and professional supporters often decide close elections and are an important source of expertise and leadership on Labour's side.[4]

Swings Within Each Party.   A similar pendulum swing may be at work within each major party. At present there are two kinds of Conservatives. One kind is highly traditional, nationalistic, nostalgic for empire, hostile to nonwhites and indeed to most foreigners, and sympathetic to the governments of Rhodesia and South Africa. Such Conservatives are strong in rural party organizations, among retired officers, and also among small businessmen and lower-middle-class conservatives in urban industrial areas. This right wing of the party supported the Suez War in 1956 and the racist policies of the former Cabinet Minister Enoch Powell who was disavowed by the leadership of his party. The other wing of the Conservative Party favors modernization, reform, economic integration with Europe, cooperation with the nonwhite countries of the Commonwealth, and a continuation of the policies of the welfare state. The Conservative Party leadership has to maneuver between both wings and try to keep them together, a task facilitated by the British tradition of strong party discipline in Parliament and the country.

[4] The Liberals, successors to the ancient Whigs, played an important role from 1832 to 1924, but since then have remained insignificant, while Labour has taken their place in the two-party system.

The Labour Party has its own internal divisions. Its left wing is concerned with the ideology of socialism and advocates further nationalization of industry. It stresses class interests and the working-class character of the Party. It favors planning and distrusts the play of forces in the market. It opposes the remnants of empire, demands sharp measures against Rhodesia and South Africa, rejects the concept of the Cold War, and is uneasy about Britain's alliance with the United States. This wing draws much of its support from the disadvantaged regions of Britain, such as Wales and Scotland, as well as from a minority of intellectuals. The right wing of the Labor Party is stronger in London and the South of England, and among many of the better-paid groups of labor and public employees as well as among a majority of intellectuals. Right-wing leaders stress evolution and pragmatism, more reliance on market forces and consumer interests, greater cooperation with the United States and Western Europe, greater caution toward nationalization of industries, and further expansion of the public sector. They stress common interests among the classes and urge restraint in the further wage demands of the trade unions.

The Labour Party leadership, like its Conservative counterpart, must manage to work with both wings of its party, and for this purpose makes heavy use of party discipline. As an added complication, the big trade unions, which for a long time cared little about ideology, insist on frequent wage increases. These unions command large blocs of votes at the Party Conference, and the Labour leadership cannot afford to quarrel too seriously with the Trade Union Congress, any more than the Conservative leadership can afford to quarrel too seriously with the financial interests in the City of London and industrial interests throughout the country.

A Continuing Support: The Civil Service

The cohesion and effectiveness of the British government is provided by the civil service. The civil service is relatively new in British history. It is a child of the great liberal reforms of the nineteenth century. Earlier, many offices, including commissions in the army, were sold for cash. Private companies, such as the East India Company until 1857, governed large territories through their employees.

When the inefficiencies of the old system became intolerable at home as well as in the colonies, the civil service system took its place. In contrast to the old practices of patronage and bribery, its members were recruited by open competitive examinations, and they were to be promoted strictly on the grounds of merit. The civil service thus became a channel for the rise of many of the brightest sons of the British middle classes—even though civil servants with an upper-class background tended to have a better chance to reach its highest levels. For nearly a century, British civil servants ran the Empire; after 1945, they superintended its replacement by new independent nations.

In the British system, civil servants are expected to remain politically neutral. With equal efficiency they are to serve Conservative ministers in encouraging private enterprise and Labour ministers in nationalizing it. In exchange for such political self-denial, they enjoy permanence of tenure. Ministers come and go but the permanent undersecretaries in their ministries remain. In practice this often means that the policy of the ministries also remains constant, and only the minister's signature changes. To this extent the civil servants actually govern the country.[5] (This practice, as we recall, contrasts with the arrangement in the United States under which a large number of top-level federal jobs are defined as policy-making, to be staffed and restaffed at the discretion of each President.)

Civil servants in Britain work well not only with politicians and fellow bureaucrats but also with businessmen, trade union leaders, scientists, and technicians. They do so on numerous *mixed boards,* of which the London Passenger Transport Board is an early and successful example. Set up in 1933 by a Conservative Government, this board, now called the London Transport Executive, brings together representatives of the government, the county of London, and the former private subway, bus, and streetcar companies which were merged into a single transport system for Greater London. The system is managed by the board, which plans new lines, construction, and investments and sets the rates and conditions for service. It also acts as a board of directors, appointing managers and supervising their work.

Boards of this type straddle the border line between public and private enterprise. They are expected to look out for the interests of stockholders and bondholders, thousands of employees, and millions of passengers or other consumers, and for the interests also of the cities as well as those of national development. Nowadays similar boards function in other countries, such as the New York Port Authority in the United States or the Northeast Swiss Power Stations in Switzerland. Britain, however, has gone farthest in developing this type of organization. Judging from the quality of London transport, which is clean, cheap, fast, dependable, and very pleasant to use, the system has been a success.

Another successful type of mixed authority, linking a plurality of public bodies, is the *University Grants Committee.* This body brings civil servants together with representatives of the universities for the purpose of distributing government subsidies among the universities in a way that protects both the institutions and their scholars from political pressures.

Finally, Britain has created a whole series of *public corporations* to manage various publicly owned services. These, too, provide for the representation

[5] Many of them are trained at Oxford or Cambridge. Loyal members of the latter university are fond of saying, "Oxford may speak for England but Cambridge runs it."

of several public organizations and interests. They range from the British Broadcasting Corporation (BBC) and British Overseas Airways Corporation (BOAC), both set up by Conservative Governments before World War II, to such creations of Labour Governments as the National Coal Board, the Electricity Generating Board, and the Electricity Council. In 1967 the Labour Government set up an Industrial Reorganization Corporation with $360 million capital to stimulate mergers in private industry; and the Land Commission was created to buy land for public purposes. Like the civil service, these various organizational devices contribute an array of stable machinery to aid the government in meeting its growing responsibilities.

Accomplishments and Unfinished Business: An Interim Score

In the generation in which 500 million people have become independent from British rule, the average Englishman has grown one inch taller than his father. The British people also have become better educated, better nourished, better housed, and longer lived. Polls show the great popularity of the national health service, and both major parties vie in promising to improve it further. With less than half of the per capita income of the United States, British life expectancy is higher.

Today Americans read in their newspapers mostly of the things that England has not done or that are difficult for it—much as Englishmen are being informed mainly about America's worst foibles, follies, and sometimes tragedies. Americans do not read of the things England has done. The jet engine is a British invention. The decisive tube that made radar possible was brought from Britain to the United States by Sir Henry Tizard in World War II. Penicillin is a British contribution. In the mid-1960s eighteen Nobel Prize winners were teaching at Cambridge University alone. Britain, as we saw, is ahead of the United States in new towns and town planning, in national health services, and in the large-scale use of nuclear energy for peaceful purposes. The British have doubled enrollment in their universities, as have the Americans. They have kept a good deal of their high quality work still going, better than in the United States, and they have struggled with many of their problems more successfully. Although they have their problems with racial differences, they are developing legal instruments to fight discrimination. After a long period of rigidity, they now have more humane laws about drugs and homosexuality than in the United States and yet have a much lower crime rate. Their streets are cleaner and safer to walk in. What they often lack in science and technology is large-scale application. Very often an invention is developed in England and applied in the United States.

The Search for Partnership Abroad.   After the 1890s, a British-American alliance began to grow. In World War II, it reached its peak. As late as 1949, American and British pilots flew their planes side by side to break Stalin's blockade of Berlin, and still later, a British brigade fought alongside United States troops in the Korean War. But although the two countries remained allied (with fourteen others) in the North Atlantic Treaty Organization (NATO), the "special relationship" of Britain to the United States faded in the 1950s.

By the 1960s, United States leaders were paying little attention to their British allies who were told of completed American policy decisions rather than consulted about them in advance. Since the decisions, as in the Cuban crisis of 1962, involved matters of life and death for both countries, the British were unenthusiastic about their new state of dependence. "Annihilation without representation," as the British historian Arnold Toynbee said earlier, "is unfair." At present, Britain still needs the alliance with the United States but it also needs to regain a greater sense of equality and independence—a greater measure of control over its own fate.

The ties to the Commonwealth can not give them this power. The predominantly white Commonwealth countries—Canada, Australia, and New Zealand—continue to accept British exports, immigrants, and capital on favorable terms, and to supply Britain with cheaper food and raw materials. The nonwhite Commonwealth nations, from East Pakistan to Jamaica, furnish Britain with cheap labor and an increase in racial and housing problems. South Africa furnishes some gold transactions, useful to the ailing British currency, at the price of grave political conflict over South African and Rhodesian race discrimination. But all these ties are no longer adequate. On balance, Commonwealth relations are becoming, to most of the British, a matter of the past more than of the future.

Yet Britain can not see any promise in a policy of isolation. It therefore has sought to tie its economy, and perhaps in time its politics, to those of Western Europe. Such a policy of *European integration* may sound great in general but has become awkward in specifics. Joining the European Common Market may mean higher food prices for British housewives, sharper competition for British industry and labor, and less freedom of decision for British voters and their government. Britain wants special safeguards for these interests, which European leaders have refused, but which British voters seem unwilling to forego. At the start of the 1970s, these problems were nowhere near solution. Britain's new role in world affairs still had to be defined.

Some Enduring Assets.   Britain's agenda for change seems impressive but so are the nation's resources. The economic growth rate, the balance between exports and imports, inflation and the value of the pound, planning for rapid technological progress, the overcoming of class or caste lines, the balanced growth of science and the humanities and the integration of these "two cultures"—all are weak points in Britain. Yet in a very important way, Britain has managed to be innovative and still remain cohesive. It can function under tremendous strains as it did in the Battle of Britain in 1940, and it can come up with new and sometimes very surprising ideas. New ideas and new dreams still are being generated in British universities. On the level of popular culture, young Britons have given the world much of the early hippie movement, the Beatles' contribution to rock and roll, and finally the miniskirt.

The British people's strange combination of tremendous persistence with unceasing innovativeness—their insistence on being both innovative and coherent—suggests that their social and political system may repay deeper study. The British are trying to build a new social order, while keeping much of their old culture and habits. This may seem impossible to do, but the British are not likely to stop trying. Though they will be harder to imitate than most other nations, the world can still learn from them.

Key Terms and Concepts

four-layer culture
public schools
Celtics, Angles, Saxons, Normans
exchequer
tradition of enquiry
Domesday Book
Magna Carta
Royal Commission
the gentleman
law of primogeniture
Member of Parliament
burgher
cross-class coalition
Crown
divine right theory
roundheads
cavaliers
parliamentary government
House of Commons
House of Lords

Cabinet
Whigs
Tories
Liberals
Conservative Party
Labour Party
parliamentary party
national party
whips
free votes
Prime Minister
Reform Bill of 1832
imperialism
Commonwealth
dominion status
the two-party pendulum
mixed boards
University Grants Committee
public corporations

Additional Readings

Beer, S. *British Politics in a Collectivist Age.* Rev. ed. New York: Vintage, 1969. Note especially new last chapter.

Finer, S. "Britain." R. C. Macridis and R. E. Ward (eds.) *Modern Political Systems: Europe.* 2nd ed. Englewood Cliffs, N. J.: Prentice-Hall, 1968.

Mackenzie, R. T. *British Political Parties.* 2nd ed. New York: Praeger, 1964.

Osborne, J. *Look Back in Anger.* New York: S. G. Phillips, 1957.

Rose, R. *England.* Boston: Little, Brown, 1964.

Russell, B. *Autobiography.* Vols. 1 and 2. Boston: Atlantic Monthly Press and Little, Brown, 1967 and 1968.

Sampson, A. *Anatomy of Britain.* London: Hodder and Staughton, 1962.

Sillitoe, A. *Saturday Night and Sunday Morning.* New York: Knopf, 1959.

Verney, D. V. *British Government and Politics: Life Without a Declaration of Independence.* New York: Harper & Row, 1961.

France

The French people have dazzled and baffled their neighbors for centuries. They have acquired so many reputations that almost everyone has an image of the French, but the different images do not easily fit together.

The Many Faces of France

Perhaps the best known image of the French is one of confusion, ceaseless change, and infinite variety. "Two Frenchmen are a political party," goes an old saying, "and three Frenchmen are a constitutional crisis." Even the French have wondered about themselves. "How can you govern a country," asked President de Gaulle, "that has 247 kinds of cheese?"

Chapter 13   Time and again in the last two centuries French governments have fallen by revolution. Even in periods of constitutional government, change has been the rule, not the exception. In the sixteen years from 1945 to 1961, the average tenure of a French chief executive was eight months. Some foreign observers were tempted to think that if one did not like a particular French government one had only to wait a while, but a French proverb seemed to know better: the more it changes the more it stays the same.

An entirely different image is that of the orderly French. This image sees the French as precise, logical, and bureaucratic. Indeed, their public gardens seem designed with ruler and compass, with long straight vistas between shrubs and trees that have been neatly clipped into shape. Their scholars are famous for close "explications of texts," their thinkers for bold Cartesian logic, their writers for French lucidity. Their provincial middle classes are known for their conservatism, and the housewives and *rentiers*—people who live on fixed incomes from pensions or investments—for their thrift.

Their orderliness makes Frenchmen put many things into compartments, including themselves. Individuals tend to join mostly those voluntary associations which fit their own social group, in contrast to Americans whose associations tend to cut across such boundaries. "The French," concludes Duncan MacRae, "are both principled and impervious to persuasion." The "typical" French landscape, observes Geoffrey Gorer, "is divided into contrasting segments . . . modified by human handiwork. The world of ideas is similarly compartmentalized. . . ." In such compartments, life can be lonely. "In no other country," says André Siegfried, "can one feel so utterly alone as in France where people barricade themselves in their homes as if they were fortresses." Neither the charms of French conversation in salons and cafés nor the eloquence of French orators and writers can overcome the divisions separating men from men and groups from groups.

A third image pictures the French as a nation of doubters. A medieval French monk, Peter Abelard, invented the scholastic method of reasoning which lines up contradictory authorities on both sides of every question. Centuries later, Descartes invented the Cartesian technique: to doubt everything as deeply as possible, so that only the simplest and most self-evident propositions will survive. And the skeptical smile of Voltaire, the great satirist, who made such merciless fun of the tyrannies, follies, and dogmas of his time, has been called "the smile of France."

A fourth image dwells on French elegance and taste, imagination and creativity. France has long furnished the models for women's dresses and men's ideas. In the arts, from modern painting to motion pictures, France has given the world the word and concept of *avant-garde*—the vanguard which does today what slower folk will do tomorrow. French thinkers have excelled often not only in their logic but also in what the mathematician Pascal called the *esprit de finesse,* the spirit of subtlety which lives on among French scientists and existentialist philosophers.

A related image portrays France as the country of the good life. "To live like God in France," is a wistful German phrase for the utmost in well-being. The French gourmet is a renowned expert on good food and wine, and French has long been the language of love, even for some English and German writers.

A final image of the French is one of courage, piety, and pride. From the Crusades and Joan of Arc to the Battle of Verdun in World War I and the underground resistance in World War II, this tradition has stayed alive.

Each of these images is one-sided and somewhat overdrawn. Yet each contains some truth. Taken together, they tell us something of the complexity of France, and of its capacity to produce surprises. How has one people acquired so many reputations and how do all these traits work together in a single political system? As with other nations, history must give us part of the answer.

The Heritage of Central Monarchy

The French were the first people on the continent—and after England, the second in Europe—to achieve a modern absolute monarchy for a large territorial state. Their centralized government was a work of art, will, and ruthless power. The English got their unified monarchy a little earlier, but as late as the fifteenth century two kings were fighting each other for England's one crown. England was not yet well centralized in the 1470's when Louis XI and his equally absolutist successors were putting France together. The first task of the English state was to consolidate a foreign conquest—that of England by the Normans. The first task of the French state was to prevent a foreign conquest—that of France by the English. A period of unscrupulousness was necessary for the successful completion of this task, but her rulers' politics of organized murder and cruelty eventually gave France a higher degree of civic peace, unity, and power than other countries in Europe had at that time.

The Weakness of Self-Government in the Cities.   One decisive choice was made by the French, perhaps unconsciously. The French cities, feeling too weak to balance the power of the nobles and the countryside, backed the King and central monarchy. They did so to the point of yielding much of their powers of self-government to the royal administration. As a result, France has had less of a tradition of decentralized, urban self-government than has Germany or England. For backing the King, the bourgeois of the French cities won much of what they had hoped to receive from him: security, order, and protection for their businesses.[1]

By 1630 the French monarchy had obtained wide support. In many other countries, such as Germany, the Church opposed a strong central government. But in France and Spain, it backed central government which in turn supported Roman Catholicism as the national religion. After the Reformation, many of the more independent-minded cities and nobles became Protestant. When they were defeated by the Catholics in alliance with the monarchy, local and provincial self-government was defeated, too.

Continuing   Centralization.   The Church in seventeenth-century France was led by a political genius, Cardinal de Richelieu, one of the

[1]In exceptional situations when the burghers of a city tried to cling to self-government they were mercilessly suppressed. In the sixteenth century the city of Bordeaux (which had been English for a time and had less of a tradition of submission to the French Crown) rose in defense of its ancient liberties. A royal army besieged the city and forced its capitulation. When the burghers killed a representative of the King, the royal army beheaded the civic consul in retaliation. The consul, who was executed for vindicating the rights of the citizens against the King, had an interesting name: Guillotin. He was beheaded by hand. More than two centuries later, another man named Guillotin, a doctor of medicine, developed a machine for beheading people, so as to make the process faster, more reliable, and, as he thought, more humanitarian; in the French Revolution his invention was applied to the King and many nobles.

great practitioners of power politics of all time. It was Richelieu who conceived the idea that the main interest of Catholic France was to destroy the power of Catholic Spain. This could be done best, he felt, through intervening in the war in Germany between Protestants and Catholics, where the Hapsburgs were uniting the resources of Austria and Spain on the Catholic side. If the French Catholic King would back the Protestant King of Sweden with money and persuade him to intervene on the Protestant side in Germany, these actions would weaken the Hapsburgs. Richelieu's maneuver succeeded brilliantly. The Swedes invaded Germany, and the Protestants and Catholics fought each other to a standstill. By 1648 two-fifths of the German people—eight million out of twenty million—had perished.

For Germany and Central Europe the hundred-year period after 1680 was a century of devastation and decline. In French history books, however, this period is called *Le Grand Siecle*—The Great Century. During these years France became the leading power of Europe and the fruits of Richelieu's work were reaped by Louis XIV—the King who so simply said, "The state—that is me." From about 1680 to 1780, France was the most brilliant, the richest, and the leading country of Europe, losing to England on the high seas, but outshining all other nations in most other respects. Throughout this period, it remained predominant both as a power and as a model of official culture and elite behavior on the continent.

Within France, Louis XIV broke the last resistance of the provincial nobles and at the same time laid the foundations of French leadership in taste and fashion. He built the most splendid palace of his time at Versailles and made the nobles reside there. He thus turned noblemen into courtiers. Far from their estates in the provinces, they had less power and were more dependent on the favor of the King. At court, they were almost constantly in each other's company, and they were encouraged to compete not only in court intrigues and love affairs but also in luxury and elegance. Court taste and court speech became the single standard for the nation. The results of this centralization have never been reversed. Isolated at Versailles, the nobles became assimilated in their own circle but estranged from most of the rest of France. The legacy of this class division has lingered, too.

Even today, after the French monarchy has been swept away by a chain of revolutions, its heritage lives on. French administration has remained highly centralized, with authority flowing from the top down. So has French culture. Paris is still the center of almost everything important in France—the arts, sciences, mass media, education, business, finance, and politics. Messages and ideas from the provinces count for little, unless their proponents move to Paris first.

The Distance Between Government and People. Communications also move most often from the top down. They flow from government to the bureaucracy; from bureaucrats and party leaders to the people; from professors to students; and from Parisian designers and avant-garde artists to consumers. Little information, if any, flows upward in return.

The little people—workers, peasants, shopkeepers, taxpayers, soldiers, and voters—may resent this situation, but they are unlikely to be heard or heeded. The best they can do is to build defenses for themselves. They defend their individuality, and their privacy. They distrust all government. If government is far away, they prefer to keep it there. They limit it legally wherever they can; and they evade it at every opportunity. Voltaire expressed the attitude of his countrymen in classic form when in the face of the powerful central monarchy he quietly announced that he was going home to "cultivate his garden," that is, withdraw to private life.

Millions of Frenchmen are still doing so, at least in a figurative sense. They keep out of politics in ordinary times, and thus make the moderate center of political opinion seem weaker than it is. But they return to political activity when stirred by unusual events, making politics in France often more exciting and less predictable than anywhere else.

The Heritage of Revolution

It is hard today to imagine how rigid the French monarchy and social system had become by the 1780s, and how long it took to gather the forces that were to transform France and in due time the world. In 1789 France finally exploded in revolution. The French did not revolt against Louis XV, a bad ruler, but rose against Louis XVI who was no worse than eighteenth-century monarchs generally were. If France could not be governed under a ruler of Louis XVI's quality, then something was fundamentally wrong with the system and would have to be changed. In this sense the revolts against Charles I of England and Louis XVI of France involved the same need: to change a system, not a person.

From the King on down, Frenchmen then showed another trait which has endured—their resistance to compromise. After the English revolution and the return of the monarchy, even Charles II accepted a bill of rights voted by Parliament. James II was driven out when he refused to compromise further; and two years later England got another monarch, William of Orange, whose reign led to the Act of Toleration. In the end the English monarchy gave in gracefully to the need of making concessions to the demands for constitutional government. The Bourbon kings of France were different. Of them it was said then and later that they never forgot and they never learned.

The French tried to establish a constitutional monarchy in 1791 with Louis XVI as monarch. But Louis refused in his mind to accept any constitutional limits to his power. He secretly corresponded with other absolute rulers of Europe (some of whom were his relatives) to persuade them to make war against France and restore him as absolute ruler. The correspondence was discovered and the King put on trial as a traitor before the National Assembly. Maximilien de Robespierre, the radical leader of the Jacobin party,[2] with brilliant French logic, made the decisive point for the prosecution. If the King was innocent, he pointed out, then he was by the grace of God the absolute King of France; he had rightfully tried to organize the subjection of his rebellious subjects; and those sitting in the Assembly were themselves rebels and traitors who ought to be beheaded. If, on the other hand, the Assembly was truly representative of the French nation, then the King was a traitor to his country and it was he who had to be beheaded. Accepting this logic, the members of the Assembly voted predictably. The King was beheaded, and the *First Republic* established.

In this case logic was used to prevent compromise rather than permit it. This tactic revealed its greatness and strength as well as its long-run onesidedness in the events that followed. Six European countries invaded France after the King's execution in 1793. But the war had already been started by the moderate *Girondist* government of France which had come to power under the First Republic in 1792.[3] It had started the war in the hope that a foreign war would increase national unity. The Girondists turned out to be grievously mistaken and perished for their folly. They started a war they could not conduct successfully, yet which became vital to the French people once it had begun. The Jacobins, the most radical middle-class leaders, took power under Robespierre in 1793 and mobilized the entire French nation.

The Nation in Arms.   In one year France brought 1,300,000 men under arms in fourteen armies, and thereby changed the scale of warfare in Europe. This could not have possibly been done by an unpopular draft. The only way of getting 5 per cent of the French people into uniform was through the voluntary support of large numbers of the French people. This voluntary support made possible the enforcement of the laws of the Republic. It seemed as if Rousseau's "general will" had taken armed shape.[4] Robespierre and the Jacobins seemed to be executing his ideas. Backed by a large part of the people, they were forcing Frenchmen "to be free." They did so with relentless logic and frequent cruelty. The city of Lyon rose against the central government and was destroyed by a repub-

[2] The *Jacobins* were the main radical party of the French Revolution. Centered in Paris, they got their name from one of their early meeting places, a former monastery of St. James whom the French called St. Jacob. Their ranks included members of the prosperous middle class as well as professional people and poor artisans.

[3] The Girondists became the main moderate party of the Revolution by 1792. Strongest in the provinces, they were named after the *gironde*, a fertile plain in southern France. Their members included the well-to-do of the smaller towns.

[4] Rousseau's views were discussed in Chapter 5.

lican army. The general in charge reported back to Paris, "Lyon rose against the Republic. Lyon is no more."

Revolutionary France was marked by extremisms of all sorts. The conservatives thought the republicans mad. The republicans, in turn, thought the conservatives to be walking corpses, men of the dead past. Each side felt that its opponents had no right to live. For a time there was a law that made it a crime to fall under suspicion.

If divisiveness and intolerance were extreme, so too were the heroism and efforts of the people. The Parisians descended to the cellars of Paris to scrape saltpeter deposits from the walls to get enough guns to blast the armies of the European monarchs out of France. In Paris alone, there were 243 open-air forges to make cast iron cannon. The Revolution first produced the massed artillery that later made Napoleon's military reputation.

The French soldiers fought with high morale; they did not run away in the field or in battle. Unlike the involuntary soldiers of the European monarchs, they did not need to fight in conspicuous uniforms, and to march in close order into enemy fire so that their sergeants could keep an eye on them. The French soldiers fought against the royal armies in open skirmish lines, firing from whatever cover they found, and then attacked in massed columns. They won, and in the process they changed the art of war in their epoch.

The Politics of Revolution.   But though they won foreign battles, they could not agree on how to run France. Not all Frenchmen favored the revolution. Not only aristocrats but also many of their servants, friends, or more loyal peasant subjects bitterly opposed the republican regime. The republican government tried to crush all resistance by public execution in a deliberate campaign of *terror*—much as the Bourbon kings had publicly executed those who resisted them or defied their laws. But soon the revolutionists turned against one another with the same ruthlessness they had used against their enemies.

The Republic introduced rigid price controls to help the poor, which then turned the middle class (which had been part of the original Jacobin movement) against the more radical Jacobins. The very radical Jacobins—"the enraged," as they were called—also rose against the more moderate radicals as the very conservative Jacobins had.

Robespierre thus had to fight enemies on both flanks. At first he used the radicals to behead the moderates. Then he used the surviving moderates to destroy the radicals. Danton on his right and Hébert on his left both died under the guillotine. But soon Robespierre himself was attacked and put to death by those who feared that their own gains from the Revolution might now be in danger.

Robespierre had not been an extreme terrorist. In fact, he had cut down the executions in the provinces, brought all the trials to Paris, and reduced the indiscriminate killing. But when he was sentenced and executed, the whole responsibility for the terror was put upon him even by those who themselves had led executions. When one provincial leader of the terror, who had voted against Robespierre, was reminded in the French Assembly of his own share in the killings, he looked straight at his colleagues and answered, "Robespierre's grave is big enough to bury our differences in."

There followed a period of domestic relaxation and corruption called *Thermidor,* and a period of government by five Directors. Under this regime, called the *Directory*, the call rose for more freedom for speculators, and more law and order against the poor. The foreign wars continued. Quietly, the nation was getting ready to hand over its problems to a general.

The General Who Set a Precedent.   Many Frenchmen in times of crisis have tended to turn to a general as their savior—Cavaignac in 1848, MacMahon in 1875, Foch in 1914, Pétain in 1940, De Gaulle in 1940, 1944, and 1958. But more than once, they lived to regret it. The general who finally stepped forward to fill the role during France's revolutionary period was a young Corsican, Napoleon Bonaparte. As a Corsican, he understood revolutions well because Corsica had had its own revolution against Genoa which had ended only when the island became French in 1768. By 1798 Napoleon's mastery of French was rapidly improving though he still spoke it with an Italian accent. Earlier, he had helped the Directory come to power by beating down the last radical flare-up in Paris. He had then won a victorious campaign in Italy which had made him a popular hero. Now, in 1798, he made himself master of the Republic. It was an inside job, done with the help of some members of the government; two of the five Directors helped bring about Napoleon's seizure of power. This occurred on the famous *eighteenth of Brumaire,* as the date was called in the French revolutionary calendar.

By 1800 Napoleon had made himself Consul and the dictatorship had been formalized. In 1804 he had himself crowned Emperor. At his coronation Napoleon took the crown out of the Pope's hands and put it on his own head. Napoleon's vast self-confidence kept growing, while his judgment worsened. Like other rulers of great power, he lost critics and gained "yes-men."

He led France into an unending series of wars—and ultimate disaster. After his fall, there was a revulsion against war in France and much of Europe. This made it possible to restore many of the old dynasties in Italy and elsewhere, and the Bourbons in France. People wanted quiet. There followed a period of withdrawal to family life and of distrust of politics.

More Revolutions, More Generals.   The next generation rose again in revolution in 1830. France became a liberal monarchy. The subversive colors red, white, and blue became official once again and replaced the lily of the Bourbons. The new constitutional king advised the middle classes: "Enrich yourselves, gentlemen!" And they did, abundantly.

The next wave of revolution swept through France in 1848. It included the poor, the lower middle class, and the working class, many of whom felt that they were becoming not richer but poorer. The *Second Republic* was set up, but the 1848 uprisings promptly produced a split between labor and the middle classes. The middle classes rallied to a new general, Cavaignac, who led the bloody suppression of the labor revolt in Paris. In 1851 the conservative, military republic was replaced by a new monarchy—the *Second Empire* under Napoleon III, the first Napoleon's nephew.

The Second Empire lasted twenty years, marked by mixed speculation, prosperity, demagogy, and minor foreign wars, until it led France into a big war which ended disastrously. Once again Paris rose, this time with the first labor government, the Communist-anarchist-oriented Paris Commune, which established itself for a few weeks before being beaten down by soldiers from the rest of France, most of them peasant sons in uniform. The other France, the conservative France, asserted its power. All subsequent French regimes show marks of its influence.

The France That Resists Change

France has produced many revolutions and many conservative reactions. Her revolutions flare up in Paris and a few other big cities and industrial areas. Her conservatism is supported by wealthy minorities in these centers but draws its main strength from the small towns and the countryside.

More Proprietors, Fewer Babies.   After 1800 French peasants became patriotic and conservative. It is this France that changes slowly, that furnishes many officers and soldiers, and that gives the nation its reputation for conservatism. The French Revolution, by making the peasants proprietors, had given them something to conserve. The Revolution also led to a long slowdown in the growth of population. This happened because in time the new laws of property had an effect on the number of new babies. The revolutionary laws of the Jacobins abolished feudalism, and gave the peasants land. These laws, later organized into a systematic legal code by Napoleon, also declared that all brothers in a family had the same right to the land, and therefore the farm had to be divided among all sons. But the more sons, the smaller a piece of land would remain for each and the poorer each would be. If a peasant did not want his land to be divided and his sons impoverished, he had to limit their number. Many peasants took to marrying later in life; those who already knew methods of birth control, now had a stronger motive to practice it; and those who did not know, now had a motive to learn.

Throughout much of the next 140 years, the population of France grew more slowly than that of any other major country. The practice of birth control had begun in the last years of the Bourbons, but the slowdown of population growth proceeded under all forms of French government in the nineteenth century, and it accelerated after 1870. French population, which had been 25 million in the 1780s, was 40 million in 1913, and is only 50 million now. Limiting the growth of population proved conservative in its effects. It preserved more of the *status quo.*

France is still one of the more slowly growing countries in the world. More recent laws, however, subsidize babies through family allowances. Also, fewer people live on farms, and more Frenchmen want more children. Now as in the past, legislation must come together with a change in human motives, if the habits of millions of people are to be changed. So far in France, habits have changed slowly.

Conservative Social and Economic Practices. Throughout the nineteenth and early twentieth centuries, the French social structure underwent little change. With more peasant proprietors, more people stayed in the country than streamed into the cities. Fewer people moved into industry. To this day, the proportions of industrial workers, of city dwellers, and of wage and salary earners all are lower in France than in Germany or Britain (see Table 13.1).

Thus the proclivities of the French peasant to stay where his parents had been, and where he liked it, went together with the proclivities of the

Table 13.1

Some Conservative Aspects of the French Social Structure

	Residence		Class	Occupation
	Population Living in Cities Above 100,000 (%)	*Workers Among Work Force (%)*	*Self-Employed and Family Members Among Work Force (%)*	*Labor Force Employed in Agriculture (%)* [1]
UK	51	60	7	3
GFR	31	51	20	11
USA	28	51 (1967)	6	5
USSR	24	46 (1959)	0	38
France	17	36	25	17

[1]Includes both farmers and farm laborers.

Source: R.C. Macridis, "France," in R.C. Macridis and R. E. Ward (eds.), Modern Political Systems: Europe, *2nd ed. (Englewood Cliffs, N.J.: Prentice-Hall, 1968); B. Russett, H. Alker, K.W. Deutsch, and H. Lasswell,* World Handbook of Political and Social Indicators *(New Haven: Yale University Press, 1964);* The 1969 World Almanac *(Washington, D.C.: NEA Enterprises, 1969).*

French middle class to slow down the growth of industry and labor in order to minimize the likelihood of further social revolutions.

A Strong Middle Class; A Weak Political Center.   This pro-agricultural bias of the French left its mark on modern-day France. In the mid-1960s, manual workers in France still were only 36 per cent of the work force, compared to 51 per cent in Germany and to about 60 per cent in England. Although workers can be highly militant in France, and about half of them tend to vote for the Communist Party, all workers are a permanent minority. Marx's prediction that the proletariat would become the great majority of society has been contradicted by the development of France, the country where the theory of class politics and the class struggle was invented.

The French class structure, in fact, remained remarkably rigid until the 1950s. Within the work force, the 36 per cent of workers are outnumbered by the large middle class, both salaried and self-employed, including government officials and officers in the armed forces, which comprises 43 per cent, and by the farmers who form another 18 per cent. The rest of the work force makes up the remaining 3 per cent. Since many middle-class people, like peasants, are keenly interested in keeping what they have, this slow-changing French social structure has not lent itself to sweeping restructuring or basic reform.

Only in the 1950s and 1960s, did the pace of change begin to quicken. Until then, the France that resisted change prevailed over all internal challenges.

The Third Republic: A Paradise for Legislators

The Third Republic, which lasted from 1875 to 1940, was a government deliberately designed to be strong in foreign affairs and against the poorer Frenchmen at home but to be weak in relation to the upper middle class in town and country.

The government of the Third Republic, like that of the United States, was divided into three branches. Its President, however, was much weaker and its legislature, the National Assembly, much stronger than their American counterparts. The legislature consisted of two chambers, of which the lower, called the Chamber of Deputies, was the more important; but the upper chamber, the Senate, also had a significant share of power which it often exercised in defense of property rights. The President of the Republic was elected by the legislature, not the people. Like the King of England, he was to reign but not rule. His powers were ceremonial rather than real. The actual head of the executive branch of government was the Premier, or prime minister, who, as in Britain, could remain in office only so long as a majority in the Chamber of Deputies backed him. Unlike his British counterpart, however, the French Premier did not have the power to dissolve the legislature and call for new elections.

The legislators thus had most of the power. They could at any time overthrow any Premier by a vote of "no confidence" without having to answer for their actions to the voters. For the length of the legislative term of four years, members of the legislative majority were virtually irremovable so long as they themselves did not vote for new elections. In effect, though the Premier and his Cabinet were responsible to the legislators, the legislators between elections were responsible to no one.

This arrangement provided not only for a weak President and a succession of weak Premiers but also for a multiplicity of weak political parties and temporary political factions. A legislator who broke party discipline had little to fear from his party so long as the next election was some years away. The rural and local character of much of French politics, and the strength of local notables and the self-employed middle class, combined with the individualism of many French voters to make the weakness of political parties and government into a tradition. Under this tradition members of the French middle class often did not scruple to evade direct taxes by filling out false tax returns, nor did they hesitate to take their money out of France and speculate against the currency of their own country whenever it seemed profitable or they happened to dislike the policies of the government. As a rule the Assembly refused to pass effective legislation that would have insured full collection of direct taxes or a real control of French currency. Under such conditions, a government could not control the world of finance, but a financial panic could easily bring down a government.

Though French political leadership was often unstable, French administration remained the mainstay of the state. While legislators played political games, civil servants ran the country. The French civil service, even more than the British, has a great tradition and commands high prestige to this day. Its top administrators, such as the Inspectors of Finance, are still drawn from the "great schools"—the *École Nationale,* the *École Polytechnique,* and the *École Supérieure d'Administration*—which are more selective and more highly respected than even the country's greatest universities. Throughout all governmental crises, the French civil service has kept the country going.

Like all bureaucrats and technocrats, the French civil servants cannot create policies. They can only administer the policies of others. In the 1930s, the Third Republic failed to produce policies adequate for the times. The depression divided labor from the upper middle class: workers demanded more welfare, proprietors less public spending. Soon, members of the French right began to mutter that they would prefer the rule of the German government under Hitler to any native left-of-center government in France. French Communists in turn, in September 1939 refused to support the French middle-class government. At both ends of the political spectrum, Frenchmen disliked domestic opponents more than they disliked foreign enemies.

The Third Republic collapsed after the Nazi invasion of France in 1940 and was succeeded by a conservative and authoritarian regime under the aged Marshal Pétain, a pathetic figurehead, and the unscrupulous Premier Pierre Laval, a willing collaborator of the Nazis. Calling itself the "French state," and located at the resort of *Vichy,* this regime was a puppet of the German occupying power. It was swept away by the invasion of the Allies in 1944 when a new republic was formed.

Promptly, most of the old political parties reappeared in it. Members of several of them had been active in the underground *resistance* movement against the Nazi occupiers, and they emerged now as candidates for leadership. But the party system persisted.

The Enduring Reality: The Parties

In the United States and Britain the main constitutional arrangements are older than the parties. In France most of the parties are older than its several constitutions. The fundamental political divisions go back to the Revolution of 1789. Those Frenchmen who favored and accepted that Revolution and the separation of church and state formed the left of the political spectrum; those whose sympathies lay with the monarchy and the unity of church and state formed the political right. The original phrases "left" and "right" derive from the seating order of deputies in a past French legislature—a seating order which later became customary in many European parliaments. In the course of time the terms have acquired other connotations. Parties on the left tend to favor workers and the poor as well as political and social change—by radical and revolutionary methods if they are far to the left, by more moderate reforms if they are closer to the center. Parties on the right tend to favor tradition, property, and privilege as well as the interests of the well-to-do and of substantial citizens in town and countryside. Parties in the center usually seek compromises between these wings and are often attacked by both sides for their pains.

In France a whole imagery has grown up around the unremitting contest between left and right. "Left is where the heart is," goes a French saying; the right is seen as the side closest to the pocketbook. But while these general political tendencies seem perennial in France, issues and problems do change. New policies must be devised to cope with them, and new coalitions formed to put these policies to work. In 1946, after World War II, 46 per cent of all Frenchmen voted for parties of the left, 20 per cent for parties of the center, 10 per cent for parties of the right, and nearly 24 per cent did not vote at all. By 1968 the left had shrunk to 32 per cent, the old center to 8 per cent, the old right to 3 per cent, but on the moderate right, a new party—the Gaullists—had risen and collected 34 per cent of the vote, enough to win a majority of seats in the Assembly (see Table 13.2).

At present the strongest party on the left is the Communists. Their main support comes from workers, and to a lesser extent, from intellectuals, white-collar workers, and even some peasants. Since 1920, they have been stronger than the Socialists. Nowadays they represent about a sixth of all French voters, and between a fifth and fourth of those who actually vote. The Socialists are only half as strong. They have lost much of their former following among manual workers, and now get most of their support from public officials, teachers, and other white-collar groups. More moderate than the Communists and Socialists are the Radical Socialists who are in fact neither radical or socialist. They are strong defenders of republican traditions, the memories and symbols of the French Revolution, and of strict separation of church and state. Opposition to any influence of the clergy on parties and education has long united the Radical Socialists, Socialists, and Communists as a coalition of laymen's parties or of the left. In 1935–1937 these three parties supported the government of the *Popular Front,* although the Communists had no Cabinet representation in it. In 1944–1947 the Communists did sit in the Cabinet which then included not only the left but also the followers of General de Gaulle, and all other groups who had resisted the Nazi occupation.

At the center, a moderate Catholic party has emerged, the Popular Republican Movement, or MRP from its French initials. This party favors public support for Catholic schools, family allowances and other welfare legislations, and respect for republican and democratic traditions.

To the right are those Frenchmen who oppose welfare legislation and non-military public spending. Still further to the right are those Frenchmen who have never fully accepted the Revolution of 1789 and the Republics that followed from it. Here one finds some of the remnants of the French nobility, many officers' families, monarchists, and those more tradition-minded Catholics who find the MRP too liberal. The candidates they vote for are often called Independents. In recent years, the Gaullist Party has brought many of these voters some way back toward the political center and to supporting the Fifth Republic that embodies Gaullist policies.

In addition, French individualism has produced a multitude of political splinter groups which often disappear after one or two elections. These are fairly negligible (see Table 13.2). Their few votes have been lumped with those of the major parties, where appropriate.

In French society, the middle class is strongest, but in French politics, the center seems weak. The politically active French are on the right and left. In the middle are the politically passive—often one-fifth or more of the electorate. As a result, French politics is often deadlocked. People often stay out of politics, until they begin to feel that something must be done.

Table 13.2

Three Aspects of French Voting: Abstainers, Parties, Candidates

French Legislative Votes by Parties

1946–1968

Year	Total Registered Voters (millions)	(%)	Valid Votes Cast (%)	Abst. & Void (%)	Comm. & Prog. (%)	Soc. & Left Soc. (%)	Rad. (%)	MRP (%)	Gaullists (%)	Ind. & Mod. (%)	Ext. Right (%)	Others (%)
1946	25.1	100	76.5	23.5	21.9	13.5	11.2	20.3	—	10.4	—	0.4
1951	24.5	100	78.0	22.0	20.1	11.0	8.8	9.8	16.7	10.6	—	0.4
1956	26.8	100	79.5	20.5	20.5	11.9	10.4	9.0	3.0	12.3	10.1	0.4
1958	27.7	100	75.8	22.4	14.1	11.6	9.7	8.7	13.0	14.8	2.5	—
1962	27.5	100	68.7	33.4	14.5	8.4	5.5	5.8	21.1	9.1	0.7	—
1967	28.3	100	78.5	21.3	17.6	14.8	—	10.2	30.0	3.9	0.7	—
1968	28.3	100	79.5	21.4	15.7	16.6	—	18.1	34.3	3.2	0.4	—

Presidential Elections, 1965 and 1969

Year	Total Registered Voters (millions)	(%)	Valid Votes Cast (%)	Abst. & Void (%)	Comm. & Prog. (%)	Soc. & Left Soc. (%)	Rad. (%)	MRP (%)	Gaullists (%)	Ind. & Mod. (%)	Ext. Right (%)	Others (%)
1965 (second ballot)	28.2	100	82.2	17.8		Mitterrand 37.4			De Gaulle 44.8			
1969 (first ballot)	28.8	100	77.2	22.8	16.6	Poher 3.9	18.1		Pompidou 33.9	2.8		1.8
1969 (second ballot)	28.7	100	64.6	35.4		Poher 27.4			Pompidou 37.2			

The slight discrepancies reflect the lack of uniform treatment of void ballots in French voting statistics. Such errors are always smaller than 0.7 million votes.

Sources: R.C. Macridis, "France," in R.C. Macridis and R.E. Ward (eds.), Modern Political Systems: Europe, 2nd ed., © 1968. Adapted by permission of Prentice-Hall, Inc., Englewood Cliffs, N.J.; Le Monde, June 17, 1969.

As in other modern countries, only more so, French politics tends to oscillate between immobilism and emergency. When many different interest groups or parties stop or frustrate each other, the result is either immobility and widespread apathy or a willingness to hand things over to a strong leader who can mobilize the otherwise apathetic nonvoters. Then the center becomes significant. The strong leader, a Bonapartist or Gaullist, sometimes can win the support of former nonvoters, together with that of the center and the moderate right, to form a majority. He is thus a compromise candidate and coalition builder who manages not to look like one. Such a strategy worked for the two Napoleons, and for De Gaulle, too—for a time. In the future it may work again for someone else.

Ordinarily much of French politics works through compromises among the parties, despite the reluctance of many Frenchmen to make compromises or to draw attention to them. Some need to compromise is built into the French electoral system. French elections come in two stages. On election day voters cast their *first ballot* for the candidate each prefers. If no candidate wins an absolute majority, a run-off election follows in which voters cast a *second ballot* for the compromise candidate whom they find least unacceptable among those likely to be elected.

These compromise choices determine much of the composition of the legislature. The multiplicity of parties makes it necessary to form coalitions, since often no party wins a clear majority. Usually, adherents of a party of the left vote for the candidate of some other party of the left; and there is similar mutual support among the parties of the right. Sometimes, similar alliances are formed among the center parties; and sometimes, Communists vote for moderate left candidates, but the latter may or may not reciprocate—as many refused to do in 1968.

Despite these deals and shifts, and many others like them, the basic pattern of French politics has remained fairly constant in recent decades. About one-third of French voters normally vote left, about half for the Communists, the other half for the more moderate left parties: the Socialists and the Radical Socialists. Another third vote for the center and the right. Among these voters, those close to the center prefer the moderate Catholic MRP; those well toward the right vote for candidates who call themselves independents or moderates; the extreme right has been insignificant in most postwar elections. The lion's share of votes on the moderate right—more than one-third—has in recent years gone to the Gaullists. Furthermore, about every fifth voter is likely to abstain from voting.

There is a *floating vote* of 15 to 20 per cent of the electorate. In some years most of this vote floats left, as in 1946, or to the moderate right, as in 1968. In other years 10 per cent may go all the way to the extreme right, as in 1956, and in still other years a similar number may increase the body of abstainers, as in 1962. Table 13.2 permits us to trace such changes. They add up to a sequence of kaleidoscopic changes on the surface produced by the floating fifth that may conceal the stable political habits of four-fifths of the French voters. The stability of the many voters and the volatility of the few have marked French politics under the Third, Fourth, and Fifth Republics alike.

The Fourth Republic: Half-Hearted Changes

The Fourth Republic, which lasted from 1944 to 1958, in many ways resembled the Third. There were the same irresponsible legislature, weak parties, weak Presidents, and quick-changing Premiers as in the Third Republic. General de Gaulle, elected its first President, tried to be strong but failed, and withdrew to private life. Politics-as-usual followed, but some of its content changed.

The leaders of the Republic placed more emphasis on economic planning and on social justice and welfare legislation. Several industries were nationalized, including mining, aircraft, and part of the automobile industry. (When overtaken on the road by a new Renault car, made in a state-owned factory, one might reconsider the time-worn notion of "creeping socialism.") There also were marked improvements in health and welfare benefits, in access to higher education, and in special assistance to families with children. But in politics, the same game of musical chairs was being played by nearly the same small group of *ministrables*— politicians eligible for Cabinet seats.

The policies of the Fourth Republic only rarely departed from those of the Third. To be sure, the Fourth Republic accepted as general and distant goals the Atlantic Community and the unification of Europe and joined a number of important European organizations, including NATO, the European Coal and Steel Community (ECSC), EURATOM, and most important, the European *Common Market*—the developing customs union of France, West Germany, Italy, the Netherlands, Belgium, and Luxemburg. During these same years, however, France rejected membership in the proposed European Defense Community (EDC) and the European Political Community (EPC). In other matters, the Fourth Republic moved further away from its European partners. It continued to send its soldiers to fight for the preservation of an empire that could not be preserved. Embittered officers and soldiers returned from Indo-China, and soon even larger numbers found themselves in a war in Algeria which the Fourth Republic could neither win nor end.

Overcommitment Abroad and Reorganization at Home

The End of Empire.   In foreign policy between 1880 and 1920 France had been successful to the point where it had taken up commitments beyond its strength. By the 1920s, France was the ruler of North Africa, the ruler of a part of the Near East (both Syria and Lebanon), the ruler of Indo-China, and the ruler of a substantial part of sub-Saharan Africa. From then on, as these countries and populations became politically active, France was involved in one bloody war after another. In 1920 to subjugate the Syrians the French killed 20,000 people in the bombardment of Damascus. From 1925 to 1927 they fought in Morocco. After 1945 they killed thousands of people in Morocco and Madagascar while trying to restore French rule. And they fought nine years in Indo-China, from 1945 to their defeat at Dien Bien Phu.

The force requirements for maintaining the Empire became increasingly larger than the capabilities of metropolitan France. Yet the ties of the French elites, the French business community, and the French middle class to the Empire were stronger in those days than the present ties of America's industrial and business groups overseas. The French middle class got more jobs out of the Empire, French industry and commerce more sales, and the French military establishment more command posts than do comparable interests in the United States today. Thus, the eventual rejection of empire by the French set a significant precedent for all large nations.

Algeria: A Choice and a Decision. Blind acceptance of the theory of *economic determinism*—the simple view that economic facts and interests determine everything—would expect to find France still in Algeria. But what happened in France in the 1950s and early 1960s is a case study of how a large, modern country broke with its tradition of empire by refusing to carry on endlessly a frustrating military campaign. The country also broke economically from imperial policy, by shifting many of its economic efforts from policing the Casbah[5] to modernizing France. Finally, the country also broke morally with colonialism. The war in Algeria had led to massacres, torture, and a decline of exactly those moral values which the defense of France was supposed to maintain. As these atrocities became known, French intellectuals, students, and some members of the armed forces spoke out in protest, often at considerable risk to themselves. France could not remain civilized, cultured, and humane, they insisted, and still continue the Algerian War in the way it was being waged in the mid-1950s.

Reorganization at Home. In late 1957 and early 1958 French public opinion turned against the Algerian War. Individuals had protested earlier in increasing numbers, but by now public opinion poll returns had to be treated as state secrets "so as not to give comfort to the enemy." In May 1958 the French army took action against the Fourth Republic which they had long accused of giving them inadequate backing in the

[5] The Casbah was the native quarter of the city of Algiers.

war. Aircraft and paratroopers moved from Algeria and Corsica against the mainland of France, and they received indications of support from the police and from the conservative parties. Moderates and members of the left called for demonstrations in defense of the Republic. Somehow a quick compromise emerged, once again disguised as strong-man rule. The government of the day legally handed over power to a former President of the Fourth Republic and hero of the Resistance, Charles de Gaulle. De Gaulle had the confidence of the military and was acceptable to the left who remembered that during his presidency Communists had sat in the French Cabinet. The right expected him to keep Algeria French; the left and an increasing number of persons in the center expected him to take France out of Algeria.

Often before in French history, factions of the right and left had balanced each other with incompatible desires and approximately equal strengths, with the richer classes calling for order and the poorer ones for change, and all demanding a stronger government to give them what they wanted. Out of such conditions Bonapartism had been born, with its skillful blend of military force and sweeping promises of social betterment. Under both Napoleons more and more force and less and less betterment had followed. Would Charles de Gaulle prove just another Bonapartist general?

This time the outcome was different. Appointed Premier on May 31, 1958, De Gaulle soon obtained full powers to govern absolutely for six months. Changing the imperial policies of nearly a century also involved changing the French domestic political system that had produced them. Therefore, during the six-month interval of absolute rule, De Gaulle had a constitution drafted. When it was submitted to a direct popular vote, to a *referendum* of the French people, they overwhelmingly endorsed it. De Gaulle reassured the military by well-chosen ambiguities that he would hold Algeria, while quietly preparing to concede its independence to its Arab majority.

At the same time he announced an accelerated program of nuclear weapons development for the purpose of making France a nuclear power independent of all others. This program split the French military. More technology-minded officers now parted company with their still empire-minded colleagues. To many new-style military professionals, nuclear weapons were more important than Algeria. They continued to support De Gaulle, even after his new policy in Algeria became visible. During this critical period, some of the colonialist military faction tried to assassinate De Gaulle (they succeeded in assassinating several minor opponents of the war); and they conspired in a secret army organization, OAS, to overthrow the De Gaulle government.

In the end the matter was decided in part by the response of the French enlisted men in Algeria who acted much the way their relatives in France had acted when they voted in the referendum on De Gaulle's constitution.

They had obeyed their commanders in the Algerian War, but now they refused to move against the government. In 1962 the Algerian War was formally ended. Thereafter nearly a million Frenchmen were evacuated from Algeria, mainly to France, where in the 1960s most of them became integrated with the mainland French. In the meantime the machinery of De Gaulle's Fifth Republic had begun to work—as it would continue working into the 1970s after his retirement.

The Fifth Republic

All Power to the Executive. The Fifth Republic was designed to avoid the weaknesses of its predecessors. Major executive powers were given to the President, not to the Premier. Its *President* is strong and is elected directly by the people. Like the President of the United States, he is fully independent of the legislature. Under the Constitution as it finally emerged in the early 1960s, his legal powers are much greater than those of his American counterpart. The French President has the legal right to dissolve the Assembly if he so chooses; his only limit is that he can do so but once each year. He nominates the Premier and thus can control him and his Cabinet. He may call a referendum or issue decrees having the force of law at any time. He may declare a state of emergency and "take the measures commanded by . . . circumstances" (Article XVI of the French Constitution). He is at no time responsible to the Assembly.

The Constitution describes the President as the "arbiter," charged with making the ultimate decision among conflicting interests and policies. During De Gaulle's presidency, the President also took on the role of "guide" to the nation. As De Gaulle stated flatly in 1964, "The President elected by the nation is the source and holder of the power of the state." Backed by a large and growing staff, the office of the presidency has become the center of policy-making in both foreign and domestic matters to the President (see Figure 13.1).

The structure of the Fifth Republic looks much like that of the Third and Fourth, but the relative powers of its various organs have changed. There still are a two-chamber legislature, a Premier and Cabinet, a President, and a system of courts. A few details have been added. But the real power has shifted.

The role of the Premier and his Cabinet is weaker vis-à-vis the President but stronger vis-à-vis the National Assembly. The Premier and Cabinet members are appointed by the President, whom no legislative vote can overthrow. The legislature technically may force the Cabinet's resignation, but its powers are much less than under the Third and Fourth Republics. Usually, a Cabinet can only be toppled through a motion of censure, which requires an absolute majority of the members, so that blank ballots and abstentions count *for* the administration. In actuality, the Cabinet is

Figure 13.1

Modern Constitutional Structure in France

The structure of the Third, Fourth, and Fifth Republics is essentially the same. The difference lies in the shift in powers to the President.

Source: R. C. Macridis, "France," in R. C. Macridis and R. E. Ward (eds.), Modern Political Systems: Europe, 2nd ed., © 1968. Adapted by permission of Prentice-Hall, Inc., Englewood Cliffs, N.J.

an instrument of the President, carrying out the policies he determines. Some of the key ministers, such as those of foreign affairs and defense, often work with the President without much intervention from the Premier. All Cabinet decrees require the signature of the President for their validity.

A Shackled Legislature.

A Shackled Legislature.   The legislature consists of two chambers. The more important one is the *National Assembly* of 487 members who are elected directly by the people for five-year terms. A change in electoral law has given the strongest party a disproportionately large share of seats to the great advantage of the Gaullist Party. But legislative seats mean less than they used to.

The Assembly legislates on all matters of law, but these are enumerated more than somewhat restrictively by the Constitution, which leaves all other matters to the *rule-making power*—that is, the power to issue binding regulations—of the executive branch. Even the enumerated law-making powers may be delegated to the executive branch by an *organic law*—that is, a law affecting the constitution—passed by a majority of the members of both houses. The Assembly's order of business is determined by the administration. The Assembly may have no more than six committees and may not meet for more than six months each year. Most important, the French legislature has lost the power of the purse. It no longer controls money. The executive alone draws up the budget and puts it before the Assembly. Any motion in the Assembly to reduce taxes or other government receipts or to increase government spending for any purpose is automatically out of order. If the Assembly fails to approve the government's budget within seventy days, it may be made public by executive decree, which makes it law.

The Senate's 274 members are elected indirectly by municipal and departmental councilors and representatives of the cities. Those directly involved in electing senators number about 110,000, more than half of them representing small villages of less than 3,000 inhabitants. Comprising only one-third of the French population, these villages through their representatives elect a majority of the Senate. Towns of over 10,000, constituting 40 per cent of the French people, elect only every fifth senator. As a result, the Senate overwhelmingly represents rural and small-town France.

The Senate, however, has few powers. Though a bill can become law only if passed in identical form by both houses, the real decision in case of disagreement lies in the hands of the Premier who is primarily a tool of the President. If he wishes a bill to pass he convenes a conference committee, which represents both the Assembly and the Senate, to seek agreement on its contents. Should they fail to agree and the Premier likes the Assembly version of the bill, he may simply resubmit it to the Assembly. A bill passed twice by the Assembly can override a senatorial veto and become law. Thus, in such cases, the Senate has merely the power to delay. If the

Premier, however, does not like the Assembly version he can refuse to convene the conference committee. The bill then dies and the Senate has exercised an absolute veto—thanks to the Premier.

Senators are chosen for nine years with one-third to stand for re-election every three years. The Senate was intended to serve as a source of advice and mild delay, and as a potential ally of the government against a recalcitrant Assembly. Actually, it has worked the other way: after the 1962 elections, the new Assembly threw its support behind the Gaullist government while the Senate turned against it. The adherents of De Gaulle did well among the mass electorate and with their allies soon captured a majority of the Assembly (see Figure 13.2). Owing to weak local organization, however, they failed to take the Senate.

The Senate has continued to represent the entrenched power structures of local governments which have remained strongholds of the traditional political parties. The Senate has also continued to represent a preference of the French voters to keep their traditional parties alive, at least at the local level, perhaps in readiness for some future return to the national scene. In the meantime the Senate remains a bulwark of opposition to the administration. It has rejected a large number of government bills which then have had to be re-passed over its veto by the Assembly. By the late 1960s the weakness of the Senate was evident; ministers stopped attending its debates and answering written or oral questions from its members.

A Sidelined Judiciary.   Other divisions of the government have still less political power. A constitutional council supervises elections and referenda and decides disputes about them. It passes also on the constitu-

Figure 13.2

French Voter Opinion, 1960

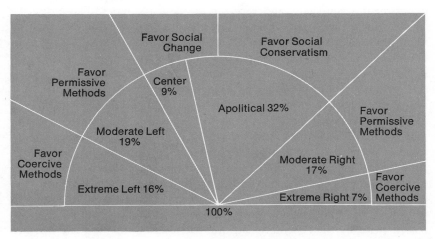

Source: R. C. Macridis, "France," in R. C. Macridis and R. E. Ward (eds.), Modern Political Systems: Europe, 2nd ed., © 1968. Adapted by permission of Prentice-Hall, Inc., Englewood Cliffs, N.J.

tionality of any bill or treaty before promulgation but only at the request of the President, Premier, president of the Assembly, or president of the Senate. Once a bill has become law, the council can judge its constitutionality only in restricted cases and upon request of the government. Judicial review in France is thus radically weaker and narrower than in the United States. The courts in general are independent but without power to nullify or modify laws of administrative actions.

Results: Successes and Surprises. The entire Constitution seemed custom-tailored to fit the imposing figure of President de Gaulle, and from 1958 to 1969 he wore his responsibilities well. During these years France acquired a great deal of prosperity, many new buildings and much productive equipment, a temporary surplus in its foreign trade, and a good deal of prestige. French technology moved forward. Acquiring a significant striking force, France became one of the world's nuclear powers. Through the development of its civilian jet plane, the Caravelle, its highspeed fighter plane, the Mystère, and the British-French supersonic plane, the Concorde, France joined the leaders of world aviation. French planning organizations were well-staffed, forward-looking, and often effective. French scientists won Nobel prizes and the government took steps to safeguard the development of a national computer industry. The enrollment in French universities grew by leaps and bounds, and new universities were added.

Suddenly in 1968, some of the new policies backfired. In the years prior to 1968 thousands of students had grown resentful at the overcrowded universities. Even where new buildings had been built, old authoritarian methods of instruction had remained, and the more numerous the students became the dimmer seemed their chance for future employment. Even where jobs loomed in prospect, they appeared dull and unattractive in a country behind whose trappings of grandeur and reforms so much was still stodgy and traditional.

When students struck and occupied the universities in May 1968, workers soon joined them for reasons of their own. Inflation had eaten into their wages which both private employers and public authorities had been reluctant to increase. "The pennies, Charlie, the pennies!" workers in the streets had cried out at President de Gaulle, but to no avail. A wave of strikes soon closed factories. Some intellectuals were delighted. "You have created new possibilities," the best-known French philosopher, Jean-Paul Sartre, told a student leader. But the solid majority of the French was shocked.

After a wage increase was granted, the workers went back to their jobs. Their unions as well as the Communist Party showed no interest in revolution and condemned the radical students as adventurers. In June 1968 French voters gave De Gaulle an increased majority. Only 6 per cent of the vote shifted from the left and center to the right, but under the French electoral system this was enough to produce a landslide in the

Assembly (see Figure 13.3). Politically, De Gaulle had won (see Table 13.2).

Figure 13.3

French National Assembly, 1968

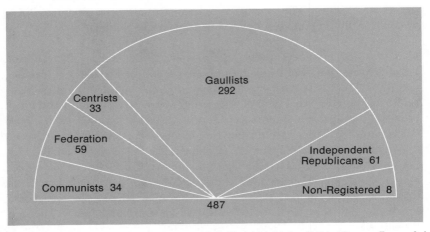

Source: R. C. Macridis, "France," in R. C. Macridis and R. E. Ward (eds.), Modern Political Systems: Europe, *2nd ed.,* © *1968. Adapted by permission of Prentice-Hall, Inc., Englewood Cliffs, N.J.*

In terms of economics he had lost, however. Once again French speculators and investors took their money out of the country. The surplus in international payments turned into a deficit. The national currency, the franc, became shaky. Inflation continued and increasingly hurt the *rentiers,* salaried employees, civil servants, and large parts of the middle class. These more conservative groups joined with labor and the intellectuals in a common resentment against De Gaulle's high-handed personal leadership which each group now blamed for its troubles. In the spring of 1969, when De Gaulle tried to put through an administrative reform providing for greater regional autonomy, he found the legislature reluctant to cooperate. As before, he presented his plan to the people in a referendum. This time he lost. A majority of voters rejected not only his plan but in effect his personal regime. The President resigned and returned to his home in a small village.

The Fifth Republic, however, survived its creator.

A New France

At the end of the 1950s, France had to choose what kind of country it wished to become. In following General de Gaulle, not toward what some thought he had promised—keeping Algeria French—but toward what he did in response to the will of the French people—ending the Algerian War—the French to a significant degree chose their own course. France today is no longer tied to its Empire and is therefore a more modern country than it was ten years ago.

France still has larger shares of its population working in agriculture, living in small towns, and remaining self-employed than do Germany or Britain. But the French occupational structure is now changing more quickly. On the average per decade, 8 per cent of the French work force has shifted from agricultural to non-agricultural pursuits, compared to only 6 per cent in the German Federal Republic and 1 per cent in Britain. If these trends continue, French agriculture will comprise less than one-twelfth of the work force in the late 1970s, and French politics will become very different from what it has been.

Already now, France is in many ways a different country. It still has a social structure that makes unity difficult, and a political culture that encourages distrust of government and withdrawal from politics. President Georges Pompidou, who in 1969 succeeded General de Gaulle, continued the policies of his predecessor, with greater suavity of style but no major change in substance. Both bankers and Communists seemed agreed that he was the best man capable of being elected. As early as the mid-1960s elite surveys had elicited the opinion that much of the Fifth Republic would survive General de Gaulle. The responses further indicated that the French elites wanted France to be an ally of the United States, but not a satellite.

Some more pessimistic Frenchmen at that time forecast that, after General de Gaulle, everything in politics would be for sale. If this had turned out to be true, domestic and foreign interests with the greatest purchasing power might have picked up new political concessions. At the beginning of 1970, they had not yet done so. Perhaps there is less for sale in the French politics of growing mass participation than both native and foreign observers suspected. In many ways, and under any government, France is likely to continue her policies of national self-government in international affairs, and her people may even develop the ability to form groups that can work with each other more constructively in domestic matters.

In the past France has been the experimental laboratory of the Western world. From the thirteenth century to the days of Jean-Paul Sartre and Albert Camus, the French have tried out more ideas than any other people. Often they have not innovated as much in practice as in thought. But what the French now try to do both in thought and practice may be— as in the past—of decisive importance for all of the Western world.

Key Terms and Concepts

rentiers	right
avant-garde	center
esprit de finesse	first ballot

Le Grand Siècle

Jacobins

First Republic

Girondists

the terror

Thermidor

Directory

eighteenth of Brumaire

First Empire

Second Republic

Second Empire

Third Republic

left

second ballot

floating vote

Vichy Regime

Fourth Republic

ministrables

Common Market

economic determinism

Fifth Republic

National Assembly

Senate

rule-making power

organic law

Additional Readings

Aron, R. *France: Steadfast and Changing*. Cambridge: Harvard University Press, 1960.

Brinton, C. *A Decade of Revolution: 1789-1799*. New York: Harper & Row, 1935.

————. *The Americans and the French*. Cambridge: Harvard University Press, 1968.

Crozier, M. *The Bureaucratic Phenomenon*. Chicago: University of Chicago Press, 1964.

Ehrmann, H.W. *France*. Boston: Little, Brown, 1968.

Grosser, A. "Nothing But Opposition." Robert Dahl (ed.) *Political Opposition in Western Democracies*. New Haven: Yale University Press, 1966.

Hoffmann, S. (ed.) *In Search of France*. Cambridge: Harvard University Press, 1963.

MacRae, D., Jr. *Parliament, Parties and Societies in France, 1946-1958*. New York: St. Martin's Press, 1967.

Macridis, R.C. "France." R.C. Macridis and R.E. Ward (eds.) *Modern Political Systems: Europe*. 2nd ed. Englewood Cliffs, N.J.: Prentice-Hall, 1968.

————. "Pompidou and the Communists." *The Virginia Quarterly*. Vol. 45, No. 4 (1969), pp. 579-594.

Métraux, R. and M. Mead. *Themes in French Culture: A Preface to a Study of French Community*. Stanford: Hoover Institute Series D, No. 1, 1954.

Pickles, D. *The Fifth French Republic*. New York: Praeger, 1962.

Wylie, L. *Village in the Vaucluse*. Cambridge: Harvard University Press, 1957.

The German Federal Republic

"To be German means to do a thing for its own sake," runs an old German saying. For good or ill, the German people often have committed themselves more thoroughly to whatever they were doing at the time—to the admiration, astonishment, or horror of their neighbors. German diligence and orderliness are renowned. "In a German train," goes another saying, "not only the conductor is on duty but the passengers as well." Yet two thousand years earlier, the Roman historian Tacitus called the ancient Germans incurably undisciplined and lazy. How did a people of such great gifts go through such changes in its character?

Chapter 14

Like the British, French, and American political systems, the roots of the various regimes by which Germany has been governed lay in part in the political culture of the country. Roots such as these may reflect images of conflict or cooperation, hierarchy or equality, which have become embodied in the things people take for granted. These images lodge in people's minds even if they are not explicitly discussed as formal political problems.

German technology is much like that of the United States, the Soviet Union, Britain, France and other advanced countries. But German history often has been radically different, and so has German politics. German politics cannot be understood by looking only at German institutions or day-to-day events. All these have changed too often in this century. To discern what German politics means and how it works, we must know something of its origins and its past.

The present German Federal Republic is among the world's youngest political systems. It came into being only in 1949. But it governs three-quarters of one of the oldest of the peoples of Europe. In a sense the German people is even older than the English people. When the German people emerged, when the word *teutiscus,* or German, was first used early in the ninth century, no Norman had yet come to England. Through a thousand years of history there has been a German people, but this people has lived in a united national state for less than eighty years. Today's divided Germany rings with the echoes of this past.

The Forming of the German People

German history differs radically from that of other major nations. While Englishmen, Frenchmen, and Russians each spent most of their history as subjects of a single centralized state, the Germans spent most of their past as subjects either of a vaguely defined empire or of many princes. The German people was put together in a 250-year period of unification and expansion between roughly 750 and 1000 A.D., which was followed by another four centuries of further expansion. But all these centuries produced no unified German state.

Six Centuries of German Expansion. At first, German expansion moved southward with the expeditions of the Frankish emperors. This expansion was formalized on Christmas Day, 800 A.D., when the roughneck Frankish leader Charlemagne had himself crowned Emperor of the Romans by the Pope. In exchange for this political service, Charlemagne made his troops available to the Papacy in the triangular war in southern Italy involving the Roman Catholic Church, the Greek Byzantine Empire, and Muslim power. The Franks were called in by the Papacy to decide the outcome. A monk of Ravenna, reporting the scene when the Frankish army arrived, called it incredible. The soldiers, he said, were covered with iron from head to foot—a stream of iron flowing into Italy. The stream of iron also moved northward and eastward as well as southward. Cities which today are in the middle of Germany were a thousand years ago frontier fortresses against Slavs and pagans. Later, and still more eastward, East Prussia was a province carved out by conquest.

Eventually some of the Slavic and Lithuanian non-German natives of these regions were exterminated; all survivors were subjugated and most of their descendants were assimilated. Today many of the German family names in Eastern Europe clearly show their Slavic origin. Thus, despite all legends of the purity of the so-called Aryan race, the German people is as racially mixed as any of the peoples forming the great nations of the world.

The expansion came to a stop in 1410 when for the first time a Polish army defeated the German crusaders in the Battle of Tannenberg. Earlier, a foray farther east had been stopped in 1242 by the Russians under Alexander Nevski, to the pleasure of a later generation of Soviet motion picture makers. (Both these battles were omitted or played down in German textbooks. German children, too, were taught that their nation hardly ever lost a war.) But a large part of the country south of the Baltic Sea remained German.

The First German Empire.   The first German empire that began in 800 A.D. with the crowning of Charlemagne was styled the *Holy Roman Empire of the German Nation.* Much of German history records how authority tried to forge one country but reality created several. For its first forty-two years, the Holy Roman Empire however, was not an entirely German state. It included both French-speaking and German-speaking people. Just as every German schoolchild is taught that Charlemagne was a German, every French child is taught that, of course, he was a Frenchman. According to the Dutch, both are mistaken since obviously he was Dutch. In fact, these nationalities were not yet sharply distinguished in Charlemagne's day. In 832, some years after his death, the Synod of Tours ordered priests in the Empire to preach in the "popular language." But what was considered to be the popular language was strikingly different in different regions.

In 842 the grandsons of Charlemagne divided his Empire. Their armies met at Strasbourg and in preference to a war swore loyalty, each to its respective new ruler. One army swore in French loyalty to the king of the West Frankish Empire, which then became France; another army swore in German to the East Frankish ruler for the part of the Empire which eventually became Germany.

Though Charlemagne had failed to bring about any lasting unity between France and Germany, he did more perhaps than even his successors in unifying Germany. His main methods were authority and force. In thirty years of warfare Charlemagne subjugated the Saxons, tamed them, and Christianized the survivors with a sword. Many of the surviving Saxons were assimilated forcibly. A number of places in South Germany contain the word *Saxon* in their name. These at one time were settlements of deported and transplanted Saxon populations who had been put into the Frankish countryside for faster fusion with the Franks.

This drive prevented the rise of two nationalities, Saxon and Frankish. Instead they became one people. Early in the tenth century one ruler, Henry I, was the first ruler from a Saxon dynasty to become Emperor of Germany. First he was king and then proceeded to have himself crowned Emperor, wearing Frankish dress and ordering his Saxon noblemen to take Frankish wives.

By the end of the tenth century, Saxon Emperors Otto I, II, and III, respectively, had led their armies again and again into Italy and built up the first powerful and splendid empire, based on a combination of German military manpower and Italian money and resources. The Holy Roman Empire was rarely holy and only intermittently Roman but it was an empire much of the time. From 1000 to 1268 it legally and symbolically claimed power and suzerainty over all of Christendom. Its Emperor was the leading symbol of secular authority in the Western world. Emotionally and intellectually it was supposed to be world government—the vision of an empire of the world in Dante's famous book on universal monarchy was its intellectual swansong. But many Germans remembered it in later ages as a German empire, and they derived from this memory an image of German world leadership and a claim to its renewal.

In actual fact the Empire, splendid as its symbols were, was a political and organizational self-deception. It had no orderly administration. It had no means of collecting taxes and no permanent body of officials. It drew its administrators, its scant supply of literate personnel, its financial revenues, and over one-half of its military manpower from the Church. More than half of the knights who rode with the Emperors on the Italian expeditions held Church lands and were subjects of the bishops or archbishops of the Church. Since most of their money and administrative personnel came from the Church, German Emperors felt that controlling the Church in Italy was vital. Forty times in 300 years, German armies rode into Italy to enforce the German Emperor's control over the Papacy. For, to lose control of the Pope meant to lose within a few years control of the German bishops. And to lose control of the bishops meant to lose money, administration, and effective power over the Empire.

The Revolution of the Pope.   Some thoughtful historians have argued that the Popes were the first revolutionaries of Western history. According to this view, the first European revolution took place in the mind of a single man—Pope Gregory VII. In the year 1075 Gregory VII in a memo to himself, called *Dictatus Papae,* wrote that the Pope and the Church must never be subject to the Emperor, but that the Emperor ought to be subject to the Pope. This stupendously bold document was the outcome of a hundred years of ferment in the Church, but thenceforth the Papacy did everything it could to make the Church free from secular domination. The hymn *Veni Creator Spiritus* (Come, Creative Spirit) became to the Church what *La Marseillaise* became to the French Revolution 800 years later.

The Papacy made an alliance with the Italian cities. The city-states agreed to furnish the Papacy militias, and in 1176 these militias defeated the imperial army at Legnano. For the first time a noble army of armor-clad aristocrats had been beaten in pitched battle by troops of European cities. The Emperor Frederick Barbarossa barely escaped with his life, and German power in Italy never fully recovered.

The wars went on. The German princes north of the Alps became more and more unwilling to supply manpower and money for an increasingly hopeless effort to subjugate Italy by German force. The Church called in Norman knights, and Normans from France and southern Italy under the house of Anjou became formidable allies of the Pope. The last Hohenstaufen prince to try to rule Italy and to regain the imperial title, Duke Conradin of Swabia, was defeated, captured, and in 1268 beheaded in the public square at Naples with the obvious approval of the Church. This

Church-inspired revolution of the thirteenth century was the first revolution to behead a monarch.

A Germany of Many States

Germany remained without a ruler until 1273 and then lived for 300 years as a shadow empire with no Emperor in effective control. For the Empire, it was a period of profitable anarchy but within the smaller regions there was a good deal of order. The real units of government were a number of territorial principalities, on the one hand, and sovereign city states, on the other. Perhaps one-tenth of the German people lived in well-governed and increasingly prosperous city states. Outside the city states, the countryside remained under the rule of nobles and the labor of the peasants made German land increasingly cultivated and fertile. Organizations of cities, such as the Hanseatic League, carried German merchants all over Eastern Europe and gave them special privileges in Venice and London. Not until the sixteenth century were German merchants in London reduced to the level of English merchants in the eyes of English law.

A substantial part of Germany was under clerical domination. What is today the Rhineland was largely under the rule of the archbishops of Cologne, Trier, and Mainz; they had the effective equivalents of church-states which they administered in their capacity as secular rulers. Medieval Germany would have been a nightmare for an adherent of a centralized modern state, but it worked for two-and-a-half centuries, economically as well as culturally.

The Reformation and the Religious Split. The prosperity of Germany created a middle class and increasingly self-conscious and self-confident princes who grew ever more critical of the ceaseless demands of the Roman Church for more money. In the meantime, Italy likewise lived under prosperous anarchy. The Italian city states flourished, fought, and produced some of the world's outstanding treasures of art. The Papacy eventually fell into the hands of a line of fabulous bankers and art collectors, the Medici, who made up in refinements and expensiveness of taste what they might have lacked in simple piety.

The German princes also acquired the expensive tastes of Renaissance rulers, together with growing needs for money to pay for bureaucrats and mercenaries. The princes wanted to keep the silver from the German mines in their own country and spend it for their own purposes. At the same time, sincere young German monks felt disturbed by the contrast between the abnegation demanded of them and the self-indulgence they saw in Rome. They were less critical of their own princes.

Martin Luther was perhaps the outstanding example of the profoundly conscience-driven revolutionist who relied on the German princes for protection. Very soon the princes discovered that Luther's doctrines could be highly profitable for rulers who wished to keep more money and power in their own hands while finding good, respectable theological reasons for taking over the properties of the Church.

Luther's doctrines on ecclesiastical purity—the desire that the Church should not be rich and arrogant, the importance of practicing Christian virtues, the value of translating the Bible so that the people themselves could read what it said, and the carrying on of services in the popular language—appealed not only to the urban middle classes but also to the peasants. And when the peasants rose, their demands became a mixture of social revolution, populism, and fundamentalism. One of the peasant songs said, "Naught shall prevail but Holy Writ!" In sum, there was to be no canon law, no ecclesiastic rules; scripture was to be directly read and literally interpreted and this would be sufficient to run everybody's lives. This is a view which still survives in some rural communities in the "Bible Belt" of the United States from Georgia to Kansas.

Authority Defeats the Peasants.   In Germany at the time, this kind of fundamentalism meant war against the monasteries and the Church. It meant plunder and violence, and, in response, the ferocious repression of the peasants by the nobles. The actions of the nobles had the blessings not only of the Catholic Church, but of Martin Luther, too. It was Luther who wrote in 1525 in a pamphlet addressed to the nobles and directed *Against the Robbing and Murdering Hordes of Peasants,* "Dear Beloved Gentlemen: There is no time in which one could deserve better of heaven by killing, hanging, burning, and piercing people through than now." He urged the nobles to do this to the peasants and restore order.

It was done to the peasants with devastating thoroughness. The victory of authoritarianism over the Saxons in Charlemagne's day was now paralleled by a second victory of authoritarianism over the peasants in Luther's day. Germany began to stagnate—politically, culturally, and economically—after the victory of the nobles and princes over its peasants; and soon the princes began to win victories over the self-governing powers of many of Germany's cities.

Germany became a plurality of authoritarian princely states. The princes who ruled the seven largest ones had the right to elect the Emperor, and they became one of the world's smallest but most corrupt electorates. Records show how the imperial crown of Germany was bought for cash in 1530. Charles V of Spain used the gold streaming in from the plunder of the New World and from the massacres of the natives of Mexico and Peru to bribe the German electors at the imperial diet into electing him Emperor, but he had to borrow additional sums to make up the full price demanded by the electors.

Religious War, Devastation, and a Legacy of Fear. The Reformation led to wars between Catholic and Protestant princes, spurred on by zealous theologians on both sides. Germany suffered. It ceased to be the source for the exercise of power over foreign countries and became a theatre for power exercised from abroad. Spanish money and later Spanish armies strengthened the Counter-Reformation and the Catholic princes in their war against the Protestants. In 1555 compromise was reached in the *Religious Peace of Augsburg* which established the doctrine of *cuius regio eius religio* (whoever rules the land has the right to determine the religion). It was freedom for the prince, but not for his subjects. They had to accept his religion, or, with luck, get out. Ever since, some German regions have remained Protestant and others Catholic; and German politics often has reflected this diversity.

The Peace of Augsburg lasted about half a century. There were disagreements within both camps whether this uneasy peace ought to last. One of the lesser-known chapters of European history is the struggle between the doves and hawks among Protestants and Catholics alike, which ended in the defeat of the peace factions on both sides. Soon the victory of the hardliners on both sides led to an increase in political warfare throughout Europe.

The worst explosion occurred in Germany in the *Thirty Years' War.* Foreign armies entered in the name of religion and stayed to fight for power. German princes on both sides abetted them. The war was fought without mercy. In its course, two-fifths of the German people perished. Germany, which had entered the war with twenty million inhabitants, left it with twelve million.

The trauma of Germany was lasting, leaving in German political culture a legacy of fear and distrust of foreigners. Foreign armies had made Germany the expendable battlefield for the conflicts of European power politics. But the Germans' fear and distrust of others was combined with a fear and distrust of themselves. At least half or more of the soldiers who had plundered and devastated Germany were Germans recruited in the name of the Pure Gospel of Protestantism or in the name of the one and exclusive Church. Either way they had been paid intermittently by their mercenary captains and had received permission to plunder and torture the population. The Thirty Years' War thus was as much an act of self-destruction as an act of the destruction by other stronger, better-organized, and more ruthless neighboring states.

A more subtle damage preceded the war and continued after it. For a hundred years, the world's trade routes had been shifting from the Mediterranean to the Atlantic seaboard following the discovery of America. Italy and Germany—to a large extent the centers of the medieval world—were becoming the backwaters of the emerging modern age. German cities had stopped growing by the middle of the sixteenth century. Germany was stagnating much as a river valley whose water supply is drying up. The Germans had no clear awareness of what was happening to them. They only had a vague feeling that unidentified, secret, alien forces were doing harm to them, and the fear of such anonymous threats to the German people became another theme in German political culture.

Two German Remedies: Discipline and Work.

After 1648, when the military and the economic misfortunes had reached their peak, the surviving Germans worked their way back to security under the rule of various absolute princes. They saved themselves through discipline and diligence. Authoritarianism scored a third victory. The most typical political entity to emerge in this period was the principality of Brandenburg, "the sandbox of the Empire," as it was called, with poor soil and few natural resources, but an incredible ability for organization, discipline, and hard work. Later it was said of Brandenburg that it had starved itself into greatness.

The key legal change was the introduction of compulsory personal service; the peasants owed not only services to the nobles on their fields in spring, summer, and fall, but from the seventeenth century onward, they also had to work indoors under supervision, spinning, weaving, and producing useful commodities. Work became a German form of psychotherapy and eventually the basis of restored prosperity. Tireless work habits, thoroughness, and order became characteristic of the German people.

The Miracle of German Culture.

Authoritarianism did not affect all aspects of German life. Despite devastation and oppression, there arose in the second half of the seventeenth century a great culture with a deeply humanist tradition in science, poetry, and music. Hermann Hesse in his book, *The Glass Bead Game,* suggests that perhaps the rise of German music was one effort toward psychological and cultural healing; music put the souls of a people together again after their lives had been shattered.

The eighteenth century brought a continuation of both German traits, authoritarianism and humanism. There was absolutism under efficient cynical rulers like Frederick the Great who wrote, "I take what I want. There will always be plenty of professors to justify what I do," and who on another occasion asserted that "prostitutes and professors can always be procured." What Frederick did not take into account was that Germany might yet produce other scholars who would do more to put the skids under monarchies than those whom he had procured to justify his exploits. The same German university culture that produced Leibniz and Goethe eventually produced Marx, Freud, and Einstein, the three men who crushed the pillars of so many of the world's former beliefs.

Whereas German politics remained absolutist and authoritarian, German culture became increasingly liberal and humanist. The work and outlook of Lessing, Kant, Mozart, Beethoven, and Goethe shows that every one of these thinkers was a liberal. Each believed in the free development of the personality of every individual, and each thought that government ought to serve this end. Lessing and Mozart were freemasons, and Kant and Beethoven were both self-confessed Jacobins—friends and admirers of the French Revolution—in their political sympathies and in their writings. Kant said, "I admire Rousseau. He straightened me out." But the silent majority of the German people remained obedient to their princes.

Liberty or Union: Germany's Long Dilemma

In France and Britain, the main struggles for popular liberties occurred within nation-states which were already unified. Likewise, "Liberty and Union—one and inseparable!" is an old slogan in American history. Germany's many states, by contrast, offered neither liberty nor union. For the German people, the choice of which goal to seek first, liberty or union, was always difficult and sometimes tragic.

A Revolutionary Era.　The issue was first posed by the example of the French Revolution, which found Germany politically and economically unprepared. Napoleon's armies overran Germany easily; the vaunted Prussian armies collapsed, proving hopelessly obsolete before the French onslaught. Soon the French occupied Berlin. But under the noses of the occupying government, German nationalism grew faster, and the German economy changed. In Prussia the civil service was reformed, the cities got partial self-government, and the University of Berlin was founded. In 1813 a wave of nationalism swept through Germany, which inspired the Germans to play a major role in destroying the Napoleonic armies in the military actions between 1813 and 1815.

There followed an age of utter tiredness with war and revolution. There were now over thirty German states, heirs of several hundred still smaller ones which they had swallowed. The average German citizen preferred to withdraw into his family and to delight in the solid comfort of his furniture. The drowsy man in stocking cap and nightshirt became the German cartoonists' symbol for the mood of their countrymen. It was an age of princes restored to nearly absolute rule over obedient middle-class burghers who held that to be quiet was every citizen's first duty.

Romanticism and an Unsuccessful Revolution.　After 1830 the popular mood began to change. A combination of liberalism, nationalism, and romanticism came to the fore. The uprising of the Greeks against the Sultan of Turkey attracted some German volunteers. Hand in hand with a growing interest in nationalism came an increase in romanticism. The first generation of romantics already had created the new images and concerns of romanticism: the love of the night and of the feelings for emotion, the thirst for intellectual powers, and the longing to transcend limits. Now the movement grew and broadened. Those contemporaries who thought romanticism was a movement of mere irrationality grossly underestimated its intellectual performance. Great philosophers like Hegel and Schopenhauer also belonged to that trend; so did Nietzsche as its last offshoot, with his vision of man and superman. The social critics coming out of the romantic decades, Engels, Marx, and others, were to prove intellectually and politically formidable. Most of the romantics, however, favored German union ahead of liberty or social change.

The revolution that broke out in Germany in 1848 was the century's high point in the struggle for liberty in Germany, but it was another failure. Some cities rose, but they were small; some students, small craftsmen, and workers from the few factories of the time manned the barricades. But many of the handicraftsmen in the cities were not interested in revolution. Germany was still overwhelmingly agrarian and the lot of the peasants had been considerably improved since the days of Luther and the Thirty Years' War. When in 1848 most remnants of feudal oppression were abolished by timely reforms, most of the peasants turned conservative. Their sons in soldiers' uniforms helped suppress the 1848 revolution. In the cities, the new factory owners had gotten into deep conflicts with their few factory workers and felt that revolution would make factory labor unmanageable.[1] Throughout Germany, the revolution was beaten easily, and the middle class turned again to authoritarian leadership, partly to keep the working man in order and partly to maintain a strong army against foreign rivals.

Middle-class Germans sought first of all stability, and they were willing to submit to authority to get it. Second to stability, they wanted wealth and power, and they sought union as the path to these. Last only, they wanted liberty—and they sacrificed it readily whenever stability or union seemed at stake.

Throughout the nineteenth century, the German middle class felt that it needed strong military protection against foreign rivals, but it never trusted its own competence to perform the great military operations. It believed that a first-class military power required aristocratic officers and generals. This is one of the deep differences between German political culture on the one hand and French, British, or American on the other.

Union From Above. In the 1850s and 1860s Germany was transformed economically through the establishment of a railroad network and rapid acceleration of industrial growth. By the end of the 1860s, Germany was producing more steel and coal than France.

[1] One should remember that European industry was built up in the first half of the nineteenth century by denying industrial workers the right to vote, and by putting all the economic sacrifices on their first and second generations. This is quite different from modern economic development where in most developing countries industrial labor cannot be treated in the way British, French, and German labor was treated between 1820 and 1848.

When Germany finally was unified in 1870–71, it resulted in the fourth major victory of authoritarianism in German history. Things greatly longed for by generations of Germans—unification of their country, equality before the law, and more rights for the middle classes and even for the common people—came as a gift of authority from on high. Prussia, the most authoritarian state, and Bismarck, its Iron Chancellor and the faithful servant of its monarch, brought it about. Bismarck's ruthless moves of power politics, his brilliant manipulation of alliances, all were undertaken without major parliamentary or popular participation in making decisions. Most Germans gratefully accepted the results. Throughout the next four decades, stability and power seemed assured. Thereafter, Germany was to become the most bellicose and unstable power in Western Europe.

Eighty Years of Unity

Germany was united from 1871 to 1945. During this short time, for less than three generations, the country went through three forms of government and two world wars.

The Failure of Steering and the Slide into World War I. The almost unlimited capacity of the Germans to trust their government made it easy for them to go wholeheartedly into World War I. In 1914, however, other people trusted their own governments no less uncritically, and this made the coming of war more certain. Other governments on both sides shared responsibility for the war, but the German failures of realistic political decision and self-control were among the worst of the great powers.

The German people loyally supported a government and a political system that in the end proved incapable of self-steering. The German government failed to understand the danger of the world war to which its own decisions were leading. It grossly underrated the numbers, strength, and determination of the foreign enemies it was acquiring; and it failed to see the character of the war into which it was blundering, and the consequences which this war would produce.

Blind leadership found blind obedience. After the German government had decided to go to war against France it announced on August 3, 1914 that French aircraft had dropped bombs on Nuremberg. This announcement, we know now, was a lie. The commander of Nuremberg knew nothing of this alleged attack. The German press, nevertheless, published it, and the German people believed their leaders. They thought themselves attacked, and they produced three million patriotic poems to express their patriotic fervor in the first nine months of the war. Never in the history of mankind was so much bad poetry produced by so many people in so short a time.

The sacrifices of the German people were vast. At the village of Langemark in Belgium, it takes a bus forty-five minutes to go past the cemetery which contains the graves of four regiments of German student volunteers who were used up by the German military command in 1914 in mass infantry attacks against British machine guns. The using up of manpower continued for four years. In the end, the war was lost, the empire collapsed in revolution, and the Emperor escaped to Holland where he lived in retirement—as the richest citizen of Germany. He kept his properties while the German people experimented with their first republic.

Between Revolution and Authority: The Weimar Republic.   In November 1918, a revolution ended the war and created a German republic. Later its constitution was drafted by a convention in the small town of Weimar, famed for memories of the poets Goethe and Schiller and safely distant from the country's restless industrial centers. From this birthplace of its constitution it became known as the *Weimar Republic* (1919–1933).

Throughout its fourteen-year existence, the Weimar Republic could only rarely count on a republican and democratic majority among its people. The Republic's main parties were the Social Democrats who put democracy ahead of socialism and averaged about 20 per cent of the vote; the Catholic Center Party, with about 13 per cent; the liberal Democrats, who averaged nearly 10 per cent until 1930, and then dropped to 2 per cent; and on the moderate right, the German People's Party which averaged about 18 per cent until 1928, but dropped to 3 per cent by 1930. Together, these moderate parties commanded a scant majority of the voters until 1928. On the radical left, the Communists averaged 11 per cent. On the far right, the conservative German Nationalists averaged another 11 per cent until 1930, and the National Socialists (Nazis) about 5 per cent. From 1920 to 1930, roughly one-fifth of German voters steadily abstained from voting (see Table 14.1).

Most often the Republic remained torn between the conservatism and authoritarianism of strong groups on the right and the revolutionary impatience of a minority on the extreme left. This struggle in the end strengthened the right-wing reaction.

But during the first few years left-wing uprisings were most conspicuous. Karl Liebknecht, the first member of the German Reichstag (the lower house of Parliament) who had voted in 1914 against war credits, (that is, in effect, against allocating money for the war), was one of a small group of radicals who from 1917 on were sympathetic to the Russian Revolution. Another was Rosa Luxemburg, one of the most brilliant women in politics of any time. They were leaders of the Spartacist League which thought that a quick uprising in Berlin in January 1919 could win Germany for

Table 14.1

Electoral Shares of German Parties and Groupings, 1871–1969 (By approximate percentage of all eligible voters)

	1871	1912	Jan. 1919	June 1920	May 1924	May 1928	Sept. 1930	Nov. 1932	Mar. 1933	Aug. 1949	Sept. 1953	Sept. 1957	Sept. 1961	Sept. 1965	June 1969
Citizens entitled to vote (in millions)	7.7	14.4	36.8	36.0	38.4	41.2	43.0	44.4	44.7	31.2	33.1	35.4	37.4	38.5	38.7
Valid votes cast (in millions)	3.9	12.2	30.4	28.2	29.3	30.8	35.0	35.5	39.3	24.5	28.5	31.1	31.3	32.6	33.0
1. Far Right: Nazis	—	—	—	—	5	2	15	26	39						
Conservatives	12	11	8 (D.V.P.)	13	19	14	10	7	7						
2. Moderate Right: National Liberals ('19–33:D.V.P.)	15	12	4	11	6	6	3	2	1	4	4	4	1	2	4
Subtotal RIGHT	27	23	12	24	30	22	28	35	47	4	4	4	1	2	4
3. Progressives and Democrats (1928: State Party)	8	10	16	7	6	10	9	2	2	9	9	6	11	8	5[1]
4. Center and Bavarian Peoples' Party	10	14	16	14	13	11	12	12	12	24	36	43	38	40	39.5
5. Particularists	4	9	1	1	1	1	1	2	0	13	7	5	2	—	—
Subtotal CENTER	22	33	33	22	20	22	22	16	14	46	52	54	51	48	44.5
6. Social Democrats	2	29	32	17	15	22	20	16	16	22	25	27	31	33	36.5
Independent Social Democrats	—	—	6	13	1	—	—	—	—	—	—	—	—	—	—
7. Communists	—	—	—	2	10	8	11	13	11	4	2	—	1	—	—
Subtotal LEFT	2	29	38	32	26	30	31	29	27	26	27	27	32	33	36.5
8. Nonvoters	49	15	17	22	25	26	19	20	12	24	17	15	16	16	15[2]
Total	100	100	100	100	100	100	100	100	100	100	100	100	100	100	100

Labels appearing within the table for the post-war period: the National Liberals (Moderate Right) figures are shown as "D.P. and D.R.P." for 1949–1957 and as "N.P.D." for 1961–1969; the Progressives and Democrats row is shown as "F.D.P." for 1949–1969; the Center and Bavarian Peoples' Party row is shown as "C.D.U." for 1949–1969.

[1]The FDP share of valid votes cast was 5.8 per cent, well above the 5 per cent minimum required by the "threshold clause" of the electoral law.
[2]Includes 2 per cent invalid votes.

Sources: K.W. Deutsch, "The German Federal Republic," in R.C. Macridis and R.E. Ward (eds.), *Modern Political Systems: Europe, 2nd ed.,* © 1968. Adapted by permission of Prentice-Hall, Inc., Englewood Cliffs, N.J.; German Consulate, Boston, Massachusetts, 1969.

communism without going through the long and tedious process of gaining the consent and support of a majority of the German people.[2]

The uprising was quickly beaten down by troops returned from the front. A new army, the Reichswehr, was largely recruited among nationalist and military circles, and Liebknecht and Luxemburg were murdered in January 1919. A series of other radical uprisings followed—in 1919 in Bavaria, in 1920 in the Rhineland, in 1923 in Thuringia, and in 1923 at Hamburg. All were bloodily repressed. The leadership of the small German Communist Party believed that it was unimportant whether an uprising succeeded or not. Coups, fighting, and uprisings were expected to have great educational value for the workers, revolutionizing them by their example. A number of left-wing leaders perished in these actions. On the whole, the *Putsch period*—the time of armed coups by small groups from 1919 to 1923—disorganized and split German labor without producing any major successes for the radicals.

Meanwhile, moderate labor and middle-class groups turned for protection to conservatives and nationalists who became entrenched in the army. Under the new democratic constitution, social reforms were enacted but soon the German government let the currency decline in value. German industry discovered that one could profit from inflation, and by 1923 the shock of World War I which had expropriated the holdings of many members of the German middle class was reinforced by another catastrophe: runaway inflation which wiped out the savings of countless others.

Many voters again turned to authority. In 1925 they chose as president the leading representative of German militarism in World War I, Field Marshal Paul von Hindenburg. This was the fifth victory of authoritarianism. Hindenburg was elected by a minority of voters. The Communist candidate, Ernst Thälmann, by insisting on running on a separate ticket, made it possible for Hindenburg to be elected rather than the moderate candidate, a Catholic politician with the surprising name of (Wilhelm) Marx. Hindenburg became President through Thälmann's insistence on not supporting the more liberal candidate. Later, in 1932, Democrats and Socialists united with conservatives for Hindenburg's re-election as the "lesser evil" compared to the election of Adolf Hitler to the presidency. They were soon to regret their success. Hindenburg appointed Hitler Chancellor in January 1933. Authoritarianism triumphed a sixth time (see Table 14.2). Hitler promptly became dictator, suppressing all parties but his own. Soon he ordered Thälmann's arrest and subsequent murder. Many of the moderates also were murdered by Hitler's regime. History can be more tragic than the stage.

---

[2] Although Liebknecht and Luxemburg personally disapproved of the uprising and considered it unwise, they loyally supported the action when the majority of the organization voted for it.

Table 14.2

Six Authoritarian Victories in German History

1. Charlemagne subjugates the Saxons, 764–814.
2. Luther and the princes smash the Peasants' War, 1525.
3. Absolute princes rule over Germany's recovery after the Thirty Years' War, 1648–1701.
4. Prussia and Bismarck unite Germany, 1862–1871.
5. German voters elect Hindenburg President, 1925.
6. Hindenburg appoints Adolf Hitler Chancellor, 1933.

Similar tables of authoritarian victories could be compiled for other nations. For Britain and France, however, they would have to be interspersed with major revolutions and popular reforms. The triumphs of German authoritarianism were more frequent, bigger, and less relieved by democratic triumphs.

Government by a Death Cult: The Nazi Period. During the 1920s, a small group of right-wing extremists was organized by Hitler under the name of the National Socialist German Workers' Party. Its main ideas were laid down in 1924 in Hitler's book *Mein Kampf.* This book extolled war as the be-all and end-all of politics. War, according to Hitler, was eternal and inevitable. Nations were determined by race, he said, and were destined to struggle perpetually against each other for survival like other species of animals in a world of insufficient food supplies. It was the duty of the German people to fight against all other nations and to turn itself into a *master race,* subjugating or exterminating all rivals, who in any case were "inferior" by definition. Jews were to be the first, but not the last marked for extermination. For the master race the only honorable alternative to victory was death, either in combat or by suicide.

Death and its symbols were made psychologically attractive by the Nazis. Skulls and crossbones formed part of the insignia of Hitler's black-clad Elite Guard; honorable death was glorified in more than half the songs in the Nazi official songbook. Hitler tried to practice what he preached. Facing defeat at the end of World War II, he gave orders for the destruction of Germany. Many Nazi leaders ended their lives by suicide; Hitler ordered an aide to kill him and burn his body.

How could such an insane set of beliefs win the support of the German people? It happened in the four short years between 1929 and 1933 when the explosive legacies of German history and politics reached their peak under the impact of a worldwide depression.

After World War I and the great inflation, the depression of 1929 was the third of the major catastrophes within a dozen years to hit the German middle class. German political culture once again showed its unfortunate tendency of reaching toward extremes in times of crisis. Once again, the more conservative people in Germany moved toward authoritarianism while the more radical shifted toward extreme radicalism. In the United

States the opposite happened: the depression was answered by a series of reform efforts, aimed at preserving not only property rights but also human rights, and serving human needs. In England, too, Keynesian economics was tried, preserving both welfare spending and private enterprise. In Germany, however, rigid and outdated policies were put ahead of people. Even the Catholic Center Party advocated an extreme response to the depression: cutting public spending, lowering wages, and reducing the power of trade unions.

Hurt by the deepening depression the masses of the middle class moved far to the right. In particular, the lower middle class flocked to Adolf Hitler's National Socialist German Workers' Party which until 1930 had been only a minor far right sect. From 1930 on, however, Hitler received massive financial and press support from big business groups. Some feared communism; others wanted "order" and a curb on democratic labor unions; still others expected profits from rearmament, or even greater profits from war and the conquest of a new empire. The Protestant middle-class parties lost most of their supporters to the Nazis, but nine-tenths of the Catholic Center Party's voters remained faithful. The Center Party, however, decided not to collaborate any longer with liberal or socialist groups and to join forces with the right. This decision led to the voluntary dissolution of the Center Party in 1933, and was followed by a Concordat between Hitler and the Vatican—which the Nazis later violated.

On the left, workers remained cool to Hitler. Both the Social Democrats and Communists kept nine-tenths of their voters. They continued to oppose the Nazis, often at the cost of their lives. The main sources of Nazi voting strength came from the middle classes, the rural population, and the newly mobilized previous nonvoters. Outside the ballot box, some of the military, like some business leaders, were useful to the Nazis.

The Nazi empire, according to its leaders, was to last a thousand years. It had a six-year period of arms prosperity and cheap victories over weaker or more timid opponents followed by World War II. From 1942 to 1945 a series of military defeats brought on the complete collapse of Nazi Germany. Those upper- and middle-class groups which had supported Hitler in the belief of serving either Germany or their own group interests now discovered that the war was destroying Germany, as well as their own lives, their homes, and their children.

By the end of the war, almost all major German cities were levelled. Today, guidebooks point out the few exceptions, such as Heidelberg, where most of the houses were left standing. The Nazis' projected thousand-year rule had shrunk to twelve. It left behind hundreds of thousands of tortured and murdered Germans, millions of dead German soldiers, half a million German civilian war dead, six million slaughtered Jews; another fifty million lives lost in World War II, and a Germany in ruins.

Another Try: The German Federal Republic

Out of the rubble crawled two postwar Germanies: a Communist-ruled *German Democratic Republic (GDR)*, encompassing one-quarter of the German population, in the east, and *a German Federal Republic (GFR)*, embracing three-quarters of the German people, in the west.

The Federal Republic was created in 1949 out of the British, French, and American zones of occupation with major economic and political assistance from the United States. The main effort for the success of the Federal Republic has come from its own people. They worked hard and they kept their heads. In the last twenty years, for the first time, Germans have reacted more often toward the middle than toward the extremes. The far right and far left parties in West Germany are small. In 1969 Communist votes amounted to about 2 per cent or less; neo-Nazi National Democratic Party (NDP) votes were less than 5 per cent. Each of these percentages could probably be doubled under the right conditions, such as an economic depression, but the far right is not likely to exceed 15 per cent even under favorable circumstances, and the far left not much more than 5 per cent.

A New Party System.   The important news came from nearer to the middle of the political spectrum (see Table 14.2). Right of center a new party has arisen, the *Christian Democratic Union (CDU)*, with an affiliate in Bavaria, the *Christian Social Union (CSU)*, which caters to local sentiment in that state but otherwise acts most often as part of the CDU. The CDU/CSU is a successor to the Catholic Center Party but it appeals explicitly also to Protestant voters. From the beginning of the Federal Republic, it has been the chief party of the middle class in town and country, and it has received generous financial support from industry. Beyond this, it has been the main political voice of farmers and rural laborers, and of people with very high and very low incomes, the latter mainly pensioners and dependent family members from the countryside. The CDU/CSU also attracts proportionately more votes from those over sixty, from women, and from those Catholics and Protestants who regularly attend church.

The CDU/CSU's share of the electorate has grown steadily, mainly at the expense of smaller middle-class splinter groups and parties. It includes on the one hand most of the former moderate right, leaving only the extreme fringe to the NDP. On its left wing it attracts a significant contingent of votes from Catholic trade unionists and from city dwellers in the industrial Rhine-Ruhr area. Some prominent CDU/CSU leaders, like former Chancellor Georg Kiesinger and former President Heinrich Lübke, once were minor members of the Nazi Party, but the CDU/CSU commitment to constitutional and democratic government has held firm for more than two decades since 1949.

The only other surviving middle-class party of any importance is the *Free Democratic Party (FDP)*, which attracted less than 6 per cent of votes cast in 1969. Apart from its lesser size, the FDP differs from the CDU/CSU in three respects. On the issues of education and culture, it is secular if not slightly anti-clerical. It favors greater separation of church and state, whereas the CDU/CSU defends public support for denominational schools and public collection of taxes for the Church. It is more hostile to censorship, whereas the CDU/CSU is more willing to invoke the powers of the state in enforcing the moral views of the Church. On most such issues the views of the FDP place it to the left of the CDU/CSU. Second, in foreign affairs and problems of German unification, the FDP favors a more conciliatory policy toward the countries of the Soviet bloc, including East Germany. Here, too, the FDP stands to the left of the CDU/CSU. Third, in economic matters, the FDP has long been to the right of the CDU/CSU. It has been more favorable to the viewpoint of employers and management, less sympathetic to wage increases and welfare spending, and more often opposed to government intervention in economic life. For this reason, the FDP has received much of its financial support from the same industrial and business interests as the CDU/CSU.

Throughout the Federal Republic, the FDP has drawn votes from the free professions, civil servants, employers, and a minority of churchgoing Protestants. The Party also used to attract regional support from North Germany, some of it conservative, and from South Germany, much of it traditionally liberal.

By the end of the 1960s some of the conservative support for the FDP was disappearing. More conservative supporters of the FDP were switching to the CDU/CSU in reaction to the Party's trying to gain ground among younger and more liberal voters. This shift in its electoral base has placed the Party somewhat more clearly to the left of the CDU/CSU. At the same time, the introduction of government subsidies for political parties has given the FDP a new source of income and reduced its dependence on business and industry as sources of funds. Together, these changes have made it easier for the FDP to form a coalition with the Social Democrats, and they may continue to influence FDP policies in the 1970s.

To the left of center stands the *Social Democratic Party (SPD)*, the direct successor of the Social Democratic Party of the old empire and the Weimar Republic. In contrast to the Weimar era, the SPD now receives practically all the votes of labor and of the left of center, which it no longer has to share with the Communist Party, insignificant since 1949 and outlawed since 1953. Throughout the 1960s the SPD has been moving from its old class appeal to workers and toward a new image as a progressive party for the entire people of the Federal Republic. During this period the Party has reduced its emphasis on nationalization and public ownership and stressed instead indirect economic policies aimed at combining economic growth, full employment, and comprehensive welfare with the flexibility of a free market. Appealing to the ambition of most Germans to own a car, one SPD poster in the 1960s showed the Party's initials on an automobile license plate.

The Party's new look has paid off in votes. German white-collar voters who did not identify themselves as proletarians have been quite willing to see themselves as progressives. The 1969 election brought the Party a substantial gain in votes, placing it only a short distance behind the CDU/CSU. This opened the way to a coalition with the FDP, which made Gustav Heinemann the first Social Democratic President since 1925 and Willy Brandt the first Social Democratic Chancellor since 1930.

Together the three parties, SPD, FDP, and CDU/CSU, have formed a new party system which is in contrast to the many parties of the Weimar era. Even now, the two major parties, CDU/CSU and SPD, poll nearly 90 per cent of all votes cast, as they did in 1969, winning 94 per cent of seats in the *Bundestag*, the directly elected chamber of the national legislature. Many observers have assumed, therefore, that the Federal Republic is on its way to a two-party system and that the days of the FDP are numbered. Despite a decade of such predictions and the decreasing votes in the 1969 elections, the FDP appears alive and well. It offers a significant alternative for those voters who are dissatisfied with the CDU/CSU but unwilling to give up a distinctive middle-class identity. By voting for the FDP these voters can support a coalition with the Social Democrats without having to entrust their political fate completely to the latter. Being small, the FDP also can offer quicker-rising public careers to younger persons of political talent, such as the sociologist Ralf Dahrendorf, in contrast to the much less hospitable bureaucracy of the two major political parties. So long as these conditions persist, the Federal Republic's "two-and-a-half" party system may well endure.

A New Type of Federalism.   The organization of the Federal Republic is laid down in the *Basic Law*. Passed in 1949, it is a constitution in fact, though not in name. Theoretically, it is to remain valid until "a constitution comes into effect which has been freely decided upon by the German people," that is, after the hoped-for German reunification. Actually, the Basic Law is entering the third decade of its validity and is now considered permanent by most West Germans.

The Basic Law created a new variety of federalism. Under its provisions, the federal government in Bonn has direct control of only a few matters, chiefly foreign affairs, defense, federal finances, the postal, telegraph, and telephone services, and the railroads. A second group of tasks of government belongs exclusively to the nine Lands (*Länder*), which are similar to states in the United States or provinces in Canada. The Länder directly control all matters of education, from grade schools to universities. They, and not Bonn, are responsible for most of the police power and for whatever regulations freedom of the press may permit. Moreover, they own and control the radio and television media (except for one competing program established in the 1960s). The Länder also have most of the administrative machinery of the country. A third group of governmental responsibilities are given to the national government and the Länder concurrently. Here the Länder may legislate, unless federal legislation supersedes. Fourth, the Länder in addition to their own tasks, carry out all federal laws and regulations, except those few directly executed by the federal government (see Table 14.3).

Table 14.3

Initiation and Execution of Laws

| | Initiation of Legislation by: | | |
	Federation	*Länder*	*Both Concurrently*
Federation	Foreign affairs, Defense, Federal finances		
Execution through:			
Länder	Most other federal legislation	Education, press, communications, police	Sphere of "concurrent" legislation

The Federal Government in Operation.   The most powerful office in the federal government is that of the *Chancellor*. He appoints and dismisses in effect all Cabinet members; in these matters, the President is bound to follow his proposals. In case of war or emergency, the Chancellor, not the President, becomes Commander-in-Chief of the armed forces. Generally, the Chancellor guides public policy. Within the limits of the Basic Law, he assigns jurisdiction among the ministries. He cannot be impeached; and he can only be overthrown if a legislative majority agrees on his successor.

The *President* is, in part, a figurehead. In emergencies, however, some of his powers can be important. In some conflicts between Chancellor and Bundestag, the President decides whether to call new elections. He thus can strengthen a weak Chancellor, or force him out of office.

Federal legislation is carried out by a two-chamber legislature. One house, the *Bundestag,* is the main source of federal legislation. It is so much more important that one might well speak of a one-and-a-half chamber system, as in Britain and France where power has shifted to the directly elected chamber of each legislature. Vis-à-vis the executive, however, the Bundestag has less power than the House of Commons, but more than the French National Assembly. Work in the Bundestag is carried on largely in committees, and it is controlled by the parliamentary party caucuses, called *fractions.* Party discipline is tight.

The second chamber, the *Bundesrat,* or Federal Council, consists of delegates from the Länder governments. The delegation from each Lands votes as a unit and follows its government's instructions. Thanks to the Bundesrat's share of legislative power, major laws and emergency laws cannot be enacted without state consent. Moreover, several states are set up in a manner that practically assures them a Socialist government, or else a coalition government with Socialist participation. The city states of Hamburg and Bremen are examples; Hesse is another. Thus there is a built-in balance between Christian-Democratic states like Bavaria and Social-Democratic ones. Finally, Bundesrat members are backed by the strong bureaucracies of their Länder, whose members may differ in view from the federal administration. This makes the Bundesrat stronger than it appears on the surface, and it makes for better laws.

In the making of laws, nearly three-fifths of all bills are initiated by the federal government (see Figure 14.1). Almost all the rest are started by the Bundestag. The Bundesrat initiates roughly one law in a hundred. A sequence of committee reports, three readings by the Bundestag, and, where needed, joint conference committee proceedings ensures careful scrutiny of each measure.

The West German court system provides for judicial independence, protection for human rights, and some limited judicial review of government actions. In this last respect, German courts have fewer powers than those in the United States, but more than those in Britain and France.

Old Interest Groups vs. New Problems. Under the new political system, most of the old interest groups have survived. Only the large landowners have lost the power they enjoyed in the days of Bismarck and in the Weimar era. Most of the large estates were in East Germany and were expropriated by the Communists. Those landowners who escaped to the German Federal Republic had to make new lives for themselves in business, the armed forces, or the civil service.

Business interests in the Federal Republic have proven far more durable. Factories and enterprises were rebuilt after World War II, often with Marshall Plan aid. By the mid-1950s the Federation of German Industries (BDI) and similar organizations were again powers in the politics of the Federal Republic. Farm groups, too, soon became well organized and influential again, but their electoral weight has been gradually reduced by the steady migration from the country into the towns. The civil service continued to function and soon was serving the Federal Republic as routinely as many of its members had served the Hitler regime. Over 160,000 civil servants discharged by the Allies after the fall of the Nazis, most often because of Nazi ties, were back on their jobs by late 1953. Nearly all civil servants and public employees, regardless of their politics, are members of strong professional organizations which press effectively for their salaries, security, and other interests.

German labor is also strongly organized. In the Weimar Republic, labor

Figure 14.1

The Passage of Ordinary Bills in the German Federal Republic

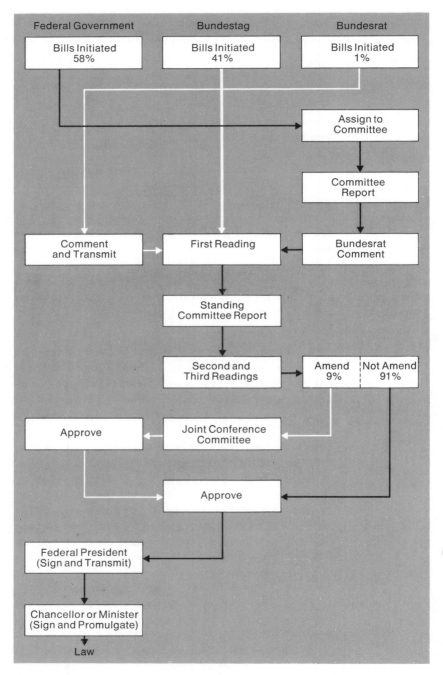

Source: K. W. Deutsch, "The German Federal Republic," in R. C. Macridis and R. E. Ward (eds.), Modern Political Systems: Europe, 2nd ed., © 1968. Adapted by permission of Prentice-Hall, Inc., Englewood Cliffs, N.J.

was divided among Catholic, Nationalist, and more or less Social Democratic trade unions; in the Federal Republic, all wage earner labor groups have merged into the German Confederation of Trade Unions (DGB), which includes over 40 per cent of all wage earners. The DGB is also the Republic's largest organization of white-collar employees and civil servants, exceeding by a moderate margin its competition, the specialized organization of white-collar employees (DAG).

Four major interest groups remain: the military, the mass media, the churches, and the universities. The military is less powerful than under either the empire or even the Weimar Republic. Although the armed forces have about 500,000 men, their leaders have thus far stayed out of German politics. The mass media have been more liberal for the most part than the average German. Radio and television are publicly owned but control of them is largely decentralized among the states. A powerful and somewhat nationalistic newspaper chain has sprung up under the leadership of Axel Springer, but other newspapers and magazines remain diversified and vigorous. The Protestant and Catholic churches continue to exercise political influence, sometimes through direct pronouncements but more often through lay organizations responsible to their leadership. The universities have expanded greatly but are now so poorly organized to look after their interests that their traditional self-government is in danger of being ground down between state control from above and student protest from below.

The first problems which faced all these interest groups after 1949 were economic reconstruction and the resettlement of ten million German refugees and expellees from Eastern Europe. Both tasks were met with remarkable success, thanks to a combination of German diligence and American aid. The next task was economic growth, and in this respect the Federal Republic, with an annual per capita growth rate of over 6 per cent during the 1950s was one of the leaders of the Western world. During the 1960s the pace slowed but remained close to a respectable 5 per cent, and the per capita income of the Federal Republic overtook both France and Britain.

Throughout the twenty years, price stability was maintained to a notable degree. Gradual inflation, common to all Western countries, remained tolerable. By early 1970 civil service salaries and many social benefits for the general population had been tied for automatic adjustment to the cost of living. The Republic also has had an excellent record in modernizing its technology. Management and unions usually have cooperated in smoothing the introduction of new machines and methods.

The problem of finding new markets for German industry to replace its traditional outlets in Eastern Europe, now under Communist rule, was solved by finding new markets in the United States and particularly in the European Common Market. West German governments steadfastly supported the increasing economic integration of Europe. Although this integration has remained gradual and partial, and made only relatively little progress in the 1960s, its importance for the Federal Republic's economy has been great.

By the end of the 1960s the Federal Republic had grown so prosperous that Chancellor Brandt's government found it advisable to revalue the national unit of currency, the Mark, upward—a step almost unparalleled in the Western world since 1930.

Other problems have proven far less manageable. German reunification has remained a widely-held desire but as a matter of practical politics it has receded to a more distant future. For over twenty years governments in the Federal Republic's capital of Bonn have refused to recognize the Communist-ruled German Democratic Republic, hoping that it would collapse and that its Soviet backers would withdraw. Nothing of the sort has happened. The westward flight of nearly 200,000 East Germans per year from 1949 to 1961 was reduced to a trickle by the building of a heavily guarded wall between the Communist and Western-ruled sectors of Berlin. Despite its unpopular government, the GDR has had an economic growth rate similar to that of the Federal Republic, even though its per capita income and particularly its consumer standards, have remained below those of its Western neighbor. Nonetheless, by 1970 both Germanies were prosperous and growing. Also by 1970, both the American and West German governments seemed agreed that confrontation tactics had brought the German problem no nearer to solution, and seemed willing to try new approaches through negotiations with the Soviet Union, and perhaps eventually with the GDR.

Another unsolved problem has become increasingly urgent within West Germany. This is the problem of the quality of life and of the conflict between generations. These are troubles which the Federal Republic shares with other Western countries but which in its own case have become particularly acute. Impoverished by the war, a generation of Germans concentrated their thoughts and efforts on restoring material prosperity and later on increasing it. Now a generation of young Germans is in revolt against what seems to its members an excessive preoccupation with material gain. In their eyes the moral authority of their elders is more suspect than in any other country: what did their fathers do during the years of Hitler's crimes? German student protest has been more vehement than elsewhere, and poll results suggest that nearly two-thirds of young Germans between the ages of fifteen and twenty-one sympathize with these protests. Whatever the cause of this unrest, it can hardly have been excessively permissive education. Most German families are still authoritarian and few German parents ever became followers of Dr. Spock.

Rising German discontent—of the young as well as of some of their elders—has extended to the political parties and to the machinery of government. The late 1960s saw the growth of a new political movement, the *Extra-Parliamentary Opposition (APO)*, which included many writers and other intellectuals and was highly critical of all three major parties. Before the 1969 elections, however, prominent writers like Gunther Grass campaigned to swing the votes of the discontented behind the candidates of the SPD, and they succeeded to a large extent. Whether the political system of the Federal Republic will manage to draw these forces of discontent into new programs of constructive change remains a major question for the 1970s. Clearly the 1970s will continue to test the Republic's capacity for political creativity and innovation.

Political Innovation.   To govern is to invent, says the political theorist Carl J. Friedrich. The German Federal Republic thus far has lived up to this principle. Its political life has been characterized by at least six political innovations new to Germany, and all of them have continued to work.

The first is the high degree of *federalism* which has given major powers, as we have seen, to the states—or Länder—of the Federal Republic, together with the *Bundesrat*. State execution of federal laws, concurrent jurisdiction of states and the federal government, and the blend of cooperation and competition between the two bureaucracies make the West German system a new contribution to modern government.

Second, there is the *constructive vote of no confidence*. The West German government is parliamentary in form, similar to the English; and, as in France, it may be overthrown by a vote of no confidence. However, in a slight variation, as we have seen in Chapter 8, the government can overthrow a prime minister (whom the Germans call Chancellor in memory of Bismarck and of the earlier Empire of medieval days) only if they can agree on a new one. In other words, a government cannot be overthrown in West Germany by a negative majority. Rightly or wrongly, this requirement has worked and seemingly has given West Germany more stability than is enjoyed by the political systems of most other large continental countries.

The third innovation is the *threshold clause*. A party that receives less than 5 per cent of the total vote in the national election gets no seat in Parliament unless it obtains a very strong representation in a particular region.

Fourth, there is a *two-track voting system*. The West German electoral system combines majority voting with proportional representation. One-half of the members of Parliament is elected in single-member constituencies which each can carry by being personally known to the voters. The other half is elected by *party slate*, lists where voters vote for the entire list by brand name, so to speak. Each list is drawn up by the party, often reflecting in effect the views of its national and regional bureaucracy. If the voters trust the party they cast their ballot for the election of the whole slate of candidates. If not, they may vote for the slate of another party, or they may refuse to vote for any slate and vote only for a single candidate. Every West German voter, therefore, has one ballot for an individual in the district and one for an entire slate of candidates chosen by the party. The result is that some reasonably obstreperous individuals can get elected by having political strength of their own, yet the parties can also maintain cohesion. In fact, parties are more powerful than individuals under this system.

Fifth, West Germany is the first country in the world that has systematically provided *public financing of competitive political parties.* This innovation has somewhat loosened the dependence of parties on their financiers. Until the 1960s the same major business organization subsidized the Christian Democrats and the so-called Free Democratic Party. As a result the two parties never voted against each other on important matters. Under the new party finance system the Free Democrats no longer have to echo the more numerous Christian Democrats. They have their own money and have used it to vote independently for the new President of West Germany, Gustav Heinemann.

The sixth innovation, the civilian defense commissioner *(Ombudsman),* involves the military sector which we shall discuss presently.

A Continuing Problem: Armament and Arms Control.   Clearly, West Germany's political innovations function. But how they will succeed in the future in containing further and heavier rearmament or in other critical areas, we do not know. Germany was supposed to be disarmed after World War II but the Federal Republic was rearmed to a limited degree in the 1950s, more upon American pressure than in response to any domestic West German demand. However, about 4 to 5 per cent of the West German gross national product now goes into defense spending. (The German Democratic Republic has had comparable rearmament, in proportion to its smaller size, under the watchful eyes of the Soviet Union.)

West German armament is limited under the Pacts of Paris of 1955. West Germany is barred from having or procuring nuclear weapons, chemical weapons, or bacterial weapons. Some West German politicians, such as CSU leader Franz Josef Strauss, have demanded that West Germany be given the formal right to possess any kind of weapons against any possible adversary. That is, Strauss has demanded qualitative equality with the Soviet Union and the United States. However, the West Germans have not won this right. Most other West German leaders do not demand it, and the West German voters have not shown any interest in pushing rearmament. In late 1969, the new coalition government of Chancellor Willy Brandt agreed to sign the *Non-Proliferation Treaty,* renouncing nuclear weapons.

The West German armies are under civilian supervision, reinforced by the sixth innovation—this one borrowed from Sweden. This innovation consists in a *civilian defense commissioner,* to hear and investigate complaints, an Ombudsman, as the Swedes call him. In West Germany the Ombudsman is a parliamentary commissioner to whom soldiers can complain directly. There is also an important office of internal leadership within the armed forces which tries to educate the soldiers to think of themselves as citizens in uniform.

Such special institutions may be needed, because the political behavior of the military posed major problems to earlier German governments. Under the Weimar Republic, the military was far more nationalistic and militaristic than the majority of the voters. It acted as "a state within the state" and contributed to the overthrow of the constitutional regime. The government and major parties of the Federal Republic were concerned to prevent a repetition. As late as the mid-1950s, one-tenth of West German poll respondents between 15 and 25 years professed open admiration for Hitler. But in another poll, only 10 per cent of German young men of military age said that they would consider military service as a career. These two groups are likely to overlap to a more than accidental degree. The Germans who are drafted into the army for a short period and get out again constitute a cross-section of public opinion. But those who volunteer to become the professional noncommissioned and commissioned officers may well be more nationalistic and more militaristic in outlook than the average German. In recent elections, small garrison towns showered significantly more votes on the neo-Nazi party than did similar small towns where no troops were stationed. We do not know whether this will be a greater problem in the future, or whether civilian democracy in the Federal Republic will somehow digest, absorb, and control it.

Germany: An Experiment in Ends and Means

Some of the most serious problems of Western civilization at high levels of industrialization and technology have occurred in Germany. In the 1920s, Germany was the most educated country in continental Europe; it had the biggest university system and the greatest intellectual traditions. Yet it fell into the worst and most murderous barbarism under the Nazis. Universities can be, as they have been in Germany, centers of humanity and enlightenment. But they can become centers of brutality and barbarism. As late as 1950, the three most pro-Nazi sections of the West German population were the peasants, the long-term veterans of World War II, and the Ph.D.'s. The new generation of West German students is different in its political aims than its fathers' generation. Though it often professes left-of-center views, it has sometimes resorted to violent means. One hopes that it can remain different in the methods it considers acceptable.

The Swiss writer Friedrich Dürrenmatt put these words in the mouth of a survivor of a Nazi concentration camp: "One tells us today one should forget these things, particularly in Germany, and that other countries, too, have had their cruelties and atrocities. I refuse to forget them because I am a human being. As a human being I refuse to distinguish between good peoples and bad peoples and to distinguish between virtuous and wicked nations. But I must distinguish between good persons and bad persons, and I must distinguish between those who inflict pain and those who suffer it. I refuse to make a distinction among any of those who like to torture people. They all have the same eyes."

What Dürrenmatt wrote in Switzerland is now being widely read in Germany. With luck it will be remembered—in Germany and in other countries.

Key Terms and Concepts

The Holy Roman Empire	FDP
Franks, Saxons	Basic Law
Dictatus Papae	Lands (Länder)
Reformation	Chancellor
Peace of Augsburg	President
cuius regio eius religio	Bundestag
Thirty Years' War	Bundesrat
romanticism	fractions
union from above	Extra-Parliamentary Opposition
Weimar Republic	constructive vote of no confidence
Putsch period	threshold clause
German Federal Republic (GFR)	two-track voting system
German Democratic Republic	party slate
(GDR)	Ombudsman
CDU/CSU	Civilian Defense Commissioner
SPD	

Additional Readings

Brzezinski, Z. *Alternative to Partition: For a Broader Conception of America's Role in Europe.* New York: McGraw-Hill, 1965.

Dahrendorf, R. *Society and Democracy in Germany.* New York: Doubleday, 1967.

Deutsch, K.W. and Nordlinger, E.A. "The German Federal Republic." R.C. Macridis and R.E. Ward (eds.) *Modern Political Systems: Europe.* 2nd ed. Englewood Cliffs, N.J.: Prentice-Hall, 1968.

Grass, G. *The Tin Drum.* Greenwich, Conn.: Fawcett World Library, 1969.

————. *Dog Years.* Greenwich, Conn.: Fawcett World Library, 1969.

Hesse, H. *Steppenwolf.* New York: Modern Library, 1963.

Hitler, A. *Mein Kampf.* Tr. by R. Manheim. Boston: Houghton Mifflin, 1943.

Montgomery, J.D. *Forced to be Free.* Chicago: University of Chicago Press, 1957.

Weber, M. *The Protestant Ethic and the Spirit of Capitalism.* New York: Scribner's, 1930.

Today and Tomorrow

Part Three

The Unfinished Business
of Politics

During World War II the story was told of an American businessman who said that he would work as hard as possible to end the war and then would shoot himself in order not to have to live in the postwar world. He was by no means the last man to be afraid of the future.

Explicit efforts by writers to imagine the future have produced some outstanding nightmares. Aldous Huxley's *Brave New World* suggested a world in which people were produced artificially in chemical solutions and "decanted" from assembly lines. Later they were taught in their sleep to repeat endlessly basic indoctrination and to retain a sense of class snobbery. They swore by the name of Ford and the secret sign of the Model T and were encouraged to indulge every whim and desire, including the abundant use of sex and drugs, provided that they did not indulge any desire for freedom.

Another nightmare, even worse than Huxley's was George Orwell's *1984*. In Orwell's world people lived in a totalitarian society in the midst of artificial squalor, dirtiness, and poverty. They were subjected to constant censorship and surveillance by their government and were indoctrinated by the state in daily "two-minute hate" exercises against a supposed national enemy with whom they were engaged in endless but inconclusive warfare. Orwell's book, like Huxley's, was exaggerated and yet to many postwar readers horribly believable, since it projected into the future some of the most menacing and unpleasant features of their own day and age.

When writers and politicians consciously tried to forecast the future in friendlier terms, their vision seemed a positive utopia. The postwar world, they predicted, was to be a world of peace, abundance, and steady progress within the confines of dependable law. People believed many of these hopes. A Soviet worker in 1936, in the first Moscow superdelicatessen, the Gastronome, was eyeing the various attractions and buying a small parcel. Asked whether he were in the habit of buying here, he laughed and replied, "Oh, no, I couldn't possibly afford it, but I come here once every month to buy something in order to get accustomed to the living standard which we'll enjoy in a few years." More than thirty years have passed since then and even at best this workman is still waiting for some of the abundance which he had hoped for then.

The politics of the present, and perhaps of the years ahead, seems characterized by a feeling of great fear—a vague dread of impending major changes. (This is not only a modern phenomenon. The French peasants on the eve of the Revolution experienced a similar "great fear.")

All of us are now living in that fearsome postwar world. Many of the readers of this book will have been born into it. At the same time they will have been born into a period in which familiar symbols of the past have taken on additional importance. In 1952, when the first hydrogen bombs were tested by the United States at Bikini in the Pacific, a fashion of coonskin caps swept the country. The homely garments which American pioneers had worn more than a hundred years earlier were worn by children, youngsters, and at least one presidential candidate. At a time when the energy of the sun was exploded on earth for the first time by human hands, people suddenly began reaching back to some familiar symbol of a safe, more stable, and more dependable past. This, too, was a kind of utopia.

Though the positive utopias have proven no more accurate or believable than the negative ones, there is another kind of utopia which may be the most unrealistic, indeed the most utopian, of all. That is the utopia that suggests that the world will stay as it is.

The Great Currents of Change

We know that the future will not resemble the fantasies of evil or abundance which people entertained in the last decades. But in many decisive ways it will be much different from the present. Of the years of the past, one cannot say what a Vice-President of the United States once said about slums: "If you have seen one, you have seen them all." The changes the world has lived through in the last half-century have been gigantic and the changes to come in the next thirty years are almost certain to be larger still.

In the coming years perhaps the first need of a political system will be to preserve a sense of identity and continuity for its people. In growing up we undergo a great many changes but we can cope with each of them because of a sense of self, a sense of personality. That is to say, we have a sense of something within us that continues through every change we experience from infancy through adolescence to adulthood. Something similar holds for groups, communities, and nations. Their members need a sense of identity, a sense of continuous growth, and a sense of belonging in order to face the dangers, the opportunities, and the tasks of reorientation which they will encounter.

In the future, the world will look very different from the way it used to. Many of the old landmarks—old governments, old institutions, old beliefs—will have disappeared. Since it was these landmarks toward which we oriented ourselves in the past, the future will impose a continuous task of reorientation. But the only landmark we will need to preserve will be our sense of who we are—our sense of identity as a group, as a people, and as a country.

For a long time the world will be inhabited by many stubbornly different peoples, each with its own culture, institutions, and social system. The Russians will remain Russians; the Americans, Americans; the Germans, Germans; and to the English, of course, there will always be an England. But someday there will come a decisive and ever-increasing orientation toward the values of mankind. It is possible that some future generation will paraphrase President Kennedy's words and say, "Do not ask what mankind has done for your country, but ask what your country can do for mankind." To reach this point, however, a sense of country, of nation, and of individual and collective selfhood will have had to be maintained in the midst of great changes. To help mankind, we must know who we are and where we are, and we must be in charge of ourselves.

But we shall have to keep our identity in a world that has changed beyond a point of no return. All continents contain watersheds. These are mountain ranges somewhere in the interior where all the water that falls on one side of them runs toward one ocean and all that falls on the other side runs toward another ocean. In North America, the Rocky Mountains is such a watershed; the rain falling on its eastern slopes runs to the Atlantic, while the rain falling on its western slopes runs to the Pacific. In driving across the American continent, when we come to the place marked "continental divide," even though the dividing line itself is invisible and the peaks and the high plateau at that point may look ordinary, we sense that we have indeed moved from the America of the Atlantic to the America of the Pacific.

There are similar *watersheds* in history. All the events that happened before them belong largely to one age in the history of mankind. Most of the events afterwards belong to a new age and lead to a new kind of historic pattern. The world is crossing such a watershed now. Or, more exactly, it has crossed a watershed in the thirty years from 1940 to 1970. Several changes in those decades have become irreversible.

For the first time in history man has the possibility to commit suicide as a species. Individuals have taken their own lives during many ages. But never before has it been possible for all mankind to end its own life. Nearly two thousand years ago, the Roman Emperor Caligula expressed his regret that mankind did not have a single neck so that he could cut it off at one stroke. Caligula died a frustrated man, but what he could not do then, modern physics has enabled us to do today. An all-out war, exploding large numbers of nuclear weapons, can end all or most of civilized life, and quite possibly all life on this planet.

But if the manufacture of death has reached unprecedented heights of effectiveness and power, so has the growth of life. Mankind, at the beginning of the 1970s is growing at a rate that will double its numbers every thirty-five years. Six to seven billion human beings are expected to live on this planet by the end of the century. Human reproduction has become a vast power, a vast problem, and, more slowly, an increasing responsibility of both individuals and government.

The growing numbers of mankind and the growing power of the mechanical and chemical devices at its service have begun to change the physical quality of life. The more than a million automobiles in use in the Los Angeles area have put a dense pile of smog over the city, and it is little comfort to its inhabitants to reflect that replacing the automobiles with their equivalent in horsepower—a quarter of a billion horses—would only make the place smell worse. The sheer numbers of people, and the amounts of energy, fire, smoke, chemicals, and waste fluids, have produced effects which are qualitatively, as well as quantitatively, new. Rivers have become poisonous to fish and men. The sun has begun to pale over many industrial cities, and the carbon dioxide that has been deposited in the atmosphere by machines has become so great that some scientists fear a permanent change in the earth's climate. In some ways all these are different aspects of one and the same process: mankind's growing too big and too powerful for its own old habits.

The difference between poverty and riches has persisted. Among a few countries the difference has narrowed. In others it has widened. But though the gap between poor and rich is an old story, now for the first time many millions of people in the poor nations are gaining access to enough science, technology, and power to do something about it. What they will do—whether it will be peaceful and constructive or warlike and violent—is not yet certain.

What many countries have done is to try accelerating their rate of economic growth. On the average, the per capita income of mankind has been growing at a rate of 2 per cent a year. Together with the 2 per cent growth rate of world population, this has meant a total annual growth of 4 per cent of world income, or a doubling of man's output of material goods and services approximately every eighteen years. In richer countries, a faster growth in the gross national product and a slower growth in population have produced a higher per capita growth rate of as much as 3 per cent a year. (All these are long-run growth rates; for a few years, or even a decade, many countries have grown faster.) Taking into account the significantly higher economic base of the richer countries, it is probable that differing growth rates alone will not reduce significantly the gap between poor and rich peoples for many decades to come.

Clearly, too, the disproportions among countries will no longer be evened out by the methods of the nineteenth century. For the first time in history, mass migration on a global scale has stopped. The few emigrants from a few countries who still make their way into the small state of Israel are less than a drop in the lake. In the nineteenth century over 60 million people left Europe for new overseas homes. Nothing of the sort seems likely or even possible in the last decades of the twentieth century. Men are penned in by the frontiers of their own states and by the unwillingness of other states to receive large numbers of immigrants.

This means that rich, relatively empty countries, such as the United States, Canada, the Soviet Union, and Australia, face poor, crowded ones, such as India, Pakistan, China, Egypt, or Indonesia's main island of Java. Other countries are both poor and empty. They have abundant land but lack capital and man power; Brazil, Argentina, and much of Latin America, the islands of Borneo and New Guinea, the Union of South Africa, and much of the rest of Africa all fit this description. Finally, a few countries are both rich and crowded. Lacking land, they have more than enough capital to make up for the shortage of square miles. Great Britain, Germany, Belgium, the Netherlands, and Japan all have proved that people can make a living in densely populated countries if they have enough machines and enough skills to use them.

The redistribution of the world's land resources, by political change, purchase, or mass migration, may become a political question in the future. But the redistribution of capital is likely to be more important. It is possible that just as in the first half of the twentieth century the idea of an income tax became accepted in all advanced countries, an international income tax within the international system may yet become a major political issue. If the experience of national income taxes is any guide, the idea will first be shrugged off as impossible, then denounced as outrageous, still later resisted as intolerable, and finally accepted as normal.

The majority of mankind is now literate for the first time since writing was invented. The crossover seems to have occurred in the mid-1950s. In terms of absolute numbers, of course, there are probably more illiterates in the world now than there were a hundred years ago because the numbers of mankind have increased. But the relative decline of illiteracy has continued so that today perhaps only 45 per cent of mankind still cannot read or write. By the end of the century this proportionality will have been reduced to only a quarter of mankind.

In most parts of the world, the importance of cities has decisively increased. During the next century the majority of mankind will be urban in residence and nonagricultural in occupation. In many highly developed countries, cities used to be surrounded by the countryside. Now the countryside is becoming surrounded by cities. Even in such formerly agricultural countries as Mexico, Brazil, and Peru a majority of inhabitants already live in towns and cities. Everywhere in the world the rural population and the farmers and peasants are becoming a minority, and the influence of their conservatism is dwindling. (In this respect, suburbanites will not replace them.) The effects of this change on world politics are bound to be profound.

Nearly everyone can now be reached by mass media of communication. Indeed the majority of the urban and industrial part of the world can probably be reached within a few days. In 1969 perhaps one-half of mankind may have heard within less than a month that men had walked on the moon. And those walks on the moon foreshadowed another irreversible change—the opening of the age of interplanetary travel.

The Information Revolution

More generally, the industrial revolution of the nineteenth and early twentieth centuries has been followed by an information revolution. This revolution has had two aspects. First, it has increased the number of people working in information-processing industries of all kinds, from clerks and librarians to telegraph and telephone operators, and to operators of computing machines and other devices. During the 1950s and 1960s, between 0.5 per cent and 1 per cent of the work force in advanced countries shifted into these information-processing occupations every year. At the same time, in the highly advanced countries, the number of production-line workers and their proportion in the work force did not increase. More and more mechanical and muscular jobs on the production line came to be handled by automation. So did some of the mechanical work of adding numbers or keeping clerical records. On the whole, the demand for human beings in the information-processing occupations continues to increase. By the end of the century we will have more people occupied with manipulating symbols, items of knowledge, and pieces of paper than we will have working on farms, in mines, or on production lines.

The other aspect of the information revolution has been the increasing intellectualization of society. All industrial growth requires ever more raw materials and other ingredients. If industrial processes remain unchanged but are carried out on a larger scale, the demand for raw materials will increase and the rarer materials will go into short supply. Production will become more expensive and eventually will slow down. This is what is called the law of diminishing returns. The only answer to the law of diminishing returns is new inventions. Men must discover new ways for making the goods they need. They must use other materials or use them in different proportions in order to break the bottlenecks of scarcity among the materials in short supply. In addition to inventions, there will be need for innovations, for changes of habit among millions of people to make them actually act in line with the new techniques.

Without a constant stream of invention and innovation the vast machinery of technology in all countries will slowly grind to a stop. As economies and populations grow, the need for invention and innovation increases and hence the need for the kind of people who produce them. The people who produce invention and innovation are the kind we often call intellectuals. They are people who are in the habit of using abstract ideas and symbols in many fields. Not only are they in the habit of thinking critically, of taking all patterns of knowledge to pieces, looking at each piece separately, and deciding which ones to keep and which to reject, they also think combinatorially. That is, they put different pieces of knowledge together in new patterns. Dissociation—breaking old knowledge into smaller pieces—and recombination—putting the pieces together into a new pattern—are the essential processes of creative thought. In the economies of the future such creative thought will not be a luxury but a necessity. The kind of people who produce it, the intellectuals, and the conditions that enable them to produce it, including security and freedom, will also be necessities.

An even greater strain on mankind will be the speed of these information changes. The number of scientific papers published in the world doubles every fifteen years. More than half of the sales of the world's largest chemical corporation, Du Pont, some years ago concerned goods that had not been known ten years before.

Rapid change, however, creates a gap between generations. Where a society changes hardly at all, parents know much more than their children. There is relatively little to learn and the parents have more time to learn it; experience counts, with little else necessary. Where change occurs a little faster, the children learn some things their parents have not learned. Parents and children now share many memories which are sufficiently alike for them to understand each other, but sufficiently different to make conversation interesting. If, however, society changes very fast, many of the experiences of the parents seem irrelevant to the children, and many experiences of the children are unknown to their elders. This accounts in part for some of the communication gap between parents and children which was discovered in recent years not only in the United States but in many other highly developed countries. The appearance in rapid succession of a "beat generation," a "hippie generation," and now perhaps a "militant generation"—and who knows what next—is a symptom of an underlying process that is deeper and broader than many observers have suspected.

The rapidity of change bewilders old and young alike. How are they to orient themselves in the world and in their society? Their plight is reminiscent of the story of troops on a ship which was torpedoed at night in World

War II. The soldiers, crew, and chaplain took their lifebelts and started swimming; and the chaplain, to cheer the men on, called out in a loud voice, "Forward, men, forward!" Out of the darkness came a plaintive plea, "But Father, which way is forward?"

If one does not know which way is forward, one would dearly like a map that provides a simple answer. When experiences follow too quickly and are too different from each other to be an easily understandable guide, one may learn to distrust the testimony of the past. Rather, one looks for simplified maps of the present or future. One looks for ideologies and seeks something simple to cling to—such as the pronouncements or the name of one's favorite politician in the West, or the thoughts of Mao Tse-tung in China.

Distrust of experience, fear of highly developed technology, and impatience with the sustained thought needed to understand complex processes and systems, all add up to the risk of massive intellectual failure. Risking a failure to understand the complex and dangerous reality now facing it, mankind may find itself confronted by a still more complex and more dangerous reality as the years go on. If we distrust anything that seems too complicated, we may be unable to deal with the realities we cannot avoid. And one cannot understand a complicated system or process without, at least for a time, accepting some information on trust. A master of political deception, Adolf Hitler, wrote in his book *Mein Kampf* that there were two kinds of people who were easiest to fool: those who believe everything they read and those who believe nothing. If Hitler were alive today, he might suspect that he would find some new easy victories among those who are approaching the age of the computer with a stone age cast of mind.

A Plurality of Political Changes

Our age of physical and intellectual dangers is also an age of growing intellectual resources. For the first time in centuries, mankind again has a plurality of social systems existing at approximately the same level of technology. Indeed, the difference between the social systems of private enterprise and communism is more profound in some respects than were the differences between, say, medieval Europe, medieval Mexico, and medieval China. And each of these different social systems has many variants. Today there are at least four kinds of communism in the world: Russian, Chinese, Yugoslavian, and North Vietnamese—and North Korean may turn out to be a fifth. There are a number of different kinds of capitalism in the world, most of them alloyed in varying proportions with the institutions of the welfare state. The systems of the United States, France, Canada, Australia, and many other countries are examples. Finally, there are countries whose societies, although based predominantly on private enterprise, have both large public sectors and governments which avowedly favor democratic socialism. (At the beginning of the 1970s, Great Britain, the German Federal Republic, and Sweden were examples of such societies.) This means that for many different policies we can find experiences in a plurality of social systems and institutions. We can not only make an experiment in a single country by keeping its social order unchanged, but we can also observe how a particular law works in the context of several different social systems, whenever such a law, or a law similar to it, has been enacted in several countries belonging to different systems.

One of the most important changes in the world has been the change in political participation and political culture. At the beginning of the 1960s, voting statistics available from one hundred countries comprising more than two-thirds of the world's population showed that among more than two billion people, nearly 60 per cent of adults were in the habit of voting. Additional countries which had not published their statistics, such as Malasia and China, were known to use voting on a large scale. At the opening of the 1970s more than one-half of the world's population (and more than three-fifths, if mainland China is included) had engaged in a vote of some kind. Never before in history had there been voting participation on so grand a scale.

To be sure, not every vote in every country means the same thing. We know that in some countries an election is a choice among genuine alternatives, such as different candidates and different parties, while in other countries it is mainly an appeal by the government for some expression of popular support or loyalty. On this last and highly restricted level, the 1960s marked the first time that the governments of the majority of mankind came back every few years to almost all of their adults for a practical confirmation of their methods.

The increase in voting is not the only form in which political participation has increased. In traditional countries today, as well as in medieval Europe in the past, the activists in politics number far less than 1 per cent of the population. In some countries they now number 3 per cent, and in others still more, rising to 5 per cent, and under special conditions even 10 per cent of the population. Something similar has happened in the increase of autonomous groups, both large organizations and small groups, which take action in many aspects of social life having political significance. Industrial workers the world over now join labor unions; farmers in many countries are organized in farm organizations; interest groups for businessmen and management have arisen in a number of places. In general, the political activity of autonomous small groups as well as of large organizations is much larger than ever.

Moreover, many of these groups and movements are primarily oriented not only to pursuit of the routine interests of their members but also to the bringing about of some more far-reaching kind of change in their society. All the organizations of the black people in the United States are working to produce such far-reaching changes in the country's race relations as well as far-reaching changes in the living conditions of its black people. The labor organizations try to produce far-reaching changes in the living conditions of industrial workers. The farm organizations try to make the life of farmers more secure and less burdened by the hazards of weather, the market, and the workings of the interest rate than the farmer's lot has been for many centuries.

Agents of change, both public and private, are at work in the world today on a larger scale and in a greater variety than ever before. A hundred years ago people used to debate whether the world could be changed; fifty years ago they debated whether change was desirable; today they mainly debate how change can be best accomplished.

Since so many people have become active in society and politics, the basis of the great empires has declined. Empires grow out of the apathy of the many which made possible the rule by the few. If the millions in a country care nothing about politics, a few thousand men brought there over land or by ship can seize control. Or a small militant minority may govern the country, perhaps aided by foreign loans or other economic ties. And the majority continue to live in their villages not caring what happens in the strange world of politics far above their heads.

For centuries, the many have been at the mercy of the few. Now that pattern in changing. With many people entering the process of politics, outside intervention becomes ever less effective. Every year sees foreign loans, foreign ambassadors, or even foreign armies less able than formerly to exercise control over a distant country. This is the shift that has liquidated the great colonial empires. It has also frustrated the ambitions of those who thought that the old imperial powers had merely suffered a failure of nerve, leaving the world in waiting for a new, brasher, or more confident power to fill the supposed vacuum. Ever more often, there is no power vacuum. No longer can the world be governed from a distance—neither by a conqueror, an ideology, nor a world policeman. The issue is not who shall succeed to these jobs, for the fact is that these jobs have been abolished.

Something similar has happened to paternalistic government. The days when a government could do things for its people and expect them to remain duly passive and grateful are disappearing. More and more it has become necessary to do things *with* people rather than merely *for* them. When the Founding Fathers of the United States said that governments obtained their powers from the consent of the governed, they were well ahead of their time. Today the world is catching up with them. George Orwell's nightmare vision of the totalitarian world of 1984 has turned out to have been completely false. Striking as his satire was in its day, and still is in ours, effective as it has been in picking up details and particular features of the political follies of mankind, it has completely misrepresented the mainstream of political development.

In country after country the inclination to take people for granted has become increasingly impracticable. Rather, it has become important to consider the responses of those affected by a public policy and to include their reactions in the planning of the policy. This is true in the running of housing projects, in the renewal of cities, in the development of educational systems, and in the operation of great universities as well as factories. Abraham Lincoln's notion of "government of the people, for the people, and by the people" must now be pronounced with a heavy stress on the word "by."

Any one of these great currents of change may undergo brief and limited reversals. At times or places the trend might head towards less participation; people might leave the towns and find themselves again scattered in the countrysides. Travel might again become more difficult and hazardous. Mass media might become scarce, and people might pay less attention to their contents. The information revolution might be halted and people once again become impoverished in knowledge and by objects competing for other attention. In some places the clocks of history might run backwards for a time. But the analysis of politics should enable us to distinguish the mainstream of a river from the eddies at its fringes. Such eddies can be powerful and lead to whirlpools in which people can drown. They should never be underestimated. Yet in the end it is still crucial to distinguish the eddy from the stream.

The Agenda for the Future

The most dangerous thing the world today can do is to continue politics as usual. If we should enter the 1970s and 1980s merely repeating the ideas and policies of the first third of the century, the dangers would be great indeed. There is a special reason for these dangers. Through most ages of man the main decision-makers have been mature men who collected their experiences and proved their competence before they reached the age of fifty. But their main image of the world was formed in most cases at the time they were twenty. Anyone born in America between 1900 and 1909, formed his images of the world in the days of Coolidge and Hoover. In Germany, they were formed in the era of President Hindenburg, in France, in the days of the conservative French governments of the 1920s, and in Russia, in the days of the coming to power of Joseph Stalin. In Britain, they were formed in the days of the conservative government of Stanley Baldwin and the abortive general strike of the British unions.

The first nuclear explosions occurred in 1945. Very few leaders of today were either young enough or flexible enough in their thinking to be able to accept the full significance of nuclear weapons and nuclear energy, not only in their thought processes, but also in their feelings, down to the very marrow of their bones. As a result, we are now governed by the only generation of statesmen that will ever have the power to control nuclear weapons but who have not fully internalized the significance of the new changes. The statesmen who come to power in the late 1970s and 1980s will be people who were twenty years old in 1945 or younger and who will have accepted the nuclear age fully. To these people war and empire no longer seem things to be sought seriously because the impracticality of nuclear war will be obvious to them.

When gasoline pumps were originally introduced across the United States, they had to be manned by a generation of attendants who had already developed the habit of smoking, and an occasional attendant might smoke near his gas pump on a hot summer day. Such attendants are no longer with us. In one way or the other, they have been replaced by a generation of attendants who have learned not to smoke near a gasoline pump. Very likely the world will be governed in the next two decades by a generation of politicians who will have learned to be as careful around nuclear weapons as gas station attendants are around their pumps.

The most dangerous thing next to a nuclear war would be to try to press all mankind into the mold of a single ideology. At the present state of our social sciences all utopias are only half thought out at best. The governments of the Communist-ruled countries do not fully understand either the economics, the politics, or the sociology of communism, even though they understand enough to stay in power. In the private-enterprise countries, too, the economic and social trends are not fully understood by either management or unions, or governments or voters. In these respects, much of the Cold War of past decades was a competition in exporting ignorance. Future efforts to force poorly understood institutions hastily upon larger and larger parts of mankind are likely to lead to worse disappointments and dangers.

In the meantime it is perhaps safer to see whether we know what we do *not* want or what dangers or conditions we must abolish. Perhaps the first emergency task will be to *abolish war.* Either we abolish all-out war or it will abolish us. Though limited war is increasingly unrewarding and impractical it may continue for a time. Yet is seems safe to say that it will rarely bring its participants the rewards they expect. Civil wars may be harder to cope with. Much as we can hope to abolish all-out war and restrict limited wars, eventually even abolishing the latter, too, it does not seem likely that we shall succeed during the next several decades in abolishing civil wars and revolutions among the local populations of many countries. Too many backward institutions, too many ideological and religious conflicts, too much impatience and intolerance, and too much poverty make it unlikely that all political and social change will be peaceful for the rest of the century. What seems more reasonable to hope for is the limiting of civil wars and revolutions to the populations directly involved. Very likely the factions in such wars will call on like-minded allies for ideological and strategic advice as well as for various types of economic aid or military hardware. But men can at least aim at restricting to a minimum or actually banning the sending of troops into foreign countries by any power, be it Russia, China, the United States, or any of their smaller allies.

Another emergency task will be the *abolition of hunger*. Many millions still go to bed hungry every night. Indian villages every year record the deaths of people from "general weakness," a polite phrase for starvation. Hunger can be abolished in our time through the use of better strains of food plants and better methods of cultivation and through the large-scale shipments of food supplies and farm tools to countries in need of such aid. For the same purpose, a great deal of technical and educational help can be given to countries to teach them to grow more of their own food supplies. For the last twenty years mankind has been in a race between increasing numbers and the difficulty of growing more food. By 1970, luckily, mankind may have pulled a little ahead; food supplies have grown a little faster than world population.

To unite the nations of the world and help them in the struggle against hunger will not be a luxury but a necessity. Any nation, Communist or non-Communist, that holds large reserves of land but refuses either to accept large-scale immigration or to grow food for the hungry will court annihilation on the day when the hungry peoples acquire nuclear weapons and rise up in desperation. That day is not yet here. But just as bicycles, machine guns, and airplanes have spread around the world and are now being used by Ethiopians, Paraguayans, and Burmese as well as by members of most other nations, so nuclear weapons will be virtually available by the end of the century to many countries, large and small, rich and poor. Some will obviously have more of them than others, but even some poor and small nations will have enough of these instruments of destruction to do terrible damage if they should despair of enough food. Clearly, mankind can no longer afford to drive any substantial part of its family to desperation.

Beyond the immediate need to reduce and end hunger lies the more far-reaching goal of *eliminating poverty*. Even under the best of circumstances, this could well take three generations. The average income of the world is about several hundred dollars per capita and very unevenly distributed. On the average, per capita income is growing at 2 per cent per year, and as we know, doubling every thirty-five years. If we could accelerate this growth rate to 3 per cent a year, average income would be $1,400 for the world in the early 1990s and $2,800 or something like it by the second decade of the next century. It would have reached a level higher than the Unites States enjoyed in the days of President Hoover. Another twenty-three years later, in the fifth decade of the twenty-first century, it ought to be at a level of about $5,600, higher than per capita income in the United States today. In terms of the average income of the world, poverty may well by then have been abolished.

But how could income be distributed in such a way as to benefit the poor classes and nations? A basic principle of economics is that of marginal utility. It teaches us that if you offer a very thirsty man one drink of water he will make great sacrifices to get it. If you offer him two glasses of water, the second glass may be worth less to him, and if you offer him the tenth glass of water he may say, "Thank you, I no longer need it."

Perhaps something similar may apply to income in terms of goods and services. When the United States was poorer, wage disputes between labor and management often were bloody. People died on picket lines. Since the income of the United States has become high, labor disputes ordinarily no longer involve the shedding of blood or the loss of life. Many leaders of major labor unions now resemble the corporate executives with whom they are negotiating, and many of the skilled men in unions, particularly those in well-organized skilled occupations, consider themselves members of the middle class. Is it possible to think that some reaction of this kind may develop during the next three generations on a worldwide scale?

So long as the United States was poorer, the idea of a federal income tax was bitterly resisted. It was considered both unconstitutional and unfair. As the American people became richer their objections to paying income tax declined. Now they are so used to paying income tax that grumbles have become perfunctory. On the international scale, nations that consider themselves relatively poor may object to paying an income tax for the benefit of their poorer neighbors. But when nations feel rich enough to send some of their citizens to the moon they may be willing to pay some taxes for their neighbors on this planet. It could even be thought that the truly rich countries of the world, the United States, Britain, and by now the Soviet Union, owe the rest of mankind a good deal in back taxes. In the next decades they will have become ready to acknowledge the obligation and start making payments.

How much could such payments accomplish? The task, as we indicated, is to increase the annual rate of growth of per capita income from 2 per cent to 3 per cent. That is, we must add 1 per cent to the growth of income for most countries of the world. To add 1 per cent to the income of a country requires an investment of about 4 per cent. It roughly takes between $3.00 and $4.00 invested once to add $1.00 to annual income in a national economy. The amount needed is approximately the arms budgets of the world today, which run at 7 per cent of world income. If we could cut the armament bill of the world in half and increase economic aid by the amount saved, we would be far on the way toward abolishing the ancient curse of poverty. Dwight D. Eisenhower was the first American President to make a proposal of this kind.

On a smaller scale, many countries can reduce poverty by doing a better job in integrating their large cities. The politics of big cities have become more like international relations, as their populations have become recruited from many races and ethnic groups. The more we become skilled in integrating our cities, the more we may develop some of the skills needed to help integrate the world.

The instruments for doing most of these things will still be the governments of our nation-states. These include all levels of the machinery of government—local, state, and national. Beyond them, we shall make use of regional organizations such as the Common Market in Western Europe and the United Nations with all its specialized agencies, as well as the many nongovernmental international organizations such as the International Red Cross.

The rule according to which all these instruments will have to be used is the principle of the *self-determination of peoples*. Insofar as the population of an area is a people—a cohesive group of persons capable of communicating and cooperating with each other with a high degree of solidarity—its members are likely to demand their rights to demonstrate their capacity and take their fate into their own hands.

Perhaps the most important task for national states, national governments, and entire peoples will be the effort to increase their *cognitive capabilities*. The nations of the world are like a fleet of ships crossing a foggy sea full of currents and icebergs. Both in the relations of nations among one another, which require the avoidance of war, and of peoples toward their natural environment, which require a more effective control of science and technology, they need to know much more than they now know in order to act in a way that prevents destroying themselves. In the United States and other Western countries this could also include an increase in integrative capabilities—that is, in the capabilities to enable people of different races, languages, religions, and geographic and other background conditions to work together effectively.

Two more problems appear on the urgent agenda for the twenty-first century. The first of these concerns *population growth*. We already have learned the importance of taking some responsibility for the seemingly automatic increase in our numbers. But most of the world's troublesome adults for the next twenty years have already been born. Hundreds of millions of peasants around the world will not change their habits quickly, and their babies will keep coming until they do. There is one comforting thought in this reflection. About one child in a thousand is born with intelligence at what is conventionally called the "genius level." If we get another three billion people in the world, we should find another three million living geniuses among them. The world could well use some of that talent.

The other problem facing us in the next century will be how to adapt to the reality of *interplanetary transportation*. Mankind has yet to enter a radically new environment without bringing back from it some discoveries that have had a profound influence on life at home. When Columbus sailed to the New World in search of spices, gold, and silver, no one expected that maize and potatoes would transform the agriculture of the old world. Yet they did. Similarly in the twenty-first century the impact of the age of space navigation will be felt in every country.

Finally, perhaps the twenty-first century will also be the age of *personal self-determination,* much as our own has been the century of the growing self-determination of entire peoples. We may do more in exploring the inner space of the human mind and spirit, and we may become more effectively mindful of the feelings and emotions of every individual. It may also be necessary to develop more devices for defending individual freedom and controlling governments by means of checks and balances.

Constitutional government may turn out to be neither an old-fashioned remnant of some Western middle-class tradition nor a luxury which only a few rich countries can afford. Freedom of the individual and freedom of opinion are essential parts of freedom in the search for knowledge, and the search for knowledge is an indispensable element in mankind's search for security and livelihood. Systems of government which are respectful of the individual, protective of minorities, and permissive of new discoveries and men's changing their minds about them, will be a necessity for the future growth of mankind. Where constitutional government and individual freedom already exist, it may be worthwhile to guard and develop these traditions and guarantees now, because all mankind will need them someday in the future.

We have no control over what our descendants will do in the next century. But we have an inescapable responsibility for what we ourselves do today and tomorrow. The fate of mankind is a do-it-yourself project.

Additional Readings

Brown, H. et al. *The Next Hundred Years: Man's Natural and Technological Resources.* New York: Viking Press, 1963.

Emerson, R. *From Empire to Nation.* Boston: Beacon Press, 1962.

Huxley, A. *Brave New World.* New York: Harper & Row, 1932.

Kahn, H. and A. Wiener. *The Year 2000: A Framework for Speculation.* New York: Macmillan, 1967.

Lowi, T. *The End of Liberalism.* New York: Norton, 1969.

Platt, J. *The Step to Man.* New York: Wiley, 1966.

Sakharov, A.D. *Progress, Coexistence, and Intellectual Freedom.* New York: Norton, 1969.

Shepard, P. and D. McKinley (eds.) *The Subversive Science.* Boston: Houghton Mifflin, 1969.

Wiener, N. *The Human Use of Human Beings.* Boston: Houghton Mifflin, 1954.

Index